Public Lives

PUBLIC LIVES

Women, Family and Society in Victorian Britain

ELEANOR GORDON AND GWYNETH NAIR

YALE UNIVERSITY PRESS

New Haven & London

Designed by Gillian Malpass

Printed in Great Britain

Library of Congress Cataloging-in-Publication Data

Gordon, Eleanor.
  Public lives : women, family, and society in Victorian Britain / by
      Eleanor Gordon and Gwyneth Nair.
          p. cm.
  Includes bibliographical references.
      ISBN 0-300-10220-8 (alk. paper)
  1. Women–Scotland–Glasgow–History–19th century. 2. Middle class women–
    Scotland–Glasgow–History–19th century. 3. Middle class families–Scotland–
Glasgow–History–19th century. 4. Sexrole–Scotland–Glasgow–History–19th century.
  5. Glasgow(Scotland)–ocial conditions–19th century. I. Nair, Gwyneth. II.Title.
              HQ1600.G53G67 2003
              305.5'5'094144–dc21
                            2003014022

A catalogue record for this book is available from The British Library

For Matthew and Robbie,
Tony and Peter

Contents

Tables

Acknowledgements

We should like to thank the institutions and the many people who have supported us over the gestation of this book. It has its origins in an Economic and Social Research Council-funded project and was subsequently aided by a British Academy Fellowship, and we gratefully acknowledge their financial support.

We are particularly indebted to those who gave generously of their time to read and comment on sections of the manuscript: Lynn Abrams, Mike French, Ruth Madigan, Megan Smitley, Pat Thane, Eileen Yeo and members of the Glasgow Women's History Reading Group. We should also like to thank the anonymous rapporteurs for the ESRC project and the anonymous readers of Yale University Press for encouraging comments and constructive criticisms.

We had help with specific aspects of the research from Joy Chusman, Fiona Dobbie, Campbell Lloyd, Debbie Nicholson and Megan Smitley. Staff at the Glasgow City Archive, Glasgow University Special Collections, the National Archive of Scotland and, especially, the Glasgow University Archive Services also patiently provided advice and expertise.

Colleagues at the Department of Economic and Social History at the University of Glasgow and the School of Social Sciences at the University of Paisley have listened and offered advice at various stages of this study. Our undergraduate and postgraduate students have contributed, perhaps more than they realise, to the development of our ideas. We should also like to thank Gillian Malpass for her encouragement and enthusiasm at crucial times, as well as her colleagues at Yale University Press, including the meticulous Ruth Thackeray.

However, our greatest debt is to our family and friends whose patience seemed inexhaustive and who sustained us with their unflagging enthusiasm for the project and their belief in our ability to bring it to fruition. We owe a particular debt to Tony Clarke, Basilia and Peter Griffin, Linda Keenan, Joan Mackenzie and Jennifer Scherr.

Introduction

IT IS RARE FOR THE ADJECTIVE 'Victorian' to be used other than pejora-
tively. Even those with a leavening of scholarly insights into the period
have probably on occasion slipped into the easy application of the term
'Victorian' to any activity or practice which could be construed as hypo-
critical, prudish, passionless or repressed. This is testimony to the power
of language and discourse to shape understandings of the past as well as
the present. One of the most potent discourses of the nineteenth century,
and one which is generally deemed to have reached its apogee in the
Victorian period, is that of 'separate spheres'. The origins of the late
eighteenth- and early nineteenth-century conception of separate spheres
has been variously attributed to the Enlightenment, Evangelicalism and
political expediency borne of the social and political upheavals of the
industrial revolution. The key component of this ideology was the notion
that men and women inhabited separate spheres: women the private
world of home and family; men the public world of the market place,
citizenship and civil society. Allied to this was the notion that, ordained
by religion and nature, the roles of women and men were complementary to each other.

The separate spheres thesis has also become the dominant historical
paradigm for understanding gender relations in the nineteenth century,
particularly among the middle classes. At its simplest and most general
level, the concept that men and women should occupy separate spheres
is seen as explaining the differentiated lives of men and women in the
nineteenth century. However, historians have interpreted separate spheres
differently, have attributed different meanings and significance to its operation, and have disagreed about its novelty in the late eighteenth and early
nineteenth centuries.[1]

One of the more sophisticated expositions of the separate spheres thesis
is to be found in Leonore Davidoff's and Catherine Hall's seminal book
Family Fortunes. Davidoff and Hall attempt to demonstrate the way in

which class and gender were mutually constitutive, and the centrality of the ideology of domesticity to the formation of the nineteenth-century middle classes. They see their task as deconstructing the fictive divisions of 'public' and 'private', of 'man' and 'woman' and of 'production' and 'reproduction'. They are sensitive to the interconnectedness of social phenomena and to the porosity of 'public' and 'private', and argue that these categories were ideological constructs rather than physical spaces.[2] They are also aware of the inconsistencies and contradictions of the dualism of 'public' and 'private', the shifting boundaries of those terms that did not always fit neatly into the categories of 'man' and 'woman'. While they acknowledge that the concept of 'separate spheres' does not capture the diversity of women and men's lived experience, they nonetheless view separate spheres as the dominant discourse in shaping male and female identity in the nineteenth century and as the prime way in which men and women mapped out their mental universe. Although aware of the empowering aspects of separate spheres and the ideology of domesticity for women, in common with numerous historians, they argue that it was a powerful discourse which shaped social institutions and practices and which ultimately created a more circumscribed social role for women with 'growing constraints on [their] physical and social mobility'.[3]

The separate spheres thesis is therefore given analytical primacy, not only in explaining gender differences, but the sharpening of the gender divide in the nineteenth century; indeed it sometimes appears that it was the only discourse which was significant in shaping gender identities. However, men and women were enmeshed in a matrix of circulating discourses, some of which competed with separate spheres, cut across it, supplemented it or even supplanted it. Moreover, discourses could be resisted, subverted and refused; material factors and individual experience played an important role in shaping the ways in which representations were absorbed, interpreted and challenged.[4] Identity or identities are mutable and multiply formed through an array and interplay of practices, habits and experiences as well as discourses. A further problem with the separate spheres thesis is the dualistic mode of thinking which it assumes to have structured ways of conceptualising the world. While binary oppositions have been an important tool for the ways in which people have organised their ways of thinking about social and natural phenomena, as Lawrence Klein suggests, they are not exhaustive of the ways in which people in their daily lives conceive of the world.[5] In addition, even when people do think in dichotomous terms, they make distinctions

on a number of dimensions simultaneously rather than on a single dimension. The category 'woman' might thus be contrasted not only with
'man', but with 'women', 'girl', 'lady', 'wife' etc.[6] Given that multiple meanings are usually attached to the terms comprising a dichotomy, the task of
mapping discourses, let alone experience, becomes increasingly complex.
Binary oppositions close off ways of thinking and lead to 'the reduction
of genders and sexualities to two counterposed possibilities',[7] whereas
the multiple meanings assigned to terms and the multiple ways of
thinking and conceiving of social relations and personal identities make
it more likely that gender roles were more complex and numerous than
suggested by the associated dichotomies of 'public'/'private' and
'man'/'woman'.

Few would disagree with the contention that the nineteenth-century
conception of separate spheres and its organisation of sexual difference
had an important role to play in structuring social institutions, social relations and material reality. However, as an interpretation of the lives of
men and women in the nineteenth century, it is far from being the whole
story. If one wants to recapture the richness and diversity of men and
women's lives, one has to move beyond the legacy of separate spheres and
the limited outlook which it provides. One needs to look for the diverse
influences which shaped men and women's experiences and identities,
and one needs to restore agency and self-reflexivity to individuals.

It has often been assumed that religion was an important prop for the
ideologies of separate spheres and domesticity. The image of woman as the
'angel in the house' has been viewed as fashioned largely from religious
discourses which vaunted female morality as redemptive and decreed that
woman by nature was supremely suited to the role of moral guardian to
the nation. Crucially it was woman's association with the home and the
family and her immunity from the corrupt practices of the public world
which were deemed to equip her for this role. Religious discourses were
certainly central to the shaping of female and indeed male identity in the
nineteenth century; however, there is a growing body of work which
demonstrates that such discourses were diverse, contested and open to
interpretation and reappropriation.[8] Although it has long been acknowledged that the language of moral motherhood could empower women,
in fact there was sufficient mobility of meanings there for women to create
a space not only to contest the effects of any repressive regulatory practices, but to reinterpret them in ways which extended their repertoire of
roles and gave them licence to enter the public arena in purposeful and
empowering ways.[9] Protestantism in its many denominational forms was

wedded to the belief that it was the duty of individuals to seek their own salvation; this could quite easily translate into a claim to enter the public world and contribute to the work which needed to be done in the world. Typical of mid-nineteenth-century feminist rhetoric was the proclamation of Barbara Leigh Smith that, 'To do God's work in the world is the duty of all, rich and poor, of all nations, of both sexes. Adult women must not be supported by men if they are to stand as dignified, rational beings before God.'[10] Evangelicalism has typically been portrayed as the religion of the home. It could also, however, provide women with the rationale for participation in the public world by its insistence on the importance of salvation and the conversion experience. In order to fulfil one's Christian duty, and win converts to the 'cause' and rescue the fallen, it could be argued that women needed to engage in the public sphere. Similarly the rhetoric of 'Women's Mission', which was constitutive of female religiosity, could provide further legitimation for a public role for women. Women could appropriate ideas about their moral and spiritual superiority to sanction their entry into the public sphere in order to exert their purifying influence.[11]

The work of historians such as Clare Midgley and Katherine Gleadle has also demonstrated how women drew on evangelical discourse and inflected it with a radical edge to sanction a political and public role for themselves.[12] The growing body of such research has shown that religious discourse cannot be interpreted merely as part of the armoury of conservative ideologues or as a discursive system which shackled women to a narrow and passive, if morally exalted, role in society. Religious belief could (and did) encourage different and even oppositional ways of thinking which lead to a questioning of separate spheres as formulated in terms of 'public' and 'private'.

Another unlikely source of middle-class female empowerment and agency has been located in imperial discourses. As Clare Midgley has observed, until recently studies of imperialism and feminism have ploughed different historical furrows. Scholars have begun to explore the ways in which middle-class women of the late nineteenth century gendered imperial discourses by drawing on them to sanction a public and political role for women.[13] Similarly, imperial and religious discourses could be drawn upon to legitimate an active role for women in the imperialist cause.[14]

Readers are now accustomed to thinking of class as a gendered experience. However, largely because of the precedence given to the separate spheres thesis, the emphasis has tended to be on the difference between the gendered identities of men and women of the middle classes. The association of women with the home and men with the world outside has tended to lead to the assumption that the factors shaping their experiences could also be compartmentalised into the 'public' and the 'private'. John Tosh's work has demonstrated that the ideology of domesticity had considerable salience for Victorian and Edwardian middle-class masculinity as well as femininity, even though the meanings of domesticity were different for men and women. Nonetheless, there has been scant attention given to the similar repertoire of discourses, values and beliefs on which middle-class men and women could draw. Indeed, Tosh does not extend his analysis of middle-class ideology to incorporate the ways in which ideologies of the 'public' were important in the formation of female identity. He concludes that while men experienced the tensions between the public and private worlds and could pass freely between them, this tension scarcely troubled most women.[15]

It is a truism to argue that women were situated by their class as well as by their gender. And yet the 'middle-classness' of women is often underestimated as a formative influence on their identity. The defining concepts of nineteenth-century liberalism, the dominant political philosophy of the middle classes, were individualism, justice, obligation, rights and freedom.[16] These values could conjoin with those of Christian duty to provide alternative aspirational models for middle-class women which were rooted in self-reliance, independence and self-fulfilment rather than dependence. The language of possessive individualism also stressed progress and improvement, including self-improvement and the 'rational pursuit of knowledge'.[17] Coupled with the emphasis on dignity, work and duty which was part of the middle-class code, it could provide powerful motivation for women to engage in the public world and to seek self-fulfilment in areas other than motherhood. It could even be interpreted by women to mean that they should go out into the world and make their own living. While it is generally acknowledged that feminists from the middle of the century drew on the language of these traditions to argue for a less restricted role for women, these values were the common currency of the middle classes and central to middle-class identity. It would be surprising if they circulated only among men or were appropriated only by a small minority of feminist women. They may have been reworked and articulated in gender-specific ways by ordinary middle-class women, but they nonetheless constituted part of their discursive world.

Protestant values of moral responsibility and bourgeois values of citizenship accorded with a central tenet of nineteenth-century liberalism that 'conduct and conduct alone, entitles to respect: that not what men are, but what they do, constitutes their claim to difference'.[18] These beliefs formed the basis of middle-class immersion in voluntary and philanthropic organisations and in civic as well as public associational life in the nineteenth century. Although it has been argued that the exclusion of women from the bourgeois public realm was fundamental to its constitution, women were not in fact absent.[19] They may have occupied a 'feminine public sphere', but public it was, and middle-class women as much as middle-class men were constituted by it as much as constituting it.[20]

More recent discussions of the middle classes have focused on cultural practices as the key constituents of middle-class identity, particularly in relation to urban modernity, public ritual and civic culture.[21] Although women of the middle classes have been curiously absent from these discussions in relation to the role they played in the creation of middle-class culture, there can be little doubt that their role was pivotal. Entertaining in the home was important in forging a common middle-class identity and in affirming one's status and standing by a display of conspicuous consumption. Middle-class identity was also marked by the acquisition and public display of 'good taste', whether in the home, in the city, or at the concert hall, public function or lecture theatre. Women as arbiters of taste, managers of display and consumers of culture were therefore central to the creation of middle-class identity and culture. Even if one were to believe that women were confined to the home, the middle-class home and family were far from being a secluded haven cut off from the wider world. The family was protean and shifting in its form and boundaries, while the home, or the realm of reproduction, was intimately linked with production and sociability, and in maintaining the social boundaries that delineated middle-class identity.

There were diverse and competing systems of meaning embedded in social practices and relations, some more powerful than others. Which ones were significant and how individuals absorbed, negotiated or refused them depended both on context and on material factors. Family culture, economics, demography, marital status and myriad other factors interrelated in complex and variable ways to structure experience and identity. Single, unsupported women were not necessarily fettered by an all-powerful ideology which decreed that they languish in the home of a male relative. There may not have been a male relative; there may have been a strong desire to achieve self-fulfilment by exporting one's piety and moral superiority to the far-flung reaches of the Empire; or there may have been a resolute belief fuelled by religious, political or moral conviction that one should be self-reliant and independent.

The discourse of separate spheres, while powerful, is not sufficient to explain how middle-class women's experience was shaped and their identities constructed. It was only one among many available to middle-class women and it could be reinterpreted and negotiated as well as refused. This book is intended to convey, if not capture, the diversity of middle-class women's lives roles and identities. The detailed information we have garnered on family and home life, marriage, motherhood, leisure and pleasure has been drawn from the Claremont/Woodside estate of Glasgow. Some of the families did not live on the estate but were close relatives of those who did. Very occasionally we have used sources drawn from families who were socially connected to those on the estate and who usually lived nearby. We have drawn on a wide range of sources, including family papers, private diaries, business papers, wills and testaments, confirmations, criminal precognitions, church records, Valuation Rolls, Post Office Directories and newspapers. We have tried to be aware not only of women's voices but of the voices that spoke to women. Inevitably, we heard the voices of those women lower down the hierarchy of the middle classes only faintly. Because of the dearth of the rich qualitative sources for this group we have gained fewer insights into the intimate lives of the lower middle classes in the area.

The book is also underpinned, however, by a quantitative study of a sample of census enumerators' returns for the area over the period 1851 to 1891. This provided us with information on family formation, household structure and occupational and demographic patterns across the range of the middle classes. The Claremont/Woodside estate, immediately west of Glasgow City centre, consisted of large, medium and small terraced houses built in the 1830s and 1840s as part of the westward drift of urbanisation. While the area contained a solid bourgeoisie of merchants, manufacturers and professionals such as lawyers and doctors, there was a degree of diversity between the north and south of the area in terms of wealth and income, as indicated by occupation of the head of household, number of resident servants and the value of the property. An important consideration was to select a sample which reflected the heterogeneity of the middle classes, thereby including a range of sizes and values of property and a range of occupations. Consequently twelve streets comprising approximately 250 households (almost 1400 households and 10,000 individuals over the period 1851 to 1891) were selected, reflecting this diversity.

By examining women's family life and marriages, how they earned and spent their money, how they filled their social, spiritual and civic lives, we demonstrate the richness of their experience and the complexities of their roles and relationships. The men and the women in this study are drawn from across the range of the middle classes. The women were not pioneers or pathbreakers but, for the most part, unremarkable in any public sense. Yet like Dorothea in George Eliot's *Middlemarch*, the effect of their being on those around them 'was incalculably diffusive: for the growing good of the world is partly dependent on unhistoric acts [of those who] live faithfully a hidden life, and rest in unvisited tombs'.[22] These women were often energetic, strong-willed, humorous, sometimes defiant. They played a multiplicity of roles: they were caring and nurturing mothers, self-supporting and independent businesswomen and active philanthropists. But they also enjoyed the pleasures of dancing, partying, flirting and travelling at home and abroad. The men were dedicated business or professional men, devout Christians, some of whom did make their mark in a public sense. But they were also home-loving, gentle and whimsical – indulgent fathers and uxorious husbands.

We can lay no claims to the typicality of our subjects, although they include a broad range of the middle classes in a large important industrial city, indeed 'the Second City' of an Empire which spanned one-fifth of the earth's surface. We do think that the evidence marshalled demonstrates that within the context of profound inequalities of power in the relations between men and women, Victorian middle-class women had scope to make their own choices, shape their experiences and make their own histories.

I

Life in the City

GLASGOW AND ITS HISTORY have long been synonymous with the notion of the industrial city. Its economy, occupational structure, architecture, housing and its class formation and class relations have all been invoked to conjure up images of a city which reaped the benefits and suffered the ravages of its emergence as a leading industrial city in the nineteenth century. This image was also assiduously cultivated in the city's civic celebrations, public displays and literature, in which Glasgow was represented primarily as a centre of manufacturing whose identity, culture, and social and physical geography were forged by an industrial economy. As with most self-representations, this image belies a more complex history and development than can be explained by reference to a single overarching concept.

Historians looking for evidence to rehabilitate the idea of an industrial revolution in Britain might have done well to cast their eye over the English border. In its early development Glasgow certainly displayed many of the features which used to be associated with industrialisation but which in recent decades have been the subject of intense debate and revision:[1] rapid and dramatic population and urban growth accompanied by profound social transformations and upheavals. The speed and character of economic and industrial changes were far more rapid and dramatic in Glasgow than in any city in England.[2] Indeed its rate of urban growth outstripped that of any other city in Europe. The population mushroomed from 25,000 in 1750 to over 100,000 in 1811. Growth was even more spectacular in the course of the nineteenth century with the City quadrupling its size between 1831 and 1911, a result of its civic ambitions to extend its boundaries as well as immigration, and changes in fertility, nuptuality and mortality.[3] In 1912, with a population of just over a million, Glaswegians were supremely confident that their city merited the designation 'Second City of the Empire'.

Urban expansion was matched by nineteenth-century economic expansion, through which Glasgow emerged as a powerful economic force. Based initially on the growth of the cotton industry, economic success in the second half of the century was more broadly based with the heavy industries spearheading developments across the board of industry, commerce and finance. As well as being the main shipbuilding centre in Britain, Glasgow was a major seaport and was the focal point of the Scottish rail and canal networks.[4] Although Victorian and Edwardian Glasgow saw itself predominantly as an industrial city, its occupational structure was more varied and became increasingly diverse as the century progressed. While the majority of its inhabitants were employed in the industrial sector, in 1911 almost a third of all occupied men and women were to be found in the commercial, professional and domestic sectors. Indeed, despite Edinburgh's reputation as the stronghold of the professions and the financial centre of Scotland, Glasgow had as many doctors and clergymen as the capital, and its thriving stock exchange dominated the capital as a provider of financial services.[5]

Glasgow was not only the unrivalled heart of the Scottish economy, it was also important to the British economy and to the world economy. The export trade boomed in the second half of the century with a glut of products mined, manufactured and forged in Glasgow, flooding into the markets of Europe, the Empire and the newly developing areas such as Latin America. These extensive links to the rest of the world economy were reflected in the location of Glasgow firms, many of which had offices in Liverpool, Manchester and London. The Mackinnon Group, a conglomeration of mercantile and shipping interests based in the city, exemplifies Glasgow's international trade and investment links. The Mackinnon Group's business empire included firms based in Glasgow, Liverpool and London, and extended across the continents to India and Africa.[6] Glasgow's imperial links were also visually expressed in its architecture and monumentalism, which spoke of a city glorying in its imperial role. The monuments and statues erected by the city fathers celebrated the great victories and figures of the Empire. Statues of Brigadier General Lord Clyde, renowned for his role in quelling rebellions in the Empire, of Sir John Moore, hero of Corunna, and of David Livingstone, explorer and foreign missionary, dominated the square in front of the city chambers. The Great Exhibitions of 1881, 1901 and 1911 not only provided a showcase for the products of the city, but carefully cultivated the image of the City as an imperial centre. One of the most impressive exhibits at the 1881 Exhibition was Doulton's Indian Pavilion: at its entrance the Doulton fountain fulsomely celebrated Britain's imperial role and 'gave expression to the untroubled imperial attitudes seen elsewhere in the Exhibition'.[7] At the base of the fountain were four pairs of figures representing India, Canada, South Africa and Australia; they were surmounted by a tier of three soldiers and a sailor, with Queen Victoria with orb and spectre at the apex.[8] Visitors to the exhibition were invited to slake their thirst in the Royal Bungalow with its Lucknow and Delhi rooms and enjoy a meal in the General Gordon buffet, 'fitted up with Punkahs' and offering as a speciality 'Indian curries by Native cooks'.[9]

Glasgow projected an image of economic self-confidence, despite the volatility of the economy and the economic vulnerability of even its most wealthy citizens. As in most cities, businesses were generally small in scale and were financially precarious with high mortality rates and often a life-span of only three to four years.[10] However, even the rich were not immune from financial failure and bankruptcies were not uncommon among those of significant wealth. James Smith, one of the city's leading architects, whose daughter Madeleine was to feature in one of the most notorious Victorian murder trials, was bankrupted in 1843 despite his friendship and business connections with some of the luminaries of the municipality, including the Lord Provost.[11]

Not only did individual fortunes vary, but the financial confidence of Glasgow's bourgeoisie was severely dented with the collapse of the City of Glasgow Bank in 1878 as a result of fraud and poor management. Most of the bank's 1,819 shareholders were middle-class Glaswegians who therefore lost either their savings or their livelihoods. Although limited liability had been introduced in 1856, most firms had not adopted it, believing that accepting full responsibility for debts was a badge of honour inspiring confidence and guaranteeing the integrity of the company.[12] The absence of limited liability meant that losses had to be met by the shareholders with only 129 of them remaining solvent once the losses had been met.[13] Guy McCrone's novel *Wax Fruit* describes the impact of the crisis and its effects on prosperous Glasgow families: for one family it resulted in the premature death of the widowed mother; other families experienced financial ruin; and for the entire middle class confidence in the probity of financial institutions was shaken.[14]

Despite such reversals of fortune, the vocabulary of depression and economic uncertainty was overshadowed by the language of economic self-assurance. The 1901 Exhibition took place while the controversial Anglo-Boer War was in progress and unemployment in the city was on the increase. Nonetheless, the exhibition was viewed as an opportunity for Glasgow to assert its status as 'the first municipality in the world and the second city of the British Empire' and to display the 'full illustration of the British Empire'.[15] There were alternative discourses which co-existed with those of civic pride and which lamented the dissoluteness and poverty in the slum districts. However, Glasgow had an image of itself as a recuperative, inventive and adaptable city.[16] Despite social problems and slum housing which was among the worst in Europe, W. H. Fraser has observed that Glasgow had 'a confidence that no problem was too difficult to be tackled by a combination of personal and public effort'.[17]

To some extent local politics reflected and sustained images of harmony, for although it could be a battlefield between competing political interests, political rivalries were muted by the overwhelming commitment to Liberalism in the city. It was not until 1874 that the Tories won their first seat in Glasgow since the 1832 Reform Act and that was largely the result of internal divisions within the Liberal Party. When the Liberal Party split in 1886, the brand of Liberal Unionism which emerged was heavily weighted towards Liberalism rather than Unionism.[18] Glasgow's local politics had its fair share of political rivalries and schisms; however, they did not fracture along party political lines. Divisions among Liberals, the dominant group in the council, were as significant as those between Liberals and other parties, with the temperance issue proving the most significant fault line in local politics for much of the second half of the century.[19] However, the distinctive stamp of Glasgow politics was not so much fierce political rivalries between contending factions as local government's enthusiasm for municipalism. There was remarkable unanimity across the political spectrum about the benefits of municipalisation, at least until the end of the 1890s. Indeed it was the Unionists in the 1880s who did most to pioneer the municipal reforms which gained Glasgow its reputation as the citadel of municipal socialism.[20] No other city in Britain embraced the municipal ideal to the extent which Glasgow did and in the course of the century the activities of the city fathers extended from the municipalisation of water and gas, to tramways, electricity and the telephone service.

Industrial cities such as Glasgow have usually been associated with class conflict and battles between the contending forces of capital and labour. However, alternative labour politics were slow to emerge in the city, which may partly be explained by the local government's willingness to mitigate the worst excesses of the market. It was not until the early years of the twentieth century that local politics began to reconfigure around class, although there was much shared ground between the political ideology of working-class parties and the radical strand of Liberalism.[21]

Glasgow's middle classes, in common with their counterparts elsewhere, were habitually concerned about the corrosive effects of rapid social and economic change on social and moral order and developed a panoply of voluntary organisations to ensure that the working-classes did not sink into godless licentiousness and drunkenness.[22] Yet despite constant middle-class preoccupations with the decline of religiosity among the working classes, the evidence suggests that church membership among the working class was maintained at a healthy level in the second half of the century. Peter Hillis's analysis of nine Presbyterian churches in Glasgow in the mid-century found that while the eldership of congregations was dominated by the upper middle classes, working-class membership comprised the highest percentage of all types of churches.[23] As Callum Brown has observed, it may have been the case that the vast majority of the working class did not go to church, but the vast majority of churchgoers were working class.[24] In a city renowned for its religious rivalries and schisms, it seems perverse to argue that religion was a potent source of social and moral cohesion in Glasgow. However, religious rivalries and schisms tended to be confined to the working classes and to cleave around the minority Catholic and majority Protestant divide.[25] Despite the diversity of denominations which multiplied after the Disruption of 1843, evangelicalism provided an overarching belief system which created a common religious culture for its citizens. Dubbed 'Gospel City' by one evangelical in the 1830s, Glasgow developed an aggressive form of Christianity which, although spearheaded by its middle classes, embraced all social classes in its ambit.[26] A common religious identity did not preclude class conflict and the development of a distinctive working-class culture and identity. As Robbie Gray demonstrated for Victorian Edinburgh, the working-class adapted and tailored dominant social and political discourses which were refashioned and imbued with distinctively working-class meanings and values.[27] However, in common with many other places, religiosity and its concomitant, temperance, were integral elements of the culture of the labour movement in nineteenth-century Glasgow, reflected in its support for sabbatarianism, temperance reform, and a belief that socialists had inherited the mantle of Jesus Christ.[28]

Whether relations between the classes in nineteenth-century Glasgow are characterised by working-class subordination, accommodation or contestation, it is indisputable that it was the middle classes who dominated the city economically, politically and culturally. However, defining who and what constituted the middle classes is another matter. There has been much ink spilt about the multiplicity of divisions within the middle classes in the nineteenth century which fractured middle-class identity and questioned notions of their socio-economic and political unity.[29] At the same time there has been increasing recognition that the middle class was not simply economically or socially constituted and that the meaning and identity of the term 'middle class' was culturally constructed.[30] The work of Davidoff and Hall in particular has been crucial in demonstrating that middle-class formation was a gendered phenomenon and that men and women experienced class differently.[31] More recently there have been those who have questioned the usefulness of the concept of class or who have reconceived the term 'middle class' as a rhetorical device and a political idiom denoting 'middle opinion' rather than as a description of a particular socio-economic formation.[32] These studies have alerted historians to the limitations of economic reductionist accounts of class, the lack of congruence between socio-economic categories and political allegiances and cultural patterns, and the centrality of culture, broadly defined, to middle-class identity. However, even those who have stripped the term 'middle class' of social and economic meanings have acknowledged the overlap between cultural patterns and socio-economic categories.[33] As Simon Gunn has observed, even in the first half of the nineteenth century, when the term had distinct political connotations, it was usually linked to other criteria such as industry, commerce, property, wealth and education.[34] If culture is defined broadly to encompass a way of life rather than simply aesthetic practice, it is likely that social and economic categories had some significance in setting the boundaries of who might participate in this culture, even if they cannot explain it. It therefore seems appropriate to look at some of the measurable social and economic structures of the middle classes as well as their cultures.

Broadly defined as the non-manual sections of the population, the Glasgow middle class was a diverse and, in the second half of the century, rapidly growing group. R. H. Trainor estimates that in 1861 it comprised some 18,000 and by 1911 as many as 54,000, with the percentage of those with middle-class occupations increasing from 17.5 per cent in 1861 to 27.6 per cent in 1911.[35] Stana Nenadic argues that while 75 per cent of the middle classes were business owners, almost two-thirds of these were petty entrepreneurs such as small shopkeepers and tradesmen. Another 15 per cent of the middle classes were professionals or managers and the remaining 10 per cent were from the rentier class.[36] These occupational differences were reflected in wide variations in wealth and income within the middle classes. Nenadic estimates that about half of the middle classes were concentrated at the bottom of the hierarchy, 'with low incomes, modest houses with few servants, and almost no tangible wealth',[37] while only about 10 per cent of the middle classes earned £300 or more, the level of income deemed sufficient to maintain the standard of living thought to be appropriate in middle-class domestic manuals of the period. These figures are roughly consistent with the estimate of one disgruntled correspondent to the *Scotsman* in 1849 who claimed, with undisclosed authority, that 'fully three fourths of the middle classes' had an income of between £150 and £400 per year. While these sums were almost certainly drawn from anecdotal evidence rather than systematic and precise calculations, the author's substantive point was the disparity of wealth within the middle classes. Although he was happy to include the 'few rich people and a few successful individuals in receipt of large incomes' within the ranks of the middle classes, his perception of the middle-class hierarchy was one in which the majority with modest and comfortable incomes were yoked together but separated by a yawning gulf from a small section of wealthy families.[38] This subjective perception of a middle-class pyramid formation by a contemporary who identified himself as 'One of the Middle Classes' has found echoes in recent studies of the middle classes in English cities. Therefore, while it has generally been acknowledged that the middle classes were economically differentiated, it would appear that both contemporaries and historians regard the most important distinction as between the substantially wealthy and the rest.

What emerges from this picture of the Glasgow middle classes is a social formation which was differentiated by wealth, by civic, religious and philanthropic leadership, and by education. The top of the pyramid comprised a small group of professionals and prosperous businessmen from across the economic spectrum. Thereafter it extended to a much larger group which consisted of a variety of white-collar workers, petty entrepreneurs and shopkeepers who lacked significant wealth and who were largely absent from the leadership of the panoply of urban institutions which swarmed in over the city. What was also significant about those who occupied leadership positions was the degree of integration and overlap of personnel. Trainor has observed that this overlap in Glasgow's public life was deep-rooted and long-standing and served to create a cohesive and stable elite intertwined by this common membership of key local institutions and shared involvement in public activities.[39]

The Claremont and South Woodside estates provide a useful exemplar of many of these features of middle-class formation and life in Glasgow.

The two estates were part of an ambitious co-ordinated development plan prepared in 1830 by their architects, George Smith and John Baird. Terraces were built throughout the 1830s and 1840s. In many ways the area appears to typify and exemplify the pattern of residential segregation which emerged in the nineteenth century, with the middle classes abandoning the centre of the city for the more salubrious and leafy havens of the newly developing suburbs to the west. It provided housing for the affluent middle classes with everything they wanted from a suburb: scenic beauty and a 'truly suburban environment'.[40] However, its social and physical geography was more complex than a spatial dynamic driven by class segregation and the desire of the wealthy to escape the city psychically and physically.

While the area was described as a 'suburb', this term had a distinctively nineteenth-century meaning. The Claremont area, built on a hill, certainly boasted splendid panoramic rustic views. There was also no shortage of trees and greenery in the form of private gardens, but in fact at its most easterly point, the area nudged the most westerly point of the city's business area, and its heart was only a mile or so from the city centre. Not only was the centre of the city easily accessible on foot, the area was well served by transport; horse buses plied the city's principal streets from the 1840s and trams, horse-drawn initially, from the 1870s. Travelling at 4 miles per hour, the horse-drawn omnibuses could guarantee the estate's passengers reaching the city's business districts within twenty minutes, enabling the continuation of the local middle-class tradition of lunching at home. In addition, most of the spacious terraced houses were provided with stabling, should the residents prefer to travel by private carriage or cab rather than by public transport.[41]

Convenient proximity to the workplace was an important requirement for Glasgow's middle classes for much of the century and one that was valued as much as, if not more than, social exclusivity. When the extension of the business district further west drove the middle classes further from the city centre, it was often not the far-flung suburban havens they sought, but the new residences that were being built nearby. Even later in the century, when the suburbs had extended much further west, the families of two of Glasgow University's medical professors, Hector Cameron and William MacEwen, moved a matter of a few hundred yards from their residences in the west of the city centre into the Claremont estate, no doubt partly so that they might still be able to walk to the nearby infirmary. The Macfarlane family, neighbours of the Cameron family in Hill Street which lay behind the main thoroughfare of

Sauchiehall Street, preferred to remain even closer to the central business area. When they moved to a larger house in the early 1880s, it was only yards west of their previous residence. This enabled George Macfarlane, who worked as a commission agent, not only to go home for lunch, but to snatch some respite from the counting house and recline on his sofa for a nap.[42] When Joseph Coats was appointed Professor of Surgery at the university, he and his family moved out of the Claremont estate so that he could be nearer his work, despite the fact that his Claremont address was only half a mile from the university. Even with the introduction of intra-city trains from the late 1880s, which enabled people to live more distantly from the city centre, Claremont still retained its attraction. It was not until the beginning of the twentieth century that the substantial bourgeoisie leapfrogged the built-up areas for the more socially exclusively middle-class suburbs outside the city boundaries, such as Bearsden, Milgavie, Helensburgh and Lenzie.[43]

Much has been made of the middle-class desire for social exclusivity of residence as the driving force behind the flight to the suburbs;[44] in Glasgow, however, proximity to the city centre seemed as high a priority as social exclusivity. Even the Claremont estate, which was specifically designed to attract the upper middle classes and to be a socially exclusive district, was close to cheaper tenement houses for the lower middle class and only a few hundred yards or so from the teeming slums of Anderston and Cowcaddens. Although there was distinct segregation by street, wealthy merchants and manufacturers and professionals lived alongside a much larger and socially heterogeneous middle class who congregated in the more modest houses at the foot of the hill. Here, there were originally fairly substantial terraced houses such as those of Queen's Crescent, built in 1840.[45] Later development brought terraces of small houses and tenements. The addition of cheaper and smaller housing to accommodate the lower middle classes and some artisans did not appear to induce those who inhabited the more august mansions to flee to more socially exclusive districts, for until the First World War property prices in the area remained buoyant, indicating the continued desirability of these residences.[46] Therefore the familiar narrative of residential segregation and the emergence of well-defined social boundaries is oversimplified; districts were likely to house varying mixes of social status groups.[47]

It is this social mix that largely determined the choice of the area whose census returns form the core of this study. In order to encompass as broad a range as possible within the spectrum of the middle classes, we chose twelve streets from the Claremont/Woodside/Woodlands area.

A further consideration was that all twelve should have residential occupation between 1851 and 1914. To the east of this area, streets that housed the middle class in 1851 had either been given over to commercial use or fallen in status by the end of the period. The westward expansion of middle-class housing gathered pace in the last quarter of the century: but the terraces and tenements of Glasgow's West End were largely built considerably later than the Claremont estate.

Within the selected streets there was considerable variation in property values. In 1851, no. 8 Claremont Terrace was bought for £3,500, while by 1892 no. 5 was on offer at £4,500.[48] In 1894 a 'mid-range' eleven-room house in Woodside Place cost £2,500, and nos 38 and 42 Carnarvon Street together could be bought for £3,300. However, many of the Claremont/Woodside houses were in fact rented by their occupiers: only a minority were owner-occupied. A house in Queen's Crescent could be rented in 1897 for £140 per annum, while 32 Lynedoch Street cost £255 per annum.[49]

The diversity of the area is represented by the occupations of heads of household. Manufacturers were chiefly concentrated in the textile and clothing industries, although there were iron and coal masters and shipbuilders too. Merchants were classified either by the goods they traded (textiles, wine, metals, sugar) or by the places they traded with (India, West Indies, South America). Professionals included lawyers, bankers, accountants, doctors, ministers and academics. In the lower middle-class streets there were teachers, grocers, drapers and above all clerks – shipping, insurance and bank clerks – as well as a smattering of representatives of the 'higher' professions. There is little change in this occupational profile across the census period. The only part of the area where new houses were being built was in the more modest Carnarvon and Stanley Streets, and this is reflected in the greater proportion of lower middle-class occupations towards the end of the century. Otherwise, the mix of commerce, industry and the professions remained similar throughout the period.

Therefore the occupational and social profile of the area reflected the heterogeneity of the non-manual classes in the city generally. The disparities of wealth and income among the residents were reflected in a multitude of ways, most obviously in the size and value of the houses and the number of servants employed. The larger and more expensive houses and mansions of fifteen and more rooms were located in the terraces and crescents on the brow of the hill, with more modest, but still substantial, houses in the streets leading up to them. At the foot of the

Table 1   Rooms per household, 1871*

Street	Range	Mean
Claremont Terrace	18–26	20.75
Woodside Terrace	12–30	18.6
Lynedoch Crescent	12–20	16.3
Woodside Crescent	14–17	15.3
Woodside Place	13–17	14.5
Queens Terrace	7–18	11.9
Queens Crescent	9–15	11.8
Woodlands Terrace	11–14	11.6
Lynedoch Street	6–16	8.8
Stanley Street	2–8	5.9
Claremont Street	3–9	5.4
Carnarvon Street	1–9	4.8

*Here and elsewhere we use the census definition of rooms with one or more windows

estate socially, economically and geographically were Carnarvon, Claremont and Stanley Streets. Table 1 shows the number of rooms per house in 1871.

Most of the more substantial terraces followed a similar design and layout: the main entrance was usually porched, pedimented and pillared. They were three storeys high with a basement, no front garden but a 'bleaching green' at the rear. Typically the front door opened on to a high broad hall which was adorned with a pair of Greek columns. The kitchen, laundry and other service rooms were located in a semi-basement, principal rooms on an elevated ground floor, and bedrooms on the floor or floors above. Servants' bedrooms might be at the very top or very bottom of the house, with some preference shown for housing the servants in the basement next to the kitchen, probably because these terraced town houses were not equipped with two staircases. In addition to the dining room and drawing room, larger houses might have a study, library, billiard room, sewing room, nursery, and various anterooms, lobbies and pantries.

The more modest houses at the foot of the hill were very different from their near neighbours at the top. The first homes built here were relatively small terraced houses, the largest having seven or eight rooms. Later, tenement housing was added, with apartments of four or five rooms

arranged two to a floor over four floors. Typical of the latter was the
home of Marion Gilchrist, victim in a celebrated murder case in 1908,
where Miss Gilchrist, despite considerable personal wealth, lived modestly
in a dining room, drawing room, parlour, kitchen and two bedrooms. Miss
Gilchrist kept only one resident servant. This was common to her neighbours in the less wealthy streets: in Stanley Street in 1851 there were forty-
seven servants in thirty-seven households, nearly all simply designated
'house servant'.

More servants were of course employed in the larger houses. In 1851
there was an average of 5.8 servants per household in Claremont Terrace.
In these grander households, there was always a cook and at least a couple
of maids. In addition, there could be a nursemaid, laundress, lady's maid,
and a butler or housekeeper to oversee them. In these large establishments, the wage bill could be up to £200 a year.[50] More typically, Andrew
and Jean Chrystal in 1881 kept three female servants: the accounts taken
on his death in 1883 list a half-yearly wage bill of £20.[51] Numbers of
servants fell steadily throughout the period, from a mean of 2.5 per household in 1851 to only 1.2 in 1891, by which time many of the less well-
off had no resident servant at all.

Despite the clear variation in material culture across the spectrum of
the middle class, there were some similarities. This is clear because in
Scotland, unlike in England, detailed probate inventories were still being
taken in this period. They provide a vivid picture of the furnishings and
appearance of the domestic interior and make it possible to reconstitute
the physical context of family life. Domestic space – whether in the grand
terraces or in the tenement flats – was crammed with furniture and orna-
ment. As an example, it is worth looking in some detail at the upstairs
landing in the Lynedoch Street home of James Thomson as it was as late
as 1905. Although this space must have been of considerable size, it was
not even a room as such. Nevertheless, there were a Sutherland table and
a writing desk by way of furniture. Two cut-glass decanters and a tea set
on a tray provided the possibility of refreshment. There were also a bronze
figure, jardiniere, three flower pots, wrought-iron stand, flower holder on
a marble stand, Japanese vases on stands, as well as numerous other vases
– two covered, two tall, three Japanese, two large and one triangular. There
were also watercolours and a 'framed copper head' on the walls and what
the apparently defeated valuer simply listed as '26 ornaments' and '35 vases
and ornaments'.[52]

As early as the 1850s, the drawing room of William Houldsworth in
Claremont Terrace was furnished with two sofas, twelve chairs, two easy

chairs, four card tables, two teapoys, four stools, a sideboard, two pole fire-screens, a Canterbury, another table, and a semigrand piano and stool.[53] This was all in addition to mirrors, books, engravings, Chinese vases, mantelpiece ornaments, brass ornaments, clocks and ornaments under glass domes and, of course, a 'bust on a marble stand'. Similarly, although Miss Isabella Campbell, in 1890 and at the lower end of the scale, had a 'parlour' as opposed to the drawing rooms of the higher middle class, its furnishings were very similar in type if not in quantity.[54] She also had a sideboard, sofa, easy chairs and tables and chairs, all in mahogany, and a rosewood piano. She too had flower pots and mantelpiece ornaments, a whatnot, figures and ferns under glass, and five pictures and a mirror on the walls.

At all socio-economic levels, colour schemes were rich and heavy. Outside bedrooms, where some pine and birch appeared, furniture was in mahogany or rosewood. Crimson was the most frequently chosen colour for curtains, furniture coverings and even bed hangings, followed by green and gold. Throughout the period, homes were lit by gas, and both drawing and dining rooms had 'gasoliers' with brackets and three, four or even five globes.

In contrast to the family areas of these houses, the service areas – kitchens, laundries and so on – appear to have had little furniture and surprisingly few appliances and utensils, given the scale of cooking and washing that was to be done there. All kitchens had a range or a grate with an oven, but several still also had an old-fashioned roasting jack or spit. In 1889 Mrs Margaret Wilson in Woodside Place had only a range, table and chairs, clock, two dish covers, scales, jack, 'odd crockery shapes' and cooking utensils in the kitchen of her otherwise opulent home.[55] In other kitchens there were dedicated pans like those for fish or jam, and several also had coffee grinders. There is, however, no sign of any labour-saving device for cooking or cleaning. Curiously, the only kitchen to have any recorded source of lighting was that of Dr Alexander Anderson of Woodside Crescent, as early as 1870, where there was a gas bracket.[56] The entire kitchen furnishings of Andrew Jack in 1885, including the fire grate, were worth £2 14s 6d, as opposed to the walnut three-door commode in the drawing room which alone was valued at £6 10s.[57] This paucity of kitchen equipment and furnishing accords with what Davidoff and Hall found for the earlier period in England. It is noteworthy that things remained so unchanged into the twentieth century, and that the over-furnishing of the rest of the house, at all social levels, was in such contrast to the sparseness of the service areas.

Nearly all homes had a laundry or wash-house, where again there is little evidence of difference according to wealth or any change over time in the way in which washing was done. Throughout the period, everyone had a mangle. Mangles were expensive: the Houldsworths' 'patent mangle' in 1854 was valued at a whopping £5 10s. Across the area, washing was still done in a traditional way, with tubs and 'luggies'. Because the houses of the lower middle class in the study area were, by and large, built later than the mansions of the very rich, they were paradoxically provided from the start with some amenities not present in the latter. Miss Gilchrist's flat in Queen's Terrace had a purpose-built bathroom: as late as the 1870s the grander houses in Woodside Crescent were still without bathrooms.

In the same way, servants' bedrooms even in the most opulent houses were sparsely – often spartanly – furnished, with beds, old pieces of carpet, a chest of drawers and perhaps a chair. The only furniture in Andrew Jack's servants' room besides the bed was a dressing glass worth half a crown. James Watson's manservant's room in 1869 contained more furniture than usual, but it chiefly consisted of 'an old Pembroke table', a 'dressing table and glass (damaged)' and, somewhat unexpectedly, an 'old gun' and two swords.

Thus parts of even the most prosperous homes were meanly furnished; and parts of the most modest lower middle-class homes were relatively expensively and showily accoutred. 'High' Victorian taste for clutter and solidity prevailed throughout the period, and across the whole middle class. Nevertheless, there were obvious disparities in the size and types of houses, which were also reflected in the wealth accumulated by their inhabitants. Table 2 shows the value of estates recorded in Glasgow confirmations: although numbers of cases are sometimes small, there is a striking correlation between the size of houses and the wealth of inhabitants in the various streets of the area.

The rich in this area were drawn from the ranks of merchants, manufacturers and even the professions. The shipowner James Allan left £371,000 in 1880; Peter White, an accountant, left £362,000 in 1881.[58] On a slightly less exalted level, there is comparability between the estates of Alexander Ewing, 'merchant' in 1876 (£23,000), Robert Ross, writer (solicitor) in 1881 (£22,000), and Agnes the widow of Alexander Johnston, a power loom manufacturer, in 1877 (£39,000). At the other end of the scale, James Fraser, a clothier, left £1,400, Robert Pinkerton, a doctor, left £558, and Andrew Clow, a 'wright and builder' left £795.

Table 2   Value of estates, 1876–1888

Street	Mean value	Estates
Woodside Terrace	£86,133	11
Claremont Terrace	£43,959	6
Woodlands Terrace	£16,585	8
Woodside Place	£13,447	3
Lynedoch Street	£13,223	7
Queens Terrace	£7,588	8
Woodside Crescent	£5,689	3
Queens Crescent	£2,489	6
Claremont Street	£1,202	7
Lynedoch Crescent	£882	1
Carnarvon Street	£770	14
Stanley Street	£551	6

Thus it is clear that our study area encompassed great social, economic and occupational diversity. However, especially at the top of the pyramid, occupational groupings were far from discrete: while the head of household might have been assigned to the ranks of manufacturers, professionals or to commerce, in practice there was wide occupational diversity within one family, making it difficult to assign entire families to one occupational category. This is particularly evident among sons: occupational scattering among siblings was commonplace. William Newlands of Lynedoch Crescent in 1881 had four sons in their twenties living at home. William senior was a 'Brazilian merchant', as was one of his sons. Another was a 'member of the Glasgow Stock Exchange'. The younger two were a theological student and a 'law apprentice'.

As well as an occupational amalgam within families, individuals' economic interests could also be diversified across a range of activities, either in terms of investments or business interests. The Houldsworths had begun in business as cotton spinners, and realising the potential of iron diversified into the foundry business and subsequently blast furnaces. According to one biographical account: 'If a branch of trade seemed to languish, they dropped it; if it promised to become a success they dashed at it.'[59] The Smith family of shipowners is another example of the ways in which businessmen diversified their interests in the nineteenth century. They began as wholesale and retail warehousemen, then, taking advantage of trade with India, acquired a barque in 1840; by the 1850s their City Line consisted of a substantial fleet of vessels which had a monopoly of the Calcutta trade.[60]

The nature of the local economy was relatively small in scale and concentrated in location and thus there developed a complex web of interconnections based on interdependence of supply and demand of services as well as goods. Therefore despite the competitive nature of the economy based on market forces, as Anthony Slaven has suggested, businessmen were propelled into a mutually supportive community.[61] Shipbuilding and shipping, two of Glasgow's important businesses, frequently established mutually beneficial 'bespoke' links, with a shipbuilding firm often custombuilding for a particular shipping line. For example Alexander Stephen of Park Terrace, shipbuilder, had a long and profitable connection building ships for the Allan, Clan, Furness, Withy and Leyland lines, and the owners were also close friends of the family.[62] It was not only businessmen who formed supportive business and social networks. Alexander Stephen was a member of a small circle of scientists and industrialists who met regularly in the home of James Brownlee, founder of the City Saw Mills, to 'study how Industry could make better use of Science'.[63] A fellow member of this clique and a good friend of Stephen's was the physicist and academic Sir William Thomson (later Lord Kelvin), brother-in-law of William Houldsworth.

The advent of limited liability had the effect of extending these interconnections with businessmen becoming involved in a multiplicity of directorships.[64] The diversity of economic interests within single families, the range of one individual's economic portfolio and the web of interconnections makes it difficult to conceive of distinct economic sectors with their own interests. As shown in chapters 2 and 3, intermarriage did much not only to cement manufacturing, commercial and professional dynasties, but also to dissolve the boundaries between sectors. Offspring of business families married into the professions, while the sons and daughters of professionals displayed no reluctance to form associations with those with a background in trade and commerce. Jessie, the daughter of George Thomson of Woodside Terrace, a clothing manufacturer, married David Greig, a merchant and partner in Leisler, Greig & Co., while the wife of George Macfarlane, a commission agent, was the daughter of a minister.

Professionals were well integrated into this elite circle of wealth. James Smith, an architect, was a business associate and friend of John Houldsworth, a textile manufacturer, and through this association introduced his daughter to her future fiancé, William Minnoch, one of the directors of Houldsworth's firm. It should not be surprising that professional families were incorporated into this circle, for it was not simply marriage which introduced them into business dynasties; these men were often, like the surgeon and academic Joseph Coats, the sons of businessmen. Indeed professionals often combined their primary career with some dabbling in entrepreneurial activity. William Thomson embarked on several business ventures which included investing in his father-in-law's textile firm.[65] Far from the upper reaches of manufacturing, commerce and the professions representing distinct economic strata, what is striking is the extent to which individuals were interconnected by overlapping business interests, common business ventures, interdependence on each other's services and custom, and by marriage.

Common educational experience was another factor to make the upper echelons of the middle classes cohere. Unlike the substantial bourgeoisie in towns and cities in England who, in the later decades of the century sent their sons to be educated in the public school system, Glasgow's wealthy citizens preferred to educate their sons in the prestigious local day schools and at Glasgow University.[66] Later in the century a few wealthy parents chose to send their sons to board at preparatory schools and then on to an English public school. In the late 1880s Frances and David Murray sent their only son, Anthony, aged about seven, to Bilton Grange preparatory school in England and then on to Rugby. However, it was only a small minority who displayed a preference for the English public school system. Most middle-class parents in Glasgow, even the very wealthy, continued to opt for the local prestigious private day schools such as Glasgow Academy and Kelvinside Academy. The sons of those of more modest means normally attended 'the College', namely Glasgow High School.

Although most of the families' social and economic activities were anchored in the locality, social and business connections ranged well beyond the city. Businesses frequently had branches in other leading British cities, or in the case of shipping, throughout the Empire. The Houldsworths and the Crums had business links to Manchester and Liverpool, while the Allan shipping empire had branches in Glasgow, Montreal and Liverpool with offices in London, Boston, Philadelphia, Baltimore and Buenos Aires.[67] The activities of professional men at the peak of their career were similarly expansive. For example, William MacEwen and Hector Cameron, eminent surgeons, were regularly invited to deliver lectures throughout the country, and occupied leading positions in their professional associations. Indeed, MacEwen served as President of the British Medical Association and became an honorary member of the Imperial Medical Academy, St Petersburg, as well as various other medical foreign academies.[68]

Despite the strong links that these elite families forged across Scotland while maintaining connections with London, their lives and loyalties pivoted around the locality. It was not until after the First World War that there was a haemorrhage of the local political elite to London, a move that coincided with more businesses, particularly those engaged in overseas ventures, moving their headquarters to the metropolis.[69] Localism did much to integrate these families, but cohesion did not rest on a narrowly conceived provincial identity. Arguably the metropolis and the nation were less relevant to Glaswegians than the Empire, which spanned many continents and included a quarter of the world's population. Not only did much of the prosperity of the Glasgow middle class hinge on imperial trade, Scots, including middle-class Scots, were ubiquitous throughout the Empire. The Scottish diaspora migrated to every corner of the Empire, staffing its bureaucracies, managing its plantations and providing volunteers for its armies. On reading of a collapsed tenement building in Edinburgh, Robert Louis Stevenson observed: 'All over the world, [. . .] fancy what a multitude of people could exclaim with truth, "The house that I was born in fell down last night!" '[70] Many of those in our study were born in other cities of the Empire, went to work there, visited relatives there or exported their Christianity as well as their goods there. The pervasive links with the Empire, indeed the role of Scots as creators of the Empire, arguably made imperial ideas central to the formation of middle-class identity in Scotland. Certainly the notion of the nation as an imperialised space is reflected in the school curriculum which included classes in Citizenship and Empire.[71] As discourses of ethnic, 'racial' and cultural identity and difference hinged on notions of superiority and inferiority, they created and legitimated a sense of cultural superiority and fuelled self-confidence among the colonisers, as well as justifying the belief that their authority was supreme and their right to lead divinely ordained.

Cohesion was further cemented by the philanthropic zeal of the men and women who became involved in urban institutions and associations. Civic roles were confined largely to men for most of the period, although women through temperance and suffrage activity played a political role and were particularly conspicuous in philanthropic and religious organisations.[72] A number of the wealthy elite in the area gained high local government offices such as Provost and Baillie, whereas at least one resident represented the city in national government. Of the thirteen Lords Provost of the city between 1851 and 1889, four lived in the Claremont estate. Robert Stewart of Claremont Terrace, an ironmaster, was Provost from 1851 to 1854; Peter Clouston, originally an insurance broker, Provost 1860–63, lived in Lynedoch Crescent; Sir James Watson of Woodside Terrace, Provost 1871–4, had earlier been the founder of the Glasgow Stock Exchange; Sir James King of Claremont Terrace was chairman and director of numerous companies and Lord Provost from 1886 to 1889. Other civic roles were held by residents of the area. James Scott, a cotton spinner, was Deputy Lieutenant of the county in 1861. James Strang of Woodside Place was City Chamberlain for many years until his death in 1863. There were also magistrates and JPs (ten resident in 1851 alone), sheriff substitutes, town clerks, procurators and town councillors.

Participation in the administration of local government was matched by membership of local hospitals and other voluntary organisations, while economic largesse was widely dispersed across the city, to fund libraries, parks, reading rooms, halls and so on. Among the most generous of Glasgow's philanthropists was John Templeton, though the recipients of his benevolence were the usual suspects found among the donations list of Glasgow's great and good. A member of the board of management of the Royal Infirmary, Templeton donated £5,000 to two other hospitals, supported the Blind Asylum and the National Association for the Prevention of Consumption, made donations through his textile firm to a Benevolent Trust run by a committee of his employees, and supported a number of educational institutions in the city.[73]

Women's participation in civic governance was limited by statute until the last three decades of the century. However, a number of mainly middle-class single women took advantage of legislation which allowed them to stand for local government offices so that by the turn of the century women sat on school boards, parish councils and, from 1907, on town councils. Typical of such women was Margaret Kerr: with a Girton certificate in mathematics and a background in teaching, she was elected a member of Glasgow Parish Council for Blythswood and Broomielaw in 1904.[74] Women were particularly active in church-related organisations and in other voluntary societies, carving out an important and influential public role for themselves, while in their philanthropic endeavours they more than matched their male counterparts. Susannah Crawford

Allan, who died in 1876, left bequests in her testament to nineteen separate charities, all Glasgow-based and many associated with the Free Church of Scotland.[75]

Another particularly munificent city philanthropist was Isabella Elder, widow of John Elder, shipbuilder and marine engineer. Isabella moved into Claremont estate after her husband's death in 1869; after briefly heading the company, she sank much of her energy and money into philanthropic enterprises. Among her many benefactions was the creation of Elder Park in Govan, where her husband's firm was based. She purchased 37 acres of ground opposite the shipyard and had it laid out as a park for the benefit of the people of Govan, decreeing that the Commissioners of the Burgh 'provide a good band of music in the park twice weekly in summer and in winter when suitable.'[76] For the university she provided additional endowments for the Chair of Civil Engineering and Applied Mechanics and some years later an endowment for a new Chair in Naval Architecture. The education of women also attracted her support and she provided several bursaries for the Association for the Higher Education of Women, capping this in 1884 by donating North Park House and its grounds to one of the first higher education colleges for women, Queen Margaret College.[77] Her charitable endeavours were legion and ranged from the establishment of a School of Domestic Economy, donations for the building of premises for the Cottage Nurses' Training scheme and the West of Scotland Technical College, the creation of the Elder Free Library and the establishment of the Elder-Ure Fund for Indigent Widows of Govan and Glasgow. During her lifetime it is estimated that she gave £200,000 in public donations over and above the many private gifts she bestowed.[78]

Public beneficence and the panoply of charitable organisations which mushroomed, particularly in the second half of the century, were usually religiously inspired and stemmed from the middle-class crusade to reform and rescue the working classes from godlessness. As Davidoff and Hall have demonstrated, religion was central to middle-class identity in the early nineteenth century and continued to be so throughout the century.[79] Church membership, church attendance (often twice on Sundays) and church leadership were all defining features of middle-class life. Religion was potentially a divisive force in Scotland. Even before the Disruption of 1843, which created the Free Church of Scotland, religious dissent was a more powerful force in Scotland than has previously been believed, and almost a third of worshippers in Glasgow and Edinburgh were Presbyterian Dissenters in the 1830s.[80] However, Evangelicalism and

the shared commitment to the civilising mission were powerful counter-
vailing forces to any divisions which might arise from interdenominational rivalries. City missions were established in 1826 to send divinity
students into slum districts to visit the working classes and spread the
evangelical truth. These interdenominational organisations grew to such
an extent that, to prevent duplication of effort and congregational rivalries, a Home Mission Union was formed in 1885: the city was thereby
parcelled up into small districts, each congregation being allocated a
number of families.[81] The shared commitment to reclaiming the working
classes for Christianity and to exercising moral leadership were powerful
imperatives which united Glasgow's middle classes over potentially divisive interdenominational rivalries.

While the social composition of church membership of all Presbyterian denominations was dominated by the working classes, the leadership
of the church was firmly in the hands of the upper middle classes. In
Glasgow membership of dissenting churches was particularly high among
the middle classes, although it was the United Presbyterian Church which
attracted the patronage of the substantially wealthy in the city.[82] The
Wellington Street United Presbyterian Church, although in the centre of
town, drew many of its members from the residents of Claremont, and
between 1850 and 1870 the area provided numerous elders, deacons and
managers for the church, the vast majority from the upper middle classes,
although there were a few from the lower middle-class streets.[83] The area
also housed twelve ministers, an army chaplain and a missionary, mostly
from United Presbyterian churches, all resident in 1861.

Middle-class religiosity was not simply a question of staffing the institutional structures of religion, congregating in church to affirm social
superiority, or displaying one's 'Sunday best', it was a matter of deeply
held faith and religious conviction. Religion was formative to middle-
class identity and religious discourses of gender were central to the construction of the meanings of masculinity and femininity.[84] Day-to-day life
was fashioned out of the fabric of Christian faith and evangelical commitment. As Brown has argued, Evangelicalism in Glasgow was a potent
force of cohesion among the middle classes, dissolving denominational
boundaries and uniting the middle classes in a religious community
dedicated to converting the working classes to Christianity and saving
their souls. Families from the Established church, such as the Murrays,
dissenting Presbyterians, like the Smiths, and Baptists such as the
Coateses, shared a commonality of purpose in their commitment to the
evangelical cause. Men may have assumed the leadership positions in

congregations, but women were central agents in the evangelical project. In religious discourses women were regarded as the moral and spiritual superiors of men and in possession of unique reformative and redemptive qualities, therefore their contribution to the business of salvation and conversion was regarded as indispensable.[85]

The Macfarlanes exemplify the way in which the civilising mission and dedication to conversion lay at the heart of middle-class religiosity. George Macfarlane was a commission agent, a town councillor, a devout Christian and an elder in the Free Church. His father and uncle had been among the four hundred or so ministers who had withdrawn from the Established Church with Thomas Chalmers in 1843. His wife, Maryanne Macfarlane, was similarly steeped in Free Church traditions; her father had also been among those who had left the Church of Scotland to establish the Free Church, and had written a two-volume exposition of his beliefs, entitled *The Bible, the Missal and the Breviary*. Both her father and his brother settled in Italy to found congregations of the new Free Church of Scotland in Rome and Florence, and the family thus played an important part in extending religious and social networks beyond Scotland.[86] George Macfarlane was President of the Young Men's Christian Association, led services at Glasgow's mission hall and was involved in providing free Sunday dinners to the poor children in the City Halls.[87] The family house, on the fringes of the Claremont estate, was a meeting point for Christian missionaries and believers from all over the globe who were accorded hospitality and welcomed as fellow devotees of the evangelical quest. Although militant Protestants, the Macfarlanes displayed a tolerance to other denominations, and a compassionate pity for those of other religions. Maryanne Macfarlane made the conversion of the local Jewish community her particular project. Poor immigrant Jews were assisted to learn English, in the hope that they might express their gratitude by converting to Christianity, while 'more selective Jews' were invited to her home, perhaps in the belief that prolonged exposure to a Christian environment might by osmosis expedite the conversion experience.[88] However, the Macfarlanes reserved most of their energies for converting the lapsed domestic 'heathen', a task in which they occasionally involved their young children. Sometimes on a Saturday night George Macfarlane would escort his brood on an exploration of the Trongate, one of the most overcrowded and insalubrious districts in the city, so that they might see the 'heathen at our doors' and acquire a loathing for alcohol and its effects. On Sunday afternoons he toured the cells of the police station and bailed out the weekend drunks on the condition that they signed the pledge and repaid the money the following week.[89]

The shipowner Robert Smith and his family were similarly wedded to the evangelical and temperance mission, although adherents of the United Presbyterian Church rather than the Free Church. They were staunch supporters of the Scottish Temperance League, Robert serving as its president for twenty-one years. When his daughter Jane married Alexander Allan of the City Line, she converted him to the temperance cause to which they shared a life-long commitment. Indeed the Allan Line vessels were manned by teetotal masters and liberally supplied with temperance tracts for the passengers. Both Jane and Alexander served on committees of temperance organisations: Alexander was director of the Scottish Temperance League for nine years and vice-president for twenty-five, while Jane was a member of the general committee of the Scottish Christian Union for sixteen years.[90] They were equally active in their church, Wellington United Presbyterian, and in numerous church-related charitable endeavours, for example providing free breakfasts to orphans, donating to the Glasgow Seamen's Friends Society, raising funds through charity bazaars and so on. They were also enthusiastic evangelicals; Alexander was the first president of the Glasgow United Evangelistic Association and provided his church with the funds to build a Home Mission. Indeed they were not simply evangelicals, they were also very much influenced by revivalism, particularly by the visit to Glasgow in 1874 of the American evangelicals Dwight L. Moody and Ira D. Sankey.

Although the evangelical alliance was forged across denominations, there remained significant differences other than the purely doctrinal among those who adhered to the civilising mission. There may have been a consensus about the imperative to save and convert, but there was no unanimity about the route to achieving this and in most denominations there was still room for individual moral choice. For example, attitudes to temperance varied among the middle classes, regardless of denominational differences, over moderation versus teetotalism, while revivalism found both enthusiasts and detractors from within congregations, let alone denominations. Although temperance was advocated by many in the middle class, it was not always practised by them. Total abstention may have been urged on the working classes, but many within the middle classes believed that moderation and temperate drinking were sufficient to demonstrate their righteousness. Joseph Coats was a Baptist and a luminary of the church in Glasgow and was mainly responsible for the foundation of the Baptist Theological College of Scotland in 1894. Baptists were evangelicals *par excellence* and also ardent temperance advocates, yet Coats was happy to down the occasional whisky, opt out of Sunday worship and deplore the emotionalism of certain aspects of revivalist evangelicalism. While on a visit to Crieff Hydro to recuperate from illness, he attended a Sunday service but drew the line at participating in a hymn which proclaimed, 'My soul is black and guilty, my heart is dead within', complaining that, 'the people who sing such a thing are either not in the least conscious of what they are saying or else they are simply going in for cant and humbug. Such is evangelical religion – a poor business.'[91] By contrast, the Macfarlanes were stalwarts of abstinence. Although neither George nor Maryanne Macfarlane had been raised in temperance households, and both enjoyed in moderation the pleasures of drink, the experience of their work with Glasgow's poor convinced them of the rectitude of total abstinence. In the words of his daughter: 'how could he even suggest to one of these men the giving up of drink if he himself were going home to refresh himself with a glass of port?'[92]

These sorts of differences must have been multiplied in the countless social, intellectual and political choices that individuals made. However, what drew the upper reaches of the middle classes together in common cause was the imperative to affirm and legitimate their moral authority and superiority, by assuming positions of moral and political leadership in the community. Although this shared commitment was often borne out of religious belief, it was refracted through class position. Common membership of a matrix of civic, philanthropic, professional and business-related organisations, the frequent encounters they brought and the shared interests they reflected and reinforced did much to foster friendships, grease the wheels of business transactions and advance professional careers. However, it was also crucial in the creation of a common identity, in constituting this group as a political, cultural and moral force and in constructing a public space where its adherents were able to display and reinforce their moral authority.

The overwhelming majority of the residents of the Claremont/Woodside estate area were drawn from the ranks of non-manual workers. Nevertheless, they were multiply differentiated. The most obvious and visible distinctions were material: the size of their houses, the numbers of servants they employed, the amount of wealth they acquired and the ways in which they displayed it. In this respect there was a gaping chasm between those who had substantial amounts of wealth and the bulk of the rest who had modest means and lifestyle. It was also the case that their involvement and leadership in associational life across the spectrum of civic, voluntary, religious and philanthropic organisations distinguished the wealthy. However, the middle classes cannot be defined solely as a social and economic formation or even on the basis of their role in urban institutions and associations. The middle classes were constituted across diverse sites and middle-class identity was a cultural construct which was mutable and multiply formed, particularly by gender. The ideology of domesticity and the cult of the home have long been regarded as central elements in the construction of the nineteenth-century middle class and it is to the site of this prime constituent of middle-class identity that we now turn, the family and household.

2

It's a Family Affair

THERE IS A POPULAR PERCEPTION that the Victorian family was a large extended unit comprising several generations of one family living together and bound by ties of affection, duty and obligation. However, sociological and historical interpretations differ widely from this, and since the 1970s or so the received view among academics is that far from a past of large, extended-family households, north-west Europe has since at least the Middle Ages favoured a pattern of nuclear family residence.[1] In early modern England, only some 10 per cent of households appear to have been of extended form at any given period.[2] While the cyclical nature of household formation, with families experiencing different forms at different stages, is generally acknowledged, the orthodoxy maintains that the nuclear family was the preferred form.

'Family', of course, is not coterminous with 'household'. Those family members with whom we live are not usually our only kin; and the household may also contain members who are not relatives. The availability of such sources as the census enumerators' books and pre-census parish listings has led to a concentration on the residential unit of the household: and the point is well made that there has consequently been something of a neglect of links with kin who do not co-reside.[3] Some studies have investigated the range of kin recognition, but these have largely concentrated on the medieval and early modern periods.[4] Others have used census returns to point to apparent familial links between separate households among the nineteenth-century working class. Michael Anderson, in his classic study of family structure in Preston in 1851, found clusters of households of the same surname and originating from the same area, and argued that the family was used by the urban working class as an employment and housing agency.[5]

Surprisingly few studies of the middle class have been written, whether investigating family or household. Consequently, no 'new orthodoxy' has emerged comparable with that for the working class. Richard Sennett, in his study of the nineteenth-century Chicago middle class, argued that there were very few extended households, although he found close social and economic links between non-resident kin.[6] In his later study of a number of industrial cities he confirmed the ubiquity of the nuclear home, arguing that extended-family forms were more common among the lower middle classes than the upper middle class.[7] In contrast, Stephen Ruggles in his comparison of middle-class families in nineteenth-century Wisconsin and Lancashire found the High Victorian period to be a 'golden age' of the extended family.[8] In fact, although interpretations of their significance vary, these studies all report similar findings: between 20 and 30 per cent of middle-class households were extended in form. Furthermore, there has been a tendency to assume that the remaining three-quarters of households conformed to the standard nuclear pattern of two parents plus children, when in fact single-parent families and even lone individuals are also included in the 'nuclear' category. Consequently, undue reliance has been placed on the stereotypical picture of the Victorian middle-class family, turned in on itself, privatised and intensely nuclear.

This book demonstrates that the Glasgow middle class, like the working class of Preston and elsewhere and like the middle class of Ruggles's study, lived in households that were often not simply nuclear in structure. In the census study area, just under 29 per cent of households were extended in type in 1851. This is higher than figures reported elsewhere for working-class households in the same year (23 per cent in Preston; 21 per cent in Oldham).[9] It is also higher than the 23 per cent found by Anthony Howe among Lancashire cotton masters, also for 1851.[10] In 1861, 24 per cent of our households were extended: in 1871 (for which Ruggles found 20 per cent), the percentage had risen to 31, where it remained for 1881, before falling back to 28 by 1891.[11] These findings support the view that the middle-class household was certainly no less likely than the working-class one to contain wider kin. The Glasgow middle class shows a higher incidence of extended living arrangements than any of the groups in these earlier studies, although the pattern over time, peaking in 1871 and 1881, accords with that found among other middle-class groups identified by Ruggles.

Significantly, Table 3 shows that 15 per cent of households classified as nuclear in 1851 were in fact one-parent units, with the corresponding figure for 1891 rising to 21 per cent. Around three-quarters of these one-parent households were headed by women throughout the period. Similarly, single-individual households by 1891 comprised 12.5 per cent

Table 3　Household Type, 1851–1891

	1851	1861	1871	1881	1891
Households listing a head	209	257	282	292	313
Single %	4.8	8.2	9.6	11.0	12.5
Nuclear one parent %	15.3	19.1	19.9	18.5	21.7
Nuclear both parents %	51.2	48.6	39.4	40.1	37.1
Stem %	2.9	2.3	2.8	3.4	3.5
Composite %	25.9	21.8	28.4	27.1	25.2
Total extended %	28.8	24.1	31.2	30.5	28.7
Total %	100.1	100	100.1	100.1	100

of the total, two-thirds of them lone women. Therefore, if one examines the incidence of households conforming to the standard bourgeois model of a male-headed nuclear unit, the figure falls to only half of the households in 1851 and to just over a third in 1891.

Anderson and others have argued that the incidence of extended-family households among the working class was a response to the pressures of poverty and industrialisation – a strategy for maximising family resources. It seems unlikely that the same factors can explain the frequency of extended families among the more affluent middle classes. Ruggles suggested that this can be attributed to the interaction of economic, demographic and cultural factors, with none of these variables having explanatory primacy over the others. Contrary to Anderson, Ruggles argued that extended living arrangements were more often an economic burden than a functional adaptation to the hardships associated with industrialisation. In other words, living with one's kin was a luxury and it was rising incomes in the second half of the nineteenth century which meant that more people were able to support dependent kin. For Ruggles, demographic factors such as rising life expectancy (resulting in greater numbers of surviving relatives), coupled with a cultural preference for living with extended kin, conjoined with economic factors to make the late nineteenth century the zenith for extended-family structures.

However, in order fully to explore class-specific variation in the incidence of extended families, it is necessary to distinguish between

Table 4   Wider kin in households, 1851–1891

	1851	1861	1871	1881	1891
Grandparent	–	–	–	–	–
Great-aunt/uncle	1	–	–	–	–
Parent	2	5	6	4	10
Parent-in-law	3	6	1	3	5
Aunt/uncle	1	3	3	1	6
Sibling	48	56	62	86	75
Sibling-in-law	17	9	17	13	10
Cousin	1	2	4	3	1
Stepchild	8	–	–	3	2
Son-/daughter-in-law	2	–	3	3	5
Niece/nephew	14	30	30	32	37
Grandchild	6	5	23	19	24
Great-nephew/-niece	–	4	2	3	1
Total	103	120	151	170	176

vertical and horizontal extension: three- or four-generation households on the one hand; and wider kin of the same generation as the household head on the other. In Table 3, vertically extended types are called 'stem' families, and horizontally extended ones 'composite', following a typology established by the Cambridge Group for the History of Population and Social Structure.[12] Single-person households and those of parents and children are also enumerated.

The table shows how the figures for extended-family households discussed in this book are made up largely of horizontal, rather than vertical, extension. Vertical extension, by contrast, has been identified as more common among the working class.[13] Rather than what Ruggles called a 'nursing home effect', with elderly parents moving in with married offspring, Table 4 illustrates a household where siblings, aunts, uncles, nephews and nieces of the head or head's spouse were more likely to be the wider kin present.[14]

Only a tiny minority of households had a parent or parent-in-law in residence. Siblings and their children, however, were much more frequently present.

Another telling feature of Table 3 is the proportion of households which conformed to the stereotypical 'privatised' bourgeois nuclear

Table 5   Household size, 1851–1891

	1851	1861	1871	1881	1891
With head	8.1	7.6	6.9	6.4	6.1
All	7.2	6.7	5.4	5.5	4.9
Stanley St	5.3	6.4	5.6	5.1	5.5
	5.7	5.8	4.2	4.3	3.9
Carnarvon St	5.9	5.3	5.3	5.0	4.7
	4.9	4.9	3.9	4.1	3.8

family. In fact, households comprising father, mother and children were only just a majority in 1851 (51.2 per cent) and thereafter never reached half. Indeed by 1891 they made up not much more than a third (37.1 per cent) of all households. Although most individuals would have experienced living in the stereotype bourgeois household of the paterfamilias, his wife and children, at any point during the period from 1861 these 'standard' families were in the minority. In particular, as examined in more detail in chapter 6, a considerable (and rising) proportion of households were headed by women, which is certainly at odds with the conventional picture of the Victorian household organised around and subordinate to the paterfamilias.

As the proportion of two-parent nuclear families fell, so the proportion of those living alone, and of one-parent nuclear families, rose. There are two possible explanatory factors: the population of the area was ageing through the period (from a mean age, excluding servants, of 20.1 years in 1851 to one of 32.9 years in 1891); and the new houses in Stanley and Carnarvon Streets were generally smaller and cheaper than the impressive residences of the rest of the area, and thus potentially perhaps more appealing to those living alone or as single parents.

There is a marked difference in household size between Carnarvon and Stanley Streets and the rest of the study area: both households and families were smaller in the lower middle-class streets. Table 5 shows size of household across the period, firstly for the whole area of this study. Two measures are used. The mean is first given for all households where a 'head of household' was present, thus excluding households where only servants were in residence, 'lodger' households where these were entered separately from the main household, and so on. It therefore probably

Table 6 Household size, excluding servants, 1851–1891

	1851	1861	1871	1881	1891
With head	5.2	5.1	4.8	4.5	4.5
All	4.6	4.5	3.8	3.9	3.7
Stanley St	4.1	5.0	4.8	4.4	5.1
	3.8	4.6	3.6	3.7	3.6
Carnarvon St	4.4	4.5	4.7	4.3	4.5
	3.6	4.1	3.4	3.6	3.6

overestimates the true figure somewhat. On the other hand, the second mean figure is for all households – and is probably an underestimate of actual household size since by definition it includes households where at least one member was temporarily not at home. Thus it can be said that in 1851, for instance, mean household size lay somewhere between 7.2 and 8.1. Household size declined over the period, to between broadly 5 and 6 by 1891. These households are nevertheless large by comparison with mean figures reported for the population at large. Peter Laslett's mean household size of 4.75 up to 1820 was subsequently argued to hold good for the period up to the 1860s. Even by 1891, mean household size in the study area was consistently higher than this. The figures for the two lower middle-class streets, Carnarvon and Stanley Streets, make up an increasing proportion of the total. Households in these streets were always smaller than the mean for the whole area, but they too followed the pattern of decreasing over time.

One obvious explanation for the relative size of middle-class households is the presence in them of live-in domestic servants. Table 6 therefore excludes servants from the analysis. Their removal shows that household size is much closer to norms recorded elsewhere among the working class. There is also a marked decline in household size after 1861. Note that this period marked the beginning of the great fertility decline among the middle classes.[15] As the figures for all households in Stanley and Carnarvon Streets show, much – but not all – of the difference in household size between the lower middle-class households and those of the area as a whole was a result of the smaller numbers of servants in the former.

Table 7   Nuclear family size, 1851–1891

	1851	1861	1871	1881	1891
With head	4.2	4.1	3.7	3.5	3.5
All	3.8	3.6	3.0	3.0	2.8

The decline in family size becomes more striking when one focuses on the nuclear family. Table 7 considers only those individuals described as 'head', 'wife', 'son' or 'daughter', and shows mean family size on this basis both for households where a head was present, and for all households (as above). We are not in a position to compute mean completed family size, and must remember that these are nuclear family members resident at a particular moment, and that child-free households are also included in the analysis. Nevertheless, the indications are that the 'standard' nuclear family was decreasing in both size and frequency right across the spectrum of the middle class.

Because of the tradition in Glasgow of educating boys at local day schools, the number of sons and daughters in early adulthood living in the parental home is remarkably similar. To take 1861 as a random example, there were fifty-seven sons between the ages of fifteen and twenty-one in parental homes, and sixty-six daughters. Given the slightly higher number of females in the general population, this is not a marked difference. Differences do become more marked at later ages. Daughters in the twenty-two to twenty-nine age bracket outnumber sons by sixty-two to thirty-seven, and among those aged thirty and over by twenty-four to twelve. Adult sons were a significant, if minority, presence in the family home.

While historians have differed over the composition and form of nineteenth-century households, they have been almost unanimous in explaining the incidence of extended-family households among the middle class in terms of the need to offer shelter – physically, financially and socially – to female relatives. Davidoff *et al.* assert that, 'As adults, sisters often took over housekeeping roles supported by their brothers in a financial and emotional bond not dissimilar to the conjugal.'[16] Nenadic, too, finds that Glaswegian middle-class sisters often acted as housekeepers to their unmarried brothers.[17] Ruggles also speaks of the need to support single female relatives, and notes that in Victorian Lancashire 62 per cent of horizontal kin – those of the same generation as the head of household

— were never-married women. According to Ruggles, the lack of economic opportunities for middle-class women and the requirements of bourgeois respectability meant that needy close relatives, who were likely to be female, should be maintained even if they were an economic liability.[18] Davidoff's and Hall's study of Edgbaston and Essex in 1851 finds that there were almost twice as many daughters over thirty living with parents than sons, and that the largest single group of extended kin were the sisters of the head of household — the archetypal spinster of the Victorian novel or the 'surplus' or 'redundant' women referred to by contemporaries.[19] There are similar findings in Howe's study of cotton masters in Lancashire, where a high percentage of extended kin were single dependent women.[20] Dorothy Crozier has suggested that marriage was the exception rather than the rule for the majority of upper middle-class daughters and that it was customary for them to live in households headed by a married man, be he father, brother or uncle.[21] These studies seem to add weight to the view that the middle-class Victorian extended family was largely made up of that pool of single women who, lacking the means and the social approbation to lead an independent and autonomous existence, sought refuge and protection in a male-headed household.

A preliminary glance at the composition of households in the Claremont estate would seem to confirm the conclusions of other historians in that the wider kin present in the households there were predominantly women. Across the period, between 72 and 80 per cent of non-nuclear kin were female. Table 8, which provides a breakdown by sex of those wider kin set out in Table 4, shows that females did outnumber males — the figures for aunts, nieces and sisters are higher than those for uncles, nephews and brothers, and so on. And in line with the findings of Davidoff and Hall and others, the largest category of resident non-nuclear kin is indeed sisters of the head of household.

Sisters and sisters-in-law of the head of household accounted for between 45 and 48 per cent of all non-nuclear kin in our sample for most of the period, declining only somewhat to 36 per cent in 1891. The mean age of these women, who were predominantly single, was just over forty, which strongly suggests that they were indeed the surplus single women who were regarded as such a problem. However, the findings also reveal a serious flaw in the argument which seeks to explain this phenomenon in terms of economically independent men sheltering economically dependent women. In many cases of households with female wider kin resident, the heads of house proved to be women. Sisters did indeed move into households headed by siblings: but they were almost as likely

Table 8   Resident non-nuclear kin, 1851–1891

	1851	1861	1871	1881	1891
Aunt	1	3	3	1	4
Brother	12	8	9	18	18
Brother-in-law	4	1	2	5	2
Cousin	1	2	4	3	1
Daughter-in-law	2	–	2	1	3
Father	–	2	–	–	1
Father-in-law	1	–	–	1	–
Granddaughter	4	2	13	11	14
Grandnephew	–	1	2	2	–
Grandniece	–	3	–	1	1
Grandson	2	3	10	8	10
Great-aunt	1	–	–	–	–
Mother	2	3	6	4	9
Mother-in-law	2	6	1	2	5
Nephew	6	10	7	10	9
Niece	8	20	23	20	28
Niece-in-law	–	–	–	2	–
Sister	36	48	53	68	57
Sister-in-law	13	8	15	8	8
Son-in-law	–	–	1	2	2
Stepdaughter	5	–	–	–	2
Stepson	3	–	–	3	–
Uncle	–	–	–	–	2
Total	**103**	**120**	**151**	**170**	**176**

to be sisters as brothers (see Table 9). In 1871, for example, the mid-point year in the census survey, fifty-two households were headed by an unmarried person: in thirty-three cases this was a woman, and in only nineteen was it a male. There simply were not many single men heading households in which their sisters *could* act as housekeepers.

Sisters were of course not the only female wider kin resident in these households. But as with sisters, other kin were by no means all taking economic and social shelter in the home of a male relative. Some categories of wider kin were actually more likely to live in female-headed households than in male. More than half of the nieces, nephews, grandnieces

Table 9 Residence of sisters, 1851–1891

	1851	1861	1871	1881	1891
Brother heads household	20	27	22	40	23
Sister heads household	15	19	30	28	31
Total	36*	47*	53*	68	55*
% with sister	42.9	41.3	57.7	41.2	57.4

*Some sisters in households with absent heads

and grandnephews present in 1881 were living with an aunt rather than an uncle. Even grandchildren were found as often in Grandmama's household as in Grandpapa's. There are also numerous examples of male kin living in female-headed households. While there are some examples of the 'classic' situation of sister keeping house for brother, there are also counterexamples of brothers living in households headed by their sisters. In 1881 Elizabeth Watson, a widow of sixty-seven, headed a household which contained her adult children and her brother George Watson, a sixty-four-year-old unmarried retired stationer. George's will reveals that he was indeed her brother – not brother-in-law – despite the shared surname.[22] Marital status, as well as seniority, seems to be crucial here. It is not known how long Elizabeth had been widowed, or if George had lived with the family before that time: but by 1881 he was definitely living in her household, rather than vice versa. In that same year, 1881, seven brothers and one brother-in-law were living in households headed by their sisters.

Census returns can demonstrate the extent and nature of extended living arrangements; but they allow researchers only to guess at the reasons behind what is recorded. However, in some cases a layer of explanation can be added to the bald statements of the census. The Murray family evidently preferred extended living arrangements across generations. David Murray's mother had moved in with her widowed mother when she herself became a widow. Generations later his daughter Eunice left home in Cardross and moved in to her grandmother's and great-grandmother's household so that she could attend day school in Glasgow. His son Anthony and family moved in to the Claremont house of Anthony's widowed father-in-law, Hector Cameron. Having become grandparents, David and Frances Murray took their grandchildren to live with them – not because they were orphans but because their parents lived abroad.[23] (Given the links between the Glasgow middle class and colonial and other countries, this must have been a fairly common situation, not confined to the Murrays.) Although the immediate reasons for the adoption of extended-household structures differ in each case, they do indicate a predeliction among the Glasgow middle class for co-residence with wider kin as a residential family strategy.

In some settings, 'family' embraced not only those related by blood or by marriage, but also those united by religious belief – spiritual kin. Studies by both John Gillis and by Davidoff and Hall point to the kin-like relations which existed between those of the same religious persuasion.[24] This is exemplified in the language of family ('sister', 'brother') employed within religious groups. In Scotland as in England, this is strongest in groups outside the established church. The Macfarlanes, Free Church members, accommodated a regular stream of visitors in their home, mostly foreign missionaries and co-religionists who were not their blood relatives.[25]

Not even all permanent members of the household were kin. The most obvious and yet often overlooked way in which family differed from household was in the universal presence of servants in this area. They clearly were not 'family' and the distinction was marked. Occasionally, however, their membership of the unified entity of the household was symbolically expressed. In the Smith household, family and servants joined together for 'family' prayers at 9 p.m. on Sunday evenings, as would be the practice in middle-class households across the city. This coming together of the whole household, including servants, in at least ostensible unity and equality before God, conveyed an important message about spiritual kinship, as well as stressing the role of the head of household as moral leader and guardian.

In some cases servants could be awarded quasi-familial status. Margaret Pinkerton in 1881 left the large sum of £100 each to two 'faithful servants', Janet Buchanan and Mrs Jane Gow or Smith.[26] The census of the same year records Janet Buchanan, a single housemaid aged forty-six and born in Callandar, in Miss Pinkerton's household. Twenty years earlier, a Jessie Buchanan, aged forty and also from Callandar, had been a servant of Miss Pinkerton's, so it looks as if the Buchanan family had long supplied servants for her. Similarly, Mrs Smith was not in the household in 1881, but a nineteen-year-old Janet Smith was, and may well have been her daughter. Miss Pinkerton seems to have maintained links with these families over a long period, and recognised those links in her will.

Servants quite often came from the same family. The Misses Fraser of Lynedoch Street had three sisters named Galloway as servants in 1881, one of whom had been with them for at least ten years. Two of the sisters, 'domestic servants in my employment', had witnessed the will of James Fraser in 1878.[27] There are several other instances of servants clearly related to each other: in these households parallel 'families' lived and worked side by side. The passage of time and presumably unstinting loyalty could result in a change of status for servants. For example the 'family retainer' could turn into a companion. Agnes Kennedy, a 'retired nurse' who was staying with Jessie Crum at Largs in 1881, had been mentioned in family correspondence as early as 1864, when she was sent to Manchester to nurse Jessie's ailing sister. Agnes Kennedy seems to some extent to have crossed the boundary between employee and family member. While never coming close to bridging that divide, Madeleine Smith's servant Christina Haggart was trusted by Madeleine to facilitate her meeting a clandestine lover in a way that her own sister was not, the two young women clearly enjoying the conspiracy.

There was usually little ambiguity, at least in terms of census categories, over the status in the household of servants. The compilers of the census were greatly exercised, however, over the exact position of non-family members who were not merely visiting but living in the household. The distinction between 'boarders' and 'lodgers' ultimately hinged on who provided meals and where they were taken. Both groups were more common in the lower middle-class streets than in the homes of the higher bourgeoisie, and were an important source of income for some householders, as discussed below. Lodgers and, particularly, boarders who did eat with the family and generally had a less separate existence, were in the ambivalent position of being with the family but not *of* the family. Table 10 shows how their numbers increased steadily across the period, though once again this perhaps has more to do with the changing socio-economic composition of the area than any other factor.

Like servants, lodgers could form 'parallel families', being related to each other. Brothers quite frequently took lodgings together, for example the two clerks aged nineteen and twenty who were lodgers in the Stanley Street home of Mrs Christina Thom in 1871. Her own eldest son was an eighteen-year-old clerk, and these may have been workmates of his. In any case, it seems likely that relations between lodgers and family were closer than a purely financial arrangement. As with visitors, 'boarders' or

Table 10 Boarders and lodgers, 1851–1891

	1851	1861	1871	1881	1891
Boarder	12	41	20	41	35
Lodger	4	18	63	38	59
Total	16	59	83	79	94

'lodgers' were likely to have been relatives of the family. Colin Strang lodged with Mrs Margaret Strang in Stanley Street, for instance. This phenomenon of kin 'hidden' in the household – another example of the web of family connections – has been noted in English census returns too.[28] While at least some family members paid for their board and lodgings, one wonders how a distinction was made between resident kin and boarders.

John Stephen, as a young single man, provides an example of how resident kin could become lodgers and visitors – in his case in the space of a few weeks. In 1864, John was living with the family of his older brother Alexander: but on 1 June the family went to a seaside house for the summer. The house in Park Terrace was 'shut up' and John noted in his diary that 'I must look out for lodgings'.[29] Because initially the lodgings were 'not ready', John stayed with friends in Woodside Crescent. In fact the friends were relatives of Alexander's wife: John for a while became 'hidden kin' in their household. Presumably he then moved to the lodgings, but his diary omits further details about them.

The comings and goings of lodgers, servants and visitors, as well as the evolving cycles in the formation of the family, reveals the household – and the family – less as a static grouping, as the census tempts one to view it, and more as an ever-changing kaleidoscope of forms. Considering the variation in household size and composition across the economic spectrum, it becomes difficult to construe 'the middle-class household' as if it were a template from which to read off universal experience. Some general characteristics do emerge, but even they do not square with the traditional view of the Victorian household. Although the residential family unit was on average quite small and getting smaller at all levels of the middle-class social scale, it was by no means always nuclear in form. Wider kin, especially those of the same generation as the household head, were often present. Furthermore, many 'nuclear' families did not follow the pattern of paterfamilias, wife and children: single and widowed individuals of both sexes frequently headed households. Household forms often changed over the life-span of the family, encompassing 'standard' nuclear, 'non-standard' nuclear and extended forms at various stages.

Just as the concept of the patriarchal nuclear family is of limited value in developing an understanding of Victorian middle-class family formation, so too is that of the isolated, privatised family. Davidoff *et al.* point out that 'families can be understood as being sited both within and between households.'[30] Certainly in our study area there is ample evidence to illustrate the family connections that existed between households as well as within them. A great web of family connections linked many of the residents, particularly in the wealthier streets of the area. This is not always readily apparent in surnames, as census returns do not observe the Scottish custom of retaining the family name of a married woman.

Mostly, these 'hidden connections' are recoverable through happy accident or idle curiosity. Who were the 'Misses Cecilia H. Fraser and Margaret P. Fraser' of Lynedoch Street, mentioned in the 1882 will of Margaret Pinkerton of Woodside Terrace?[31] At first, there is no apparent link, no obvious reason for Miss Pinkerton to have left money to these two unmarried middle-aged daughters of James Fraser, retired clothier, who appear in the 1881 census at 29 Lynedoch Street. However, we found that Cecilia Hamilton Fraser was born in 1832 to James Fraser and Margaret Pinkerton. This Margaret (herself born in 1801) was the niece of James Pinkerton, father of her namesake Margaret, who died unmarried in 1882. In other words, the Fraser sisters were not only neighbours of Miss Pinkerton, but also her second cousins.

Once begun on tracing this particular family connection, we quickly found ourselves enmeshed in a whole series of further links. Miss Pinkerton also left legacies to her nieces Eliza and Isabella Lumsden, daughters of Sir James Lumsden. They seem not to have lived in the Claremont estate. But James's sister Janet had married Peter White, and they and their family lived at 2 Woodside Terrace. Their children all had Lumsden as a middle name: and James Lumsden was an executor of Peter White's will in 1881. So far, then, this family web connects three Claremont families who appear from the census to be completely unrelated. Meanwhile, at 6 Woodside Terrace lived Janet, the widow of James White, a brother of Peter. Janet was a daughter of the Orr family, wealthy thread manufacturers of Paisley. Still in Woodside Terrace, at no. 21, were the family of

John Orr, thread manufacturer born in Paisley, and certainly a relative of Janet White.

Probably even more dizzying ramifications could be discovered, and the chain pursued even further. Serendipity revealed that the Pinkertons, Frasers, Whites and Orrs were all related by blood or, importantly, marriage. Quite possibly, all the residents of Woodside Terrace had some family connection to each other. No clear distinction can be made between friends and family, neighbours and family, for very often friends and neighbours *were* family. Moreover, it is not the case that painstaking detective work can uncover relationships of which the protagonists themselves were only dimly aware (or not aware at all): for these people recognised quite distant kinship in their naming patterns, in their wills, and in their business dealings.

Intermarriage was common both within and between upper middle-class families. The three families in our area in the late nineteenth century named Playfair were all related, and all the result of a cousin marriage between Patrick Playfair and Jane Playfair which took place in the early years of the century. Marriages between cousins may reflect the frequency and extent of contact between wider kin: they were also a way of keeping property within the family.[32] Two such dynasties sit at the top of the pyramid of wealth in the Claremont estate – the Houldsworths/Ewings, industrialists and landowners, and the Smiths/Allans, shipowners – families whose complex intertwining illustrates the importance of marriage and family in the continuation of a business empire (see figs 1–3). There are examples of cousin marriages, of two sisters marrying two brothers, and of marital unions between the great shipping dynasties. George Smith and Ellen Service were first cousins, as were Robert Smith and Eliza Service. Two other marriages were between more distant cousins. Robert and George Smith were shipowners. Robert's daughter Jane married Alexander Allan, son of Hugh Allan who had emigrated to Canada in 1826 and founded the Allan Line in 1852.[33] Nevertheless, Alexander was in Glasgow in 1854, when the marriage took place. This marriage was crucial in uniting two shipping families, for Robert and Eliza Smith died without male heirs, and their grandson Robert Smith Allan was their chief beneficiary. But it was not the full extent of 'shipping' marriages in the family. Eliza's sister Margaret was married in 1849 to James Corry, who is named as an executor of Eliza's will in 1883 and described as a shipowner and MP of Belfast.[34] Robert Smith Allan married Lizzie Kincaid Greenhorn, who may also have been a member of a well-known West of Scotland shipping family.[35] These family members maintained

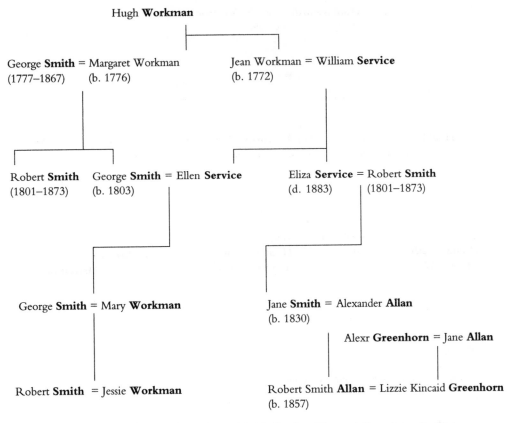

Fig. 1   Descendants of Hugh Workman (Smith, Service, Allan and Greenhorn families)

close links. In 1861 Margaret Corry and her four children were living or staying (though not recorded as 'visitors', so the stay may have been extensive) with the Smiths in Woodside Terrace. In 1851 Eliza's brother William Service was living with the couple. The Smith family tradition of marriage 'within the family' to cement business links and achieve personal advancement continued into the twentieth century. Robert Workman Smith, who married Jessie Hill Workman, was born in 1880.

Similarly, the large and successful Houldsworth family illustrates the importance of family connections in the social and business life of the Glasgow middle class. The clan all stem from Henry Houldsworth, born in Nottingham in 1774, who had settled in Glasgow by 1795. Over the

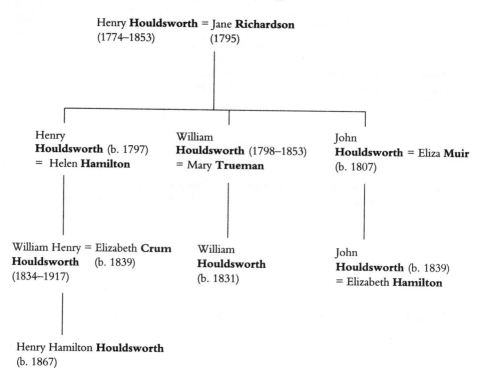

Fig. 2   Descendants of Henry Houldsworth

next thirty years he established himself as one of the leading cotton spinners in the city – before branching out in 1839 to set up the Coltness
Iron Works. As a cotton spinner, Houldsworth had maintained links with
the textile-producing Manchester area, as did his son Henry. In fact Henry
junior's children were born in Manchester in the 1820s and 1830s. Nevertheless one of them, William Henry (b. 1834), was married in Glasgow
in 1862, although he and his bride, Elizabeth Crum, returned to Manchester to live. Family connections remained strong despite distance. In
1881 William Henry was back in Scotland as a visitor. He described
himself as a 'landowner and cotton spinner': in fact he had set up the
enormous Houldsworth Mill near Stockport in 1864. William's wife
Elizabeth (they later became Sir William and Lady Houldsworth) was
the daughter of Walter Crum. The Crums were also cotton spinners, with
a large mill at Thornliebank in Renfrewshire set up in the late eighteenth
century. This was very much a marriage within a business sector. It also
connected the Houldsworths with another wealthy and influential family,

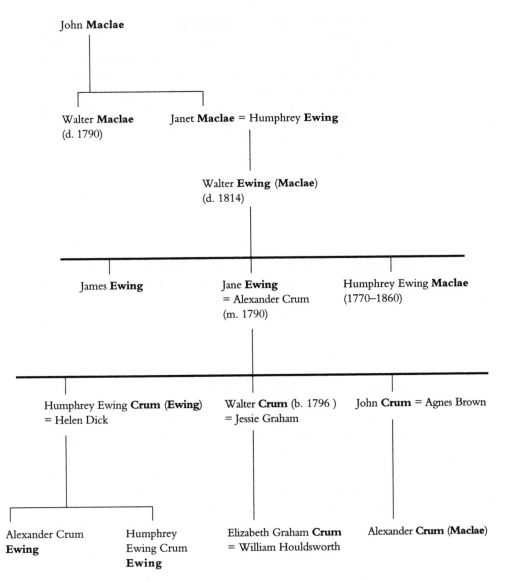

Fig. 3   Descendants of John Maclae (Ewing and Crum families)

the Crum Ewings, who further serve to illustrate the importance of family and family name.

As fig. 3 shows, three individuals changed their surnames. They did so when they inherited through the female line. Walter Ewing adopted the name Maclae; one Crum adopted the name Ewing and another the name Maclae. The custom of using one's mother's maiden name as a middle name resulted in some unfortunate children acquiring names such as Humphrey Ewing Crum Ewing, a testimony to the centrality of family to middle-class experience as well as a potential embarrassment to the bearer. The Ewings were Glasgow merchants, originally the 'tobacco lords' of the city and still retaining business links with the West Indies throughout the nineteenth century. Their name would have died out early in the nineteenth century, had not the son of Jane Crum (née Ewing) taken his mother's surname: and she herself was only a Ewing because her father had changed his surname to that of *his* mother after she was born.

William Houldsworth and his wife Mary lived at 9 Claremont Terrace, where she remained during her long widowhood. The Crum Ewings lived at 7 Claremont Terrace, illustrating yet again the way in which family connections linked neighbours in these upper middle-class streets in much the same way as Anderson found for the mid-century Preston working class. The Glasgow middle classes were not faced with the same economic pressures: yet their families were close-knit within a small geographical area. These interconnections were clearly an important part of family life even though they did not involve co-residence.

Attention has been drawn to the need to look beyond the residential unit of the family to the 'functional family' – that network of kin upon whom one can draw for legal, financial and social support.[36] The concept of the functional family is a useful one and clearly played a crucial role in the Glasgow middle classes. For them too, it did not merely encompass family members with whom one lived, or indeed whom one regularly saw. 'The family' could mean different things on different occasions, and to different people. It could be a set of business connections, a marriage pool, or an important source of financial support. It could also be a set of obligations and responsibilities. Sometimes, of course, 'family' was a residential unit – people with whom one wanted to live or felt obliged or needed to do so. But it was also much more than that and it would be a mistake to let household-based census listings blind one to the extent to which family ties transcended co-residence.

As described above, close contact was maintained between Houldsworths, Allans and others despite the scattering of these clans across Britain and North America. The level of communication which was kept up between kin sits oddly with the stereotype of the beleaguered nuclear family pulling up its drawbridge like Wemmick in *Great Expectations*. Not only the immediate nuclear family, but grandparents, aunts, uncles and cousins maintained frequent and intimate contact, either through correspondence or by visiting. Ritual occasions like family weddings, parties and holidays drew relatives together. The penny post and the advent of rail travel made it easier than ever before to maintain family networks.

Census returns offer no more than glimpses of the extent of visits exchanged with kin. First, they provide merely a snapshot of one night each decade: visiting might have been more prevalent at other seasons. Second, of course, they list only visitors who stayed overnight and not the myriad fleeting visits which are more typical of visiting patterns. Most problematic of all, they do not consistently record family relationships of visitors even where these did exist. In 1851 fifty-one individuals are listed as 'visitors' in our study area. Of these, only eight are specified as related to the head of household. By 1881 and 1891, none of the visitors (thirty-nine and thirty-seven respectively) is apparently a relative of the family. Yet further investigation shows that some of these visitors *were* kin. As just one example, Alexander Dick was simply a 'visitor' in the home of Humphrey Ewing Crum in 1851: but the family tree (fig. 3) shows that he was in fact Humphrey's brother-in-law. In 1881 Margaret Rae, unmarried and aged thirty-seven, was a visitor in the house of George Thomson, a seventy-seven year-old retired manufacturer and widower. It is only the evidence of George's will which bestows respectability on this arrangement, for it reveals that Margaret was almost certainly his niece by marriage.

Family correspondence and family memoirs supplement the partial picture of family visits provided by the census. William Henry Houldsworth's Glasgow connections were cemented by his marriage in 1862 to Elizabeth Crum. Although the couple lived near Manchester, they seem rarely to have been without family visitors from Glasgow. From at least April to September 1864 Elizabeth's parents, one or more of her sisters and an aunt descended on the household in quick succession, sometimes overlapping with each other. Elizabeth's illness and pregnancy and the concern which this aroused probably accounts for the flood of visiting kin. Her father wrote of his gratitude that he had daughters 'where affection places them, so entirely at the disposal of their sister in trouble.'[37] But even in less troubled times, the comings and goings between the family were legion, especially as the Crums also had business in Manchester and Elizabeth's husband business in Glasgow.

Marriage served to multiply the number of visits and visitors to a household. Elizabeth's sister Margaret visited with her husband, while her brother William was accompanied by his wife when he visited the

Manchester couple. The traffic was not only one-way. Three months
before the marriage of Elizabeth and William Houldsworth in 1862, the
couple and her sister were visiting Elizabeth's parents at Rothesay,[38] ensuring that William was inducted early to the level of family contact that he
could expect. Neither were family visits among the Crums confined to
siblings. Jessie Crum stayed with her aunt in Birmingham during this
same period, and accompanied her on another family visit to Hereford.
Meanwhile brother Walter, before leaving for Bombay, was staying with
his uncle John on a shooting holiday.[39] Earlier that summer, sisters Elizabeth and Mary had been to stay with the senior branch of the Crum
Ewings at their estate, Cathkin.

The Crums were not exceptional in the frequency with which they
visited each other. Throughout the period, diaries and correspondence of
the Glasgow middle class record a near-constant round of comings and
goings, especially but not exclusively during summer months. As with
Elizabeth Houldsworth, women could expect lengthy visits from female
relatives when they were pregnant or had given birth. When Maryanne
MacEwen had a son in 1874, 'upon the announcement Grandmother set
off to nurse Maryanne and Dr MacEwan's heir apparent. [She] has been
with Maryanne constantly since she left us and is there at this date.'[40]
Similarly Georgiana Coats abandoned husband and family to be with her
sister during her lying-in period.[41]

Family weddings necessitated quite long visits. John Stephen, for
example, spent a week in Broughty Ferry, on the east coast, for his sister's
wedding in 1864.[42] Rites of passage like weddings were crucial to a sense
of family cohesion and identity among the middle class – part of the web
of mythologies that formed and informed class identity.[43] They recognised
that marriage both united the family for the ceremony and formed new
alliances. Thus the Stephen family gathering was recorded for posterity,
when 'twelve of us went to St Andrews [. . .] and got our likeness taken
in a group'.[44] That the occasion marked the linking of two families as
well as individuals was recognised at the wedding of John McCallum
and Margaret Macewan in 1862, when there were 'no end of toasts and
"suitable replies", the Macewan and McCallum families being given in
succession'.[45]

It was expected that the whole family would gather for weddings, and
the presence and support of male as well as female relatives was vital.
Archibald Allan wrote to his brother James before the wedding of their
sister imploring him to come home as 'Mimma is already in tears.
Her heart she says is broken. The very idea of you not coming will

incapacitate her for the myriads of duties which are now becoming urgent.' Slightly tongue-in-cheek, Archibald added, 'I dare say the marriage will be a complete failure if you don't come': but his brother's presence was genuinely needed: 'This is no flattery of yourself, but a confession of our and more especially of my own helplessness.'[46] Families were also a source of support and solace as well as being participants in the rituals which cemented family identity. When Archibald Allan was ill, his brother-in-law called on his own family connections to provide convalescence. 'His Uncle has a farm about three and a half miles from Rothesay where I would get an abundance of warm milk. He is going to write asking them if they would take me.'[47] They did, and Archibald stayed there for some time.

It was not all happy families, of course, and friction and conflict were no strangers to middle-class families. Janet Story recalled the difficult relationship her parents had with their relatives, particularly her father's sister, who 'was very interfering' in his domestic affairs. To avoid 'open rupture' her parents left Cheltenham to go and live in Edinburgh, where 'daily intercourse' would not be possible.[48] Alexander Stephen's son Andrew resorted to even more drastic measures when he and his father came into conflict over Andrew's expenses for his medical studies. Andrew took his father to court, suing him for £240 to cover expenses 'in the name of Aliment and Expense for Education'.[49] Andrew was apparently a sickly child and young man and therefore did not enjoy 'the advantage of an ordinary liberal education'. His father apparently 'required' Andrew to follow a course of medical education which was interrupted by illness. The protracted nature of his studies meant that he was still studying and incurring expenses at the age of twenty-eight and was no longer being supported by his father. Not all family feuds or conflicts would have been as intractable as these, but they are salutary reminders that families could be sources of sorrow and antagonism as well as tranquillity and nurture.

The different stages of the life-cycle were certainly occasions which drew families together. More usually, however, there was no special reason for family visits. Family members simply went to stay with each other, and took long holidays together, for the pleasure of being in each other's company. In 1880 the Allan siblings had been in Troon on the Ayrshire coast from July. 'It is now a month since we became dwellers by the melancholly [*sic*] ocean and during that time I can assure you we have engaged ourselves thoroughly', Hugh Allan wrote to his brother. 'The girls are delighted to think that there is still something to live for seeing that Archie will be down on Friday and you on Monday.'[50]

Contacts between family members were not confined, of course, to lengthy visits. Many families lived close enough for short visits which did not involve staying overnight. These could be informal and indeed unexpected: Walter Crum wrote in 1864: 'I was going to answer your letter when Mr Steven arrived with Janet and Mary Crum, and I must go out with them.'[51] On other occasions, relatives turned up to look over the family works at Thornliebank. The party which the Crums held in April 1864 was attended by several Grahams, Houldsworths and Crums, who were all kin of some degree.

When not in each other's company, family members would correspond. Letters – often long and detailed, intimate and jocular – flew to and fro. They linked relatives over great distances. In 1856 Madeleine Smith reported in a letter to her lover that she had 'written a great many letters today – two very long ones to India – one of them to a cousin who has been shipwrecked'.[52] In the 1870s Margaret McCallum received a stream of letters from her sister-in-law in Alabama, typically ending 'with *much* kind love to Mother, Bella, Brother John and James and *his* Maggie and with kisses to all the little ones from Uncle Harry and Aunt Molly' – all relatives by marriage whom, it seems, she had never met.[53] It was not only those separated by oceans who corresponded; people wrote to each other regardless of the fact that they had only recently parted company, or would shortly be seeing each other. Sometimes there were specific reasons for the letters – to make arrangements, pass on a particular piece of news, and so on. But more usually they were simply a means of keeping in touch, of sharing with family the minutiae of day-to-day life. John Macewan acknowledged as much when he wrote to his daughter in 1855: 'There is not much need to write, as I have nothing to communicate save that we are well and enjoying ourselves to the best of our ability.'[54] He nevertheless went on and filled a page or two.

Walter Crum used to write to his five daughters almost daily, providing an endless supply of local and family gossip. They not only responded to him, but also wrote to each other and to their mother. When Walter's son William was in Manchester on family business between 1860 and 1864, he wrote letters to his sisters that were full of chatty and intimate detail about his daily life.[55] The eldest son Alexander also wrote copiously to at least one of his sisters, and the brothers had also corresponded with each other since their schooldays.[56] Family gossip circulated widely – sometimes letters written to the parents were forwarded for circulation among the scattered children. In Hugh Allan's family it was not unknown for a letter written to one of the clan to be opened and read by other family members in their absence. Typical letters would chronicle daily events, with detailed health reports, discussion of political events and long expositions upon sermons heard. Walter Crum's Sunday evening letters to his daughters regularly summarised and offered a commentary on the sermon he had heard that day.[57] William Crum expressed political vehemence in a letter to his sister Agnes, explaining that he would support the Universal Suffrage candidate 'because he is such a low rascal and an ignorant uneducated villain, and would show up the real meaning of universal suffrage nicely [. . .] proving by reductio ad absurdum that we ought rather to raise than lower the franchise.'[58] Interestingly, female relatives were routinely included in political and religious discussion.

It is interesting, too, that many of these letters are from men. It is often supposed that letter writing was the preserve of women with leisure to write and with the moral responsibility for maintaining family cohesion. Yet fathers and brothers also valued family correspondence, and found time to undertake it. One evening in 1864 Walter Crum had at 7 p.m. 'still plenty of work before me' before he could go home: yet he was completing a letter to his daughter first.[59] Hugh Allan praised his son James for having 'gone the round of the family with your epistles', and Hugh's wife Margaret commended James for 'sending so many interesting letters we feel as if you were living amongst us'.[60] James obviously was a good correspondent, writing to all his siblings including the baby, Peter:

> (The following is to be read to the gentleman to whom it is addressed and then preserved for him.)
> My Dear Peter,
> Did they reckon you nobody? Did they fancy that Peter was not going to have a letter like his brothers and sisters? I have not forgotten you mon petit frere and although you are not fond of me I am fond of you. [. . .] Have you got your supplies of liquor cut off yet – or are you still a "sucking baby"? [. . .] Are you walking about more – or still creeping and standing? How many teeth?[61]

Where there was less of an age gap between siblings, letters took on a different tone: although brothers often favoured affectionate teasing, they were also happy to express emotion. It has been suggested that the relationship between brothers and sisters could be quasi-marital when they set up house together.[62] The Crum siblings did not do that: but William writing to his (married) sister rather wishes that they had, and uses language reminiscent of a romantic relationship:

Yesterday as I was walking home from my business, tired and discontented with the day, I began to think about you. 'Someone to love, someone to cherish' or rather the pretty plaintive air of that song came into my head when I thought of going home to my somewhat too regularly recurring dinner with my one companion, Walter [his brother], and the course of ideas led me to you and I thought how nice and cheerful it would have been had you been there.[63]

Two years later, after a misunderstanding between them, William wrote: 'How grieved I was and am that you have allowed yourself for a moment to think that I was in any way altered in my love for you.'[64] In less sentimental moments, William addressed his sister, married to William Thomson, as 'My Dear Old Thomsing', and took a keen interest in her wardrobe: 'I am very glad that you do not spurn any idea of a "silken ground", and we must get a good one if possible. I should have mentioned Madame Elise as the best person to make it up.'[65]

John Tosh has done much to dispel the notion that Victorian men were uninvolved and detached from family and domestic life, by demonstrating that domesticity was central to the formation of masculine identity in the nineteenth century.[66] The surviving correspondence of the Glasgow middle class suggests that men, as well as women, defined themselves in terms of the family. Men saw themselves as fathers and brothers as well as businessmen and civic leaders. Correspondence reveals that men were not just paying lip-service to an ideology which elevated home and family (although they did that too), but that much of their lived experience passed through a prism of familial affections and obligations. This should not be surprising when so frequently domesticity was hailed as the antidote to the corrupt and immoral practices of the market place. Prescriptive literature tended to portray the domestic domain as the refuge for men and to value it for its redemptive role. However, men as fathers, husbands and brothers were also expected to play an active role in family life and not simply to bask in its warm and restorative glow.

The pressures of breadwinning were acknowledged to limit some men's time with their families. A. J. Hammerton and others have noted that contemporary authors of prescriptive literature were aware of the practical difficulties for men of accommodating the canons of the domestic ideal given the competing demands of business or a profession. Advice was regularly dispensed on how these difficulties might be overcome.[67] Certainly the demands of business could entail frequent absences from the family home. Sir William MacEwen's grandson recalled that his grandfather's 'professional activities entailed long absences from home not only by day but often by night as well' and that MacEwen joined in family musical evenings 'when he happened to be at home'.[68] As noted above, many of the wealthy families had business connections in England and even abroad which required frequent attention, and which obviously placed constraints on how much time men could spend with their families. However, if such trips were likely to be lengthy, families usually made extended visits, and even temporarily relocated. Such was the case with the Crums, who had a branch of the family firm in Manchester, and the Macfies, whose Greenock sugar refining business had a branch in Liverpool. These families regularly divided their time between two different cities in order to preserve the routines and the intimacies of family life. Not infrequently a wife would accompany her husband, occasionally with their children, on business trips, particularly if they were extended or foreign trips. For example, David Murray was accompanied by his wife and one of his young children when he went to the United States, and Robert Blackie, a book publisher, toured North America on publishing business with his wife.[69]

Nineteenth-century working life is customarily characterised as consisting of long hours and few holidays. However, this is probably truer of the working and lower middle classes than of the more prosperous commercial or professional classes. Many historians have attributed Britain's relative decline in the nineteenth century to the gentrification of the bourgeoisie and their preference for the pleasures of the country and an aristocratic lifestyle rather than the daily grind of the counting house. Although this argument no longer has much credence, it does suggest an alternative conception of the working lives of the middle classes to that invoked by the self-improving literature of a Samuel Smiles or the Gradgrind employers of Dickensian fiction. By the second half of the century, many of the tasks of the early nineteenth-century entrepreneur would have been devolved to salaried specialists or, in smaller concerns, foremen. The diaries of John Stephen, one of the two brothers who owned the Stephens' shipbuilding company, reveal a working schedule which left ample scope for pleasure, recreation and family celebrations. Although John Stephen regularly worked long hours, including Saturday mornings, he frequently did not return to work until early afternoon on Monday, having spent the weekend at the family home of various relatives. As mentioned above, when his sister married in 1864, he took a week off, two days before the wedding and a few days afterwards which he spent on excursions, visiting and parties.[70] Before his own wedding he spent several weekdays house hunting, buying furniture and making legal arrangements for the marriage. Although the annual 'fair' holiday in July lasted only a week, in the course of the year the working schedule was regularly punctuated by breaks and holidays. John Stephen's brother Alexander, for example, made three-day yachting trips, usually a few days before the annual summer holiday. However, other interruptions to the working schedule were more prolonged, such as John's three-week continental holiday in 1865, his thirty-six-day tour of Italy and France in 1866, and his month-long stay on the Firth of Clyde in April the following year.[71]

The life of an academic left similar leeway for recreational pursuits. James Thomson, Joseph Coats and William MacEwen, all professors at Glasgow University with busy schedules, were able to spend significant amounts of time on travelling and holidays, usually with their families. Nineteenth-century businessmen, professionals and politicians probably had a more relaxed timetable than their modern-day equivalents. Demands could vary according to the size and scale of the business, the extent of an individual's direct involvement, the age of the party concerned, competing interests and perhaps even temperament. However, what is clear is that even such businessmen as John Stephen, who was fully committed to his enterprise and involved in the day-to-day running of the business, still had a considerable amount of free time, much of which was spent with family.

Men delighted in their roles as grandfathers, fathers, sons and uncles. James Allan became an uncle in 1874:

> Well to confess the truth I am awfully proud about the event myself. As an Uncle my feelings are beyond expression. I am assuming airs over the head of it. My Lochaber friends wonder why I have become proud, haughty and distant. To the inquisitive my cold yet dignified reply is Remember Sir (or Madam as the case may be) I am now an Uncle![72]

Of course, James was writing to the mother of the new baby, and exaggerating for effect. Yet the letter makes him sound genuinely pleased by his new status, and ends by 'humbly expressing a wish that you would kiss the baby for me'. James retained a lifelong closeness to his nephews. More than thirty years later he wrote: 'Kind hearted William came out to see his old Uncle and we had a very happy meeting. [. . .] Hugh also came out to see me and we had a very pleasant day together. [. . .] I had a very kind letter from Jack.'[73]

There seems to have been no reluctance on the part of middle-class men to demonstrate physical as well as epistolary affection. In 1870 James Allan wrote to his baby brother Peter, saying that 'if I were beside you I would give you a kiss.'[74] As a child, the young William Thomson (Lord Kelvin) 'would fling his arms about his [father's] neck and smother him with kisses and stroke his cheeks endearingly'.[75]

Ideologies of acceptable (and indeed 'natural') male behaviour tempered men's displays of familial pride and affection. Even if they felt deeply, it was acknowledged that they might properly be more reluctant to show emotion than were women. James Allan, again on the subject of his sister's baby, wrote to her: 'I suppose you would swallow any amount of praise and flattery of that child, and so would its worthy father the doctor – although perhaps he would conceal his feelings much better than you, just so. This is human nature.'[76] Sir William MacEwen's grandson recorded: 'there was much hidden sentiment in my grandfather's heart – it was not shown by speech but now and then one would find it.'[77] He went on to recount how his grandfather decreed that his own childish handprint, inadvertently left on an outhouse wall, should not be cleaned away, but be preserved for the rest of his life.

Victorian fathers have often been portrayed as aloof patriarchs presiding over their family with stern authority. Gillis has suggested that middle-class fathers became 'distant figures, strangers even to their own children'.[78] Yet the evidence from the Glasgow middle class shows fathers' care and concern for their children at all stages of their lives. The widowed father of the Thomson children greeted so rapturously by William 'was indeed both father and mother to us, and watched over us continually'. He 'generally took a walk' with the children in the morning, read aloud to them, taught them lessons and William 'for some years [. . .] slept in a small bed in our father's room because he had a tendency for sleep-walking'.[79]

Concern for the well-being of children did not end with childhood. In 1869 Hugh Allan wrote to his son James (aged twenty-two) in terms that one might expect to come from a doting mother: '*See* and *take your food well and mind your Porter regularly* so that with the blessing of providence you may get your body strengthened.' He enjoined James to 'tell us something about your own health, and [. . .] be very regular and particular in that respect as we are very fond to know about all that concerns your welfare.'[80]

In temperament and demeanour the eminent doctor and academic Joseph Coats conformed to the stereotype of the stern Victorian patriarch. One of his daughters commented that 'many people who did not know him very well were decidedly afraid of him'.[81] She herself claimed always to have been 'in awe of him', and that 'instant obedience' was his rule.[82] His ideas of fatherhood were grounded in his strong Baptist Christian beliefs and he saw it as part of his role to provide moral and spiritual guidance to his children. His letters to them were littered with admonitions to behave, work hard, and to 'do your duty'. He wrote to his daughter Olive when she turned eight: 'it is much better on your birthday to be wondering what you can do that is useful to yourself or to others than thinking what you can get.'[83] Yet he could not be accused of being distant or uninvolved with his children. He read to them, took them on holidays on his own, and took careful measurement of their heights as they grew. He was capable of displays of tenderness and affection. When his nine-year-old daughter Vicky was taken ill with rheumatic fever during a family stay in the country, she came home by carriage sitting on her father's knee, and 'at every specially trying jolt he said "Poor Lassie! Poor Lassie!"'.[84] Professor Coats encouraged independence of thought and action in his daughters: he increased their pocket money so that 'they should learn how to spend', and gave the elder – then thirteen – a sum of money to furnish the hall at their new house. His letters to his children were loving and, above all, characterised by teasing good humour.

> My Dear Infant,
> There is something wrong with your fountain pen. Not only is it spelling (as usual) in a quite peculiar fashion . . . the writing is quite distinctly worse than usual . . . Your letter is short and not of ravishing interest.[85]

Physical displays of affection were clearly the norm when Coats was at home. He ended one letter 'Sweet kisses to you all, from Old Fad': another to his daughter Olive Mary enjoined her to 'Give Vicky a kiss, a rub-noses and a knockheads from me,' and was signed 'Old Joe'.[86]

The reality of paternal relations was much more subtle and complex than the stern and remote patriarch so frequently invoked as the norm of Victorian fatherhood. Prescriptive injunctions and societal expectations to convince men of the importance of their domestic role did not always create a Victorian version of the 'new man' who selflessly devoted himself to his children. The Victorian father who was stern and distant was as much a reality as one who entered his children's world and was their companion and playmate. However, no matter how individual fathers

enacted their role, it is clear that being the breadwinner did not consti-
tute all that it meant to be a father.

The lack of reticence in men's correspondence and the warmth and
informality of their familial relationships suggests that they were not aloof
and detached from the domestic sphere. Men could even voice their
preference for the private realm over the public. Walter Crum regularly
expressed a preference for home above anywhere, for example: 'The
temptation to go where three daughters are listening to the Birmingham
organ [they were on a family visit] is very great, but the organ in our
own drawing room with the said three daughters tempts me infinitely
more.'[87] He once even professed to be truly comfortable only in the
domestic sphere, confessing himself 'less at ease abroad than at home'.[88]
This may have been mere rhetoric: but the whole tenor – and indeed
the very fact – of his domestic correspondence suggests otherwise. For
all his wealth and business commitments, he was truly a 'family man'.
Women have often been identified as the prime agents in maintaining
family contacts, the main guardians of home, family tradition and sentiment. Although there is some evidence to support this – in the sex of
visiting family members, for instance – other evidence shows that men
too acknowledged the power of family. They, too, were concerned with
symbolic as well as monetary bequests; they were deeply engaged in
family matters; they held firmly to their familial identity, seeing themselves as indulgent fathers, benevolent uncles and so on. Men as well as
women were upholders of family ties and traditions; they located themselves in the sphere of home and family as much as in the world of work
and they expected to and often did find the domestic sphere a source of
happiness and fulfilment.

When it came to financial matters, family clearly came first, as is clear
from the extent to which the business empires of the Crums, Smiths and
Houldsworths relied on family connections. These examples could be
replicated many times over. Kin were chosen as executors of wills; and
of course they made up the great part of the beneficiaries of those wills.
A sample of confirmations of wills recorded between 1878 and 1881,
mostly involving testators from our study area, was examined to see just
who was being chosen to act as executor. Most confirmations record four
executors, one of which was often a writer (solicitor). Of the 209 named
executors, seventy-six were specified as being related to the testator. A
further fifty-nine had the same surname as the testator, and obviously
were relatives although the precise relationship is not stated. The remaining seventy-four, including writers, had different surnames – although

even here, some might have been related without sharing a surname. Of the seventy-six with a stated relationship to the testator, seventeen were spouses. Of the remainder, twenty-eight were males (sons, sons-in-law, brothers and nephews) and thirty-one were females (daughters and sisters). Testators preferred to entrust this important job to a relative, and had no qualms about placing a female relative in this responsible position.

Similarly, wills show a preponderance of bequests to family members. It is not surprising that close kin – surviving spouses, sons and daughters – were the principal beneficiaries. But the range of kin recognised in wills is wide. Typical is that of Janet Broom, a sixty-five-year-old widow who lived alone in Woodlands Terrace. She died in 1881 while on a visit to her sister Margaret Auld. 'The key of Mrs Broom's writing desk, which was locked, was got from Mrs Auld' so that her business papers could be examined.[89] She left bequests to her two sisters, to nine named nephews and nieces, and to the three siblings of her late husband. Mrs Anna Loudoun, who died in 1879, left her whole estate to be divided between nieces, nephews, greatnieces and greatnephews, and a 'niece by marriage'.[90] It was not only the childless or, importantly, only women who show a wide range of kin recognition in their testaments. In 1870 Dr Anderson left bequests not only to his own children, but also to his brother, his cousin, and to the children of his wife's brother.[91]

Testators showed an appreciation of the importance of family in the nature of their bequests, too. They were anxious that family belongings stayed in the family, and that more distant kin, even if they were not to receive substantial monetary bequests, were remembered, and would remember them. 'Uncle Wemyss is to get his choice of anything belonging to me as a remembrance', specified Euphemia Guthrie in 1901, and 'my daughter Elizabeth Grant Guthrie [is] eventually to inherit the silver tea set which belonged to my grandmother'.[92] Bequests could be very personal. Another Euphemia, Euphemia Johnstone (d. 1883), left 'to my sister Mary my clothes', in the expectation that Mary would be happy to wear them.[93] Janet Mitchell (d. 1881) left 'sentimental' bequests to her brother as well as to her sister. He was to receive 'my father's small locket miniature, my mother's diamond ring and silver pencil case, and a ring of my deceased sister Jane'. Distance was no bar to this kind of bequest. Janet's sister was married and living in Australia: one wonders how she was to get 'a dozen silver knives and forks that belonged to my uncle Benjamin Cowie'.[94]

Yet it was not only women who remembered family in this way. Men could also be conscious of the symbolism of family continuity invested in objects. James Fraser, for example, in 1881 left to his grandson James Fraser Readman 'my gold watch, chain and seal'.[95] There was, nevertheless, a scrupulousness about ownership among kin. Several testators were careful to note that possessions which might appear to be theirs were in fact owned by other family members. Mrs Anne Munro added a codicil in 1878 to note:

> whilst I am in good health I think it better in case of any confusion in the future to write these few lines to say that all the furniture I have used in this house almost entirely belongs to my daughter May Annie Munro (there is mearly [sic] the exception of the book case equal share of the books Easy Chair in Morocco and half the silver plate) most of the furniture being bought with the money my daughter received in a legacy from Miss Strachan of Cortes.[96]

Anna Playfair, a single woman who died aged thirty-four in 1892, was at that time living in the Woodside Terrace household headed by her widowed mother. The inventory of Anna's estate records among her debts to her dentist and dressmaker, one of £50 as a 'proportion of board due to Mrs Playfair'.[97] It seems, then, as if adult offspring, female as well as male, were expected to pay their way and that at least in some cases this could be quite a formal arrangement.

The practice of contributing to household expenses, if widespread, has interesting implications for the household structure discussed in this chapter. Who retained headship of the household was not just a matter of formal record in a census: it had practical financial implications, and may in part explain the reluctance of widows, for instance, to move in with their children. One such was Agnes, widow of Alexander Johnston, 'merchant' of Shieldhall, Glasgow, who had died in 1844. When she moved into the Claremont estate, she chose not to live with her daughter Rachel and son-in-law Walter Paterson in Claremont Terrace. Instead, she set up home nearby in Woodside Terrace together with her unmarried sister Cecilia; in 1861 they were recorded as 'retired ladies' aged sixty-eight and sixty-six, living in an eighteen-room house with two servants. The Patersons had twenty rooms in Claremont Terrace, so space can hardly have been a problem. Agnes seems simply to have preferred the autonomy of her own household; the sisters remained there until Agnes's death in 1877.

Where family members stayed on a temporary basis, however, at least one host household expected to foot the bill, which with accompanying retinue would not have been small. Walter Crum's married daughter was visiting, and 'thinking of parting with her horse because the groom goes away. [. . .] My business was never so bad as it is just now, but I can yet afford hospitality to her horse as well as to herself. If she likes the horse, someone can certainly be got to attend to it.'[98] He wrote in a brief postcript to another daughter embarking on a trip: 'If you want money let me know.'[99] Walter Crum seems to have been an indulgent father, at least financially.

It was not only immediate family who showed financial generosity to one another. Jessie Crum clearly gave her nephews money and presents quite often: one of them wrote in 1871 of two such gifts: 'It is a great joy to me and I am sure to you also, to think that the money which you formerly furnished me with has not been thrown away; and it shall be my endeavour to make an equally good use of the last sum which your kind insistence has made me accept.'[100] Jessie gave another nephew a writing desk in 1872, and as early as 1857 a third had received a 'most appropriate and comfortable gift'.[101]

Family was an important source of financial support in business as well as personal matters. Gillis has stated: 'in the second half of the nineteenth century, banks and the stock market replaced family and kin as sources of capital.'[102] However, British capitalism has been renowned not only for the dominance of the family firm in its business structure, but for the short life and small scale of most of these firms.[103] Most businesses were in fact small single-owner ones rather than true family partnerships and tended to survive only one generation.[104] The start-up capital required for these firms was very small and generally did not require formal capital markets such as banks and the stock market to fund their entrepreneurial venture. Sometimes family provided capital or sometimes suppliers would provide credit. Even where the family and kin had not been required as a source of start-up capital, often the continued survival of a small concern was dependent on the owner's ability to use the family as a cheap and reliable source of labour and as a source of financial support in times of difficulty. Small firms, operating in a highly competitive and unstable environment, often looked to kin to bail them out of financial difficulties. Walter Paterson bought his house in Claremont Terrace in 1851, having borrowed the money from the trustees of the estate of his late father-in-law. 'I have purchased a lodging in Claremont Terrace [. . .] at the price of £3,500. [. . .] As it would be inconvenient to take such an amount from my business, I am desirous of obtaining a loan secured on the property from the funds of my father-in-law.'[105] He got £3,000 at 4 per cent, and his business was obviously spared any inconvenience.

Genuine family firms which were based on partnerships of family members and which had a life-span of several generations were in the minority and tended to be larger concerns than the single-owner, single-generation firms.[106] The advent of limited liability in 1856 and even the company merger movement of the 1890s did little to dislodge family control of these firms. The adoption of limited liability usually involved very little change to the family form of ownership and the firms continued to be private concerns. Funds were raised by issuing 'outside' shareholders with preference shares or debentures which did not have voting rights. Similarly, the large mergers which took place at the end of the century failed to weaken family control as a high proportion of issued share capital was retained by the original partners or their relatives. Even as late as 1951 one-third of Britain's largest businesses were owner-controlled.[107]

The history of the shipbuilding company of Alexander Stephen & Sons Ltd is fairly typical of the dynamic long-running family firm and illustrates how the family was at the centre of the business world and integral to its operation well in to the twentieth century. The firm had been founded in the 1750s by Alexander Stephen who began building at Burghead on the Moray Firth. His grandson extended the firm from the east coast of Scotland and set up business at Kelvinhaugh in Glasgow. The fifth generation of Stephens, Alexander and Frederick John, joined the firm in 1887 after substantial academic and practical training in naval architecture. When their father, Alexander Stephen senior, retired in 1894 at the age of sixty-two, a new deed of co-partnership was formed whereby financial control of the firm was passed on to the two sons. Alexander senior, his brother John and two salaried employees who had been taken into the partnership retained a minority share in the business. The reconstitution of the company's partnership is instructive of the ways in which the importance of family affiliation and family ties was blended with hard-headed business economics. The new partners rented the yard from the founder and it was arranged that the sons should take over the heritable property and pay off the price in ten years.[108] At the turn of the century the firm converted from a partnership to a limited liability company with John Stephen, uncle of Alexander and Frederick John, becoming the first chairman. However, the changed status did not weaken the family's ownership or control of the business. Although salaried managers were employed, family members held executive managerial positions and exercised decisive influence over company policy.[109] It was not until after the Second World War that the company became a public one, with A. Murray Stephen, the sixth generation of the family, as chairman. He clearly regretted the fact that the company had been forced to adopt public status and with a hint of defiance declared: 'traditions are still strong enough, and it would seem probable that members of the family may take in the future as full a part in the management as others have taken in the past.'[110]

Not all families were fortunate in producing either sufficient progeny or ones who were both willing and able to take control of the family business. In such instances daughters could prove their worth to the family firm, sometimes attracting new talent into the firm through prudent marriages. Alexander Stephen's in-laws and near neighbours, the Templeton brothers, owned a successful carpet-manufacturing firm in the city. In 1884 the Templetons recruited a salaried professional into the firm, D. H. Young, who successfully created and developed new product ranges. He was rapidly promoted to partnership in the firm and within a year had married a daughter of one of the brothers. When the Templeton brothers retired from active involvement in the business in the early years of the twentieth century, control passed to the son-in-law, D. H. Young.[111] Family continued to be central to recruitment to the firm, with Young's son taking over the management of one of its branches and his brother replacing him as senior partner when Young died in 1921.[112]

Family loyalties did not always work to the advantage of the firm and there were occasions when they were a source of weakness and instability. George Macfarlane's export business suffered several reverses of fortunes, some of which stemmed directly from his unpropitious employment of family members. His daughter observed, with a hint of rancour which seemed to stem from the nationality of the relatives: 'Twice he was swindled by partners, both Englishmen, one the husband of his favourite sister Jemima.' She also claimed that he had 'unfortunate experiences with the various nephews whom he had taken into his business by way of starting them in life'.[113]

Family and kin were integral elements in the network of business and economic relationships throughout the nineteenth century and beyond. Family members could not only provide capital, loans and labour, but act as surety in bonds and even provide business premises on flexible terms for small firms.[114] Large businesses could also take advantage of family affiliations and networks to counteract the uncertainties, volatility and risks of the market. It has generally been acknowledged that kinship networks were particularly useful in the early stages of industrialisation, when information flows were extremely imperfect; however, it has often been argued that by the second half of the century the family basis of business organisation had become a burden and an impediment to growth and development.[115] Whatever the long-term effects of the family factor in business performance, there is little doubt that it was commonly exploited throughout the nineteenth century as a market advantage and an emblem of respectability and repute in an environment not noted for either. Nenadic has noted that in nineteenth century Edinburgh it was not unknown for a firm to fabricate a family name in order to signal respectability.[116] Kinship networks and personal connections provided a basis for mutual trust which could offset risks in a market environment characterised by fierce competition, volatility, limited regulation and corrupt practices. In the absence of a well-established network of institutions and agencies which relieved the individual of the costs of conducting transactions, a premium was placed on trust and honour, virtues which were commonly associated with family morality. As Yoran Ben-Porath has observed, the value of family affiliations was their signal of personal traits such as honesty and fidelity as well as the degree to which the family took responsibility for the obligations and actions of its members.[117] The lag of thirty or forty years between the advent of limited liability in 1856 and its adoption by companies in Glasgow[118] is in part a reflection of the privileging of locally based networks of trust, often organised around myriad family firms, over legally based guarantees of security, and is testimony to the dependence of the business world on non-market relations.

Gillis argues that during the nineteenth century the British and American residential family was 'shrinking to the nuclear core', a process well advanced by the end of the century.[119] There is no evidence from the middle-class households in the Claremont estate that they became more confined to the nuclear unit during the period. Nor is there any evidence that kinship networks became less important in the second half of the century as sources of capital or in marriage and family formation. Rather our findings point to a continued role for the extended family in business and social life, right through to the end of the century and beyond. The point about continuity is a crucial one. In the context of changes in women's roles Amanda Vickery states that such change is always located in some period other than the one under immediate investigation.[120] Rosemary O'Day also argues for continuity when she points out that many of the features that Davidoff identifies as typifying the eighteenth-century family can also be found in an earlier period; that they are, in her words, 'an extension of an earlier world'. It is instructive to look at this list of features:

> The fact that the family network supported commercial enterprises; the training of the young in the families of relatives; the cementing of business partnerships by sibling and cousin marriage; the late age at marriage [. . .]; the proximity and interchangeability of home and work; the strengthening of family bonds through visiting, feasts and celebrations of rites of passage.[121]

As discussed here, and as explored further in later chapters, these are for the most part also characteristic of the Victorian middle-class family. 'The family' of course shifts over time: it is dynamic rather than static, and its form, its rituals and its meaning of course change – not just over time but according to location within the socio-economic spectrum of the middle class. However, despite the assertions of some historians of the family that during the nineteenth century (or the eighteenth, for that matter) there was a discontinuity with the family of an earlier period, the 'extension of the earlier world' was a longer one even than O'Day suggests. Throughout the century, family remained at the heart of 'public' as well as 'private' experience, and was a prime locus of male as well as female identity.

3

What's Love Got to Do with it?

IN TERMS OF COURTSHIP AND MARRIAGE, the nineteenth century is frequently depicted as a time when love conquered all. The rhetoric and the ideal of romantic love and companionate union are often affirmed to have taken hold over economic and social considerations in the selection of marriage partner.[1] This rather Whiggish view of the development of marital relationships has not been uncontested and has been subject to intense criticism for its evidential base, chronology and explanatory basis.[2] The correspondence of elite groups, the middle classes and the evidence of working-class marriage litigation suggest that there were expectations across the social spectrum that love and companionship should be aspects of the marital relationship. However, much of the evidence for the supremacy of companionate marriage in the late eighteenth and nineteenth centuries is based on prescriptive literature and the discourses of political theorists. Enlightenment thinkers, who were more interested in expounding on the doctrine of separate spheres than on marriage, nonetheless linked the growth of private property and commercial society to the improvement of the condition of women within marriage and the emergence of a companionate ideal:

> Inequality of wealth soon sets in and causes property to be valued. At this point the bonds of marriage are no longer made at random. One wants them to be good matches. To be accepted, one must please, and this necessity brings with it greater consideration for women and gives them a kind of dignity.[3]

Complementarity and accommodation were the virtues most frequently invoked in the copious writings of political and moral ideologues as the ones on which the union of husband and wife should be based. However, these authors were virtually unanimous in either assuming or explicitly stating the supreme authority of the male both inside and outside of marriage. One of the leading figures of the Scottish Enlightenment, Lord

Kames, while opining that 'a woman of sense prudently educated, makes a delicious companion to a man of parts and knowledge', was equally adamant that 'woman defined by nature to be obedient, ought to be disciplined early to bear wrongs, without murmurings'.[4] Therefore the model of companionship which was propagated in discourses of marriage was expected to be forged within a framework that sanctioned male authority as supreme. Indeed, Susan Moller Okin has argued that idealised conceptions of the family and companionate marriage propounded in the late eighteenth and early nineteenth centuries undermined female claims for equality and reinforced patriarchal relations between men and women.[5]

Whether popular ideals of companionate marriage advanced or hampered women's equality is a moot point. However, as A. J. Hammerton has noted, the contradiction between the prescriptive ideals of married life and actual experience could be intense, when ideals of companionship vied with entrenched and vaunted notions of male dominance which were embedded in custom, beliefs and institutional structures.[6] Prescriptive and cultural injunctions favouring a more companionate relationship within marriage sat beside the unleavened patriarchal basis of the law in the nineteenth century. However, Scottish divorce law in common with other European Protestant states was not so comprehensively patriarchal or inegalitarian as its English counterpart. Papal authority – and with it the absolute prohibition on divorce – was abolished during the Reformation. A Commissary Court was established in 1563 to deal with all questions relating to marriage, divorce, legitimacy, bastardy and so on; divorce was made available to men and women on an equal basis, solely on the grounds of adultery.[7] In 1573 the grounds were extended by an Act of Parliament to include desertion and these remained the only grounds for divorce until the twentieth century.

Despite the formal abolition of canon or papal law, it continued to exercise considerable influence over the decisions of the Commissary Court.[8] Moreover, equality before the law in regard to divorce was not replicated in other areas of husband and wife relations. As one historian of the law of husband and wife in Scotland has noted, 'in 1830 the husband's legal supremacy was undoubted'.[9] The legal inequalities which wives were subjected to were multifarious and had the cumulative effect of a wife being 'in a manner, in a state of wardship or minority under the husband'.[10] As in England, the position at the beginning of the nineteenth century was that the wife's movable property, whether owned at marriage or acquired later, passed to the husband by virtue of the *jus mariti* and he could dispose of it at will. The *jus mariti* did not apply to heritable property, although the *jus administrationis* gave the husband the right to administer the wife's heritable property and its rents or produce fell under his *jus mariti*.[11] Formal legal subordination was compounded by interpretations of the law laid down by a succession of Scottish legal writers in the late eighteenth and early nineteenth century which gave husbands a large measure of personal control over wives. Baron David Hume pronounced of a wife: 'She is liable to his control in her conduct and mode of life and measure of expenses (always within certain bounds).'[12]

Church attitudes to marriage echoed the patriarchal basis and principles of the law by unequivocally endorsing the supreme authority of the husband and advocating female submission and obedience to his will. As an article in the *Christian Journal* acidly observed in 1840: 'Had she kept her proper place, and been guided by man, instead of attempting to guide him, the great disaster would not have befallen our race.'[13]

Therefore religious and cultural discourses as well as the institutional framework of marriage for much of the nineteenth century clearly sanctioned the authority of the husband and the subordination and deference of the wife. It was expected, however, that the relations between husband and wife would be based on love and mutual respect, and that the authority of the husband would be tempered by affection and consideration. Although both parties to the union of husband and wife were expected to meet exacting standards of behaviour, it was the behaviour of the wife which came under greater scrutiny and prescription and, ultimately, responsibility for the success of the marriage was adjudged to rest with women. In 1781 Lord Kames had observed: 'To make a good husband, is but one branch of a man's duty; but it is the chief duty of a woman to make a good wife. To please her husband, to be a good economist, and to educate their children, are the capital duties.'[14]

Handbooks, advice manuals and religious literature of the first half of the nineteenth century continually exhorted women variously to maintain a well-ordered household, be a helpmeet to their husbands and to minister to the needs of their family. However, the conception of femininity that constructed woman's nature and role as complementary to man's also invested in woman a spiritual and moral authority which enabled her to shape the moral character of her children. A lecture delivered by the Reverend F. West in Liverpool in 1856 is illustrative of the continuing emphasis in hortatory texts and sermons of the separate spheres ideal, the complementarity of the sexes and the moral authority invested in women: 'Our social and moral character is chiefly of woman's formation, and in woman's keeping. Raise woman, and you elevate man; for life takes its form from her.'[15] Therefore, while women were expected to be all duty and self-sacrifice, the morally redemptive role accorded them some standing and influence within the family, which may have induced them to have higher expectations of their husbands and of the marital relationship. Hammerton has suggested that it was rising expectations among women that partly engendered the debate about marriage which ensued in the second half of the nineteenth century, with husbands' behaviour rather than women's coming under close scrutiny.[16] From the middle of the century the focus of debates on marriage centred on husbands' abuse of their power and their unreasonable behaviour, with complaints voiced by campaigning feminists as well as ordinary women.[17]

In the 1880s and 1890s there was an even more rigorous debate on marriage and there were those who came to question the sanctity of marriage itself.[18] However, the institution of marriage proved to be sufficiently robust to withstand the slings and arrows of sundry critics, including the feminist 'New Woman', the sexual radicals and the ordinary women who paraded their private sufferings in the public arena of the divorce courts. At the turn of the century the institution of marriage emerged intact but chastened by a raft of legal reforms. In Scotland changes to the property laws usually followed swiftly on the heels of English legislation; consequently, the egregious injustices of the property laws were swept away by a series of reforms, culminating in the legislation of 1881 which abolished the *jus mariti* and restored to married women the right to own and control their own property. There remained significant legal inequalities, including the *jus administrati*, which gave the husband the right to administer his wife's separate property and to make his consent necessary should she wish to dispose of it.[19] The fact that patriarchal authority had been only curbed rather than abolished and the principle that a husband's authority was supreme remained intact, as is illustrated by the adjudication of Frederick Walton in 1893: 'The husband as *dignior persona* is the head of the house. As his duty is to love and cherish his wife, so hers is to love and obey him.'[20]

Whatever its defects, marriage was still the destiny of the majority of Victorian women in Scotland. There are a variety of interpretations of the statistics on marriage in the nineteenth century, but it appears that the most significant feature of marriage rates was a steep rise in the 1840s to a level which was more or less maintained into the last decade of the century.[21] Once married, most women remained so. Despite the availability of divorce for both men and women in Scotland since the Reformation, few availed themselves of this option. There was an average of fourteen divorces per year in Scotland between 1830 and 1854 and only one decree of separation.[22] Leah Leneman has speculated that the reason for so few seeking a divorce was related to its cost. Although divorce was relatively cheap in Scotland, the cost was approximately equivalent to four to eight months' wages for a working man and proportionally more for a working woman.[23] In addition to cost, the iniquitous matrimonial property laws undoubtedly provide part of the explanation for the low divorce rate. It was surely no coincidence that in the four years after the introduction of the 1881 Married Women's Property Act the average number of divorces increased by fivefold compared with the figure for the years 1850–54.[24] However, entrenched economic inequalities, coupled with social opprobrium, probably provided the most powerful obstacles to women seeking divorce and judicial separation.

Can the popularity of marriage and the low rate of divorce be interpreted as an index of the ubiquity of wedded bliss in Scotland? Did couples marry for love, in the belief that they were embarking on a partnership for life, and once married, were their expectations met?

It is generally accepted that arranged marriages or marriages where parents exercised a decisive influence on their children's choice of marriage partner were a thing of the past in most Western European countries by the nineteenth century.[25] The importance of individual choice in the selection of marriage partner has been assumed to signal the triumph of the love-match and the establishment of companionship and love as the foundation of marriage. This did not mean that romantic love had replaced material interest as the basis of marital unions in the nineteenth century even when individual choice was paramount. As Amanda Vickery has noted of eighteenth-century England, it is overly simplistic to posit a simple polarity between love and money as the basis of matrimony.[26] Choice of marriage partner could be governed by unvarnished material considerations or unalloyed sentimental ones. More frequently the choice was not so stark, as a range of factors combining elements of both these extremes and many other criteria came into play.

The hortatory marriage literature of the nineteenth century may have been preoccupied with questions of emotion and sentiment, and middle-class spouses may have had increased expectations of companionate unions; but this did not mean the absence of economic imperatives governing the choice of marriage partner. The nineteenth-century bourgeoisie were noted for forming marital alliances which cemented business partnerships and prolonged political and economic dynasties.[27] Liaisons between the children of business partners or prominent business families could ensure the economic survival or consolidation of a firm in a competitive economic climate. As discussed in chapter 2, marriage inter-linked prosperous families such as the Houldsworths, Crums, Smiths and Allans. These alliances did not give rise solely to social connections, but linked families and businesses and often cemented business empires.

Despite the economic prudence of these marriages, they were far from being the instrumental and often loveless unions which were alleged to have been typical of the arranged marriages of the aristocracy in earlier centuries. These marriages may have been convenient for all parties, but they were far from being marriages of convenience. Rarely was dynastic survival or financial acuity the sole reason for marriages. More subtle forms of economic and social regulation characterised the choice of marriage partner for the middle classes, and the overriding concern was as much economic and social compatibility as economic aggrandisement. When the renowned surgeon Joseph Lister married Agnes Syme in 1855, both fathers made settlements on the young couple. As Lister's bio-grapher Richard Fisher remarked, the arrangement had the hallmarks of a 'hard-headed business transaction'.[28] Fisher also records how Joseph's father expressed some disappointment at the size of Agnes's dowry and complained of the sum given by Mr Syme: 'I had hoped for rather more, but he knows best his own circumstances.' In this instance it was not the survival or promotion of a business empire which was at stake. Joseph was the son of a proseperous wine merchant and Agnes was the daughter of a surgeon. Their settlements were perhaps significant in allow-ing Lister to pursue his medical career unencumbered by financial anxi-eties. However much of a love-match the Lister-Syme marriage was, and there is much to suggest that it was, shrewd economic considerations coexisted with ideals of romantic love. Just as the characters in Jane Austen's *Pride and Prejudice* sought to achieve an equilibrium between their purse and their heart, the Victorian match saw romance, passion, shared interests, and no doubt many other considerations, jockey with material calculation in the final decision.

As already emphasised, the extended family was an important source of marriage partner. While at least one historian has attributed cousin marriage to a convenient and acceptable way of displacing love towards a nuclear family member, it is more convincing that the role of the family in the marriage market was indicative of social and economic

compatibility in considerations of future spouses.[29] Most marriage partners were of course chosen from outside the extended family circle.
However, the family friendship network was fertile territory for meeting
potential suitors, as it was usually a guarantee of suitability. The Thomson
family was regularly provided with partners by their friendship network.
In 1816 Margaret Gardner married her cousin's friend James Thomson,
whom she had met while visiting her relatives in Belfast. Almost thirty
years later their daughter Anna married a former pupil and friend of her
father's, and their other daughter, Elizabeth, married the Reverend Dr
King, also a friend of her father's.[30] Frances and David Murray's circle of
friends was equally rich fodder for marital unions, their only son marrying the daughter of Frances's childhood friend.[31] Brothers were particularly useful for providing suitable young men for their sisters: Elizabeth
Crum, Mary Allan and Mary Stephen, for example, all married close
friends of their brothers.[32]

Important as the family was as a source of appropriate suitor, the market
for socially and economically suitable matches was more expansive than
this. It has long been argued that social distance and segregation characterised class relations of the nineteenth century, particularly in the arena
of leisure and recreation.[33] These segregated class relations ensured that
the young bourgeoisie inhabited a circumscribed, although by no means
small, social circle and made it unlikely that they would encounter a
socially unsuitable partner. This generally made the heavy hand of parental
control redundant in the selection of a marriage partner and conferred
on young middle-class men and women a considerable degree of choice
in the matter.

Occasionally, however, the self-regulation inherent in the ordered social
arrangements of middle-class life failed to operate perfectly and unsuitable matches were the product. It was at this point that the invisible hand
of the middle-class marriage market was replaced by parental regulation
to guide the luckless lovers towards social conformity and propriety.
Perhaps one of the most celebrated and notorious of these social mis-
matches was the case of Madeleine Smith and Emile L'Angelier. The consequences of the affair between these two, she the daughter of James
Smith, a successful, prosperous and well-connected Glasgow architect, and
he an impoverished warehouse clerk from Jersey, scandalised not only
Victorian Glasgow, but the world beyond. Madeleine was put on trial for
the murder of L'Angelier after he died of arsenic poisoning in the spring
of 1857. The interest in this case was willingly stoked by the Victorian
newspapers, which covered – often at prurient length – the details as they

unfolded in the ten-day trial. The evidence itself, the extensive legal documentation and the several hundred letters that the twenty-year-old Madeleine Smith wrote to L'Angelier provide a valuable source for the historian and illuminating glimpses into intimate as well as humdrum aspects of middle-class life in a Victorian city.

The voluminous correspondence between Madeleine Smith and her lover offers a one-sided picture of their liaison; only one or two of L'Angelier's letters to her survive. She scrupulously disposed of them, presumably in the hope that they would not be read by anyone in her household. Her letters are suffused with artifice and read as a scripted melodrama. Their tone suggests that she was well versed in the idiom of nineteenth-century romantic fiction and that she took care to craft a narrative of her affair, casting herself in the role of doomed heroine. But the dénouement was not part of her planned scenario. Whether Madeleine murdered L'Angelier or not, the entire story illustrates the social conventions of middle-class courtship and the considerations which governed the operation of the marriage market.

Emile L'Angelier came to Glasgow in 1852 via Edinburgh and Dundee, having arrived in Britain from Jersey ten years earlier to take up employment as a trainee estate manager with Dickson's & Co., an Edinburgh nursery. He had worked in his father's seed shop in Jersey and went on to train in all aspects of the nursery trade. A wealthy Scottish client offered him a position on his estate in Rosshire, proposing that he complete a training with Dickson's before joining the estate staff.[34] By the time he reached Glasgow, he had abandoned a career in market gardening and had taken employment as a warehouse clerk in the firm of Huggins & Co. The evidence suggests that he was something of a social climber; not only did he set his cap at a woman who was his social superior, he counted among his acquaintances Monsieur August de Mean, the French consul in Glasgow, and several young scions of the more prosperous Glasgow bourgeoisie. By all accounts, the thirty-two-year-old L'Angelier was a dapper suitor, but as a match for a young middle-class woman whose social circle included the eminent Houldsworths, he was seriously unsuitable. Not only was he an impecunious clerk, whose social origin was several notches beneath the Smiths, he compounded his social disabilities by being patently not Anglo-Saxon.

L'Angelier was indefatigable in his pursuit of Madeleine. He inveigled his way into the company of a family who were acquaintances of the Smiths and on several occasions unsuccessfully tried to persuade them to effect an introduction to her. His persistence eventually paid off and in the early spring of 1855 he managed to contrive an introduction to her. Their affair rapidly blossomed and soon they were involved in arranging secret trysts. When Madeleine and her family left Glasgow for their summer residence at Rhu, near Helensburgh on the Firth of Clyde, the two were exchanging letters almost daily. L'Angelier's efforts to secure an introduction to Madeleine from someone of her own social circle reflected the etiquette of Victorian courtship rituals, as well as the intensity of his ardour. Not only was it regarded as unseemly for a man to introduce himself to a young woman, it was expected that he would be known within her social circle, signalling social acceptability. A letter from Madeleine to L'Angelier, written immediately after her father had found out about their relationship, highlights the primacy placed on social cachet and propriety by the respectable bourgeoisie:

> Some 'friend' was 'kind' enough to tell Papa that you were in the habit of walking with us. Papa was very angry with me for walking with a gentleman unknown to him. I told him we had been introduced, and I saw no harm in it. Bessie joined with Papa and blames me for the whole affair. She does not know that I am writing you, so don't mention it.[35]

Madeleine's entire family put pressure on her to stop seeing L'Angelier once the father had made his views known. Her sister Bessie, who had at first been a fellow conspirator and ally, now distanced herself from any involvement in the liaison. Their mother was equally hostile, telling Madeleine that L'Angelier was 'poor [. . .] but a clerk and that she should look higher'.[36] Even her younger brother Jack joined in the chorus of opprobrium:

> Jack came to sit with me in my bedroom, and he was telling me all the news he knew, I said, 'I wish you would tell me something about a person I love.' 'L'Angelier,' he said. I was in fun, [so] I said, 'No.' 'Well,' he said, I am ashamed of you. Do you know he is only a clerk in Huggins?' I said I knew that, but 'if I love him, then that was enough.' He tried to tell me I was expected to marry a rich man – not a poor one. He got a little cross and told me not to think of you, as he knew Papa would be angry, very angry.[37]

At first Madeleine was keen to prolong the relationship, provided it was conducted in secret, although she also professed to be immune to the censure of society. Affecting a tone of wisdom and experience, she proclaimed: 'I know from experience that the world is not lenient in its observations. But I don't care for the world's remarks so long as my own heart tells me that I am doing nothing wrong.'[38] This was palpable melodrama and performance, designed to display Madeleine's romantic credentials. Aged twenty, only recently returned from a London finishing school, and thoroughly bourgeois by birth and upbringing, Madeleine had very little experience of anything, let alone the odium dished out to those engaged in an illicit affair. Despite Madeleine's protestations that love should conquer all, when confronted by the united opposition of her family, her resolution rapidly crumbled. She tried to break off the affair at least twice. The first time was two weeks after her initial declaration that she intended to follow the injunctions of her heart rather than the dictates of her head. However, Emile's importunings, or perhaps his amorous prowess, persuaded her to rekindle the romance and the affair continued illicitly. Her second attempt, after she claimed that her father still refused to countenance the relationship, also foundered, and once again the two continued their romance, planning their wedding and eventually reaching sexual consummation. It was only when a more suitable match entered the scene, adroitly introduced by Madeleine's father, that her ardour began to cool. By this time the affair had lasted almost one and a half years. Although she professed to be indifferent to this new suitor, in time her letters to L'Angelier became rather more curt than affectionate. She also began to echo the sentiments and views of her family with regard to Emile's financial and social position. On one occasion she wrote: 'Dear me, dear Emile. Have you only £50 [per year] from Huggins? I thought you had £100. How could I make such a mistake? I wonder you stay for such a small sum. You could have much more.'[39]

Despite breaching social conventions throughout this relationship, Madeleine in many respects was thoroughly conventional. She had absorbed the fundamental values of bourgeois society, namely that money and breeding were the *sine qua non* of a successful bourgeois marriage. Her dalliance with L'Angelier and the allure of the forbidden ('Perhaps if you had been well off, I would not have loved you as I do') could not withstand the compelling demand to make a good marriage.[40] If she had prized love and sentiment over money and social convention, she could have risked her parents' wrath, defied the social codes of her class, and eloped with L'Angelier. Madeleine had demonstrated that she could be strong willed and stubborn. Her teacher at Mrs Gorton's Academy for Young Ladies in London remarked to her parents that Madeleine was subject to sulks and flares of temper.[41] Madeleine elected instead to opt for the more socially acceptable and more solvent William Minnoch, a family friend and partner in the firm of Houldsworth & Co. In spurning L'Angelier, she either allowed propriety to triumph over sentiment or had simply lost her appetite for the drama of a clandestine affair. When Madeleine wrote to him to break off their affair, L'Angelier refused to reconcile himself to her decision. Sloughing off any vestiges of gallantry, he threatened to reveal her letters and the intimate details of their relationship to her father if she broke her promise to marry him. He disregarded her anguished pleas to him to return her letters and not to destroy her: 'Emile, for God's sake do not send my letters to Papa. It will be an open rupture. I will leave the house. I will die. Emile, do nothing till I see you.' In another letter she again begged him not to show her letters to her father: 'Emile, my father's wrath would kill me – you little know his temper. Emile, [. . .] do not denounce me to Papa. [. . .] He will put me from him. He will hate me as a guilty wretch.'[42]

Madeleine's purchase of arsenic on two separate occasions from local chemists, Emile's death from arsenic poisoning and the discovery of her letters in his lodgings provided sufficient evidence for her to be tried for his murder, a charge which culminated in the uniquely Scottish verdict of not proven. Cynics have claimed that verdict to connote guilt without requisite proof. Madeleine certainly garnered a good deal of sympathy in the course of the trial from all sections of the press. L'Angelier was portrayed as a ruthless fortune hunter who had seduced a young, naïve middle-class woman. Her youth, her class, her sex and her beauty persuaded most contemporary observers that she was either innocent or that she had taken rightful revenge on a scoundrel who had callously ruined her reputation.[43]

The Madeleine Smith case illustrates *par excellence* that for the middle classes decisions about marriage were not a simple matter of personal choice based on romantic love. A romantic idiom may have prevailed and love undoubtedly featured in the final choice. However, as Peter Borscheid has argued for nineteenth-century Germany, 'one did not marry for love but often with love'.[44] Economic considerations were not eclipsed and the suitors had to observe the rules and conventions of the social and economic hierarchy. If the existing social arrangements were disturbed, there was a high price to pay. Madeleine was no doubt indulging her characteristic flair for melodrama when she claimed that her father would kill her if the letters were discovered, but it is not unlikely that she would have suffered social exclusion and could probably have waved goodbye to her inheritance and any financial support from her family if she had married Emile. Individuals may have made the ultimate choice in marriage decisions, but it was not an unconstrained choice and the family and its social peers played their part in shaping that decision.

As well as revealing the importance of material factors in the marriage market, Madeleine's letters also offer glimpses into some of the rituals of bourgeois courtship practices and romantic conventions. A recurrent theme in Madeleine's letters is her claim to have abjured 'flirting' once she had formed a relationship with L'Angelier: 'I feel confident you will trust me with society. I made a promise to you that I would not flirt that promise I shall keep.'[45] In fact Madeleine's frequent references to flirting were clearly part of a ploy to make him jealous and to inflame his passion. On one occasion, when Emile had obviously been chiding her about her conduct, she assured him that she had 'flirted with no one this year'. Madeleine, no doubt realising that this was no great testimony to her fidelity, since the letter was written on 14 January, added in parentheses: '(or rather since we were engaged.)'[46]

Madeleine's disavowals of flirting are usually juxtaposed with references to the attentions she had been receiving from rival suitors: 'I got 4 such pretty valentines this morning. I don't know where they came from and I don't care'; 'I write to one or two gentleman friends – but if you wish it I shall give it up.' She also liked to keep Emile informed of her many social engagements and social encounters: 'We have had a great many friends with us last week (four young men) (Englishmen) but I tried not to flirt with them. I did not tell you how much I enjoyed my visit to the Trossachs. I never enjoyed a trip more (it would have been perfect if you had been with me)'; 'Living in the house with me are two very smart young fellows, both of them 6 feet tall you know they won't please my fancy.'[47] In another letter, saturated with conceit, her coquettish disingenuousness must have tested Emile's patience to the limits:

> K has been with us this evening – came in without invitation. Papa seemed pleased – he has got the length of calling him 'John'. What shall be the next. Thank God he leaves in two weeks. Everyone is speaking to me about him. I cannot fancy why they have fixed me. It used to be B. [Bessie] He is to dine with us on Wednesday. [. . .] I do not intend to go to the Ball in January – I shall go out as little as I can. I dislike so many parties now. I believe we are to have a small dance on Wednesday.[48]

Such constant tattling about her social life appears to be part of Madeleine's courtship strategy and is deployed with other devices designed to fan the flames of Emile's desire and to test his commitment. Clearly she considered herself *sui generis* and had a highly developed sense of melodrama; however, this intricate dance with the emotions of one's suitor seems to have been a common and accepted part of courtship ritual. The period of courtship was one in which a woman, however briefly, reigned supreme. Her hand was the prize that was sought, and the man had to prove himself worthy of victory.[49] For some women, no doubt, the temptation to capitalise on this welcome and fleeting reversal of gender power relations was too great and they may have abused their temporary ascendancy and indulged, as L'Angelier complained of Madeleine, 'in playing with affections . . . pure and undivided'.[50]

Courtship often was formalised by an engagement, though this was not necessarily a signal of serious intent to marry. A common function was to provide a proving ground to test the depth of the lovers' affections. In a letter to L'Angelier, Madeleine remarked of her maid Christina Haggart: 'She intends to be married in November. But she may change her mind.'[51] Madeleine's references to at least two other young women in her social circle whose engagements did not end in matrimony suggest that this was an unremarkable occurrence. Indeed, Emile had also been engaged previously to a young woman from Fife, who had broken it off in favour of another.

Engagement could also serve as a mechanism to sanction the kind of intimacies between young people which would otherwise have occasioned censure. After a visit by her fiancé, Duncan McKenzie, to her bedroom in the Smith household, Christina Haggart gave an account to the procurator fiscal, explaining: 'I am engaged to be married to him on June next.'[52] Her intention was almost certainly to suggest that they had licence for their behaviour and that it was not entirely reprehensible. The engagement between Madeleine and Emile probably similarly permitted their physical, written and verbal intimacies, which would have been unacceptable even to themselves had they not been betrothed. During their 'engagement', Madeleine and Emile addressed each other with terms of endearment such as, 'My Own Beloved Darling Husband'; 'Ever thine, thy own fond wife'; 'My Dearest and Beloved Wife, Mimi'. Although it was to be some time before they consummated their relationship, the use of these terms indicates that they thought of themselves as bound together and as intimate as any married couple.

Given her parents' opposition to their relationship, Madeleine's and Emile's meetings had to be carefully orchestrated to avoid detection. However, she seemed to have ample opportunity to meet him alone.

Contrary to popular belief that young single Victorian women were subject to constant supervision and regulation, Madeleine was frequently left to her own devices. For example, at the family's country house at Rhu she and Emile were left alone to enjoy at least one tryst.[53] She also contrived a meeting on the steamship on which she travelled on her own between Glasgow and Rhu.

The long courtship of Frances Stoddard and David Murray was evidently also free from the restrictions and the chaperoning conventions generally associated with Victorian Britain. They spent most Saturdays together, making 'many excursions together under the guise of a day's "archaeologising", "geologising" or "botanising",' as their daughter put it.[54] Nevertheless, they almost certainly did not engage in the same level of physical intimacy as Madeleine and Emile. The notoriety of the Madeleine Smith case arose as much from the revelations of their sexual encounters as from the fact that the daughter of a respectable and prosperous businessman had possibly callously and premeditatedly murdered her lover. The notion that the Victorian woman was passionless and that sexual gratification was for her to provide rather than receive has been successfully debunked by a number of authors.[55] However, if women enjoyed sexual intimacy, it was expected that it would be confined to the marital bed, as would any expressions of sexual fulfilment. The details of the Madeleine Smith case were grist to the mill of the Victorian press, whose circulation was doubtless boosted by a public eager to digest the latest revelations of the case. It is all too easy to imagine the collective sexual frisson that was aroused: a young, female, unmarried, middle-class woman had indulged in and enjoyed premarital sexual intercourse, and had written about her experience with some frankness. Rarely were so many Victorian sexual taboos simultaneously broken.

Although relying on customary Victorian euphemism, Madeleine expressed her ardour to Emile in candid and sensual terms. In December 1855, for example, on hearing that he had been feeling unwell, she wrote to him: 'I hope that the pain in your chest is much better, I wish I had been with you to have put on your mustard plaster.'[56] Immediately after their first sexual experience, Madeleine was unprecedentedly explicit, writing that she 'did not bleed in the least last night, but [had] a good deal of pain during the night.' She went on to express the pleasure and enjoyment she had experienced, betraying only a hint of shame at having breached the ultimate sexual taboo for respectable single women: 'Beloved, if we did wrong last night, it was in the excitement of our love. Yes, beloved, I did truly love you with my soul. Oh, if we could have remained, never more to have parted, But we must hope the time shall come.'[57] If Madeleine did regret making the ultimate sexual transgression, it was not sufficiently so to prevent the sexual liaison continuing, nor was it solely at Emile's behest. She admitted that it was 'hard to resist the temptation of *love*' and concluded one of her letters by regretting that they could not spend the night together: 'But I must go to bed as I feel cold – so good night. Would to God that it were to be by your side, I would feel well and happy then. I think I would be wishing you to *love* me if I were with you – but I don't suppose you would refuse me.'[58]

Clearly Madeleine's experience of premarital sexual relations was untypical of single middle-class women. However, she was not alone in her enjoyment of sexual intercourse, or of giving expression to it. When Mary Allan married William MacEwen in 1873, she wrote to her brother, his best friend, on her return from honeymoon. That letter does not survive, but her brother's response shows him clearly relishing, indeed taking vicarious pleasure bordering on the homoerotic, in her pleasure:

> I have not the least doubt about your having enjoyed your Honeymoon at Lochranza – No doubt Lochranza was Paradise and Willie and you played Adam and Eve to your hearts content. I suppose you both lived in a sort of day dream – in a state of ecstacy long drawn out.
>
> I am not a bit surprised at your gushing admiration for your big manly husband. You may indeed well be proud of him – and I know that you love him with your whole heart – as well you may.[59]

Who knows whether the promise of that first sexual encounter was sustained in the course of the marriage. In the case of Joseph and Georgiana Coats, however, ardour was still evident several years after their honeymoon. While on holiday with their children, Georgiana wrote to her husband: 'they [the children] are longing for your sweet company. So am I . . .'[60] As published in a memoir compiled by their daughters, the letters contain several unfinished sentences such as this, the result of censorship applied by the daughters in the interests of propriety and privacy. Frances Murray was more reticent about expressing her desire for intimacy, though she clearly missed David when they were apart. Such phrases as 'would that you were here, dear husband' suggest more than a mere spiritual longing.[61]

Protracted engagements may have served primarily to establish the compatibility of partners; when prolonged, they may also have reflected the uncertainty and doubt which surrounded the prospect of marriage for many. There could be competing pulls on the emotions and commitments, and marriage was not necessarily the summit of expectations for all women. Janet Maughan, Elizabeth Thomson, Georgiana Taylor and Frances Stoddart all expressed some wariness about taking marriage vows. Janet Maughan was thirty-five in 1863 when she met the Reverend Robert Story and had gained a reputation in her native Edinburgh as a society hostess and *bon viveur*. She admitted that her apprehension about her marriage to a minister was related to her fear that she might find life in a rural parish rather dull in contrast to the 'whirl to which I had been accustomed'.[62] When in 1842 the Reverend Dr King declared his feelings in a letter to Elizabeth Thomson, she was not in the least interested and responded curtly 'giving him no hope'.[63] Her response was perhaps influenced by the Kings' lack of conviviality: she had glumly remarked of a party at their home that it was 'a grave and solemn' affair. Explaining her resistance to King's overtures, she claimed: 'Deep, clinging love for the dear old home was the chief obstacle.'[64] Her suitor, bolstered by the support of her father, who had inserted an encouraging note of his own with the letter from the incognisant Elizabeth, persisted with his attentions. Although she began to warm to him, she still harboured serious doubts, again explaining it in terms of the rival attraction of her single life in the comfortable bosom of her family:

> I am glad you are coming to Knock, but you must not talk on only one subject. I am quite afraid of it. [. . .] From my former letter you will perceive that I am in great doubt – indeed I feel both afraid and sad when I contemplate the possibility of change in my lot. At home I am so happy. I think scarcely ever any one had so many blessings to be thankful for.[65]

While lacking Madeleine Smith's manipulative streak, Frances Stoddard also kept David Murray waiting several years after their engagement, eventually agreeing to marry him in 1872, when she was twenty-nine. Their daughter Eunice, writing from the perspective of a late nineteenth-century suffragette, was convinced that her mother's lengthy courtship was related to her 'reluctance to bind herself and give up her independence'.[66] There is certainly evidence from Frances's correspondence that she feared that marriage would shackle her and prevent her from pursuing her intellectual interests. She had been an avid reader all her life of biographies, philosophy, poetry and religion, as well as a student of astronomy and English literature. In 1867, at the age of twenty-four, Frances wrote to her mother from America complaining about the lot of women:

Indeed, here as at home, I find a woman better not have too decided views on any matter, literature, historical, social, reform or politics, if she wishes to be a man's favourite. It is hard that brains in a woman except to give herself satisfaction, are a hindrance not an asset. Well, Mamma dear, I would rather have the brains than live on empty compliments the plaything of any man. Though I find men very pleasant, and their company very charming.[67]

Eunice's belief that the length of courtship could be attributed to her mother's reluctance to surrender her independence is given some credence by the observation of an uncle who wrote to congratulate Frances on her engagement:

I confess to some surprise when I heard that one who has enjoyed for long her entire liberty and freedom of action and who has found so much happiness in it, should be willing to forego it all and come under the 'yoke of bondage', but not withstanding my surprise, I am very glad my dear niece, that you have found a friend in whom you have such perfect confidence, that you can without hesitation give him your entire love and trust.[68]

David Murray, a Glasgow lawyer, was a staunch supporter of women's rights and active in the campaign for the education of women, which no doubt found favour with Frances. Indeed he sent her a pamphlet on the Women's Question, for which she thanked him, adding that: 'although initially fired by it [. . . , by] this time I have relapsed into indifference.'[69] Frances may have been more of a faint-hearted feminist than a committed one, but she placed a high premium on her independence. During a sojourn to London, where she drank copiously from the fountain of art, literature and the theatre, she replied to a letter from David in a manner which bordered on callous indifference:

Many thanks for your letter, but you wrote too soon after mine. You ask do I think much of *you*, to tell you the truth, I'm enjoying myself too much to think of anyone. My life has been so bright and happy and I have enjoyed it all, that to tell you the simple truth I have put all diversions from me.[70]

David Murray's love and devotion to Frances must have indeed have been constant to endure the slight of being consigned to the order of a 'diversion'.

Georgiana Taylor was one of four sisters who had lived with an elderly companion since the death of their parents. Although the eldest sister had married with no obvious qualms about leaving her younger siblings, Georgiana's sense of duty appears to have been more highly developed, or at least this was the reason she gave Joseph Coats for her reluctance to enter a serious relationship with him. He had to pursue her to Switzerland and promise that her two younger sisters could come and live with them before they eventually married in 1879.[71]

The initial reluctance of the four women just discussed to enter into matrimony may have been fairly widespread among prosperous Victorian women. As Frances Stoddard Murray's and Janet Maughan Story's experience testifies, there was no shortage of time and money for these single women to indulge their pleasures and passions, within the bounds of bourgeois conventions, while as Elizabeth Thomson and Georgina Taylor declared, there was the competing pull of the security and familiarity of family bonds. On the other hand, although marriage held out the promise of love and companionship, it also entailed subordination to the authority of the 'master', and the loss of their liberty and freedom to do much as they pleased. It would not have taken a committed feminist to express some anxieties about taking the plunge. While married couples may have been counselled to love, honour and respect each other and husbands to temper their authority with affection, rarely do complex and intimate human relations neatly correspond with cultural prescriptions. Once married, how did couples negotiate the potentially conflicting injunctions to make marriages which were complementary and companionate, and yet based on a model of male independence and authority and female dependence and submission?

Although Madeleine Smith and Emile L'Angelier did not marry, their correspondence reveals details about prevailing ideas of the marital relationship. Madeleine's letters are replete with studiedly melodramatic expressions, which in all likelihood were influenced by romantic fiction of the period. Despite the fact that her prose was transparently artifice, Madeleine was clearly drawing on a well-established model of conjugal idiom to address L'Angelier. Her rhetorical mode, based on a relationship where the husband was the supreme authority and was morally and intellectually superior, might well have been a plagiarised version of any one of a number of prescriptive texts or romantic novels. She repeatedly cast herself in the role of pupil and L'Angelier as teacher: 'My dear husband it is your duty to give your foolish wife advice so I may try and improve'; 'I am trying to break myself of all my very bad habits – it is you I have to thank for this, which I do sincerely from my heart.' Although L'Angelier's exotic good looks attracted Madeleine, there is also a suggestion that he had an air of sophistication and intellectual solemnity which added to his allure and set him apart from her customary beaux. 'But it is not only your appearance that makes me feel proud of you – but your superior mind and ways of thinking different from other young men. I look upon "fast" men now with horror!' L'Angelier embraced his role as tutor to the unsophisticated Madeleine and frequently suggested appropriate and 'improving' literature for her to read and chided her for any behaviour or habits he perceived as deficient. She in turn relished the role of pupil and eagerly responded to his suggestions, anxious to display her dedication both to him and to cerebral improvement: 'I shall practice music and drawing and I shall read useful books. I shall not read Byron any more. I shall do all I can to improve myself and shall not spend any time idly.' Not that she always found his recommended reading to her taste, as she tentatively complained of Gibbon's *Decline and Fall* and Pollard's *Ancient History*, that they 'are rather dry are they not?'[72]

Madeleine delighted in parading her obedience to Emile: 'I shall be thine own dear dutiful wife'; 'I shall make it my study to please you in all things. [. . .] It is the duty of a wife to study her husband in all things'; 'You are my husband dear and you have a right to dictate to me.'[73] Echoing much of the prescriptive literature of the early nineteenth century, she also promised to provide a haven for him where he would not only be obeyed, but also be comforted and cosseted: 'When we are married, it will be my constant endeavour to please you and to add to your comfort. I shall try to study you, and when you get a little out of temper, I shall try and pet you, dearest – kiss and fondle you.'[74] Madeleine's conception of a wife's duty was as a helpmeet who would minister to the spiritual and indeed carnal needs of her spouse: 'Is a man not more happy with a wife? Is she not a happiness and a comfort to him? A solace to him in his sad hours?'[75] There were few references to her own needs or how Emile might reciprocate.

By the same token, Madeleine consciously distanced herself from those women who sought to gain equality for their sex, or at least equal value. She wrote to Emile that she had declined to take a subscription out for a new publication, the *Waverley Journal*, which was published by 'Ladies for the Cultivation of the Memorable, the Progressive, and the Beautiful'. She explained her disapproval of the paper in terms of the poor quality of the writing: 'it was all milk and water writing – you know the style.' She was dismissive of the ability of women to produce writing of quality and linked this to their general inferiority to men: 'I have a very poor opinion of my sex. There is no doubt man is a superior being and that is the reason why I think a wife should be guided and directed in all things by her husband.'[76]

Madeleine acknowledged that her views did not reflect those of other women in her circle who subscribed to a more egalitarian notion of the relationship between the sexes and the role of women in society: 'I get few ladies who agree with me. They all think "woman" is as good and as clever as a man.'[77] If Madeleine's observation of the views of her contemporaries has any credibility, it would appear that the conventional and uncompromisingly patriarchal model of the marital relationship, which she fabricated for Emile's benefit, was an outmoded one. However, there is some reason to doubt that Madeleine was as subservient and deferential as she purported to be. L'Angelier may have been open to intellectual stimulation and political ideas (he had enlisted during the 1848 Revolution while living in Paris) but he had conventional views about the relationship between a man and a woman. Madeleine was well aware of L'Angelier's opinions and was probably telling him what he wanted to hear and tailoring her discourse accordingly. His two surviving letters reek of priggish self-righteousness and he rarely missed an opportunity to berate Madeleine for her failings: 'You are not stupid Mimi – and if you disappoint me in information, and I have cause to reproach you for it, you will have no one to blame but yourself. I have given you warning long enough to improve yourself.'[78]

The proposition that Madeleine was carefully constructing an image of uxorial deference is supported by her own assessment of her character. Her self-descriptions suggest that compliance and submission were alien to her character. She wrote of having a 'fiery' temper, one which was 'like her father's'. Although she never openly defied her parents in her relationship with L'Angelier, she reports herself as 'standing firm' in the face of her father's opposition, of not being 'easily frightened', and as bragging to L'Angelier 'that her father would find out that his daughter has a mind of her own'.[79] This may, of course, have been bravado, or an attempt to convince Emile that she was making an effort to secure the sanction of her parents. Nonetheless, despite Madeleine's many declarations of self-sacrificing duty and obedience, all the evidence points to a strong-willed, spirited, stubborn young woman who would not meekly submit to the will of another, whether bound by marriage vows or not. L'Angelier was certainly not wholly convinced of her ingenuousness. He once complained: 'Sometimes I do think you take no notice of my wishes and desires, but say "yes" for mere matter of form.' Had their affair culminated in marriage, L'Angelier may have found that his submissive betrothed had transformed into a feisty and less malleable wife.

In its outward appearance, the marriage of Joseph and Georgiana Coats resembled the Victorian romantic stereotype invoked by Madeleine: the patriarchal marriage of an acceptably older and more educated man to a younger woman. Joseph Coats, a pupil of Joseph Lister, became a successful doctor who secured an appointment as lecturer in pathology at Glasgow University, eventually becoming the first Professor of Pathology in 1894. As mentioned above, he was also a luminary of the Baptist Church. Besides playing a leading role in a number of the city's philanthropic organisations, he was a prodigious walker and moutaineer and a keen golfer. He was, *inter alia*, one of the founders of the Glasgow Co-operation of Trained Nurses, the Baptist Theological College of Scotland (of which he was the first President), the Glasgow University Club, the Scottish Mountaineering Club and also helped to start the Glasgow Students' Union. By contrast, Georgiana's activities revolved around her large extended family and her two daughters, and there is little evidence that she engaged in such a full public life, although her daughter noted that her father 'in all his enterprises was aided and abetted with enthusiasm by his no less venturesome wife'.[80] It is likely that this support was provided in the background rather than in the public eye, for her daughter Olive refers to the fact that her mother made only one public speech and that to a garden fête in connection with the girls' auxiliary of the Baptist Missionary Society. When she became a lay member of the Glasgow Lady Artists Society, it was at the suggestion of her husband, according to her daughter. The intellectual relationship between Joseph and Georgiana resembled one of tutor and pupil in that he seemed to provide suggestions for reading matter and tried to expand the breadth of her knowledge. He certainly displayed many of the qualities of a patriarch; from time to time in his correspondence he would reprimand her for what he perceived as her failings. His daughter commented that those outside the inner circle of his friends were 'apt to judge him severe', while others referred to his 'cold demeanour'.[81]

However, it is clear from their correspondence that Georgiana was not in awe of her husband. On the frequent occasions when they were separated, they wrote daily to each other and their letters express affection and tenderness which transcended the prescriptions of conventional conjugal endearments; they also include plentiful domestic details. From the tranquillity of her bedroom and observing her child at play, she once wrote: 'And Ole is being put to bed and Moritz [their dog] lies panting below and the pony is eating grass and whisking away the flies with his tail. It is all too tragic – but I have to leave tragedy and attend to hubby Dubby. . . .'[82] Again, this was not originally an unfinished sentence but this was one of the letters subject to the censoring hand of their daughter. Georgiana was more effusive than Joseph was in his letters, which display a masculine reserve at public demonstrations of emotion; he 'hated anything gushing or sentimental'.[83] However, he displayed enough self-knowledge to mock his reserve when he commented: 'I saw you waving from the pier this morning, but do you think I was going to make a spectacle of myself by waving in return? No, Madam. I am too old a bird to be caught in that way.'[84] On another occasion, when she was away for a few days visiting family, he wrote: 'My Dear, – How shall I tell you how much we are longing for you here? It seems such a time since you left and we are counting the days and hours till you come back.'[85] On the eve of his fiftieth birthday he reflected: 'My Dear One, – Tis the end of another year in my journey. This day I finish 49 years of travel, of which over fifteen have been in your sweet company.'

The couple's letters also display a healthy measure of irreverence towards each other. Georgiana would often upbraid her husband for his failure to discharge his duties or would harry him to perform a task she had set him. She certainly assumed primary responsibility for organising the household tasks, but she expected support and practical help from her husband and not infrequently dispatched him on domestic duties. The chronic illness of their younger daughter necessitated long periods spent away from the city and this frequently left Joseph and their elder daughter in their town house where he was expected to carry out some of the household tasks. He was not always punctilious about performing them, and she was quick to reproach him, although her reprimand was usually laced with playful banter. For example, having forgotten to take blinds back to Glasgow with him, he received the following note from the holiday home:

It *was* a pity that after all you forgot the blind. I did not find them till fully five minutes after you left, and sent Jessie spinning after you, but it was too late to be any use.

I suppose you would have the gumption to order the blinds all the same – at the shop in Buchanan Street. There is, of course, no news to relate. I simply write to commiserate you on being such a numbskull as to leave behind an object which had been so frequently before your eyes and which had been such a bone of contention. [. . .] Thanks for the money which caused you to forget – oh no, it didn't, for you were at the door before I asked [for] money – the blinds. You stayed in fact too long in the Palace of Delight.

Yours very sympathetically.[86]

On another occasion, Georgiana wrote a letter heavy with irony in which she detailed the multifarious tasks she had undertaken that day:

I got a *new key* for you for the Gardens (good little woman!). I wrote to proprietor of Tummel Bridge Inn for terms and Post-Master at Braemar for information about lodgings with attendance for September (excellent small person!).

I sent off various parcels ... all by *new* post, just over 3lbs so had to pay 9d. instead of 6d. (But very good, Mrs Coats – excellent!). I also sent off the 12/6 for old books and 3/- for wastepaper (so that I might not be tempted to spend it). (Wisdom far above rubies, young woman!)

And what else did I do? – Oh, yes.

I invited Minnie.

I wrote to A. Clark, Esq. (Insurance)

To Girls.

To Mrs Fleming – a discourse about Isa.

To Miss H. S. Lamont.

To Shetland about account.

And what more shall I say?

...... The cayenne has *nearly* killed the moths! But alas, what havoc they have made!

A small wee mouse was drownded this morning.

His remains were committed to ashpit!

Further news in *Herald* of the day. With love.

Yours most intellectually and devotedly.

Although the irony is apparently self-deprecating, the letter also suggests that recognition is being sought for how much she had accomplished in a single day, not only household chores but administrative tasks. She certainly embraced her role as helpmeet to her husband with enthusiasm and regarded herself as a partner in his public role. When he was to give an address to the congregation of the Baptist Church in Paisley she offered him advice, penned his script and went along to lend support:

My Dear, – This is me. Two umbrellas, three sticks and one poker, come to inspire and applaud.

If you look up to the right hand corner (as you come in) just behind a person with a Black Bonnet trimmed with Crimson you will see my beaming face.

Look well – don't put your specs on, for they are lying on the chimney piece!

Don't pitch your voice too high.

Don't roar at your audience.

And

Don't emphasize every fifth word!

. . . Now I am sure you have succeeded very well. . . .

Did you hear the plaudits of the multitude – some of the 'External World'?

Was it very 'susceptible' to the flow of oratory so badly penned by the Secretarial Wife – or had the micro-organisms and the ill-ventilated condition of 'Storie Street' too depressing an influence?

Mind I am listening. Pull your cuffs well down and push your hair well up, take a sip of water – now go on.

[. . .] This is a Bright (with a capital) Cold (with a capital) day. Put on your gloves and Button (with a capital) up your coat.

Good luck – Ta-Ta

The reference to 'the Secretarial Wife' implies that Georgiana saw herself as a partner in Joseph's public life, albeit an unequal one. While he may have inspired deference and even awe in his public life, in the home he did not reign sovereign. Indeed he seems to have believed that he deferred too often to her more finely attuned social and emotional antennae. Reflecting on their life together, he wrote:

As to you, I rather fear that my respect and deference for your wisdom and understanding of people may lead me to leave you too much to follow your own way. You must be aware that you are, more and more, getting things arranged exactly as you want. Well and good; in the main your way is better than mine.'[87]

This comment might have been motivated by a fear that his authority was being usurped rather too often, rather than indicating a reversal of traditional authority relations in the Coats household. However, Georgiana was clearly not without domestic clout. The couple's personal relations were based on reciprocity, mutual respect, companionship and love. Perhaps the spirit of their relationship is encapsulated in the last phrase of one of his letters: 'Well, we shall not have any dispute about it and we will take the way together that either of us convinces the other to be the best.'[88] In their private life together there is little evidence that the power relations of the marriage were marked by Joseph's authority and Georgiana's submissiveness. Is this to be explained simply by their love for each other which tamed and mellowed this apparent martinet while conferring private power on Georgiana? Besides their love, it is likely that their religious beliefs infused their relationship with a mutual regard and respect. Both were Baptists, a religion noted for its egalitarian principles in Church governance, although not necessarily for championing women's rights.[89] However, Joseph's deeply held belief in the equality of souls before God was one which he translated into day-to-day life. He criticised Hinduism for being elitist and neglecting the labouring masses, so that it 'could never be a people's religion.'[90] It was conceivably this egalitarianism which led him to invite the foremen and some of the workmen who had built their new home to a house-warming party at which a toast was proposed by Joseph to 'the British Workman'.[91]

Although advocates of equality in human relations do not always translate their principles into their private lives, apparently Joseph Coats did. His daughters recalled that he did not seem to regard them as inferior beings and that his attitude to their mother was 'not so much one of chivalry as of comradeship'.[92] His view that women were different but complementary and equal to men was derived from his religious convictions. One of his reasons for marrying was that he believed that the 'influence of a woman is useful to deepen the religious life'. He explained this belief by arguing: 'there is a need for action and reaction [. . .] the religious convictions coming from the man would be very strongly impressed on the woman, and in her nature would be transformed into religious feeling, and in this shape be reflected on the man.'[93] Their daughters claimed that they were initially bemused by the cry of 'Women's Rights', because in their household it was the unquestioned assumption of woman's equality with man that held good. This observation may need to be shorn of retrospective gloss, but in the context of the couple's correspondence contains more than a shard of truth.

Madeleine Smith's reference to her views on women meeting with opposition within her circle indicates that there were rival interpretations of women's role within and outside marriage by the middle of the century. The publication of which she was so caustically dismissive, the *Waverley Journal*, evinced a current within Victorian society by the middle of the century which advocated an expanded role for women and a greater premium being placed on their worth. However, there was no attempt to jettison the Enlightenment model of separate spheres which had held sway in prescriptive and advice literature for so long. The greater appreciation of women was still to be achieved through the recognition of her different and indispensable qualities:

> Woman is happily endowed with qualities of a gentle and endearing nature, which are often suffered to lie dormant or run riot. She is eminently qualified to be a worker of benevolence – an inspirer of high and generous sentiments – an instigator of noble deeds; let her not sink into the thraldom of vanity – let her not be [. . .] 'an animal that delights in finery'. Let her awake to her own responsibilities, and feel conscious that her influence, well-intentioned and wisely directed, is a regenerative principle [. . .] let her cultivate her intellect, and true to her own feminine attributes, prove herself the kind, genteel, intelligent creature man needs, cherishes, and esteems.[94]

The interpretation of separate spheres to be found in the journal's editorials differed in one respect from the more conservative version propounded in other prescriptive literature. Women were urged to develop their intellectual faculties and to forgo superficial preoccupations with appearance so that: 'woman would find her influence more powerful and unfailing.' The cultivation of the mind was promoted as a 'loftier ambition' than to be admired for 'the graces of the person'. While accepting and embracing their distinctive qualities, this view perceived women as having intellectual capacities that matched those of men – a view at odds with those expressed by the Reverend F. West in his lecture 'Woman: Her Position, Power and Privileges', reproduced in the *Waverley Journal*, that women lacked the mental constitution of men, although they may have shared his view that 'our social and moral character is chiefly of woman's keeping'.[95] There was some recognition in the journal's articles that ideals of complementarity were no guarantee of equality of esteem, value or treatment in practice. One article complained of the hypocrisy of men and contrasted their public politeness and congeniality with their private irascibility: 'The champion of female rights and seeming worshipper of a woman's gentle influence is alas! too often a household tyrant, a stern, unbending task-master. The smiles and seeming cordiality of the festive hour, are no true index to the hidden feelings.'[96]

The editorials of the *Waverley Journal*, a Glasgow publication aimed at the city's middle-class ladies, subscribed to the view of the family and the home as the site of spiritual and moral renewal and as 'the place in which to train souls for heaven'.[97] However, they also accorded men a role in this process and were critical of husbands who neglected their domestic responsibilities. Indeed, their views on marriage, and on husbands in particular, could be both scathing and jaundiced. One particularly misanthropic editorial warned of the disappointments in store for those seeking a husband: 'Some will go husband-hunting, and practice the arts of that trade – throwing the matrimonial lasso, by fond mothers prepared, at the shy necks of desirable matches: some shall catch fortune, and some respectability, but more disappointment, and more, alas, anything worth catching.'[98] Although there was no suggestion that the institution of marriage should be radically transformed, let alone abolished, these sorts of criticisms indicate that a robust critical discourse on marriage, particularly on the behaviour of husbands, was taking root by the middle of the century.

The correspondence of Frances Stoddard echoes many of the views contained in the *Waverley Journal*. Although seven years younger than Madeleine Smith, Frances could very well have been one of her circle who believed that 'woman was as good and clever as a man'. As an avid reader, she could well have been a subscriber to the journal, although only fourteen at the time of its inception. Frances strongly adhered to the journal's belief in separate spheres and the distinct and elevating qualities of women. The tensions inherent in coupling an assertion of sexual difference with a belief in the equality of the sexes were captured in Frances's own ambivalence to the Women's Movement and to women's rights. During a visit to her American relatives in 1867, she wrote to her mother:

> Aunt Agnes and Aunt Clara Nicolson are very strong on 'Women's Rights' and great advocates of the cause for which they work hard. . . . Many of the cleverest women here favour 'Women's Rights'. I vacillate. [. . .] My conclusion is – that if you have a strong mind and force of character it is a misfortune to be a woman, and no voting papers, or removal of disabilities will compensate for the mistake; but for those sweet and loving beings like you, Mother, or our own sweet Mary, their very softness and sweetness is a glory power which they exercise in a circle very different from the hustings and the pulpit. Yet with true inconsistency, the wrongs of my sex fire in me a flame of anger, and I feel we should be up and doing.[99]

The marriage of Frances and David Murray was a union of hearts and minds; they were soulmates whose marriage was founded on a bedrock of mutual respect, shared interests and love undiminished by the passage of time. Griefstricken by the death of her brother, Frances wrote to her husband: 'My darling, I cannot see for tears, if ever you were to leave me I should die – I could not live without you.'[100] For Frances emotional and intellectual compatibility were the solid foundations on which to base a marriage rather than unbridled passion. As she wrote to her daughter's friend on her engagement: 'I like to hear of my friends pairing off with those they know thoroughly well – for otherwise I have an uneasy feeling that the transaction partakes of the nature of a lottery.'[101] In many respects their relationship conformed to all the prescriptions of a middle-class Victorian companionate marriage: Frances became a wife, and in time a mother, never fulfilling her early desire to find employment. Once they had moved from Glasgow to the more rural retreat of Cardross, she busied herself with the task of managing a large household and caring for their four children, while David pursued his legal practice in Glasgow. Her life in their new home in Cardross took on all the aspects of the wife of a typical middle-class professional in the mid-Victorian period, revolving around home, children and the local community. She took responsibility for the children's education in their early years but also embraced the role of hostess and enjoyed 'entertaining and being entertained'. In addition she busied herself with 'her horse, her dogs, her music, her garden and her books'.[102] However, Frances also engaged in cultural and intellectual pursuits which were shared by her husband: they were both keen advocates of higher education for women and played an active part in setting up the Glasgow Ladies Higher Education Association in 1877.

Frances had clearly relished her single life, and the happiness which she appeared to attain in her marriage may be attributable to the fact that she retained considerable freedom and autonomy and did not experience the relationship as a 'yoke of bondage'. Frances was certainly not immured in domestic seclusion and had a very active public and social life even when her children were still young. She attended lectures, went to concerts, travelled widely and delivered a regular series of public lectures on Scottish song that she organised herself; occasionally her young family, even a five-month-old daughter, would accompany her to the lecture.

Superficially a conventional Victorian wife, Frances obviously had a strong independent streak, doubtless fuelled by her commitment to women's rights. Eunice wrote that her mother never wore a wedding ring: 'presumably she had one for the marriage ceremony, but immediately afterwards she discarded it, as she saw no reason why a wife should wear one unless her husband did likewise.'[103] Frances's feminism evolved from her radical liberal beliefs which she had inherited from her family.

Indeed her family background strongly influenced her views on politics, religion and women's role. Her American-born parents had a long association with radical causes in the United States, particularly the anti-slavery movement. In 1844 they settled in Britain, where Frances's father became active in his support of the agitation to repeal the Corn Laws. Frances's correspondence indicates that she had inherited her parents' liberalism, which instilled in her a love of freedom and liberty and a hatred of tyranny and oppression in whatever form it took, though she also fashioned her beliefs from deeply held Christian convictions. She interpreted Christian precepts through the lens of her political radicalism and they were invoked to rationalise her arguments for equality for women:

> Lord Macaulay's dictum concerning women is true. Certainly the Greek civilization, which reached so high a point in morals and metaphysics, in the arts and poetry, yet failed to raise women to anything like social equality, and certainly the female in any of the Semitic races (including Hebrews) was still worse off. And yet there were Deborahs and Miriams, Sapphos and Aspasias, here and there, and in their mythologies many countries have done justice to women − witness Pilas and Isas. They say it was Christianity that first gave woman her place, and truly I think it was, for the law that lays down that none but little Children can enter the Kingdom of Heavan and that if any man will be master among you let him be your servant is purely meant to teach that the weak and tender were not meant to suffer disabilities for the same; so I read it.[104]

Frances clearly adhered to an understanding of femininity which was informed by the doctrine of separate spheres, but which she inflected with the language of equality by interpreting Christianity as a liberating theology for those defined as 'weak' by nature, status or creed. Therefore the political and religious beliefs which she inherited from her family were braided with her feminism to create an identity based on self-value and independence. According to her daughter, Frances's public lectures were considered 'very bold and unwomanly conduct'. She also enjoyed the company of men and when visiting Cannes for the winter with three of her young children, complained to her husband about the lack of male companionship. Fortunately, family friends, the McGrigors, were also wintering in Cannes, and Frances found solace in the company of Mr McGrigor: 'He and I go long walks, oh, he is a charming man, so well read, so sympathetic with me in the things I care for.'[105] There was no hint of impropriety in this admission, which was apparently expressed ingenuously and without intent to inflame David's jealousy. Frances's predilection for male company may have stemmed from a belief, shared with Madeleine Smith, that by and large men were more likely to provide intellectual stimulation than their own sex. Her enthusiastic approval of Mr McGrigor certainly did not seem to aggrieve her husband, who made no efforts to summon Frances home and seemed content to await her return some six months later.

Although Frances found both personal fulfilment and autonomy within her marriage, she was not without regrets. As she put it in 1917: 'I have never had sufficient will force to determine my own life, but have let circumstances guide me.' She was evidently disappointed that she never earned her own living: 'In my young days the aim of a mother was to make her daughter pretty and attractive and sufficiently accomplished to let her marry well. Few other careers presented themselves to women'.[106] Born in 1843, she belonged to a generation of women who seldom embarked on higher education or pursued a professional career. While her marriage to David could be characterised as a 'marriage of true minds', the economic and social power which resided with men prevented the partnership from being a truly equal one. The rhythms of the Murray household were to a great extent dictated by David's business and civic concerns. Eunice observed that her mother was 'always anxious to spare my father in his busy life, and she it was who superintended the garden and the stables, who saw tradesmen and attended to matters affecting the upkeep of the place.' Rather than unquestioningly accept this role of helpmeet to her husband, Frances occasionally implied that it was one she stoically endured. In 1917, aged seventy-four, she wrote to a friend from the Holy Loch: 'In many ways I should be glad to end my days here, and never should miss a more strenuous life, but my husband is still active in business, and we must follow the Master and attend his comings and goings as long as he and I are together.' The use of the term 'Master' may have been intended ironically or figuratively, but it nonetheless conveys the limits on a truly companionate union when economic and social power relations were so unequal.

The crucial difference between Frances Murray and Georgiana Coats was the different aspirations and expectations they brought to their marriages. Despite considerable autonomy and independence, Frances occasionally felt constrained, but Georgiana's private correspondence expresses no such regrets, although it does contain an element of rationalisation and self-justification. For Frances, the emotional intimacy and the intellectual partnership which she and her husband forged were balanced

against the unfulfilled aspirations and the limits to her personal autonomy imposed by marriage. Frances had been chary of the potential self-
sacrifice, whereas Georgiana's reluctance to enter matrimony was related
to her family obligations rather than fear of the loss of her freedom and
independence. Her role as a helpmeet was not undertaken with resigna-
tion or dutiful self-sacrifice, but with enthusiasm and vigour. However,
she clearly expected a good deal more than mere material support from
her husband in return for ministering to his needs in his private and
public roles. Of course expectations were not the whole story; individual personality and cultural prescriptions jostled with aspirations and
expectations in determining whether there would be a happy outcome
for both parties.

Women negotiated the given patriarchal structures of marriage in different ways to carve out a role which gave them personal satisfaction and
fulfilment. The marriage of the Reverend and Mrs Story was also a partnership based on complementarity and mutual respect. As described
above, Janet Story initially had misgivings about marrying a rural parish
minister on the west coast, where she missed the social sparkle of her
Edinburgh days, and complained that 'the members of the dining society
were only 17'. However, she successfully re-created the role of society
hostess even within the constraints of marriage to a member of the clergy,
and regularly attended and gave dinner parties, teas and musical
evenings.[107] Mrs Story and her husband clearly had different temperaments and predilections. She admitted that her 'unfortunate love of hospitality' could create tension as he was 'less sociably disposed' than she.
However, the resolution to the potential conflict was not achieved by her
deferring to his wishes, but rather by his withdrawal from the frantic
'hubbub'. While the Reverend Story gained a reputation as an eminent
theologian and progressive force in the Church of Scotland, Mrs Story
gained an equally impressive reputation as a society hostess. The success
of their marriage was founded on a mutually agreed accommodation and
a division of roles which not only accorded with societal prescriptions, but also corresponded with their different personalities and
predispositions.

Although it is impossible to quantify and state with any certainty
whether harmonious marriages were the norm, it is certain that not all
marriages were as happy as those discussed here. Many middle-class
women would have enacted their role dutifully with neither expectation
or realisation of personal happiness and fulfilment. Others would have
endured marriages devoid of affection, where obedience was the vow that

took precedence over love and honour. And there would have been marriages where patriarchal authority was not only vigorously exercised, but also abused. Although divorce was uncommon, there were certainly many unhappy marriages. The divorce courts were generally the last stage in marital breakdown, partly because of the cost of divorce, so that many couples continued to live under the same roof, being united only in a legal sense. Others separated by mutual consent and simply lived independently. An uneasy coexistence may have been the only realistic choice for working-class women; however, living apart may have been a practical and preferred option for some middle-class women. Marriage settlements (discussed in chapter 5) gave women legal rights to their movable property, irrespective of the formal legal position, and were commonly made among the more affluent middle classes in the nineteenth century. Thus many middle-class women were often legally guaranteed financial independence and did not have to seek the sanction of the courts for aliment.

The prevalence of the marriage settlement among the middle classes can also be seen as an indication of the willingness of husbands to forgo their legal rights and acknowledge the right of women to own and control their own property. However, there were those who chose to abide by the letter and the spirit of the law and allow their husbands full authority in matters financial. When those marriages broke down the financial consequences could be severe. Janet Story's memoirs recount the cautionary tale of an older cousin who had married in the 1850s and had refused to make a marriage contract. The husband's health began to fail and he developed epilepsy, 'which told seriously on his temper, never a good one'. He became so violent that his wife could not deal with him and he went to live with a doctor to whom he subsequently left all her money as well as his own.[108]

Agnes Gardner, the aunt of William Thomson, later to become Lord Kelvin, may also not have been so fortunate as to have made an antenuptial contract. In 1826 she married a man who worked in her brother's firm, against the advice of her family. The marriage rapidly ran in to difficulties because her husband was 'a drunkard and unreliable'. They emigrated to Brazil where he sought work, but returned after a couple of years and stayed with various relatives. He went off to Lisbon, ostensibly for employment, and she remained with her sister's family and became a surrogate mother and housekeeper after the death of her sister. However, another attempt was made to revive the marriage and she joined him in Lisbon four years later. This attempt at reconciliation floundered as her husband was 'so cruel', and she returned alone to Glasgow where she again stayed with her sister's family.[109]

While some separations were doubtless caused by violence, cruelty or maltreatment from husbands, others were caused by incompatibility. Another of Mrs Story's anecdotes concerns a couple who on the day of their wedding had had a disagreement which had never been resolved. They lived not only apart for the rest of their lives, but in separate countries, although remaining legally married.[110]

The debates about marriage during the 1880s and 1890s were evidently more widespread than they had been earlier in the century. Elaine Showalter and others have suggested that the emergence of the 'New Woman' who looked outside marriage for personal fulfilment and the growth of a homosocial culture might have contributed to an increasing disenchantment with domesticity and to declining rates of marriage.[111] Although towards the end of the century there probably was a mushrooming of exclusively male associational life, and there may even have been a periodic crisis of masculinity, there is no definitive interpretation of marriage statistics in the second half of the century, let alone an explanation for these statistics.[112] Even if there was a flight from domesticity and a rejection of marriage at the end of the nineteenth century, what about those who did marry? Did they become disillusioned and disaffected with the institution of marriage? Were the largely harmonious marriages discussed above islands of conjugal tranquillity in a sea of troubled marital waters?

John Tosh has argued that the questioning or rejection of masculine domesticity led to a redefinition of masculinity and an intensification of gender divisions. For example, the growth of all-male clubs and societies is attributed to an unconscious desire to recapture a definition of masculinity free from the 'taints' of feminine influence.[113] There is some evidence in the contemporary press to support the contention that men were shunning female company and heading for the billiard tables, the golf courses or the hills. The *Glasgow Herald* sporadically published articles that served as apologias for men's discomfiture with marital intimacy. One of them, discussing the proposal that the honeymoon should be shortened, includes the comment: 'Concentrated life "a deux" is, as some one (doubtless a much-married person) has said, "a terrible test" [. . .] the male mind is less able to concentrate itself on these happy hectic days than the female mind.'[114]

The fact that Victorian and Edwardian married couples were often – and long – apart is striking. However, this cannot be easily ascribed to a rigid demarcation of the sexes, polarised gender roles or to a crisis of masculine identity. The times spent apart were not always in sex-segregated activities or associations. Nor did these activities neatly correspond to a division between a male 'public' and a female 'private' sphere. Both husbands and wives, independently as well as together, spent a good deal of time visiting relatives and friends who were scattered across the country. Such visits were not confined to the domestic setting. Frances Murray, for example, on her frequent forays to cousins in England or her friend on the east coast of Scotland, would spend time sampling the cultural fare on offer and attending dances and balls. When she visited her married daughter in Glasgow, she was drawn by the concerts, plays and public lectures as much as by a desire to be in the bosom of her family. Joseph Coats made regular visits to his family in Paisley as well as more lengthy visits to his relatives in the north of Scotland. He was occasionally accompanied by one of the children while his wife remained at home with the other.

The practice of separate holidays and summer exiles of the family to the coast or the country long predated any putative masculine identity crisis. Wives and husbands often took lengthy holidays or travelled abroad independently. While Frances Murray, Georgiana Coats and Janet Story sometimes took their children on their trips abroad, it was just as common for the children to remain at home with their father and servants or a governess. As the children grew up and school commitments kept them at home, these women would travel with a friend or another family member, often to exotic destinations. This applied equally to men, including David Murray, Hugh Allan and Joseph Coats, who, without their wives, accompanied their children on continental holidays. The free time which businessmen and professionals enjoyed was often spent travelling, sometimes in the company of other men. William MacEwen, for example, enjoyed a foreign trip with a wealthy patient, while Joseph Coats took several all-male golfing holidays; when he was convalescing at Crief Hydro in 1885, however, Coats's party included several women.[115]

There could be few organisations that conformed so comprehensively to the late nineteenth-century model of male associational life than the Scottish Mountaineering Club, although it lacked the imperial connotations of the hunting and shooting fraternity. Founded in 1889, it was exclusively male until the 1990s; the annual dinner, the 'meets' and even the usage of huts were restricted to men. Yet the club was not a refuge for men fleeing the emasculating clutches of women. Although women were excluded from membership, they were welcomed on their excursions and wives frequently accompanied their spouse.[116] Joseph Coats, a founder member of the club, was not accompanied by his wife on his many expeditions in the Scottish Highlands and the Swiss Alps, although he often took one of his daughters.

In the language of popular psychology, the Victorian middle-class marriage in both its companionate and patriarchal forms allowed both parties acres of 'personal space', or at least, space from each other. Rather than trying to explain the relative autonomy of middle-class married couples in terms of the doctrine of separate spheres, or in terms of the aggressive form of masculinity that sought to flee from domesticity, it may be the case that some answers might lie in attitudes to intimacy and privacy. In the marriages discussed in this chapter, the most companionate were characterised by a strong emotional bond and an intellectual partnership, yet the individual husbands and wives did not seem to expect each other to be the sole source of companionship or even of intimacy. The intensely private conjugal relationship may be a product of the twentieth century, when declining fertility rates, contracting family size and nuclear units were well established rather than incipient. Only when the nuclear unit was stripped of its extended-kin supports did it became the focal point for the fulfilment of emotional and psychic needs, with the conjugal unit expected to meet diverse needs which had previously been diffused among a large and extended network of kin relations.

The examples discussed here cannot of course be taken to suggest that companionate unions were universal. Patriarchal marriages did not disappear but continued to exist alongside marriages based on mutuality. They do, however, reveal that a legal and institutional framework of patriarchy and a cultural assumption of the supremacy of male authority were compatible with marriages based on love, affection and companionship. Husbands and wives mutually accommodated and negotiated the contradictory injunctions to embrace both companionship and patriarchal authority in ways that produced a variety of conjugal relationships. Public and private power did not always coincide, and power relationships within marriages did not necessarily reflect culturally sanctioned authority relations. Intimate human relationships do not always neatly comply with cultural and institutional prescriptions, and ordinary men and women with different temperaments, expectations and foibles could forge relationships that tempered or even flew in the face of cultural imperatives and prescriptions. By the same token, there were many marriages that remained untouched by edifying public discourse, where women's subordination was unleavened by affection or mutual accommodation and where patriarchal power was unreined.

The character and quality of a marriage did not rest solely on the vagaries of individual temperament or the contest of wills. The relations between husband and wife were mediated, if not determined, by cultural prescriptions and institutional structures which sanctioned and legitimated structural inequalities in gender relations.

4

Let me Entertain you

Our mother was always waiting for his return with the children about her. Very eagerly we listened for his knock and ran to open the door, and helped him to take off his things; and then heard some stories from him of what was going on in the world.[1]

THIS IDYLLIC EVOCATION OF CHILDHOOD MEMORIES from *Lord Kelvin's Early Home Life* resonates with a common view of Victorian family life as a private enclave, cloistered from the public gaze and the disorder of the public world. Indeed 'home' and 'private' or 'domestic' and 'private' are often used interchangeably when referring to nineteenth-century home life.[2] Furthermore, 'private' has often been defined implicitly through its juxtaposition with 'public'. The counterpoising of 'public' and 'private' and the conflation of the category 'private' with 'home' and 'domesticity' has led to a cluster of assumptions about the nature of Victorian home life which revolve around the themes of retreat, domesticity and moral regeneration.

In large part we have derived our view of the Victorian home from the prescriptive literature of the period which sought to delineate the home as a spiritual enclave, a source of psychic and emotional comfort, particularly for men, as well as a source of physical sustenance.[3] Davidoff and Hall have discussed the emergence and development of this literature from its origins in the Enlightenment to its mutation and secularisation amidst the social and political upheavals of the early nineteenth century.[4] By the middle of the nineteenth century the family was also seen as a vehicle for promoting social harmony and cohesion which would counteract the fissiparous forces of the industrial revolution.[5] Therefore the home was also seen as a moral training ground and inextricably linked to the production of good Christian citizens. Although this literature proliferated in the early nineteenth century, attempts to define and confirm the idea of the home as a spiritual and religious haven continued throughout the Victorian period. For example an editorial of 1856 in the *Waverley Journal* declared: 'As the holy family is the fairest emblem of heaven, so it is the place in which to train souls for heaven.'[6]

Academic literature, often drawing on this literature, is also laden with references to the private nature of the home. However, many writers have been sensitive to the problematic nature of the term 'private': Davidoff and Hall, for example, have explored both the theoretical and empirical limitations of the binary division of 'public' and 'private', while Tosh has observed that, as a code of living, 'Victorian domesticity was shot through with contradictions'.[7] Indeed a central tenet of the constitution of the 'private' for Jürgen Habermas was its audience-orientated nature as an object of the 'public gaze'.[8] For despite the claims about privacy, middle-class domestic life had to be paraded and ostentatiously displayed in order to vaunt its superiority and become the model of home life. Despite these qualifications, it has been the conflation of the 'private' and the 'home' which continues to lie at the heart of our understanding of Victorian home life. Historians have tended to identify the mid-nineteenth century and the Victorian era as the point when the ideology of domesticity and the private character of the home became consolidated.[9] Gillis is unequivocal in demarcating the middle of the century as the point at which 'the family had cut itself off from the wider world'.[10]

The separation of home and work is one of the influential narratives of the history of the family in the nineteenth century and is deemed to have been both cause and consequence of the retreat of the middle classes into domesticity. Davidoff and Hall chart the process of the separation of the home and family from the enterprise in the first half of the century. Although they acknowledge that this process was incomplete and partial, they comment that by the 1830s and 1840s most contemporary writers on domestic ideology were assuming that this separation had taken place.[11] Of course the separation was not intended to be only physical, but also to preserve the home as a spiritual enclave, free from the pressures of the market place. There are indications that some families may have made a conscious effort to ensure that business affairs did not intrude on home life. For example, Madeleine Smith, whose family relationships are described in chapter 3, wrote to her lover in 1856 that she had 'not the least idea of what [my father's] income is he never mentions business or money matters in the household. I know that he is an architect but that is all.'[12]

Writing in the 1940s, Catherine Carswell – whose father George Macfarlane was a prosperous merchant in late nineteenth-century Glasgow –

still seemed uncertain of her father's specific occupation: 'My father was, I believe, a commission agent.'[13] Like Madeleine Smith, Carswell professed to be ignorant of 'money matters': 'Money was a subject I never remember as a topic of conversation in my youth. [. . .] I had a vague idea that consequent upon certain mysterious ceremonies enacted before his large desk, of which he was sole master, coins in sufficient quantity insinuated themselves through a hole in the office roof.'[14] However, she recounts how both she and her sister launched ships built for her father's business and took part in their trial trips down the Clyde. She also remembered him bringing home yards of printed cotton to display to the family as the purchase had brought great commercial success.[15] Nor was it unusual for her and her siblings to visit their father at his workplace, although she claimed to 'be awed when we went there'.[16] Madeleine Smith was also familiar with her father's business premises and on occasion called in there during her shopping expeditions.[17]

Therefore the claims by the daughters of these two prosperous middle-class families to be ignorant of the commercial world need to be treated with some caution; they might stem more from a desire, in the case of Madeleine Smith, to underscore the fact that she was in the throes of a passionate romance and was unconcerned with worldly and 'vulgar' matters such as money. Catherine Carswell's memories suggest the fantasies of an imaginative child. Both cases may also reflect the desire to show a socially acceptable innocence about business matters rather than real ignorance.

In fact the penetration of the home by the world of work and business among the Glasgow middle class is a more common occurrence than one might expect, even taking account of the fact that the process of separation was protracted and incomplete. Even in an estate designed for residential purposes such as Claremont, work was inextricably linked with home. As one might expect, the separation of home and work was less clear cut among the old professions such as medicine, the ministry and academia. Although William MacEwen's professional activities as a surgeon 'entailed long absences from home not only by day, but also by night', he did not confine his work to the infirmary or the lecture theatre, as his daughter recalled her father working in his study 'till late into the night'.[18] His daughter acted as his secretary and occupied a study in the family home in Woodside Terrace to carry out her secretarial tasks.[19] In a practice long familiar in academic circles, James Thomson, Professor of Mathematics at the University of Glasgow from 1832, and the father of Lord Kelvin, routinely retired to his study in the evenings to work.[20]

The interpenetration of home and work was perhaps most marked in the households of Victorian doctors. Not only did many general practitioners have consulting rooms attached to their homes, a practice which continued well into the twentieth century, but some doctors performed surgery in those rooms. For much of the nineteenth century the medical treatment of the middle class largely took place in private, outside the hospital system, which was the province only of the poor. Middle-class patients were commonly treated in their homes.[21] One Glasgow general practitioner, J. Stuart Nairne, claimed to have performed ninety-seven serious operations in private practice.[22] In the Claremont estate, Woodside Place housed many of the doctors in the area; Joseph Lister, for example, would frequently work long into the night in his laboratory at home. The household effects of George Wilson, a doctor in the same street, included 'medical books and medical instruments in his house'.[23] The detailed household inventory of Dr Alexander Anderson describes his consulting room as 'the library': however, it contained a 'consulting table', microscope, a 'mouth basin & ewer' and other items that suggest Dr Anderson saw his patients there.[24] There were also several china vases and plates and other ornaments; nineteen framed photos, watercolours, engravings and medallions; and 'a musical instrument'. In short, the room displayed a blend of the professional and domestic which is, interestingly, also evident in the drawing room. Here, alongside the rosewood work table (for sewing), the piano and the stereoscope which all indicate family activities, were also letter weights, ink stands and ink bottles and no fewer than 715 books.

Some doctors with a modest practice would have a shop attached to their premises which served as a pharmacy for the preparation and sale of medicines. This was particularly common in small towns which did not have a chemist shop. William Walker, a general practitioner in Pollockshaws on the outskirts of the city had a practice in the 1870s where the shop was inside the house. His son, writing in the 1930s, remarked that this arrangement 'made it easier for my mother to supervise the shop, but must have interfered with the privacy of the household'.[25] One can only speculate whether Walker was articulating a nineteenth-century conception of domestic privacy which may have been that of his parents, or whether he was reflecting a peculiarly twentieth-century version, the product of a more privatised and nuclear family form.

Besides medical men, architects, ministers and teachers also commonly worked at home. The library in the Lynedoch Street home of the architect James Thomson, for example, contained a green baize folding table, two other tables, a wastepaper basket and a large collection of architecture books.[26] The several ministers resident in Claremont over the forty-year period of the census lived sufficiently near their churches to allow parishioners, invited and uninvited, easy access to their homes. The Reverend Mr Robert Story wrote his sermons and lectures in his study in the manse at Roseneath, where he also frequently interviewed parishioners, entertained visiting theologians and held meetings.[27] In fact he took to writing late at night in his study to avoid interruptions. As a diary entry noted: 'Writing – but a good deal interrupted by people out and in.'[28] His study was not isolated from the rest of the house, nor did he wish it to be; his father, also a minister, had installed an extra door to shut off from the rest of the house the little passage leading to the study. However, Story junior refused to use it and insisted on leaving the door of his study slightly ajar, ensuring the interpenetration of the day-to-day business of both God and the home. Thirty or so years later, when he became Principal of the University of Glasgow, his daughter Elma worked as his secretary, occupying a study in their university residence to carry out her duties.[29]

As far as teaching was concerned, several residences in Claremont doubled as schoolhouses. In 1851 there were four such schools in the area and in 1891 two. Typical of such establishments were the Establishment for the Board and Education of Young Ladies run by Mrs Allan and Miss Ritchie at 2 Woodside Crescent and the Misses Garies' Ladies' Seminary at 22 Lynedoch Street. In addition, throughout the period there were those who taught singing, painting and languages all, usually, from home.

Among businessmen such as large-scale manufacturers and merchants the physical separation of the enterprise and the home was more common by the second half of the nineteenth century. The process whereby manufacturers ceased to live 'above the shop' is illustrated in the living arrangements of William Houldsworth and his relatives, the Crums, who were textile manufacturers in Thornliebank, on the outskirts of Glasgow. The Houldsworths had occupied a house in the grounds of their cotton spinning factory until the 1850s, when they moved into the Claremont estate. Similarly, the Crums' family residence and the offices of the firm were all within the grounds of the printworks at Thornliebank House, until the family moved to Rouken Glen Mansion House in the late 1850s. The reason for the move seems to have been the more spacious accommodation afforded by the new home rather than a desire to retreat from the family enterprise.[30]

The separation of home and work was a gradual process; furthermore, it did not necessarily proceed in a linear fashion, as there were a number of businessmen who did not move their place of residence away from the enterprise but closer to it. Robert Brown, a member of the Glasgow Stock Exchange, lived in Paisley, as did most of his clients. In the summer of 1847 he decided to move his family from New Sneddon Street to a house in the High Street as it was 'more central for persons calling on me'. He subsequently converted the back bedroom of the house into an office, which he recorded was 'a great convenience to me in conducting my business in Paisley'.[31] In 1863 the firm of Messrs Randolph, Elder & Co., marine engineers and shipbuilders, moved their premises away from the centre of town downriver to Govan; John Elder and his wife Isabella followed suit, leaving their town house for a villa in Govan Road near the new premises.[32] After her husband's death Isabella became head of the family shipbuilding firm, but ill-health forced her to relinquish her nine-month tenure and in 1870 she moved to the residential estate of Claremont.[33] Among those who did not move at all were Thomas Allan, of the ironfounders Thomas Allan & Sons, who continued to live in the grounds of his Springbank works in 1880, and James Aitken, owner of the Mallsmire Brickworks.[34]

Where works were out of town, the trend whereby families lived close to the enterprise persisted well into the twentieth century. The brothers James and Robert Couper lived near their paper mill business at Cathcart, a village to the south of Glasgow in a villa built for them in 1853. In the mid-1850s they decided to move even closer to the business so that they could observe the works from the window of their home. James commissioned the Glasgow architect Alexander 'Greek' Thomson to build Holmwood, while his brother's villa was designed by James Smith, the father of Madeleine. Interestingly, Thomson himself moved out of the city centre at Hutchesontown in the Gorbals, after four of his children had died of cholera between 1854 and 1857, choosing to move into a residential estate which he designed on the south side of the city.[35] This suggests that moving into residential suburbs might have been motivated by a desire to escape the noise, pollution and general insanitary conditions of the city and the town, rather than being driven by an ideological imperative.

Lower down the middle-class social hierarchy, it was not unusual for the home to double as working premises. The expansion of the retail sector in the second half of the century contributed to the proliferation of small businesses as well as the growth of the department store. This possibly increased the number of businesses which combined home and work. The Post Office Directory for Glasgow of 1879–80 records hundreds of retailers such as hosiers, drapers, tobacconists, stationers, grocers, wine and spirit merchants, restaurateurs and so on, whose residential and business addresses were the same. Even in the building trades there were firms which continued to operate from the home. From a dataset of 1,206 building firms extracted from the Glasgow Post Office Directory for 1875, it was found that seventy-nine had identical workplace and home addresses. As the authors of the study observed, the necessity of storing plant and materials made proximity to the workplace crucial.[36] The home was also the site of work for the many women who took in boarders or lodgers to supplement the family income. In the lower middle-class households in Claremont, this was common practice. In 1851 seven households had boarders or lodgers: by 1891 this had risen to seventy-three.

Thus for a good number of the residents of the area the home was the site of business, including those who appeared to have no occupation. There were a number of people who were listed in the census as proprietors of houses or land, as fundholders or annuitants, or simply as having no occupation. Andrew Jack, who in 1881 was listed in the census as living on 'house dividends', owned and rented out several houses in Lynedoch Street and also property in Charlotte Street. The fact that he was engaged in business activity is confirmed by the advertisements placed in the *Glasgow Herald* after his death, inviting creditors to submit accounts, and by his inventory, which records that he kept business papers in a 'repository' in his home.[37]

The example of Andrew Jack and those who had no 'official' occupation presents an important point in terms of the separation of home and work in the Victorian middle classes. It is by no means easy to make a clear distinction between the two, when for many people 'work', in the sense of financially productive activity, was carried out in the home. In addition, as feminist historians have demonstrated, if the definition of work is expanded to include that of housewives, a non-traditional form of labour central to the production and reproduction of economic relations, then the home was the workplace for many women.

Even in households where the physical separation of home and work was complete, the world of business was never entirely sealed off from the home. It was not uncommon for business meetings to be held in the home or to have a study where business papers could be consulted. John Stephen and his brother Andrew regularly entertained business associates, taking them sailing in Andrew's yacht, or simply hosting a dinner party for them.[38] Conducting business required nurturing and maintaining social networks as well as demonstrating the sound basis of the enterprise. Therefore the wealthy middle classes hosted a good deal of business-related entertainment. Ian Gow describes Holmwood, built circa 1857 on the south side of the city, as a small suburban villa which 'reflects the importance attached by Glasgow merchants to business entertaining, with its disproportionately large dining room and extensive service accommodation of larders and kitchens close at hand.'[39]

Professionals were also likely to entertain work colleagues or associates in the home. When Robert Story became Moderator of the General Assembly of the Church of Scotland in 1894 and four years later Principal of Glasgow University, entertaining became an integral part of his duties. He and his wife hosted parties, dances and dinners for the eminent members of the Church of Scotland, the City Fathers of Glasgow and the luminaries of the academic community. While Mrs Story appeared to relish her role as a hostess and take delight in the range of personalities she encountered, Joseph and Agnes Lister offered dinners as opportunities for exchanging medical and scientific information. On one occasion, when Lister wished to propagate the gospel of carbolic acid to a navy surgeon, the crucial guest was at the last minute unable to attend. According to Lister's cousin, a doctor who had also been invited, there was now no *raison d'être* for the dinner, so the remaining guests had a 'quick dinner by [them]selves'.[40]

The most striking feature of the home life of middle-class families is not the increasing physical separation of home and work, but the continued symbiosis of the two. For many members of the middle class, particularly professional men, the boundaries between home and work were blurred or indistinct, for others the home was an extension of the business, a place where business associates were entertained, business deals clinched and business papers stored and consulted. The continuing close links between family and firm was another factor conjoining home life and the world of work. When kin were also business partners, it was unlikely that work and business matters would be consigned to a separate sphere. There was no *cordon sanitaire* around the middle-class home to ward off the evils and corrupt practices of the business world; the home was more frequently an adjunct to the business world, a world with which it was fused and which was permeated by its practices, ethos and values.

It was not only the public world of the market place which entered the home. The 'public' had many forms and meanings of which the world of work was only one.[41] Religious and philanthropic activity was central to the creation of middle-class identity, as was demonstrating one's good character through good works. The Macfarlanes, a deeply religious family, entertained a wide range of people in their home. As remembered by their daughter, the household was 'full of interest for the young': 'Our own contribution to the variety of the street was made by our visitors, who were of every colour and nation – freed negro slaves, Indian rajahs, South Sea Island royalties, Jewish evangelists and all kinds of white missionaries.'[42]

The rich web of interconnections in religious, political and associational life described in chapter 1 made it unlikely that the family and home could ever be entirely cloistered from the public world or visitors confined to only family or close friends. In fact women who were active in the temperance and suffrage movements made very public use of the 'private' realm of the home by holding meetings there, usually in the drawing room.[43]

The sociability of the household also ensured that the family was constantly in the public gaze, for the Victorian household entertained a stream of visitors, most staying only a matter of hours, although others remained for days or even weeks. Despite the supposed ubiquity of the calling card and the prearranged 'at homes', frequently visits were undertaken on a casual basis with very little evidence of the ritual and formality associated with the Victorian era. Edith Napier recounted how her father had taken her and her brother out walking one afternoon and on the way home they had called in on a Mrs Harvey. They were given a 'nice drink of milk from the servant as Mrs Harvey was not in'.[44] Diaries and letters frequently refer to impromptu visits to either family or friends. The personal journal of Helen Wahab, of the MacFie family, has many references to such visits, often undertaken when on shopping trips; she might be invited to stay for lunch, or might invite similarly informal callers to stay to dinner.[45] Mrs Story, fondly recalling her early home life in Edinburgh, wrote:

> What scenes have been enacted behind those long glass windows! And oh! the many different eyes that have looked out of them, the countless feet that have trodden those well worn steps! While the tingle of that richly pealing bell I could distinguish among all the other bells of a city! How it rang – morning, noon, and night, bringing callers, male and female, young and old, joyful and sorrowful![46]

Not all uninvited visitors were made welcome. Mrs Story described how her father, in ill temper and not keen to see some unexpected callers just before lunch, left the room and requested a private talk with his wife. When she returned to explain the situation, the visitors beat a hasty retreat, remarking 'husbands will at times be very unreasonable'.[47] Not that visiting was an activity which was exclusively female as indicated by Janet Story. Morning and afternoon visitors were predominantly female, but not exclusively so.

Although most visiting was of the informal sort where friends or family might simply drop in for an hour or two, others visited for longer periods. The extent of overnight visiting is borne out by census figures. In 1851 there were fifty-nine 'visitors' in the 209 households, of whom eight had a specified relationship to the head of household. There is some decline in numbers of visitors across the period. In 1871 there were fifty recorded visitors (including seven visitor/relatives) in 282 households: by 1891 this had become thirty-seven visitors in 315 households. All of these visitors recorded in the census had stayed over at least one night. Nearly two-thirds (64.9 per cent) were female. Some young women seem to have been visiting friends whom they met at school, as Madeleine Smith did. This is particularly the case when the visitor had been born in England: Susanna Robson (twenty-one, born Durham) was staying with the family of Katherine Maclay, aged twenty-two in 1891; and nineteen-year-old Margaret Bridges (born in London) was staying with the eighteen-year-old daughter of Peter Clouston, Lord Provost, in 1881. But older women were both guests and hosts: Janet Fullarton, aged seventy-nine, was in 1871 entertaining sixty-nine-year-old Margaret Shannon, a widow, and Margaret's twenty-three-year-old daughter Bessie. Men also visited, however, and not just when accompanying wives or daughters. John Hunter, aged fifty-five and born in Aberdeen, was in 1871 visiting James Pitkethly, a cloth manufacturer, and his wife Isabella.

Homes across the middle-class spectrum hosted visitors. There is no evidence from the census that those in the lower middle-class streets with smaller and fewer rooms were less likely to have visitors. Of the total of thirty-seven visitors in the area in 1891, fifteen stayed in Carnarvon and Stanley Streets, which were made up of the smaller terraced and tene-ment houses. Dugald and Christina Macleod of 8 Stanley Street lived in four rooms with their two children and two lodgers; in doubtless cramped conditions, they had a thirty-eight-year-old male visitor on census night. At 23 Carnarvon Street the Craik household consisted of two brothers (both draper's assistants), their mother and aunt, a schoolboy cousin and both a boarder *and* a lodger. They had only five rooms. Nevertheless, they were also welcoming a visiting fourteen-year-old schoolboy from Fife.

Some visitors brought an entourage of servants and copious amounts of luggage; others arrived alone and travelled very lightly. Mrs Story was once chagrined to discover an overnight visitor had brought only a small bag and would therefore be unsuitably attired for the dinner party which had been arranged for her.[48] The reasons for short overnight visits were as numerous as the visitors who made them. Some may have made a short sojourn in order to do some shopping in town, or to attend a meeting or a function. In March 1856 Madeleine Smith and her sister left Glasgow to stay for two or three nights at the home of John Thompson and his family at Gogarburn, near Edinburgh, so that they could attend the United Services Ball.[50] On this occasion, the hosts spent very little time with their guests, the two daughters being occupied with tending their sick father.[49] In the winter of 1910 Frances Murray stayed at the home of her sister-in-law in order to be nearer her daughter who had rented a house in Park Terrace while visiting Glasgow from her home in India.[51] Transport difficulties and the relative dearth (and presumably expense) of hotels meant that the Victorian home would offer accommodation not only to family and friends, but also to acquaintances. The eighteenth-century aristocratic custom of relying on letters of introduction to secure hospitality when travelling seemed to have been adopted in a modified form by the Victorian middle classes, who facilitated their travels through friendship networks. The practice was particularly prevalent among religious communities, but was more widespread than this.

Some visitors stayed for lengthy periods when they were using the host household as a base from which they could visit or even stay with other friends, attend functions, and generally engage in a variety of social pursuits. This seemed to be the case when Frances Murray visited family friends in London for several weeks, combining a hectic social schedule with a few days' visit to another friend in Streatham, a visit to her sister at school outside London and a Christmas visit to a friend in Cheshire on the homeward journey.[52]

Visiting in the nineteenth century has often been characterised as a ritualised acitivity, carefully orchestrated and regulated. Its function has generally been attributed to either the consolidation and nurturing of professional and social networks or as part of the culturally prescribed rituals of bourgeois female social life.[53] Yet the frequency, popularity and informality of much social visiting suggests that it was an activity whose purpose could have many possible interpretations. Too often the Victorians have been portrayed as obsessed by appearances and ritual to the exclusion of other considerations. Rational calculation and social obligation could coexist with or even be eclipsed by more personal, sentimental or altruistic motives. Soirées, parties, musical evenings, dances and balls were all held within the confines of even modest middle-class homes. The rich provision of publicly provided entertainment in the city did not stem the tide of private functions but merely added to the array of entertainment on offer to the Victorian city dweller.

Davidoff and Hall have contrasted the public social life of the eighteenth century with the home-centred entertainment of the early nineteenth.[54] Their characterisation of it as 'private', albeit lively, masks the range, scale and frequency of entertainment within the home in the Victorian era. The abundant hospitality offered to family, friends and sometimes strangers gave the Victorian household a sociability and public character which seem far removed from the rather sedate and claustrophobic family-centred life portrayed in some of the literature. Entertaining and being entertained lay at the heart of Victorian social life. Mrs Story averred that she loved 'entertaining and being entertained', a phrase also used by Eunice Murray of her mother, a Victorian of a later generation. The Victorians opened their doors to their kith and kin to an extent which the modern household would almost certainly not countenance. Some forms of hospitality were modest affairs, while others were quite lavish and required the employment of extra staff. Mrs Story also remembered that her parents 'abounded in hospitality'. A typical large dinner party of the 1840s in their Edinburgh home had at least twenty-two guests, requiring a good deal of preparation as well as an additional cook and a head waiter.[55] The fare provided was sumptuous, not to say dyspeptic, as her father 'liked everything to be of the best':

> Two soups . . . two large dishes of fish, and these were all placed on the dinner table, my father serving the one, my mother the other. [. . .] In succession to the soup and to the fish, four massive entrée dishes were placed heavily on the table. [. . .] One of them was invariably a curry. The silver entrée dishes were removed, and a huge roast of beef or a leg of mutton was placed before the host: the opposite end of the table being graced by a gigantic turkey, roasted or boiled. [. . .] Half way down the table on each side was deposited another large dish containing a still further variety of solid viands, – ducks, a ham or tongue, beefsteak pie – so that every guest might be safe to have his or her particular taste gratified.

Then came the sweet course. At the foot of the table there was usually a dish of macaroni and cheese, more especially for masculine tastes; while at the other end towered a magnificent erection of spun sugar and pastry, filled with luscious preserves. [. . .] Two side dishes, one occasionally a simple pudding, duly appeared; while four handsome cut crystal dishes took the place of the previous entrée, containing a white vanilla and a pink raspberry cream, a pale wine jelly, and one tinted crimson drop of cochineal.[56]

Forty years later, when her husband was appointed to the Chair of Church History at the University of Glasgow in 1886, Mrs Story experienced Glasgow hospitality on a similarly lavish scale. She recalled that punch, oysters and caviare were *de rigueur*. 'Very luxurious dinners were given in these days; some of the old city magnates rivalling one another in the excellence of their banquets, for indeed they could be called nothing else.'[57]

The hosts of these dinner parties, often former civic leaders, were perhaps trying to recreate the sumptuousness of civic banquets in their homes, as a totemic reminder of their former civic status and their current social standing. Therefore these 'banquets' may not have been typical of sociability of the period. Writing in 1913, Mrs Story welcomed the more ascetic conviviality which she affirmed was then current: 'let us be thankful that we live in less luxurious times.' It is difficult to establish whether there was a real shift in the form of home-based hospitality between the later years of the Victorian period and the reign of George V, or whether Mrs Story was indulging in the growing fashion of anti-Victorianism that prevailed soon after Victoria's death.[58] It is certainly the case that not all dinner parties were as extravagant or elaborate as those given by the elite of Glasgow society. Even fairly modest dinners, however, such as those offered by the business and professional classes, might cater for large parties of guests. Luncheons and dinners for ten to twenty people were not unusual. Two nights after the death of her lover, Madeleine Smith and her fiancé dined with fourteen others at the home of the minister of the Smith family's church.[59]

The letters of Madeleine Smith to Emile L'Angelier provide some insight into the pivotal role of dinner parties in the social life of the Glasgow middle classes. In 1855 she wrote: 'We very seldom dine alone, some one is with us every day.'[60] Her account of a not untypical week included several dinner engagements at the home of family and friends:

'Last evening [. . .] I was at a card party at Aunts. Mr K dined here tonight. [. . .] Tomorrow we dine at the Houldsworths and on Wednesday we dine at Hillhead. [. . .] We had another invitation from the Griersons but we were fore-engaged.'[61]

Food, conversation and usually alcohol were the staple fare at dinner parties; occasionally the evening would be rounded off with a game of cards or billiards. Cards were extremely popular: everyone had at least one card table, and William Houldsworth had six. Good conversation was regarded as a *sine qua non* of a successful dinner party. Those unfortunate enough to have been seated beside someone lacking conversational aptitude or sparkle would lament the absence of an agreeable dinner companion. When Janet Story dined at the home of Sir James King in Claremont Terrace, she remarked that it had been particularly memorable as two of the male guests 'were masters of the art of conversation, and the one seconded the other in every way, anecdote, repartee, apt quotations passed from one to the other in rapid succession'.[62] Not that it was only men who were deemed to possess these qualities; she commented of another dinner party that the hostess had been 'a brilliant conversationalist and a very clever and well-informed woman'.

There is little evidence of Presbyterian censure policing sociability, although Robert Brown complained bitterly about an all-male dinner party he attended in 1885: 'as there were no spirits or wine at the entertainment the proceedings were rather flat and far from being cheerful. I think it is a great mistake for anyone to ask gentlemen to dine with them and not to treat them according to the custom of the country.'[63] Brown, an eminent member of the Established Church in Paisley, seldom missed a public or private dinner party where alcohol was usually available. Having quaffed a large quantity of wine, he once confessed that he 'got quite gracious' and had to leave early as he 'was so thoroughly wearied'. Brown himself did not stint when it came to entertaining his own guests and bought whisky literally by the gallon. In the notes for his autobiography he observed that in 1841 he had paid 23/- for 2 gallons of whisky while 'at present [1885] the price of a gallon of whisky is 12/-.'[64] Janet Story recalled that in 1886, when her husband had been elected second clerk to the General Assembly of the Church of Scotland, they held a 'jolly dinner and drank the new Clerk's health in bumpers of champagne'.[65] While some of those present at such gatherings were abstemious, if not teetotal, and disapproved of card games, it seems that they could be accommodated with little infringement of the enjoyment of others less constrained by Calvinist precepts. The Storys' appreciation of liquor did not extend to card games and Janet Story recounted that at parties held by two wealthy spinsters, the evening was usually rounded off with a 'rollicking game of cards'; however, the hosts always waited until the Storys' departure before proposing a game.[66]

Besides dinner parties, Victorian home entertainments often revolved around piano playing, singing, dancing and assorted games. Mrs Story described the parties of her youth in 1850s Edinburgh as being very informal:

> No floor-cloth was deemed necessary for the improvised 'dance', and the refreshments were of the lightest nature, a table in the corner of the room, with jellies, sandwiches, and other slight fare, iced cup the chief, sometimes the only beverage. One young lady after another provided the simple music. [. . .] Those impromptu parties were never very late, very rarely lasting beyond one o'clock.[67]

Evening parties in Glasgow during the later years of the century were evidently similar to that description; they might involve a game of whist for the more mature partygoer, while younger people might indulge in 'round games', such as Old Maid, Catch the Ten or Happy Families. At some stage in the proceedings someone would offer to play the piano or be pressed into doing so, with others following suit. Inventories indicate that most middle-class homes possessed at least one piano. Singing songs, usually light popular pieces, was also standard practice.[68] Some homes would arrange more serious musical evenings, at which the invited guests were seated to listen to piano solos and duets as well as songs and operatic excerpts.

Rather less often, the middle-class household hosted a grander occasion in the form of a 'carpet dance' or ball. This involved the removal of all the furniture from the drawing room, except the piano; the door was removed from its hinges, the curtains taken down and a white cloth with a smooth surface was stretched over the carpet.[69] The very wealthy would have hired a group of musicians, while those of more modest means relied on members of the household or relatives or friends to provide the music. The scale of these dances varied according to the size of the host's purse. However, even in the ordinary middle-class home these occasions involved a great deal of planning and preparation, including hiring caterers for the refreshments. Although essentially informal occasions, the programme of dances was planned in advance and publicly displayed in the drawing room for the guests to consult.

While Victorian sociability played a central role in constituting middle-class identity and culture, hospitality in the home not only served a variety of purposes but took a variety of forms. Dinner parties might cement a business transaction, be a display of open-handed generosity, or a means of affirming one's identification with guests as part of a circumscribed middle-class community. Larger social gatherings could provide a forum for articulating one's social standing and status, or be a display of conspicuous consumption, or in celebrating a family event, involve a form of hospitality which temporarily extended the family to embrace a wider grouping. Felicity Heal has observed that middle-class concerns to maintain social and physical segregation from the working classes in the nineteenth century created a more exclusive hospitality than the all-embracing conviviality of the early modern period.[70] Certainly hospitality was not routinely offered beyond the bounds of one's social peers; indeed, it was a means of affirming who one's peers were. When Joseph Coats entertained the tradesmen who had been working on his house, this must have been a departure from the customary form of entertaining one's social peers. Yet despite the more restricted nature of Victorian home-based hospitality, the scale and frequency of it suggests an integration of the public and private realm and a malleability of those categories in relation to the home.

The descriptions of dining rooms in the probate inventories of the Claremont estate serve to underscore the permeability of any public/private distinction in the Victorian and Edwardian middle-class home. They were equipped for entertaining on a large scale. Twelve was the minimum for dining chairs. Cutlery, drinking glasses and so on routinely came in sets of twenty-four. Families were also equipped for lavish entertaining. Dr Anderson of Woodside Crescent had, in 1870, 179 wine glasses of various types – and one 'patent corkscrew'. This was quite standard: William Houldsworth in 1854 had 184 wine glasses. The Houldsworth cellars were extremely well stocked. For a start, there were fifty-five dozen bottles of sherry and twenty-six dozen bottles of port and madeira, as well as brandy, whisky, champagne, claret and assorted other wines. The Houldsworths were at the top of the middle-class social scale: but James Watson, with a much more modest total value of household goods, had no fewer than 1,478 assorted bottles in his cellar. The value of these amounted to £139 10s out of the total of £820 for the whole nine-bedroom house.

All the homes had great quantities of silver and silver plate – ice buckets, dish covers, epergnes, strawberry dishes, nutcrackers and grape scissors. Every culinary eventuality was catered for. Mrs Mackenzie of Claremont Gardens had a second home in Ayr which was probably rented furnished: very little furniture is listed in the inventory of her property there. Nevertheless, the articles which she had chosen to take or keep at Ayr for her visits included a vast range of silver cutlery, marmalade dishes, toast racks, cheese scoops, wine funnels, biscuit boxes, egg stands, tea services and so on which suggest large-scale entertaining at meals other than dinner. Inventories do not convey information on how often such entertaining was undertaken: but they do make it abundantly clear that families expected to be able to serve elaborate meals, with all possible appropriate accessories, to large groups of people. Even Isabella Campbell of Turner Street, at the bottom of the middle-class scale, had cutlery in sets of twelve.

Not only does this kind of evidence illustrate the public character of the home, it also demonstrates how the home served both outwardly and inwardly as a symbol of success. Middle-class homes, from the Pooteresque to the extravagant villas of the wealthy merchants and manufacturers, served as showpieces for an – albeit limited – public gaze. The main rooms, usually the drawing rooms and the dining rooms, were 'on display' to colleagues, friends, acquaintances and wider kin. Inasmuch as they represented a retreat from the world, it was in terms of displayed domesticity, a contrived 'privacy', an image of 'private' family life for relatively public consumption.

To those who visited, these public rooms spoke of prosperity. Robert Napier took delight in conducting his guests round his large house at Shandon on the Gareloch to view his lavish collection of paintings and *objets d'art*.[71] Napier may have been unusual in that he was sufficiently wealthy to indulge his eclectic artistic taste, but he was not alone in enjoying the conspicuous display of his rich assortment of treasures.

Nenadic makes the point that eighteenth-century bourgeois Scottish homes were less concerned with fashion than with quality and durability, and with the sentimental associations of objects.[72] This is to a large extent borne out by the Claremont inventories. Quality there certainly was: vases from such prestigious factories as Worcester; a great deal of silver; furniture in mahogany and satinwood; soft furnishings in silk, velvet and damask. Display cupboards, mantelpieces, shelves and tables held scores of ornaments. These were carefully chosen to reflect the 'taste' and creativity of the family – there could not be too many objects, provided that all were beautiful.[73]

There is plenty of evidence of sentimental attachment to possessions.

Drawing rooms spoke not only of prosperity but also of family. There were the signs of shared leisure pursuits – the piano, music stands, card tables and work tables. In the late nineteenth century there might be a magic lantern or 'stereoscope'. There were 'sewed covers' on footstools and chairs, probably worked by the women of the family in fashionable Berlin woolwork. The oil paintings usually included 'family portraits': in most cases it is not known whether these were of current or past generations. Mrs Mackenzie had, in addition to portraits, marble busts of herself and her late husband. Testaments indicate that great store was set on the family associations of possessions. Women, in particular, left items of furniture to those who had some sentimental or familial claim to them. Jessie White, who died unmarried in 1880, left to her nephew her 'dear Willie's things' – the books, pictures and a clock which had belonged to her late brother.[74]

The drawing room, then, displayed the family past and present, its wealth and its good taste. Commentators on domestic architecture and those who have explored the gendering of domestic space have acknowledged this public aspect of the home. However, they have also subscribed to a private/public dichotomy within the home and have tended to conflate female and private and male and public and to apply the terms unproblematically.[75] Those who have been concerned with the gendering of domestic space have focused on the dining room and the drawing room; the drawing room is seen as feminine because it was light, glittering and shiny, or because it was cluttered, soft, red and womb- or nest-like. Indeed, for Juliet Kinchin, 'the drawing room came to represent the woman of the household.'[76] The dining room, with its harder, plainer furnishings, was essentially masculine. Such equations lead to the argument that the masculine dining room is somehow more public than the feminine drawing room: the drawing room becomes private/female space. Yet Kinchin is aware of the contradiction here – this is only a kind of privacy. 'On the one hand, the drawing room was to provide a haven from the external world of work and the corrupting aspects of commerce. On the other, it was still the showpiece of the home, the focus of high-profile expenditure.'[77]

The principal danger in equating the drawing room with the feminine or with the private is that it involves superimposing ideological hindsight; such significance may not have been apparent to the families themselves. Most drawing rooms were cluttered, opulent and probably rather dark: velvet and damask in green or red seem to have predominated for curtains and soft furnishings; furniture was massive and in dark wood.

Neither do they seem lighter than dining rooms in terms of mirrors (found in both rooms, over the mantelpiece and, often, between two windows) or the level of lighting. Drawing rooms do not sound particularly 'feminine'. An image of domesticity was certainly being presented – and of a certain kind of domesticity at that. But as described in chapter 2, men were intimately involved with domesticity. If there was gendering of domestic space, what did that mean for these families? Drawing rooms may have been furnished in a softer, lighter way than dining rooms. But drawing rooms were intended for intellectual and creative activities (if not productive ones) – and for the family. Did men playing cards in the drawing room think of themselves as encroaching on female space?

One should be similarly cautious with the 'masculinity' of the dining room. Certainly furnishings were less soft – but this was largely because of their function. Dining rooms were only marginally, if at all, less cluttered than drawing rooms. They had a similar range and style of ornaments and paintings. The principal colours were the same: green, red and possibly gold. Dining rooms may indeed have carried connotations of masculinity, but this is not readily apparent in their furnishing. Nenadic, describing the increasing specialisation of rooms in the eighteenth-century home, refers to the dining room and its function for 'male hospitality'. There was certainly an association of this room and the men of the party in that they remained in the dining room while the women 'withdrew' after eating, although this practice was criticised as old-fashioned and uncivilised well before the end of the century. It is also true that *exclusively* female hospitality may have been more likely to take place in some other room: but women dined too. Madeleine Smith and her sister Bessie went to dine with their parents' friends the Houldsworths without either parent or, it seems, any male companion. The dining room, then, was used for *family* hospitality. In the numerous cases of all-female households, this can hardly have been 'male'. Mrs Mackenzie's dining room in 1902 also had a 'bamboo afternoon tea table', which shows that here at least the dining room was not only used for formal evening meals.

There was no apparent gendering of domestic space in the home, either in the physical sense of carefully delineated areas designated 'feminine' or 'masculine' or even in the metaphorical sense of particular domestic spaces being associated with either gender. However, the occupation of space may have been diachronically gendered in that particular spaces were given over to men or women at certain times of day. The most obvious example of this is the practice just mentioned, whereby men enjoyed their port and cigars in the dining room while women retired to the drawing room. All-male dinner parties, held in the dining room, and all-female gatherings in the drawing room in the morning or the 'forenoon', a custom which was in decline by the end of the century, are other instances of the gendered regulation of space. However, such gendering of interior space as there was in the middle-class home was characterised by flexibility and contingency rather than stasis.

As those who have written on interior design have demonstrated, the drawing room was in a real sense public. By the late Victorian period, interior design manuals were calling for an 'openness' that, as Jean-Christophe Agnew argues for the USA, invited the 'performance of private life as public spectacle'.[78] However, the swathed and crowded drawing room could also be viewed as the epitome of 'home and hearth': the 'private' sanctum of the family. But for family members in large households (as most were) there could also be an element of 'public' about the drawing room even if the audience consisted entirely of others in the household. Madeleine Smith felt she 'was not fit for the drawing room' when upset, and had to retire to her bedroom.[79]

While historians of interior design have ascribed a public character to the home, this is seen as confined to particular spaces, such as the drawing room, or in lower middle-class homes, the parlour. To modern eyes, however, there is a distinct lack of privacy about all areas of the Victorian middle-class home. A string of people brought deliveries to the kitchen; servants shared bedrooms; the housekeeper or cook came to the drawing or morning room to receive instructions. Conditions in prosperous and well-appointed Victorian homes fostered a kind of physical intimacy that is rather at odds with the commonly held view of Victorian prudery. People washed and used chamber pots in bedrooms that were often shared, whether by married couples or by siblings. Servants emptied the slops and helped women to dress. The 'washbasins and ware' in all bedrooms needed hot water brought by servants, who also lit the fire there. Although bathrooms gradually made their appearance, they were not universally provided, and all bedrooms throughout the period nevertheless contained washstands, towel rails, 'night stools' or commodes and often foot baths or pails and sitz baths. People were still washing in bedrooms into the twentieth century: a single bathroom in large households could not cater for everybody at once.

Generally, bedrooms seem to have been designed exclusively for sleeping, washing and dressing. Some, like those of the Anderson family in 1870, contained books and bookcases. Dr and Mrs Anderson's bedroom also had a small desk, a writing slope and ink stands, though, as noted above, Dr Anderson also had a study cum consulting room elsewhere in the house. Writing equipment and desks or escritoires appear in the inventories for bedrooms of several houses, suggesting that reading and writing took place there. Mrs Mackenzie had a card table in her bedroom, and several people had chairs, easy chairs and small tables, though whether these were used exclusively *in situ* is a matter of speculation. One bedroom in the Thomson house had a brass afternoon tea stand. In his memoir of the Glasgow middle classes in the 1870s and 1880s J. J. Bell recalled that his grandmother, who lived with the family, used to retire to her bedroom in the evening to knit and read; members of the household would occasionally join her there for a chat.[80] On the whole, however, it does not look as if much entertaining went on in bedrooms. Lighting was often poor. Bedrooms did not always have any obvious source of lighting: no lamps are listed for William Houldsworth's many bedrooms in 1854. By 1869 the Watson home had gas lighting in some but not all bedrooms, as well as bedroom candlesticks and snuffers. This was still the case in the Claremont Gardens home of Mrs Margaret Mackenzie in 1902. For much of the Glasgow year, this would have made bedrooms dim places after late afternoon, though the presence of fire grates suggests that they were at least kept warm.

Unlike the aristocracy, the middle-class couples in the Claremont/Woodside estates shared bedrooms and beds. The husband may have had a separate 'dressing room', but this had neither bed nor washstand. In fact there are few single beds listed in the surviving inventories: not only married couples but also siblings and servants appear to have shared beds. In the family's town house, Madeleine Smith had to share her bedroom with her younger sister, which restricted her amorous assignations with L'Angelier. It was not unusual to share beds with visitors; in the 1880s Catherine Carswell did so with the nurse of visiting cousins.[81]

These nineteenth-century middle-class homes show little evidence of sharply delineated private and public spaces in the home. Not even the notion of a gradient of privacy can fully capture the complexity of the use of space. Within the supposedly private domain of the home there was evidently a proliferation of public spaces and a fluidity of meaning to the terms 'private' and 'public'. Domestic spaces had multiple uses which defy the ascription of either 'public' or 'private' to them, as evinced most clearly by the use of domestic space for conducting business. The 'private dinners' such as those alluded to by Robert Brown could involve fourteen of one's closest friends rather than the intimate dinner *à deux* with which the term is now associated. The nineteenth-century distinction between 'private' and 'public' clearly did not coincide with family and home on the one hand and the world outside on the other.

The holiday homes to which the middle classes customarily migrated during the summer might be regarded as corresponding to the notion of the home as a retreat, sheltered from the malignant influences of the urban world and from the corrupt practices of the public one. Since the early nineteenth century it had been fashionable for the Scottish middle classes to take a summer residence on the coast or in the country. The reason that so many families left the city in the summer months was less to do with the ideology of separate spheres than with changing conceptions and philosophies of childhood and a romanticised notion of the rural idyll. Whereas in the eighteenth century the habit of 'taking the waters' was developed for adults as beneficial to their health, in the nineteenth century it came to be recognised that children's health should also be considered. In the interests of both spiritual and physical welfare, families sought a clean and unpolluted environment in the countryside or by the sea. Long summer holidays were not within the means of those families lower down the social scale and even the lower middle classes, such as clerks, shopkeepers and artisans, had to be content with only a few days by the sea or in the country.

The Glasgow middle class adopted the Firth of Clyde coastal resorts as their favoured holiday spot, although a significant minority headed for the hills and countryside. The small villages around the Gareloch and Loch Long were particularly popular with Glasgow's prosperous merchants and manufacturers, whose summer residences often became their retirement home. In the Claremont estate several of the more affluent middle classes had holiday homes within a few miles of each other: in 1864 Alexander Stephen, of Messrs Stephen & Son, rented a villa at Cove; in 1866 his brother rented a house nearby at Kilcreggan; in the intervening year John Templeton, a carpet manufacturer, and his brother-in-law, Alexander Stephen, rented summer premises at Dunoon; and George Thomson, a manufacturer of Woodlands Terrace, died at Cove in 1881, almost certainly while on holiday. William Houldsworth of Claremont Terrace preferred the other side of the loch at Rhu, as did the family of Madeleine Smith, while Robert Napier, head of a large engineering works, had a home at Shandon, also on the Gareloch. Some families spent time at their holiday homes outwith the summer months. At the time of the 1851 census, taken in early April, thirteen houses had been left in the sole charge of servants, all family members being away. Testaments and confirmations record place of death, and indicate that quite frequently, especially in the summer, Claremont residents died while away from home, whether at their own country houses, while visiting relatives or while taking holidays or convalescent trips to spas such as Great Malvern or Peebles.

Those families who did not own country homes could rent them. The exodus to the coast (or loch-side) began in May. The *Glasgow Herald* of 4 May 1860 listed houses offered in sixteen different locations. Two days earlier a detailed advertisement appeared offering the 'beautiful marine villa of Fairlieburne, three miles from Largs' on the Clyde coast. It had 'three public rooms, seven bedrooms, servants' apartments, bath rooms etc. Double coach house, three-stalled stable, fully-stocked kitchen garden, lawn and good sea bathing and yachting.'[82] Not all middle-class families would have been able to afford such capacious accommodation. Bell's memoirs recall that his family holiday home on Arran was a small cramped cottage with no water supply which had to accommodate a family of seven, plus maid and sundry visitors.[83] Even the affluent Macfarlanes sometimes opted for a simple cottage, although more often they rented a roomy, water-supplied villa.[84]

The *Herald* also contained notices informing middle-class Glaswegians that 'parties sending furniture to the coast [. . .] may have it conveyed by luggage steamer on moderate terms by the Glasgow and Greenock Shipping Co.'[85] The volume of luggage transported could be considerable. Some indication of this is given by Catherine Carswell's account of her family's journey to their holiday home on a farm in Perthshire: 'Leaving Glasgow by an early train for the long journey to Perth, we had transferred ourselves and our vast baggage – strapped tin baths, laundry baskets, trunks and holdalls [. . .] into the little single line for Abernethy.'[86] In addition to these 'essentials', the Macfarlanes took their parrot, although unlike some families, they chose to leave their piano in their town house.[87] However well-equipped the rented house, it seems that middle-class Glaswegians travelled like snails with their shells, taking their own furniture as well as servants and horses to their summer 'home from home'.

It is generally supposed that during the summer months mothers and children went to the holiday residence, where they would be visited at weekends by the paterfamilias, who otherwise remained in the city home.[88] However, the pattern of this annual pilgrimage was usually more varied than this. Some husbands ensured that they had a good deal of time available for family holidays, while for others work took precedence. Alexander Stephen, the brother of John, commonly rented a house on the Firth of Clyde during the summer. However, he chose to commute there daily rather than be separated from his family for lengthy periods. There must have been others who did the same, as contemporary steamer and train timetables stressed the convenience of their connections and how they allowed a more-or-less full day in the city. Catherine Carswell's father followed the more familiar pattern and made the trip most weekends, even when the family took a summer cottage in Perthshire, a round trip of over 200 miles by train and then a short journey by horse-drawn carriage. The remoteness of the Murray holiday home in the Hebrides made weekend visits impossible, so David Murray made few but lengthier visits there. William MacEwen's position at Glasgow University regularly took him away from home, but he was usually able to spend the long summer vacations at Garrochty, the family's holiday home on the Isle of Bute. Robert Brown, despite the commitments of his varied business interests, was able to spend April and May with his family at the house he had rented in Dunoon in 1863, a pattern he maintained for at least the next few years.[89]

Mothers and children were not ensconced in these summer residences for the entire season. The school holidays were in June and July but, as 'A Mother' complained to the *Glasgow Herald* in 1871, the rest of the family, 'fathers and elder brothers in business', took their holidays in July and August. Since, she argued, 'it is by no means pleasant never to have all the family united while away from home', compromise was needed.[90] There were frequent trips back into town for all members of the family, as well as travelling to other parts of the country and visits to friends and relatives. Rather than being viewed as a protected refuge from a hostile urban world, the summer residence can be viewed as a base, valued for its restorative and salubrious properties, from which one could organise one's summer social calendar and sometimes even business activities. John Stephen's diaries refer to a number of business meetings held in his brother's summer residences in the lochside village of Cove and at Dunoon.[91]

The conviviality and hospitality of life in the city was to some extent replicated in these summer retreats. There were so many visitors to the MacEwen family's holiday house on the Isle of Bute that it was necessary to regulate numbers and timing. Understanding that Lady MacEwen was 'busy with guests at the moment', Mrs Macdonald, who was to become the mother-in-law of one of the MacEwen daughters, wrote suggesting that her own visit with her husband should be delayed 'till it is convenient for you'.[92] The Smiths' summer residence in Rhu on the Firth of Clyde also had a steady stream of visitors, and their lodgings in the spa resort of Bridge of Allan was seldom reserved for the exclusive use of family. The Macfarlane farmhouse in the remoter parts of Perthshire with its relative inaccessibility and austerity did not deter regular visits from family and friends. Household numbers swelled in the summer months with young cousins, older relatives and 'humble friends from Glasgow who were recovering from illness'.[93] In 1871 Dr Charles Blatherwick, a friend of the Storys and 'a man of great social ability and charm',[94] produced a mock newspaper, the *Kilmahonaig Journal*, during his family's holiday in the Highlands, recording the numerous 'arrivals' and 'departures' of friends. Robert Brown and his wife became acquainted with four other couples when holidaying in Dunoon in the 1860s, and 'met frequently in one another's houses at night in a social way' – so much so that they called themselves The Clique.[95]

For the reasons outlined in this chapter, it is now generally acknowledged that the actuality of separate spheres was a myth. Nonetheless, the Victorian home has still tended to be viewed as a space apart from the public world and the private nature of the home and the seclusion of women within it is often taken for granted.[96] Historians have talked variously of the family becoming cut off from the wider world by the mid-nineteenth century; of the home becoming a haven where spiritual renewal and comfort were sought; of the home as the repository of order and a refuge from the chaos of the industrial world; and of the home as a place to escape the tensions of one's public role. However, far from domestic and family life being an island cloistered from the robust exchanges of the commercial world and insulated from the hustle and bustle of social life, the Victorian home was an ocean of sociability and was steeped in the practices and processes of the business world. This was not an aberration from ideological prescription: the ideology of domesticity was riddled with contradictions and those promoting the publicity of the home were as common as those declaiming its private nature.

The separation of home and the market, in both the physical sense and in terms of processes, was far from complete; symbiosis rather than separation more accurately reflects the nature of the relationship between the two. Social life was as often conducted within the so-called private realm of the home as in the public concert halls, assembly rooms and theatres, and home entertainment was far from being exclusive to a select family group. Dinner parties and dances were 'public' in that they involved work for servants, for women of the family, sometimes for outside caterers or servants, and a degree of sociability which matched that of many public gatherings. The intertwining of social life, business life, work, leisure and home is far more striking than the distinctiveness of these many spheres. Like the fibres of a thread, they wound together to create the fabric of middle-class day-to-day life in the nineteenth century.

The public character of the home obviously has ramifications for how the role of women is viewed. Women were participants and to a large extent the creators of the public aspect of the home as agents of sociability, and in their key role of displaying domestic life for public consumption. Even if the ideology of domesticity had confined women to the home, it did not confine them to a private role. The Victorian home may have been private in the sense that it was the preserve of intimacy and emotional succour, although the evidence of correspondence and diaries suggests that it cannot be assumed that Victorians looked only to resident family for this kind of nurturing. However, it was by no means private in the sense of being inward-looking or cut off from the wider social world. Admittedly the abundant hospitality offered by households was not all-inclusive, but limited to family, friends, acquaintances or friends of friends, and therefore may be described as a 'private' sociability. However, limited access or exclusivity was also a feature of middle-class public life where status, standing or financial resources were the requirements for participation. Although the family in the nineteenth century and beyond has been a metaphor for 'the private', the unproblematic use of the term and perhaps an anachronistic application has created a cluster of false assumptions about the Victorian home which have connoted insularity, intimacy and distinctiveness from social and public life. Yet it is the openness, sociability and ties with social and public life which are the striking features to the modern reader.

5

A Woman's Touch

The small and loving assembly gathered round her knee, in the
genial atmosphere of home and lisping its responses to prayer and
catechism and hymn from lips that quiver with maternal devotion, is
the audience she may fearlessly and effectively address by God's own
appointment and from Nature's inspiration.[1]

THIS ARCHETYPAL AND IDEALISED portrait of sacred motherhood is from
an article entitled 'Woman in her own sphere: A voice from the other
side', published in the *Waverley Journal* in 1856. The notion prevalent in
the nineteenth century, as already emphasised, was that a woman's place
was in the home as moral and spiritual guardian, as ordained by religion
and nature. Ironically, however, the article stands as testimony to the contested nature of the meanings of motherhood and femininity and to their
socially constructed nature rather than their 'natural' status. The author, a
man, disquieted by what he perceived as a worrying trend towards the
'amalgamation' of the qualities of the sexes and the disordering of the
relations between them, urged women not to step beyond their sphere
and to fulfil the duties for which God and Nature intended them.

Motherhood had been long sanctified in religious discourses. It has
been argued, however, that from the end of the eighteenth century
the coalescence of diverse influences, particularly the Enlightenment and
Evangelicalism, privileged female religiosity and that the role of women,
particularly as mothers, was elevated to that of moral guardians of the
nation.[2] There are long-standing debates about the timing of new conceptions of motherhood and of parent–child relationships and about
whether notions of these intimate human relationships can be more
readily characterised by continuity of ideas than by change.[3] Historians
of the medieval and early modern periods have been sceptical about the
supposed 'invention' of motherhood in the eighteenth century and also
of the novelty of idealised conceptions of women which stressed their

morally redemptive role and hence their suitability as nurturers of children.[4] Although religious writings may have feminised piety in the nineteenth century, it is doubtful that they newly elevated motherhood, a status long valorised in religious literature and imagery.[5] The weight of evidence suggests that the mother–child relationship had an enduring primacy and a longer pedigree than those who locate key shifts at diverse points since 1500 would admit. However, there have been cultural and historical variations in how this relationship was conceived and in the meanings attached to it. Nineteenth-century secular attitudes to the mother–child relationship emphasised the special importance of childhood as a stage in the human life-cycle and conjoined with religious discourses on female piety to exalt motherhood and to conceive it primarily in terms of moral and educative responsibilities to children.

If histories of motherhood and childhood are viewed interactively, it is possible to argue that from the end of the eighteenth century a new vocabulary of motherhood was created, offering different meanings and definitions to the role. Hugh Cunningham has argued that by the middle of the nineteenth century there had evolved a body of ideas on childhood, which were sufficiently coherent to be regarded as an ideology. Although there were competing ideas about the essential elements in child-rearing practices, there was a shared idea in the importance of childhood as a distinct phase in the life-cycle and a shared interest in the ways in which children learned.[6] The reformulated view of childhood which elevated its importance in the stages of human development and which Cunningham argues was predominantly secular in tone had important implications for the role of the mother. As the early years of the child were the subject of increased focus, the mother–child relationship was endowed with a new intensity which gave rise to new sensibilities surrounding motherhood and placed more emphasis on their time-honoured role as the carers and nurturers of children.

The importance of the instruction of the heart rather than the head is the theme of Lord Kames's prescriptive text, *Loose Hints upon Education chiefly concerning the Culture of the Heart*, written in 1781. Echoing Rousseau, he described the 'cultivation of the heart during childhood' as a vocation 'with which females only are charged by providence' and one which was 'not inferior in dignity to any other that belongs to the other sex'.[7] He urged that this task not be abandoned to nurses and servants and that the dignified occupation of educating their children should be the chief duty of married women. While acknowledging that it was also the duty of a woman to make a good wife, he accorded the task of educating children equal status with pleasing her husband as the 'capital duties' of a wife.[8] Directing his text at elite women, whom he perceived to be neglecting their duties for a 'perpetual round of pleasure', Kames was perhaps reasserting the traditional role of women rather than delineating new ones. Kames's emphasis on moral instruction differed from Rousseau's somewhat libertarian injunction to 'leave childhood to ripen in your children.'[9] Nevertheless, his emphasis on childhood as the most important stage in the human life-cycle chimed with much contemporary thought which revered and sanctified children and childhood.

As Cunningham has noted, Romantic notions of childhood as a time of innocence and of the special nature of childhood had only limited relevance to the mass of the population, as the conditions enabling children to be regarded as other than economic assets did not exist for most families until the advent of compulsory education in 1871.[10] However, they did gain currency and influence among the nineteenth-century middle classes, whose rhetoric was full of references to the innocence of children and even to their redemptive qualities. Childhood was often sentimentally idealised, children themselves indulged, and certainly deeply mourned when they died. Frances Murray's grandmother lost her only son in the 1820s, when he was four; so overwhelmed with sorrow that 'for months [she] lay severely ill', she always kept his clothes in a small wooden box beside her bed.[11] Janet Story's account of the loss of her first child in the 1860s is a reminder of the hazards of pregnancy as well as the high incidence of infant mortality in the nineteenth century:

> To me, after a time of great and critical illness, the knowledge that it had all been in vain, the total disappointment of all my long and cherished hopes, brought anguish that was almost overpowering, and only my husband's thankfulness for my own preservation reconciled me to a life which seemed to have been shorn of everything that made life desirable.[12]

Infant mortality in Scotland never fell below 120 per 1,000 live births during the century.[13] Neither medical intervention nor the prosperity which bought it could shield bereaved middle-class parents from their grief. Ideas of childhood as the best time of life and as a time of innocence, coupled with the knowledge that it was also a precarious stage of life, perhaps fuelled sentimental and indulgent attitudes towards children. Mrs Story reflected that children were often present at adult dinner parties when dessert was served and that 'kindly and foolish people then amused themselves in stuffing the youngsters with a variety of fruits and

sweetmeats most injurious to their digestions'.[14] When Frances Stoddard
Murray's parents went on a trip to the United States, accompanied by
only the youngest of their three children, her mother wrote letters with
fulsome expressions of love: 'My dearest eldest child my heart beats
quicken at the thought of thee, thou sharest my sleeping and waking
thoughts. [. . .] Pat Freddy's hair, smooth his brow, kiss him goodnight,
kiss my Budda and know dear Fanny, that you have the affectionate devotion of your loving mother.'[15] This archaic, almost biblical, language suggests a synthetic idiom, possibly drawing on the vocabulary provided by
Romantic conceptions of childhood. Given the proverbial 'absence makes
the heart grow fonder', her maternal devotion was possibly inflamed by
the considerable distance between her and her children. Although such
expressions of devotion to children were commonplace among the
nineteenth-century middle class, it remains unclear how they were integrated into the practices of child-rearing. As Cunningham has tersely
observed of Romantic notions of childhood: 'the overall influence of
romanticism, whilst all-pervading, was short on specifics.'[16]

As discussed in chapter 2, while the father–child relationship was often
a central feature of family relationships, the absence of most fathers from
the household during the day meant that the day-to-day task of child-
rearing generally devolved on mothers. So how did prevailing notions of
childhood and child-rearing affect what middle-class women actually did
with and for their children? As far as formal education was concerned,
that of middle-class children was more likely to take place outside the
home than in it, particularly towards the end of the nineteenth century.[17]
In the first half of the century middle-class girls' education in Glasgow,
in common with their English counterparts,[18] consisted of a mix of small
private schools, private classes, governesses and mothers, and from the
1830s large private secondary schools. There was a large army of private
teachers who held classes in their own homes, a practice that continued
into the early twentieth century, as can be seen from the many advertisements in the *Glasgow Herald* for private classes in dancing, deportment
and an assortment of accomplishments. There was also a clutch of small
private schools, often run by women. The Woodside Crescent school,
owned and run by the four Miller sisters in the 1850s, was probably typical
of these establishments.[19] As Lindy Moore has observed, these small
private schools and private classes came to be eclipsed by larger and more
structured establishments as the century progressed.[20] The School Boards,
established in 1872, introduced girls' secondary high schools and post-
elementary education and began to attract girls from the lower middle

classes who previously might have been educated at small private schools, private classes and perhaps also by their mother.

One of the most significant developments in the education of more affluent urban middle-class girls in Scotland was the formation of Young Ladies' Institutions from the 1830s and 1840s. Some of them were short-lived, but others survived for forty or fifty years. Their existence meant that Scottish girls were more likely than their English counterparts to be educated outside the home.[21] The Young Ladies' Institutions were large, urban and mainly secondary day schools, although there was provision for boarders. The curriculum was designed to raise the academic standard of education for girls, which had previously been 'very fragmentary and disjointed'.[22] The fees of between 15 and 24 guineas a year tended to limit the selection of pupils to the wealthier sections of the middle class, particularly where there was more than one girl in a family. However, in recognition of the prohibitive costs, some schools charged a cheaper rate which enabled them to widen the social base of their recruitment.[23] The Glasgow Institution, established in 1845, initially charged 10 guineas a session, although it was at pains to emphasise in its prospectus that this did not detract from the quality of the education which it provided.[24]

These schools were the forerunners of the English secondary schools which were established later in the century to promote an academic secondary education for middle-class girls.[25] Some of the institutions offered preparatory classes for younger pupils, but the majority of the pupils were receiving a secondary education.[26] The curriculum in most of the schools was fairly broad and included English, modern languages (with Latin and Greek as alternatives to French and German), geography, writing and arithmetic as well as the usual 'accomplishments'. The Glasgow Institution in 1857 offered instruction in English, French, German, Italian, geography, arithmetic, drawing and painting, writing, pianoforte, vocal music, dancing and needlework.[27] An innovative feature of the institutions was the teaching of mathematics and science, including chemistry, botany, zoology, natural philosophy and astronomy; the success and popularity of the science and maths courses often depended on the teacher and his style.[28]

Most of these schools enrolled over 100 pupils, and the largest Glasgow school, the Glasgow Institution for Young Ladies, boasted 300 pupils in 1847.[29] Indeed a survey of the most affluent district of Glasgow in 1865, Blythswood, established that about one-fifth of middle-class girls at school were attending the Glasgow Institution. With approximately three or four of these schools existing simultaneously in Glasgow at any one time

between 1845 and the end of the century, they must have been responsible for educating significant numbers of the daughters of Glasgow's
prosperous middle class.

Middle-class boys in Scotland, like their English counterparts, were
usually educated outside the home from an early age. By the middle of
the century the sons of the upper bourgeoisie were generally educated
in the local private day schools rather than boarding schools or public
schools favoured in England, and the sons of the less well off were usually
educated in burgh schools. The trend for more formal and structured
education in schools rather than the home, for middle-class children, is
reflected in the census figures, which record small numbers of children
educated by governesses or by mothers. Although census practices were
not consistent, in 1851 children who were educated at home were usually
designated 'scholars at home'. In the Claremont/Woodside estate area in
1851 there were only twenty-seven children of 277 between the ages of
five and sixteen, predominantly girls, who were described in this way.
These were children from eight families in the more prosperous streets
in the area and with one exception were educated by governesses. The
three daughters of George Skene, an advocate, and his wife, Georgina,
were designated 'scholars at home'; the live-in servants comprised a tablemaid, a cook and a nursery maid, but no governess, suggesting that they
may have been educated at home by their mother or perhaps both
parents. However, it is by no means certain that these were the only
children who were educated at home as there were sixty-one children
between these ages who were given no designation, some of whom may
have been educated by mothers. By 1891 no children were described as
'scholars at home' and only thirty-three had no designation. There were
still three 'governesses' employed by and residing with families in the area,
although in each case the children were boys, mostly under the age of
six (two were only three) not yet attending school. In 1884 the Mac-
Ewens of Woodside Crescent employed a governess for their two eldest
daughters, but by the 1891 census there is no reference to a governess
and the children are described merely as 'scholars'.[30] It is possible that the
girls by that time had graduated to school education, or that the governess did not reside with the family. The decline in the number of
children described as 'scholars at home' and the near-absence of resident
governesses in the later years reflect the preference for schools over home-
based education. This is also suggested by the smaller number of governesses recorded in the census for Glasgow in comparison with districts
in England. In 1881 in Liverpool there were over 800 governesses

recorded in the census for a population of around 800,000, whereas Glasgow reported only a little over 200 for a population of about 600,000.[31]

Although the increase in schools limited the role which mothers played in the formal education of their children, most middle-class mothers continued to play some kind of role in their children's education and there were a few who were the main providers of formal education. Mothers tended to play a more active role in formally teaching their children in the early decades of the century when educational provision was less structured. Elizabeth Thomson King's mother and father were closely involved in their children's education in the 1820s and 1830s. Although Elizabeth went to Latin and French classes, she was also taught by her parents, as were all her siblings. Elizabeth recalled reading Goldsmith's *History of England* with her mother: 'and if she went up to town for a day I had to read my portion by myself and tell her about it on her return.'[32] Mothers were expected to provide some rudimentary education in the pre-school years, as Janet Story's mother did until she went to a local kindergarten at the age of five in the 1830s. Even when a governess was employed or the children attended classes outside the home, many mothers took responsibility for some aspects of formal learning. In the 1840s and 1850s, Frances Murray's mother was closely involved in her children's education, even though the governess, Miss Dickinson, supervised most of their lessons and the children also attended small private schools as well as receiving private lessons in music and dancing.[33] When in 1854 Frances's parents went to visit relatives in America, leaving the governess in charge, Frances, aged eleven and the eldest, was given innumerable instructions to care for the younger children and to become a surrogate mother. Part of her daily routine with the children included reading to them, as her mother, a great reader herself, encouraged the children to read widely, including philosophy, poetry and religious texts.[34]

When Frances had her own children, in the 1870s and 1880s, she came to play an even more substantial role than her mother had done in educating them. Her daughter Eunice claimed that she and her sisters were educated entirely by her mother until they were twelve, at which point they were sent to boarding school in Fife. When Frances spent several months in Cannes with three of her four children in the winter of 1888, she continued to be 'busy teaching' them, although her lessons were supplemented three times a week by Professor Rouvier, who taught the two girls French, Latin and maths.[35] By the last decades of the century Frances Murray was probably unusual in treating her educative role as a full-time vocation. Most middle-class mothers in the second half of the century performed a much more informal role in instruction, one which was confined to reading to their children, listening to them recite their psalms and catechism and superintending their lessons. Reading to children was not merely a pastime or leisure activity; it was regarded as a means of moral and intellectual instruction, which was integral to a mother's duty to imbue in her children the appropriate virtues. Helen MacFie, the wife of a Greenock sugar manufacturer, read diligently to her children, recording the texts in her diary.[36] Georgiana Coats also 'heard' her daughters' psalms and paraphrases. Mary Ann Macfarlane dutifully listened to Catherine reciting her prayers and catechism, while the child's academic education was assigned to local day schools. Mollie McEwen's daughter recited 'her ABC's' to her mother nearly every day.[37]

Obviously the nature of a mother's involvement in the day-to-day care of children varied considerably: some mothers could delegate the more arduous tasks to nursemaids and servants, while others devoid of an army of servants had to undertake the bathing, feeding and dressing for themselves. Mrs Margaret Muir, wife of a muslin manufacturer and mother of eight children aged between eighteen and two in Carnarvon Street, must have had her days and hands full, without the support of any servant, or at least none who was recorded in the census as living in the family home. In contrast, the life of Elizabeth Hannay of Woodlands Terrace might have appeared enviably effortless: with one baby son, she was able to call on the services of four servants.

Indeed the contrast between the households in the prosperous streets and the lower middle-class streets is particularly marked in terms of the employment of nursemaids and children's nurses. In 1851 thirty-seven families employed between them a total of fifty-one nursemaids/children's nurses. The greatest numbers were in the 'middling' streets, reflecting the concentration of young families here rather than in the most prosperous three streets. Only five of the families employing nursemaids or nurses lived in the lower-middle class part of the area. One of these, the household of a solicitor, employed both a nurse and a nursemaid: but there were five children living at home, four of them under six. The family of a portrait painter had a nurse to help look after two young children. The remainder – headed by a maths teacher, a sheriff substitute and a shipping agent – had nursery maids to assist in looking after one or two children.

The 1851 returns distinguish between nurses, under-nurses and nursery maids or nursemaids. The latter were less specialised, often younger and cheaper to employ. 'Nurses' were employed when children were three or younger. Nursery maids were still working in families where the youngest child was eight or more – in one case as old as twelve. Some households, of course, employed both. There is only one specified wetnurse, although many families had children of less than one year old, suggesting that maternal breast-feeding was the established practice by the middle of the century. By 1891 the number of nurses/nursemaids had fallen to thirty-one, a reflection perhaps of declining family size by the end of the nine-teenth century or the 'servant problem' which so exercised the middle classes towards the end of the century. However, the majority were still employed in the more prosperous streets: there were none in Carnarvon or Stanley Streets, for instance.

Households staffed by nursemaids, cooks and general servants no doubt contributed to the notion that middle-class wives did not have to con-cern themselves with the daily toil of household chores and child-rearing. Indeed the term 'angel in the house' might have been coined especially for Helen MacFie whose daily journal records a life seemingly unen-cumbered by the duties of child-care. After the birth of her son on 9 December 1872, Helen had a lying- in period of several weeks. She may have had a difficult birth as she refers to 'severe pain' on two separate occasions some four weeks after the birth. It was six weeks before she was brought down from the upstairs bedroom to the front room. For the next five weeks she seemed to spend her time between her upstairs bedroom and the front room, where she regularly entertained visitors. Not until 12 February did she venture into the nursery 'for the first time'; a further two weeks passed before she considered going out.[38] Although she had three children under five, her journal of 1873 records a life which revolved around regular church attendance, various ecclesiastical and philanthropic activities, interspersed with the leavening of shopping, vis-iting and entertaining. Her children make occasional appearances in her diary as companions on walks or visits, but by and large her daily life appears relatively uninterrupted by the demands of child-care. Yet she was by no means a detached or uncaring mother; as mentioned above, she read regularly to her children, recording the titles of the books in her diary, where she also charted their heights and weights and noted when they had grown a new tooth. Her own reading matter, listed at the end of her diary, contained a hefty dose of religious and prescriptive litera-ture such as *Christian Training*, *Discourses by Reverend Lewis Ferguson* and *Doing and Suffering*, alongside novels such as *Good Wives* and *Little Women*. Of course she may have been keen for her diary to be a selective account of her life, one which reflected the depths of her piety and the extent of her social intercourse rather than the details of raising children. Helen MacFie seems to embody the dual images of women as both redemptive and idle that are inherent in the idiom 'angel in the house'. Motherhood may have been important in the construction of her identity, but it did not occupy much of her time or energy. Her affluence enabled her to interpret discourses of moral motherhood as a license to proselytise and export her piety outside the home.

In stark contrast to Helen MacFie, who limited the time with her children to afternoon or early evening reading sessions and escorting them on outings to the shops or countryside, the early motherhood of Mollie Macewan, as reflected in her letters, was filled with the minutiae of childcare. The correspondence between Mollie, who lived in America, and her sister-in-law Margaret McCallum gives some indication of how absorbed women were in the lives of their young children and how unremitting the business of child-rearing could be when servants could not be called upon to relieve some of the burden. Margaret's husband, John, was a coalmaster and they lived in St Vincent Crescent, a prestigious development of large tenement flats built around 1850. The *Glasgow Herald* referred to the houses as 'fine middle-class dwellings whose rents ranged from £40–£70' per annum, indicating a fairly typical middle-class rent.[39] The Crescent was on the other side of Kelvingrove Park from the Claremont estate. Indeed the Macewan children went to school in one of the streets on the estate.

Mollie and her husband Henry lived in Alabama. It is not clear what Henry's occupation was, although he seems to have been involved in some kind of business activity (his father's profession had been in medicine). At the time of her correspondence with her sister-in-law (only Mollie's letters survive), Mollie had three daughters, born in 1867, 1868 and 1870. Margaret had three sons and one daughter, born between 1864 and 1869. The letters are replete with references to each other's children as they traded the details of their health, weight, birthdays and general well-being. Children, child rearing and fecundity were Mollie's preoccupations. Not even the details of her children's bowel movements went unremarked: 'Our little ones all keep well, although they have been more or less troubled with their bowels this last month of May, but I have been very careful of their diet, and have not allowed them any ice water or fruit which I think it bad for them in that month.'[40]

We do not know whether Margaret was similarly immersed in the details of her own four children's lives, although she certainly shared intimacies with Mollie including details of planning and limiting the size of her family. The two women had obviously discussed Mollie's imminent pregnancy and possible names for the baby:

> Our first *boys* name is to be Henry Clow, but *we* seem partial to the fair sex. I had been hoping to *you* would have been the first to change the order of things by having a daughter (as your time comes next) and then there would have been hope of Maggie D. and myself following with sons, but you told me some time ago you were going to take a rest.[41]

There is certainly an element of Mollie's parading her maternal role in the correspondence. Margaret was some twenty years older than Mollie, who was barely into her twenties. The younger woman may have been anxious to gain approbation and respect from her sister-in-law and therefore flaunted her role as mother to highlight their common status and perhaps accrue some gravitas. She certainly did not assume the mantle of motherhood lightly, as attested by her letters, inscribed with references to the minutiae of her maternal role: 'you who are a mother can understand what it is to commence a letter and then have one child cough and another wake and cry for water and at other times when we have actually seated ourselves company comes in to spend the evening, (I may as well say that I never write in the day) as I believe the annoyances would be greater then.'[42]

There was probably some truth in Mollie's claims that the rhythm of her day was dictated by the demands of her children. Having dispensed with the services of an erstwhile nurse or 'house-girl', she once lamented that she had time only for practical clothes making and mending and none for more elaborate work: 'I live in hopes someday of knowing how and having time to do little fancy things [. . .], of course I mean if God spares my life until my children grow up around me to be a help.'[43] She clearly found the task of caring for young children demanding and arduous. She frequently referred to feeling tired or sleepy, which she often used as an excuse for not writing more often to her sister-in-law. The McCallums in Scotland employed a cook and a housemaid, though Mollie acknowledged that this did not necessarily free them from child-care responsibilities. She remarked of another relative, who had not written since the birth of her child: 'I suppose that she finds very little time to write with 6 children to attend to.'[44]

Those middle-class mothers who employed nannies or nursemaids might not have used much energy in tending to the needs of their young children, but they did spend time organising cultural excursions and parties as well as ensuring that lessons in dancing, music, drawing and painting were provided. Unlike the working-class child, whose playground was the street and whose playthings were fashioned from the detritus to be found there, the middle-class child's play tended to be more supervised and confined when they were in the city, in contrast to the freedom they generally experienced on holidays.[45]

Georgiana Coats had the benefit of a young nursemaid to help her care for her two daughters and the family also employed a housemaid and a cook. However, she did not relegate all child-care activities to the nurse. She regularly escorted her 'clan' on numerous outings to parks, exhibitions and visits to friends, with the nursemaid in tow. After an energetic day with her children, she dispatched a letter to her husband providing an account of her round of activity:

> We went yesterday – the cavalcade – Janie, Mary, Baby, perambulator, Nurse, and Moritz, to the Botanic Gardens: tied Moritz at the gate and saw Winter Gardens and Plant Houses – found the hour for Musical promenade changed from 4 till 7 – provoked: took cavalcade to Sophie's where we had tea, and returned at 7; heard three tunes by the pipes.[46]

The role of the nurse was clearly not intended to supplant that of the mother. As Amanda Vickery has noted of elite women of the eighteenth century, there was probably a division of labour between the mother and the nurse, although it is difficult to establish its precise nature.[47] The nurse might have been responsible for the more menial tasks, while the mother would undertake such pleasurable ones as accompanying them on outings, reading to them and supervising their education. The dividing line was not necessarily that clear. In one of Georgiana Coats's letters to her husband, for example, she mentioned having taken her elder daughter, aged six, for a walk in the country, but the next day, '*she* took the nurse herself to the spot, through all the gates, and up to the house – and showed her all the sights – I could hardly have given her credit for knowing the way'.[48]

The Thomson nursery boasted a nurse and an under-nurse, with Nurse Sally 'reigning supreme' there, according to Elizabeth Thomson. Nonetheless, it was Elizabeth's mother who mended and made their clothes with 'her own dear hand', as well as being their teacher. Catherine Carswell's nurses took her and her siblings for walks in their pram around the West End of Glasgow, but it was their mother who nursed them when they were sick, consoled and sang to them when they could not sleep at night, taught them to float, and fell into the sea fully clothed when taking them on a boating trip.[49] Frances Murray regularly spent the summer months on the island of Oransay with her four young children. A nurse accompanied them, but when she left for her holidays, Frances remarked in a letter to her husband: 'We are getting along beautifully without her.'[50]

It was far from the case that middle-class children were closeted in the nursery with the occasional visit from a distant mother more preoccupied by the demands of her social life than those of her children. Even wealthy mothers, who could consign some of the duties of child-care to nurses or servants, chose to spend much of their time ministering to the needs of their children. The ill-health of Georgiana Coats's younger daughter meant that she spent much of her time nursing or entertaining young Vicky in the family's coastal retreats while her husband and older daughter remained in the city. Even church-going was an activity which was circumscribed by the responsibilities of motherhood. Maryanne MacEwen's minister wrote her a sympathetic a letter on this topic: 'I know it is often difficult for Mothers to be away from home for any length of time. You should know that we pause for 2 or 3 minutes in the service about 12.20 or 12.30 to give time to any who may not have been able to come at 11 to enter the Church.'[51]

Maryanne MacEwen was probably typical of many middle-class women of modest means. Although her husband William was later to become an eminent surgeon, in their early married life his salary as casualty surgeon at the Central Police Division was £250 per annum and they probably did not have the means to employ a live-in nurse. In 1881, when their three children were aged six, four and ten months, the MacEwens had only one 'general servant'. On the birth of the first child in 1874, it was Maryanne's mother who provided the nursing care, and who was with her 'constantly' thereafter.

It has become customary, particularly among the middle classes, to approach child-rearing with a studied self-consciousness. The Victorian and Edwardian middle-class mother, however, was equally absorbed with the business of bringing up children. Inasmuch as she was a slave to her children, she would be a more than willing one, and she went to extraordinary lengths to ensure that her brood were entertained and amused, educated and edified, and above all cherished and loved. Yet it should be remembered that what it involved to be a mother differed according to the material circumstances and culture of the middle-class woman as well as the stage of the family cycle. As children got older, mothers obviously acquired more freedom. Often the eldest daughter would undertake certain household tasks as she approached adulthood. Madeleine Smith, aged twenty, was evidently responsible for writing the daily orders for the servants. Eldest daughters would also often act *in loco parentis*, even when servants were present. Sometimes this was a symbolic gesture which portended future responsibilities, as when a mother wrote to her eleven-year-old daughter from America. 'Be very considerate and attentive to Fred, three times as much as you would if I were there. He is just the age when a boy needs a mother.'[52] When Margaret Mcewan's parents left for their summer holidays on the Clyde coast, she was left in the city to look after her five younger brothers who were attending school. Margaret may have been wilting under the burden of her responsibilities or her father may merely have been keen to ensure that she did not bear them lightly. In any case he wrote to stiffen her resolve:

> Mamma says you are to have her bonnet trimmed and ready. Hope James and Henry got safe home on monday and are none the worse for the shower. Hope that you are also enjoying yourself and finding much pleasure as Housekeeper, Strive more and more to govern your temper and allow the consciousness that you are doing your duty bear you up under all the ingratitude of others, Count it all joy when ye fall into divers temptations and resist evil and render not evil for evil but contrarywise good for evil. I hope you are all getting up betimes in the morning and you as the Oldest especially shewing the example.[53]

It was partly the assumption that woman's destiny was to be a wife and a mother which meant that eldest daughters were expected to deputise in the absence of their mother. However, it was no doubt one effective way of mothers shedding tasks and lightening their load so that they could occupy their time in other ways. Certainly once children were older or were away at school, the calls on a mother's time were significantly reduced. Frances Murray, whose children were born when she was in her thirties, was able to indulge freely her taste for socialising, cultural outings and intellectual gatherings when she was in her forties and fifties. Once Georgiana Coats's brood were grown up, she spent a good deal of time travelling abroad. As discussed in chapter 7, these women also became increasingly involved in public activities.

Sometimes children were left with relatives and servants for fairly lengthy periods. In 1887 Frances and David Murray chartered a yacht for a month's cruise in the Western Isles, taking their two elder children and leaving the two youngest with their grandmother (it will be recalled that

Frances herself had been left in the charge of a governess as a child, and that she followed suit in leaving her own children with servants). Margaret Allan, Maryanne MacEwen's mother, chaperoned two of her older children to Paris, where they received lessons in painting and enjoyed trips to art galleries, churches and other cultural haunts.[54]

When Joseph and Georgiana Coats visited Germany in 1886 they were unhampered by querulous children, having left their two young daughters with their grandmother and aunt; it is not clear whether they had servants to help them. Madeleine Smith's parents frequently left the household in the charge of servants. Indeed Madeleine complained to L'Angelier that her parents were too often out and about socialising.[55] When Helen MacFie's husband moved to Liverpool to take charge of the branch of the family business there, her eight children did not seem to provide much of an obstacle to the couple becoming celebrated members of county society in Cheshire.[56]

Prosperity and material circumstance alone cannot explain the differences in how dominant ideas of motherhood were conceived, interpreted and practised. Family culture and the predilections of individual women were also important influences on how the middle-class woman conceived of her role. Frances Murray was something of an intellectual who before she married had harboured hopes of earning her own living. Perhaps the fact that she chose to make motherhood a vocation and educate her children was a way of realising her ambitions and usefully employing her talents as much as being a reflection of dutiful motherhood. On the other hand, Helen MacFie came from a deeply devout background of evangelicals and had spent much time travelling before her marriage, visiting churches abroad and attending religious gatherings. Therefore her interpretation of her role once she had married and had children was to emphasise the redemptive and spiritual aspects of female identity as much as the nurturing and educative ones.

Motherhood was certainly pivotal to the construction of female identity, yet how that role was enacted and the meanings given to it varied considerably across the middle classes. While women may have been defined by the home, the family and motherhood, not all were confined by it; some of the wealthy women were able to combine motherhood with socialising and travelling even when their children were young. Middle-class mothers were not simply the products of domestic discourses; the family cycle, their material experiences and their cultural world shaped their lives, as did their own interpretation of what it meant to be a mother.

The notion of the idle and decorative middle-class Victorian wife has been largely dispatched to the historical dustbin by Patricia Branca and others who have demonstrated her essential contribution as a household manager.[57] Supervision of a large household staffed by a retinue of servants could resemble the management of a small business. Elizabeth Bower, wife of the Episcopalian Bishop of Glasgow, living in Claremont Terrace in 1851, superintended a household comprising her husband and three teenage daughters, and a governess, housekeeper, lady's maid, cook, two housemaids, kitchen maid, butler and footboy. The housekeeper and butler would traditionally have supervised the other servants, but their overall management, as well as their hiring and if necessary firing, would have fallen to Mrs Bower.[58]

Few households had a domestic staff as large as that of Bishop Bower, although in the rest of Claremont Terrace there was an average of six servants per household. But where the housewife had fewer servants to direct and, it seems, worry about, the more housework she would have had to do personally. In the 'middling' households, servants were less likely to be differentiated, except perhaps for the cook. A typical complement in 1851 would be two women simply designated 'servant' or a cook and one general servant. By 1891 there were only forty-three resident servants in Carnarvon and Stanley Streets, out of 158 households. These were practically all 'general servants'.

By the end of the century the 'servant problem' had become a constant preoccupation of the middle classes. In fact the decrease in the percentage of women employed in domestic service began rather earlier in Scotland than in the rest of Britain.[59] The increasingly difficult business of finding servants, whether by word of mouth, newspaper advertisement or use of an agency, exercised middle-class women for most of the period. Agencies existed to act as liaison between employer and prospective servant: the Misses Miller were running one on Sauchiehall Street as early as 1857.[60] Many wives placed advertisements in local newspapers detailing their often exacting requirements: 'Nurse – wanted now for one little girl; superior, well-educated, about 25. References and particulars by letter to Mrs Newman, 28 Woodside Place.'[61] Servants had to be interviewed, appointed and inducted into the nature of their duties and the ways of the household.[62] Then they had to be 'managed'. The housewife probably wrote out daily orders, as was done in Madeleine Smith's family, saw to household accounts, planned menus and supervised the smooth running of the household in matters such as spring-cleaning, replacing linen and so on. In the more modest households of the lower middle class, housewives must have worked side-by-side with their servants. In addition, many housewives saw themselves as standing *in loco parentis* to their servants. Mary Ann Macfarlane found that servants 'only added to her cares, because their lives, too, became her responsibility'.[63] The mistress of the house was to safeguard the moral well-being of her staff, as well as to remain constantly vigilant against pilfering, skimping on tasks or the entertaining of visitors in the kitchen.[64]

As described in chapter 4, entertaining in the home was a regular occurrence, and in wealthier families it could be on a scale requiring the time, planning and organisation of a military campaign. Entertaining not only added to the normal burdens of managing a household, it swelled the numbers of servants to be instructed, supervised and reprimanded and often involved the hiring of additional servants. Furthermore, the problems attendant on securing the services of workmen, ensuring that the task was carried out to specifications, completed within the specified time, and with minimal upheaval to the household, are easily recognisable to the modern reader. Georgiana Coats once had occasion to complain that 'painters and plumbers are not all – all honourable men – no, no'. Her frustration with the procrastinations of Mr Leitch, a plumber, was compounded by the fact that she was away from the household and unable to issue her orders directly. Lacking faith in her husband's ability to deal with the situation, she wrote to him with terse instructions:

> And first and very much so – will you please arrange for Mr. Leitch to wait upon you by *return* of post and agree to do the Conservatory job – it must be done in July before Lisbeth leaves and before William gets charge of the place.
>
> There are two plants of Miss Watson's – one is a smallish pot of ivy, the other is a large pot containing long leaves which grow up straight from the soil. Pray do not let these be tampered with and see also that the stair carpet is carefully turned away before commencing operations – even if the job were not finished before you came up it could at least be well begun. Now, don't forget.[65]

Maintaining domestic standards that would reflect the social standing of the family could place a heavy burden on the Victorian housewife. In 1881 Mary Ann Macfarlane employed three servants to execute the domestic duties involved in running a house and a family of two children. She evidently found the business of housekeeping irksome and a trial, partly because of her own exacting standards, but also because she felt 'bound to maintain the convention of her husband's condition' and had strong principles 'concerning the health and happiness of a house-hold which included children and servants'.[66] Nor were women released from the responsibilities of supervision when they were absent from the household. When Georgiana Coats was in Rothsey preparing the family summer home for the season, she wrote to her husband: 'I have written to Bella with directions about feeding you – and ordered things from Annacker for you.'[67]

Bonnie Smith has suggested that the rituals of domesticity for the bourgeois women of northern France in the late nineteenth century were essentially symbolic, being related to the preservation of gentility and the display of opulence rather than being utilitarian or having economic sig-nificance.[68] Account keeping, in particular, she views as a largely symbolic ritual which was unrelated to the requirements of domestic economy. However, the economic experience of the middle classes varied enor-mously; even among the more affluent sections, the vagaries of the economy could inflict wounding blows to the financial health of the household. Many of the families in this study similarly suffered down-turns in their fortunes, some of them being bankrupted several times. Janet Story, for example, recalled how her father lost most of his fortune in the 1830s, when the Indian bank in which he had invested his savings crashed. In a short space of time the family fortunes experienced a climacteric shift which necessitated financial stringency and a search for alternative sources of income. Her mother began the more stringent regime by dispensing with the services of some of the servants and selling off some of her jewellery. When it looked as if the family would have to give up their large town house, her mother concocted a scheme to augment the family income; she obtained the services of a joiner and the upper floor of their spacious house was partitioned off and transferred to the next house; the three spinster sisters who lived there were thus able to accommodate many more visitors than before. Many women in similar straitened circumstances would have derived some satisfaction and status from such displays of competent housekeeping. Catherine Carswell's father, a commission merchant, was twice swindled by part-ners, and on another occasion was advised to go bankrupt when a ship which he had bought was found to be unseaworthy. These serious financial reverses required her mother to exercise strict budgetary control and to pore 'more anxiously over her little account books'.[69]

Bankruptcy, bank failures, poor investments and economic uncertainty were no strangers to the middle classes of the nineteenth century, particularly before the widespread adoption of limited liability in the

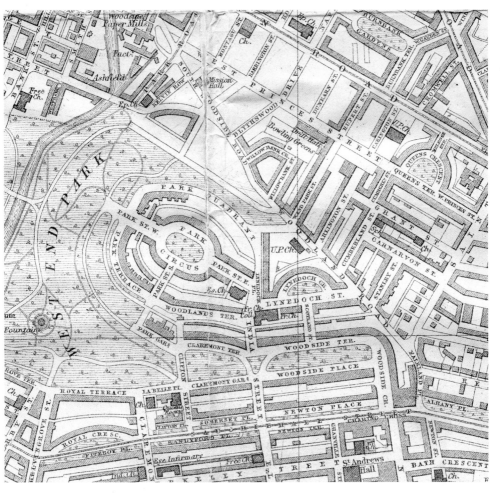

1   Street map of the Claremont/Woodside estate, 1883.

2 Woodside Crescent, 1852. These impressive houses, with their porticoed entrances, were the homes of 'carriage folk' at the top of the middle-class hierarchy.

3 *(facing page, top)* The hall of Marion Gilchrist's home in Queen's Terrace, 1907. Although personally wealthy, Miss Gilchrist lived in the more modest part of the area, in a flat of two bedrooms and two public rooms.

4 *(facing page, bottom)* Great Western Road (here *c.*1905) was a bustling thoroughfare which flanked the Claremont/Woodside estate.

7   The Coats family, 1856. Joseph, the youngest child, who subsequently married Georgiana Taylor, is seated next to his father.

5 *(facing page, top)* Wellington Church, 1905, attended by many of the Claremont/Woodside residents.

6 *(facing page, bottom)*   Crowds flock to one of the many attractions at the Glasgow International Exhibition, 1901, held in Kelvingrove Park. The Canadian pavilion was one of several exhibits representing the Empire.

8 Three generations of the Lorimer/MacLaren family on holiday together at their Clydeside summer residence, *c.*1880s.

9   The Napier family holidayed at Shandon on the Clyde in the 1880s.

10 The wedding of Rosa Mirrlees, 1901. Weddings often provided opportunities for grand celebrations of family and for affirming family identity.

11 Portrait of David Murray, drawn for *The Bailie*, 1893.

12 Joseph Coats triumphant, having at last overcome the reluctance of Georgiana Taylor to marry him. The photograph was taken to commemorate their engagement in St Moritz in 1879.

13 William MacEwen at the age of forty, *The Bailie*, 1888.

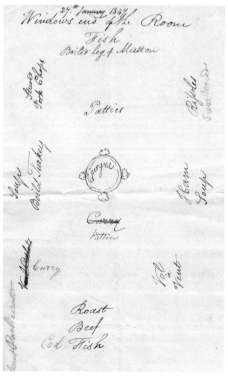

14 Dinners had to be planned with military precision: Janet Story had clearly given a great deal of thought to the menu and table setting for this dinner in 1847.

15   The dining room of the Mirrlees home, which was just off Great Western Road, rep-
resents the height of middle-class luxury. Robert Mirrlees was a wealthy engineer, and his
wife Helen was President of the Glasgow YWCA.

Within the illustration the following captions appear:

"House (Slated) Splendid Situation"

"4 Beds"

"Crag View; Easy Access"

"On Shore; Water in House; Steamer passes daily"

"School-House to let; Good Accommodation for small Family"

"Use of Kitchen"

"Boat"

"Piano; Very Moderate"

"Only 15 minutes from Pier"

"View of Bay Unsurpassed"

"Apply Post Office"

—Our Coast Residences

18   The annual move to the coast was full of potential hazards for the middle-class house-wife, to whom it fell to make the domestic arrangements. 'Our Coastal Residences', *The Bailie*, 1890.

16 *(facing page, top)*   The dining room of Miss Marion Gilchrist's flat in Queen's Terrace, 1907.

17 *(facing page, bottom)*   The interior of the Edgar family home, typical of modest, lower middle-class Glasgow, 1895.

19 Helen MacFie and her daughter Janet, 1870.

20 Maryanne MacEwen and her children, c.1890.

21 Professor William Thomson (Lord Kelvin) and his second wife, Frances Blundy, *c.*1890. She continued the tradition of providing 'secretarial support' to her husband – note the pencil in her hand.

22 Isabella Elder, 1894.

23 The Taylor family, c.1870. As orphans, the four sisters and a brother lived with an elderly companion. When the eldest, Sophia, married, Georgiana took on responsibility for her younger siblings. This contributed to her initial reluctance to marry Joseph Coats.

24 Miss Cranston's tearoom empire was already well established by 1885. A shrewd businesswoman, she prospered partly through catering to women's desire for a public space in the city. *The Bailie*, 1885.

25   Dr Joseph Coats, 1897. He is shown here breaking with tradition by allowing a young woman doctor into his postgraduate class.

THE ROYAL CLYDE YACHT CLUB BALL

26 The Royal Clyde Yacht Club ball was one of a host of such events in the Glasgow Season. *The Bailie*, 1891.

CITY HALL, GLASGOW.

MR

TEMPLETON

Has the honour to announce that he will make his FIRST APPEARANCE in Glasgow, since his return from

AMERICA,

IN A GRAND

MUSICAL

MELANGE,

On Thursday Evening,

MARCH 4, 1847.

Mr LODER will Preside at the Pianoforte.

Part First.

Introduction—Lyrics of Sir Walter Scott—His Minstrelsy of the Scottish Border—The value of old lyrical fragments—His excursions to Liddesdale—Ancient ballad on which he founded his 'Jock o' Hazeldean.'

BORDER BALLAD—"JOCK O' HAZELDEAN."

Sir Henry R. Bishop—His genius and compositions—The Romance 'Orynthia, my Beloved'—Dr Johnson's 'Hermit Hoar'—Bishop's Glees—His round, 'When the Wind Blows'—Anecdote of Bishop and Weber.

ROMANCE.

RECITATIVE—"ORYNTHIA, MY BELOVED."
ARIA—"A HERMIT WHO DWELLS."

Burns' scorn of the flame of Love when kindled at the altar of Mammon—His remarks on the subject of 'My Tocher's the Jewel'—The knowing lass an overmatch for her covetous suitor.

SONG—"MY TOCHER'S THE JEWEL."

The Ballet Opera of 'Le Dieu et la Bayadere'—Its Oriental origin—Its plot—The 'Indian Divinity'—Maid of Cashmere'—Success of the unknown—Reward of truth and sincerity—Object of the song.

SONG—"BEATS THERE A HEART,"
From the Opera of 'La Bayadere.'

The Poet and Composer Henry Carey—His contemporaries, Dryden, Addison, and Pope—The Augustan Age of our Literature. The National Anthem. Carey's descendant, Edmund Kean—Carey's vocal powers—The incident which occasioned 'Sally in our Alley.'

SONG—"SALLY IN OUR ALLEY."

AN INTERVAL OF TEN MINUTES BETWEEN THE PARTS.

In the course of the Evening, the
GRAND SCENA,
From Donizetti's Opera of 'Anna Bolena,'
"CHERISH LIFE, I DO CONJURE THEE."—Vivi tu!

Part Second.

History of the Air—Character of the old words—Adapted to verse by the Poet Thomson—John Mayne, Author of the present Song—Its early popularity in England.

SONG—"LOGAN BRAES."

America—Her Patriotic Songs—New England—Americans not all Yankees—Anecdote—Freedom of Intercourse—Personal Anecdote—Patronage of Art—National Music—its power.

NATIONAL AMERICAN ODE—" THE STAR-SPANGLED BANNER."

Matrimony—Quaint remarks thereon by an Old Writer—The Young Lady and Middle-aged Bachelor—Sketch of the Song—Cupboard Courtiers—Disaster of the Wooer.

SONG—"THERE CAM' A YOUNG MAN TO MY DADDY'S DOOR."

Meeting of the Old Harpers—Ireland's Great Lyrical Bard, Thomas Moore—The Planets—The Moon in the Ascendant—Habitual Grumblers.

SONG—"THEY MAY RAIL AT THIS LIFE."

King James V. of Scotland—His popularity among his people—' King of the Commons'—His eccentricities and curious adventures—His Poetical and Musical talents.

SONG—"JOLLY BEGGAR."

Prices—Reserved Seats, 2s ; Second Seats, 1s ; Gallery, 6d.

N.B.—Books of the Words, Price 6d. each, to be had at the Hall.

DOORS OPEN AT 7—TO COMMENCE AT 8 O'CLOCK.

MR TEMPLETON'S SECOND ENTERTAINMENT
Will take place, in the above Hall, on Monday Evening, March 8.

THEATRE ROYAL,
HEAD OF HOPE STREET, GLASGOW.
SOLE LESSEES and MANAGERS   BY ROYAL LETTERS PATENT.   Messrs GLOVER & FRANCIS

CARL ROSA

OPERA COMPANY

FOR FOUR NIGHTS ONLY.

ARTISTES:

MISS JULIA GAYLORD	MISS LUCY FRANKLEIN
MISS JOSEPHINE YORKE	MRS AYNSLEY COOK
MDLLE. IDA CORANI	MISS L. GRAHAM

MDLLE. OSTAVA TORRIANI

MR HENRY NORDBLOM	MR LUDWIG
MR PERCY BLANDFORD	MR AYNSLEY COOK
MR J. W. TURNER	MR ARTHUR HOWELL
MR CHARLES LYALL	MR MULLER
MR FRED. C. PACKARD	MR STANLEY POTTER
MR F. H. CELLI	MR H. BROOKLYN

AND
MR SANTLEY

FULL BAND & CHORUS
Conductor - - - - Mr CARL ROSA

Stage Manager	For CARL ROSA	Mr ARTHUR HOWELL
Acting Manager		Mr JOSEPH D. M'LAREN

On WEDNESDAY Evening, 7th March
FIRST PRODUCTION IN GLASGOW OF WAGNER'S ----1847

FLYING DUTCHMAN

THE ENGLISH VERSION BY JOHN P. JACKSON.

The Dutchman (Van der Decken)	MR BARTLEY	Erik (a Forester of Daland)	MR FRED. C. PACKARD
Daland (Master of a Norwegian Ship)	MR AYNSLEY COOK	Mary (Senta's old Nurse)	Miss LUCY FRANKLEIN
Senta (his Daughter)	Mdlle. OSTAVA TORRIANI	The Steersman of Daland's Ship	Mr J. W. TURNER
	Crew of the Norwegian Vessel.	The Crew of the "Flying Dutchman."	Village Maidens.

Scene - - - - - THE NORWEGIAN COAST.

Thursday	F. H. Cowen's PAULINE.
Friday	Beethoven's FIDELIO.

Saturday, March 10th, GRAND

DAY PERFORMANCE
OF WAGNER'S

FLYING DUTCHMAN

SATURDAY Evening   Benedict's LILY OF KILLARNEY

The GASCON COMPANY

Including MISS CARLOTTA LECLERCQ will shortly appear.

Doors open every Evening at 7, commence at 7.30. SATURDAY—Doors open at 6.30, commence at 7
PRICES—Private Boxes, £5 5s, £2 2s & £1 10s;
Dress Circle & Stalls, 7s 6d; Side Boxes, 5s; Pit Stalls, 4s;
Pit, 2s 6d; Amphitheatre, 1s 6d; Gallery, 1s.

CHILDREN IN ARMS NOT ADMITTED

Scenic Artist	Mr D. S. SMITH
Musical Director	Mr GEORGE PURDY
Acting Manager	Mr E. L. KNAPP

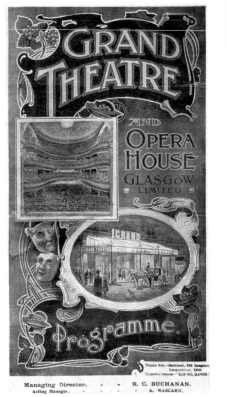

27　Throughout the period of this study, the Glasgow middle classes were offered a range of cultural events, from popular musical recitals to grand opera and Shakespeare, as advertised on these posters.

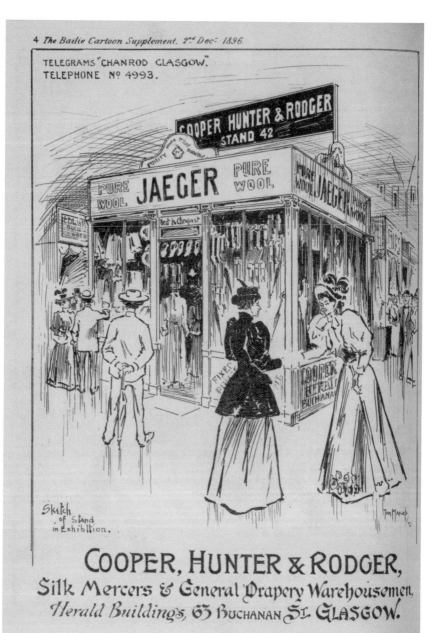

28 Two fashionable Glasgow ladies out shopping, one of the perennial pleasures of city life. 'Cooper, Hunter and Rodger', *The Bailie*, 1896.

BAZAAR, KELVINSIDE (NORTH) UNITED PRESBYTERIAN CHURCH.

29   Not only were the names of stallholders at charity bazaars published in newspapers: their portraits were reproduced in *The Bailie*, a magazine devoted to the affairs of the Glasgow middle class. 'Bazaar, Kelvinside United Presbyterian Church', *The Bailie*, 1895.

30 (*above*) By the last decades of the nineteenth century women frequently undertook cycling trips, often unaccompanied. In this photograph of the Napier family, *c.*1900, the women were joined by two men and a dog.

31 Two women in a rowing boat, *c.*1900. By the 1880s rowing had become a common pastime for women, especially for those with holiday homes that bordered the Clyde.

1880s and 1890s. Even when it did not result in financial ruin, economic crises dictated harsh economies and a tougher financial regime than was enjoyed in the halcyon times of prosperity. Far from evincing the affluence of the bourgeoisie and assuming a purely symbolic significance, in hard times the account books could be a tyranny which enslaved many middle-class housewives.

Personnel management, supervision and book keeping were only some of the skills that the Victorian housewife had to master. Recent studies of consumerism in the nineteenth century have focused on shopping as a pleasure and its role in modernity and the creation of a public space for women.[70] However, shopping for provisions or for household goods was also a business which required time and careful management. It is likely that it was the wives of only the lower middle class who personally had to shop for basic necessities, though even they may have preferred to have their provisions delivered. Cooks were more likely than wives to scour the butcher, baker or greengrocer stores for quality produce, though once the goods had been delivered, the lady of the house doubtless checked them.

Shopping for other household items was another matter and clearly one for which the middle-class housewife took personal responsibility. In Georgiana Coats's account to her husband of one particular morning's activities, shopping loomed large:

> This morning I went to the church with *old clothes* for the Mission – and to a music shop to get 'exercises' for O.M. [her daughter] and 'Rest in the Lord' for you – then to the Arcade to recover my feathers which were being curled – then to MacLehose for *Story of Ida* then to 'Registry for Girls' with some *newspapers* and *old shoes* and *brown paper* and a soap-box for *firewood*. 'Julius Caesar' is to be acted by Mr. Beerbohm Tree on Saturday night. I am trying to get tickets for Olive and me. She says it would be such a help to her in understanding the play. We may not likely get seats, there will be such a rush. [. . .] I went to More's (stationer) and bought (without paying) 6/- of copy books for 5/-, 4 dozen pencils, 3 dozen penholders and nibs, and 2 dozen 1/2d india-rubbers, all for 10/- for the Zenana Box . . . and then to Miss Japp with the 'copies'.[71]

Shopping as pleasure and shopping as business could clearly shade into each other. While none of the errands recounted by Mrs Coats could be categorised as 'necessities', they were very much part of her household duties and ones in which she took some pride in executing with efficiency and thrift. Certainly when she was away from home helping her sister after childbirth, and Mr Coats had to deputise for her, he found the tasks time consuming. After she had reprimanded him for not writing, he complained that he had had 'not a minute' for letters: his morning had been taken up going to the 'bank, Foulis [bookshop], printer, hat shop, etc.';[72] admittedly, he had spent some time at work in the afternoon, before returning to read to the children, have supper and entertain a guest in the evening. His rather plaintive tone suggests that he categorised these activities as chores rather than pleasure.

While married women could enjoy a degree of autonomy in relation to household expenditure, Rappaport has noted that credit could be a source of tension between husbands and wives, especially when the latter overindulged their taste for the latest fashions.[73] When Maryanne Mac-Ewen secretly bought a new carpet for one of the rooms in the family home, the reason given for the illicit purchase by her grandson was not that his grandfather wanted to keep a tight rein on the household budget, but that he disliked 'ostentation and up-to-date furnishings'. Whether William MacEwen was merely cloaking his parsimony in self-righteous frugality is speculative, but what is clear is that his wife was able to buy such an expensive item without his consent or indeed his knowledge.[74]

As already emphasised, Victorian women treated housekeeping as a serious enterprise, requiring an array of skills in which they took pride and from which they derived a sense of satisfaction and self-worth. Whether they held their role in the same high regard as the editor of the the *Waverley Journal* is less certain. The journal took a progressive view on employment for middle-class women and was equally positive about the worth of the unpaid work of the mistress of a household. The role of the housewife was equated with the role of any professional who was charged with the task of training subordinates:

> The mistress of a family should feel it to be a part of her mission to teach those who are under her care, the best way of doing housework. There is a right and a wrong way of cooking, washing, churning, sweeping, etc. There are principles of economy which a good housewife must recognise in the use of fuel and food, in the adaptation of means to ends, and in the time and use of different departments of labour. The mistress of a family has quite as good a right to feel proud of a notable housekeeper, the wife of some farmer, mechanic or common labourer trained under her care, as a lawyer has to feel proud of some eminent advocate or jurist whom he trained to the profession.[75]

Training, and by implication delegation, were the quintessential compo-
nents of housekeeping. To train someone properly in the skills of domestic economy, however, presumably required some direct knowledge and
experience. Janet Story's description of her aunt's fastidiousness gives
credence to the view that at least some women felt compelled literally
to roll up their sleeves and muck in with the servants:

> she not only knew how the work of a house should be done, and how
> to keep her servants well up to the mark, but she could put a hand to
> it herself if she thought it advisable, and work with the best. A light
> duster lay handy in every room of her well-ordered house, and how
> often have I watched her carefully removing the layer of dust that will
> form in spite of the most careful morning cleaning, or deftly polish-
> ing her beautiful Oriental vases and lacquered boxes and making them
> shine with a double radiance.[76]

The servants probably awaited this formidable aunt's inspections with
trepidation, and may have found her exacting standards too high a price
to pay for sound training in housekeeping. She was similarly rigorous
about bed linen and mattresses, which she insisted be aired with great
regularity, often doing the task herself as she doubted that others would
perform it to her satisfaction.

The experience of the young Elizabeth Thomson suggests that there
was more than simple delegation involved in the running of a household.
When Elizabeth's mother died in 1830, leaving a young family of four,
and her aunt who had taken over her sister's responsibilities left to return
to her husband, Elizabeth, then about sixteen, and her younger sister were
left in charge of the household, with only a cook to help. Elizabeth found
the task of maintaining a well-ordered household and the sheer hard work
of housework extremely onerous:

> We brought down all the spare blankets and had them shaken and
> washed, and then put them by nicely folded and covered. We counted
> and classified linen and laboriously mended some that needed repair.
> [. . .] I sewed long seams of old sheets, overcasting the selvedges
> together, cutting them up the middle and hemming the sides.[77]

Elizabeth was unusual in having such responsibilities so early in life. In
time her duties took their toll and she had to be treated for headaches
by being bled with leeches. Janet Story's opinion of her aunt, a contemporary of Elizabeth Thomson, that she 'was of a type much more common
than it is now', might indicate that such direct involvement in physical

labour by the mistress of a prosperous household was rare by the end of the century. However, while the burden of the daily physical exertions of housework undoubtedly fell on servants in the wealthier families, *in extremis* it was not uncommon for the lady of the house to undertake some of the more arduous toils of housework.

Georgiana Coats employed two general servants in her town house. As described above, she directed and supervised household operations with vim and assurance, though even she was driven to distraction by the amount of work required to prepare the family's summer holiday on the island of Rothesay. The house had lain unoccupied over the winter and, much to her chagrin, was cold, damp, musty and dirty. Her usual staff was reduced to one house-girl, 'Wee Mary', who was aided by a local woman. Despite their combined efforts, Georgiana needed to tell her husband to delay bringing down the children. Obviously fraught and weary, she nonetheless managed to lace her letter with her usual humour and self-mockery:

> Picture of Red House as follows – Woman and wee Mary out in the field (11.30) beating carpets. Dining-room first wash and first fire – still only 'two bags' in house – drawing room furniture, pictures, etc., all in glorious confusion – first fire on by which I am seated feeling neuralgic.
>
> [. . .] Pillows and blankets were positively wet with damp and beds steamed as they were put to the fire. [. . .] It would be utter madness to bring down the bairns tomorrow although the day is gloriously fine. The house is cold and raw and decidedly *damp*; [. . .].
>
> Oh, I wish I was up on the top of the Eiffel Tower, for there I would be high up away from painters and varnish and islands that can't get coals handy. It's an awful nuisance picking one's way out of confusion. [. . .] The men are very decent, although they did take our pails and tubs and baths for their paints – four of our utensils aforenamed were in their possession thus.
>
> [. . .] What a dreadful waste of time this letter is! I ought to be washing potatoes and dusting pictures and grumbling.
>
> Oh what a waste of time! My feet were so cold with slippers I had to put on boots and I have a shawl on my *shoulders* and one on my *head* – yes and rings, real diamonds, on my hands.[78]

Georgiana Coats's cavilling at the amount of work she had to do was partly related to the magnitude of the task which confronted her, but it probably also had something to do with the fact that she was not used to physical toil. Her reference to the incongruity between her disheveled clothing and jewelled hands indicates that she felt menial work of this kind to be inconsonant with her status.

The burdens involved in housekeeping duties were recognised by the Hydro hotels, which specialised in providing healthy holidays for the middle classes. By the 1890s their advertising literature was making its pitch as a more comfortable and enjoyable alternative to the tradition of renting a holiday home for the summer, particularly for the wife: 'businessmen return to work, refreshed by their holiday [. . .] their wives and children also having benefited very much from the relief of housekeeping follow.'[79] The rituals of domesticity were certainly thick with social meaning and spoke of the status and prosperity of the family as well as reflecting the competence of the mistress of the house: however, they also had functional significance, involved heavy responsibilities, considerable time, and on occasions physical labour.

Mollie McEwan, with no servants to call on, expected her young daughters to pitch in to help with the housework. Mollie wrote to her sister-in-law, with some pride, that her five-year-old middle daughter was an excellent helpmeet:

[she] can do more work than Isabel and delights in doing it, she has lots of work to do now as I have not kept a nurse or house-girl for some months past, it is really a pleasure to see her so willing to do anything that is to be done. Tonight she set the table nicely for her Papa to eat dinner, as he does not come home until night.[80]

Revealingly, her description of the activities of her youngest daughter illustrates the power of the cultural construction of 'angel in the house' to shape contemporary perceptions if not actual experience. Maggie, at only two and half, did 'nothing much' but lace and unlace her shoes, read and sing hymns, eliciting the wry comment from her mother that 'she will no doubt be the lady of the house if one is required'. Those who did not have the means to employ servants to relieve them from the drudgery of housework perceived those who did as idle ladies of leisure.

Although the work of most married women was in the realm of reproduction, many middle-class women did have a productive or economic role. However, as with working-class women, their contribution was generally not reflected in the official census of employment. The percentages of married women recorded as having a source of income, let alone an occupation, was tiny in the Claremont estate, between 3 and 4 per cent until 1891, when the figure rose only to 6.2 per cent. As might be expected, most of the eighteen married women recorded as having an occupation over the five census years lived in the lower middle-class streets. Interestingly, only a minority of these women were actually living with husbands, suggesting that separation by choice or force of circumstances was responsible for these women taking employment. In 1851 all three of the women recorded as having an occupation lived with their husbands: one was a milliner whose husband was an 'attendant upon the insane', another was a teacher of dancing who was married to a miniature painter, and the other was head of a private school whose husband was a foreign wine agent. In 1891, when six wives were recorded as having an occupation, only one lived with her husband; she was employed as a dressmaker and her husband as a printer's compositor. Of the remaining five employed women, one was a lodger, three lived with one parent or both parents and one, Margaret Watson, a ladies nurse, was recorded as head of the household.

Although they occupied similar types of housing, sometimes almost next door to each other, the following women, all with young children, lived in remarkably divergent circumstances: Martha Low of 15 Carnarvon Street, an architect's assistant, had a resident husband who was an architect, three children, but also two servants; Margaret Johnston, a dressmaker of 11 Carnarvon Street, also had a resident husband, one baby son but no servants; Katherine Findlay, an artist of 23 Stanley Street, lived with one servant and four children but no husband; and Janet Findlay, a dressmaker of 8 Stanley Street, had a one-year-old son and lived with her mother.

The low numbers of married women working recorded in the census largely reflects the 'hidden' nature of their work, and the fact that it did not conform to the male norm of work which was salaried, full time, permanent, and mainly conducted outside the home. In some instances it might reflect the flawed nature of the census, for valuation rolls which recorded every piece of property in Scotland and showed the name, the value of the property, the name of the owner and the name of the tenant and occupier, indicate that women's direct participation in the market was greater than recorded in the census. For example, Mrs Agnes Austin of 77 Renfield Street was recorded in the 1881 census as having no occupation, and yet the valuation rolls record her as a dentist.[81] Many historians have documented how the census is inadequate as a complete record of women's employment.[82] Although these shortcomings have usually been pointed out in relation to working-class women, the same factors – the instructions to the enumerators, the temporary or home-based nature of much of women's work, and the ideological bias against recording female work – would appear to apply equally to the middle class.

In the 1861 census, enumerators were instructed to tabulate women under the domestic heading, 'no matter what trade or occupation she might occasionally follow', and in the 1871 census and all subsequent ones, the working population did not include shopkeepers' wives, farmers' wives, innkeepers' wives, shoemakers' wives, butchers' wives and so on, although they had previously been included.[83] This has the effect of excluding the wives of small businessmen from the occupational tables, although there may have been no real change in their role. The practice of prefixing 'wife' with the occupation of the husband was partly related to interest in occupational health, but it might also indicate that there was implicit recognition that these women performed a role in the enterprise, although in official documentation this role was unacknowledged. In 1861 fifty-seven of 168 wives were given the prefix of their husbands' occupation; by the next census in 1871, however, only twenty-three wives of 150 are so described. While this may have reflected the withdrawal of wives from the family business, it is just as likely to reflect changing census practices and the increasing tendency to define women solely in relation to the domestic sphere. For example, being described as a stationer's wife, the wife of Robert Adam, who owned a stationer's shop, was very probably involved in the business in some capacity. Similarly, Agnes MacEwan, an accountant's wife, and Marion Duncan, a minister's wife, might also have assisted in their husband's work, yet these women were classified as 'dependants' and were formally placed in the 'unoccupied' category. Very occasionally, a wife was formally recognised as assisting her husband in his profession or business, as was the case with the above-mentioned Martha Low, recorded in the 1871 census as an 'architect's assistant'. This was almost certainly a more frequent practice than the census indicates, but such an overt acknowledgement of a wife's role is rare in official documentation.

As described in chapter 4, work and home were far from being distinct and separate realms, even by the end of the century. A number of professionals within teaching, medicine, the law and of course the ministry remained home-based throughout the nineteenth century and indeed the twentieth, making it more possible for wives to continue to play a role in their husbands' business or occupation. In Glasgow and other urban centres there were married women who, alongside their husbands, managed and sometimes owned important educational establishments. The Young Ladies' Institutions, for example, were owned mainly by men, but some were run by a husband and wife team: the St Vincent Street Seminary was originally owned and managed by the Reverend George Panton and his wife; about 1872 it changed premises and proprietors, with Mr and Mrs William Begbie as managers and Mrs and Miss Sturrock taking over around 1878.[84]

The wives and daughters of the many ministers who lived in the area at various census points undoubtedly played a central role in the life of the church. As Mrs Story self-effacingly put it:

> I did not neglect the duties of a clergyman's wife, but carried on the various organisations commenced by my mother-in-law, herself a model minister's wife. A Sunday School was new to me, and I found it rather hard at first. [. . .] I had so large a class that I felt that I could not properly attend to them all and I looked about among the young ladies of the parish for one who would be kind enough to assist me in my not very arduous work.[85]

The wives of academics often played an equally vital role in their husbands' working lives. Although it was the husband who was recognised as having the career, and it was he who gained the public credit for the work performed, the wife was often his unacknowledged partner and unpaid assistant.[86] Anna Geddes, wife of the eminent sociologist Patrick Geddes, was *de facto* his secretary as well as running the home and raising a family; she even took responsibility for moving all his books from one room to another and putting his study in order. After one particularly busy day she wrote: 'Have been busy with your multitudinous papers all morning and now must go and attend to some business re home etc.'[87] There are other fairly typical examples from Glasgow University: the MacEwen family acknowledged Sir William's eldest daughter as his secretary when he became Professor of Surgery, and Elma Story served in the same capacity when her father was Principal in the 1890s. Such roles were not formally recognised in the census statistics.

William Thomson, later Lord Kelvin, received advice from his wife Margaret when negotiating business and professional matters. Margaret, the daughter of the textile magnate Alexander Crum, was perhaps more consonant with this world than her physicist husband and consequently more shrewd in her judgements. When he was negotiating a post with a London firm in 1867, she not only counselled him on how to word his letter of application, she urged him to undertake some 'hard bargaining'.[88]

There are occasional indications that the wives could wield influence as well as a pen. When two appointments were to be made at Glasgow Royal Infirmary, a letter was written to Mrs Story suggesting a possible candidate for one of the positions. The writer no doubt believed that while Principal Story was the member of the Board of the hospital, his wife would not only be a conduit for this information but perhaps even influence his decision.[89]

Throughout their thirty-seven years of married life, Agnes Syme, wife of the scientist Joseph Lister, had been not only his intimate daily companion, but his professional partner. As the couple had no children, she was able to give Joseph and his work her undivided attention. Her father had been a surgeon and, according to one of Lister's biographers, 'She was as much at home in the laboratory as in the drawing room.'[90] In a letter to his father, Lister described the part his wife had played in his preparing a paper to be delivered to the Medico-Chirurgical Society of Edinburgh: 'she wrote for seven hours one day and eight the next, and was most helpful in suggestions as to words and arrangement of sentences.'[91] Mrs Lister was not only her husband's amanuensis, she regularly assisted with experiments in the laboratory of their home in Woodside Place. On at least one occasion, in a display of selfless devotion to either her husband or to the pursuit of knowledge, she helped Lister in experiments to determine safe quantities of chloroform for anaesthesia by breathing the gas herself.[92]

On a financial level, women occasionally revealed an intimate knowledge of family business and its accounts. In 1883, for example, Jean Crystal, wife of a recently deceased wine merchant of Queens Crescent, submitted a detailed inventory as one of his executors, demonstrating considerable familiarity with the business.[93] The many letters and speeches of Isabella Elder demonstrate her knowledge and familiarity with her husband's shipbuilding business; this stood her in good stead when she took over the helm of the business on his premature death in 1869 (her role as a widow is discussed in chapter 6).[94] Kate Cranston, on the other hand, had established her business as a restaurateur a dozen or more years before her marriage to John Cochrane, an engineer, in 1892.[95] Her husband's financial support, however, did allow her to acquire new properties and to employ the foremost Glasgow architects, including Charles Rennie Mackintosh, to design the interiors of her famous teashops. She continued in business throughout her twenty-five years of marriage. Not only was Miss Cranston (as she continued to be known) a successful businesswoman: employing the best avant-garde architects to work on her restaurants and her family homes, she was a significant patron of the arts in turn-of-the-century Glasgow.

As described in chapter 4, it was not uncommon for doctors with a modest practice to have a shop attached to their premises. In the 1870s William Walker's practice in Pollockshaws had a shop adjacent, the back apartment of which served as a consulting room. His wife supervised the chemist shop and 'not only produced and maintained order in the shop, but learned to dispense and even prescribe for common ailments'.[96] There were still a number of small business premises in the second half of the century, particularly in retail, which were either nearby or adjoined to the home, where any boundary between a purely domestic realm and a business sphere was a fiction. As the Claremont estate was built specifically for residential purposes, there were no retail outlets in the area. However, there were a number of married women who contributed to the family income by taking in boarders and lodgers. Most of these women lived in Carnarvon and Stanley Streets, the lower middle-class areas. In these two streets alone, in 1891, sixteen married couples took in boarders or lodgers, although none of the wives had a recorded occupation. Alfred Bury, a mechanical engineer, and his wife Catherine, both in their forties, lived with their five children as well as Catherine's sister and a young male boarder, also a mechanical engineer. Already large households might still take in a lodger. Thomas Stokes, an iron worker, and his wife Sarah had eight children at home, ranging in age from twenty-eight to five. Sarah's elderly mother also lived with them. Nevertheless, they found room in their eight-roomed home for a twenty-one-year-old civil engineer who boarded with them. Both of these examples are of boarders rather than lodgers, which means that the provision of meals was added to the work involved in offering suitable accommodation. As Mary Ryan has observed of women who took in boarders in Oneida County, New York, the domestic location of these women occluded not only their economic contribution to the family income, but the fact that they were effectively managing the equivalent of hotels and restaurants. Thus if the definition of business is expanded, these women could be conceived as being involved in business activity and market relations, even though they operated within the domestic sphere.[97]

The numbers of middle-class married women who engaged directly in the labour market or independently in business were clearly small, as their economic role was circumscribed by the law, their responsibilities as mothers and by prevailing ideologies. However, despite these constraints numbers of married women, sometimes driven by necessity, found ways of contributing to the family income, often from within the domestic sphere where they could combine an economic role with housekeeping and child-rearing. For many more married women, Peterson's pithy observation that men's work *was* women's work seems apposite.[98] The wives of professionals, academics and businessmen regularly assisted and supported their husbands in their careers and their businesses in numerous ways and frequently demonstrated a familiarity and expertise with the world of work. Indeed the extent of wives' involvement in the work and career of their husbands suggests that women were routinely expected to acquire some knowledge of the business or career of their husbands and assume some role in it, albeit a subordinate one. This should not be altogether surprising. As historians of the early modern period have repeatedly pointed out, wives had long made an important (though supplementary) economic contribution.[99] The 'hidden' nature of women's contribution to enterprise has been well documented by Davidoff and Hall for the early nineteenth century; the evidence indicates that there was no diminution of this role as the century progressed. For women throughout the hierarchy of the middle classes, motherhood was probably the most constraining factor limiting their active participation. It was surely no accident that the women who were most directly involved in productive, commercial or professional activity were those without children, such as Isabella Elder, Agnes Lister and Kate Cranston. This is not to deny the influence of ideologies of domesticity in constraining women's economic role; domestic discourses did not preclude such a role, but – in conjunction with a number of other factors – they shaped the form it could take and defined how it was viewed.

The notion that nineteenth century middle-class wives were economically impotent derives as much from the formal legal position of women's property rights as it does from their absence from the census of employment. The accepted wisdom is that married women, who were granted no separate property of their own until 1881 in Scotland, were not significant property owners or wealthy in their own right.[100] Under the common law, the husband assumed legal possession and control over all movable property that she might have owned as a single woman, and any property and earnings that might come to her during marriage was further designated as belonging to him; as discussed in chapter 3, this *jus mariti* was enshrined in Scottish law until abolished by the Married Women's Property (Scotland) Act 1881.

Until the last two decades of the nineteenth century, however, Scottish wives had greater legal rights of inheritance and legal protection of their property than their English counterparts.[101] In that a bilateral system of inheritance operated, Scottish property laws were a variant on the system which was widespread throughout continental Europe and similar to the English law in the early modern period. Marriage was spoken of as bringing about a communion of goods between the spouses, the *communio bonorum*, which related only to movable property. While the husband was given complete power of administration over this common fund, by virtue of his *jus mariti*, on the husband's death, the wife or her representatives were entitled to a fixed share of these 'goods in communion', commonly a third if there were children, and half if there were no children. If the wife predeceased the husband, then her representatives took her share. With regard to heritable property, on the husband's death the wife was entitled to terce, a liferent of a third of the property, while on the death of the wife, the husband was entitled to courtesy, a liferent of the whole his wife's heritable property.

Although the Scottish system was by no means based on a married couple's equality of rights, nonetheless there were community property elements in it; on marriage the spouses' movable goods merged into one fund, albeit the husband's, and on the dissolution of the marriage the fund was split up again into certain defined shares. Thus in Scotland the position with regard to women's property rights was much more complex than in England, where the conventional trajectory is portrayed as one of increasing constriction and a decline in rights and status in the course of the eighteenth and nineteenth centuries.[102] By 1881, through a series of statutes in the second half of the century, this system had changed to the type of separate property system which existed in England, and had lost most of its communal elements. Despite the greater recognition of wives' property rights in Scottish law, the *jus mariti* was under vigorous attack in the second half of the century in Scotland as well as England.[103]

A more common form of resistance to legal inequalities was the practice of making marriage contracts. These were important legal devices for circumventing the normal property consequences of marriage. The practice had originated among the upper classes in earlier centuries and owed more to the desire to protect family property from being squandered by a spendthrift husband than to any concern to preserve female independence. However, both legal and anecdotal evidence suggests that this was not the main reason underlying the practice among the middle classes during the nineteenth century and that they were used as a means of negotiating the law rather than being subject to its control. As Eric M. Clive and has noted, the most compelling reason for contracting out of the normal property consequences of marriage was to exclude the husband's *jus mariti*; after the introduction of the Married Women's Property Act in 1881 there was thus a decline in the incidence of marriage contracts.[104] Janet Story recounted an anecdote that gives further credence to the view that marriage contracts were used as a deliberate strategy by middle-class women to guarantee proprietorial autonomy and independence rather than as a means of protecting family property. One of Mrs Story's cousins had married late in life and refused to draw up a marriage settlement, 'insisting that her little fortune should pass entirely into the control of her husband, arguing that the restrictions of a legal settlement showed great want of confidence in the honour and integrity of the husband'. The observations that her cousin 'had imbibed a rather medieval view as to the inability of women to manage their own property', and that all her cousin's friends had counselled her to make a settlement, are suggestive of the way in which marriage settlements were regarded routinely as mechanisms to protect women's property and as a means to give them control over their wealth.[105]

This tale, cautionary in itself, had a bizarre dénouement: the cousin and her husband separated; when she predeceased him, all her property went to him instead of to her younger sister. To compound the sister's financial misery, when the husband died, he left every last penny of his estate, which had been considerably augmented by his wife's fortune of £7,000, to the doctor with whom he had been residing. This seemed such a breach of the principles of natural justice and equity to a spinster aunt of the husband's that she left a legacy of £7,000 to the hapless sister, 'as she considered her nephew had unfairly appropriated his wife's money, to which her sister ought rightfully to have succeeded'. Women, married and single, also demonstrated this particular brand of female solidarity by commonly making legacies to their female relatives, expressly excluding the legacy from the jurisdiction of the *jus mariti*. Indeed one of the justifications for changes to married women's property law was that the law should be altered in order to reflect beliefs and practices which were commonplace in society. One supporter of the 1880 Bill argued that it 'proposed to do nothing more than was now done every day by such as ante-nuptial contracts'.[106] Therefore the legal changes that culminated in the 1881 Married Women's Property Act were not simply the result of campaigns by women's rights activists, but reflected more broadly based beliefs, expressed in lived legal relations, that women should have full rights over the use and disposal of their own property. As Amy Erickson has noted of the early modern period in England, common practice often departed significantly from common law in the settlement of inheritance and marriage.[107] Thus there was a marked disparity between the disadvantaged position of married women under the law and the actuality of the powers given to them by marriage contracts.

Antenuptial contracts, exclusion clauses in wills, and trusts, ensured that wives had more control and rights over the property they had before marriage, and any that might come to them in the course of the marriage, than the formal legal position would allow. There were several ways by which the husband's *jus mariti* and rights of administration could be excluded from the marriage settlement. In some cases the husband explicitly renounced his *jus mariti* in the antenuptial contract, as did Robert Orr Sawyer when he married Jessie Patrick White in 1862, and Humphrey Crum Ewing did when he married Janet Creelman Robson in July 1862.[108] In other cases the wife could convey her property to herself antenuptially, excluding, with her husband's consent, his *jus mariti* and the right of administration. Such was the case with the marriage contract trust made between William Henry Houldsworth and Elizabeth Graham Crum in August 1862:

> And this indenture further witnesseth, that in consideration of the said intended marriage, the said Elizabeth Graham Crum with the consent of her intended husband, assigns, disposes, conveys and makes over from her and her heirs and successors to and in favour of the said trustees, the estate real and personal now belonging and pertaining to her, or which she may acquire or succeed to during the marriage, or whatever belongs to her at the time of her death, to be held by them in trust.[109]

This marriage contract ensured that all property Elizabeth owned as a single woman and all property that she might acquire during her marriage would remain her own property, and would usually be held in trust for her. It also ensured that any income and interest resulting from this separate property belonged to the wife, and the wife alone. Davidoff and Hall have suggested that trusts essentially gave power to male family members to use women's property as capital, while women received only income from the trust. Essentially they characterise women as passive recipients of unearned income, whereas the power to invest or dispose of the capital resided with men.[110] There is evidence from these marriage contract trusts, however, that women were certainly not without power and influence with regard to their property and how it was disposed. In the marriage contract of Elizabeth Graham Crum, any decision to sell or give away her property rested upon her sole judgement as 'her receipts alone shall be sufficient discharges to the said trustees'. The contract also stated that 'no investment shall be made during the life of the said Elizabeth Graham Crum, without her previous consent in writing'.[111]

Women could also have considerable autonomy over their financial affairs and were not necessarily dependent on others to organise their business affairs. Constance Robertson Blackie's pre-marriage property of £3,000 worth of stocks and shares was transferred over to the control of trustees upon her marriage to Hugh McMaster Ewing. However, referring to her business dealings, her father noted in a letter that 'her investments have been made in concert with her brothers, but whilst I have advised on them, she has always looked after them herself'.[112] Marriage contracts could also enable women to retain aspects of their separate property outside the confines of a trust fund. Constance Robertson Blackie's contract contained provisions by which she was able to retain parts of her property. Similarly, any legacy of £200 or less was not to be signed over to her trustees.

So intricate and detailed were the provisions of marriage contracts and so frequently were they used, that for many middle-class couples, with varying degrees of wealth, marriage was an occasion to visit the solicitor's office as much as an occasion to celebrate. The resultant contract bestowed at least some economic rights to married women whose formal legal position was otherwise hedged with restrictions. The evidence from these contracts suggests that the disjuncture between the theory and the practice of the law allowed married women a certain degree of independence, autonomy, freedom of action and a separate legal identity with regard to their own property.

Nineteenty-century married women may have been defined primarily by domesticity and motherhood, but the meanings and experience of both varied significantly. Women with little or no domestic help, mainly those in the lower middle class, would have spent most of their time and energy on child-rearing and housekeeping with little opportunity to escape either. If these women were mired in domesticity, with lack of money and social cachet denying them access to a recreational public life, some at least seemed to embrace those roles and to derive some gratification and self-worth from dutifully carrying them out. Mollie Macewan's and Margaret McCallum's correspondence exemplifies the contention made by many feminist historians that conceptions of moral motherhood empowered women and were a source of personal pride and public credit. While women of the more affluent middle classes were also charged with the responsibilities of housekeeping and child-rearing, their physical labours were significantly lighter. However, they invested much of their time and emotions in their children and commanded authority and respect for demonstrating efficiency as household managers. For some, such as Mary Ann Macfarlane and Elizabeth Thomson, the effort of discharging their duties efficiently drove them to illness and nervous exhaustion. The time and money available to prosperous middle-class women extended their world beyond the home and enabled many to enjoy travel, widely socialise, attend balls, dinners, theatres and concerts and participate in the feminine public sphere of philanthropy. Discourse of domesticity certainly played a role in structuring middle-class women's lives; however the material reality of their lives varied significantly and there were different ways of interpreting and enacting the meaning of domesticity and motherhood; for some it involved immersion in the world of home and family, for others it could also sanction engagement with the public world of church and philanthropy, and for others it meant judicious juggling of their private commitments with their social and public life.

6

I Will Survive

THROUGHOUT THE NINETEENTH CENTURY, attitudes towards lone women, especially spinsters, were not only ambivalent and shifting, but occasionally contradictory. For much of the century, single women supposedly constituted a problem as they were unable to support themselves: they became a 'problem' in the later nineteenth century when they could and did choose to support themselves. So although concerns about the financial burden represented by unmarried women remained a constituent part of prevalent attitudes, moral opprobrium was additionally directed towards those who elected to pursue financial independence. That some women actively chose singledom over marriage was held to be responsible in large part for the *fin-de-siècle* 'crisis in masculinity'. By this period too, female celibacy was frowned upon in a context of falling birth rates and eugenicist concerns about the quality of the race and the future of the Empire.

So, despite some attempts to portray spinsterhood in a less unfavourable light, it remained the case that single women were viewed through the prism of dominant gender ideologies which saw marriage and motherhood as the true destiny of women. Those whose experience was outside the normative bounds of womanhood were viewed as aberrant. Spinsters were regarded as a social anomaly, usually as objects of pity. As Harriet observed to the eponymous heroine in Jane Austen's *Emma*, 'You will be an old maid! And that's so dreadful!'[1]

Bourgeois respectability required that women live in a state of social and economic dependence on men: those who could not achieve this by acquiring a husband needed the protection of another male relative so that they could be contained within the safe haven of a family unit. Those women who did not live under the protection of a man and who were not attached to a family were regarded as a social problem, prey to the twin dangers of poverty and sexual impropriety. At worst, they could be seen as presenting a sexual threat to the married: at best, they were viewed as 'incomplete' and probably embittered if they were unable to

fulfil their biological destiny as wives and mothers. The terms used –
redundancy, superfluity – serve to underscore the view that the *only* role
for woman was as wife and mother: only then could she be needed, be
useful. This is the view epitomised by Harriet's exclamation to Emma.
The spinster could not be fulfilled, was bound to be marginalised and to
lead a 'peripheral existence'.[2]

There was certainly also a school of thought which regarded single
women as morally pure, and which sought to offset the pejorative por-
trayal of the embittered spinster by investing the role with qualities of
virginity and sacrifice.[3] For this view, the single state could be 'blessed',
imbued with the 'virtues of celibacy and spiritual love'.[4] These were,
however, negative virtues: like the nun, the spinster was not distracted by
carnal or maternal concerns, and was free to devote herself to a different
kind of service to others.

Official discourses about unmarried women were imbued with an
ambivalence that is epitomised in these two views. Consequently, when
single women sought economic independence or pursued a life outside
the confines of the family unit, they did so in the light of a dominant
ideological construction of spinsterhood as a problematic category.
Prevailing attitudes towards spinsterhood meant that the countless
single women who immersed themselves in philanthropic work, who
tended the sick, or dedicated their lives to converting the 'heathen' at
home or abroad, did so in an ideological climate which saw them as
sublimating their frustrated maternal or sexual drives into a form of
surrogate motherhood.

Nevertheless, the dominant images of nineteenth-century spinsters
should not be confused with their actual experience, nor should they
blind one to the extent to which it was possible for these women to
exercise agency and choice. The middle-class spinster could subvert
such imagery to construct a more positive view. As Martha Vicinus
has pointed out: 'Women did not reject the Victorian myths but reinterpreted them.'[5] A more positive role could also be constructed from the
alternative ideologies and discourses which circulated among the middle
classes.

Although the rhetoric of separate spheres stressed the complementarity of gender roles, an integral element of this ideology was the notion
of female dependence. The concept of dependence had a variety of meanings: as well as encompassing economic and social dependence, it was also
emblematic of the established gender and authority relations of Victorian
society. For Victorians, dependence on men was not only regarded as the

Table 11   Female-headed households as a percentage of all households, 1851–1891

	Overall	Carnarvon/ Stanley Streets	Other streets
1851	23.0	29.2	20.1
1861	25.3	35.1	19.4
1871	36.5	49.6	26.1
1881	35.5	46.3	25.6
1891	40.0	49.4	30.5

norm, but as a badge of respectability, the natural and proper state of womanhood. For William Greg, writing in 1868, domestic servants were admirable because 'they fulfil both essentials of woman's being; *they are supported by, and they minister to, men.*'[6] Women were assumed to need and to seek the support and protection of a male, whether father, husband, brother or even a more distant male relative. Yet, as discussed in chapter 2, the predominance of the male-headed nuclear family is not supported by our analysis of middle-class family and household structure in Glasgow. Only a minority of families, across the period 1851 to 1891 and across the spectrum from higher middle class to lower, conformed to this type. Even that most 'dependent' of groups, unmarried women, were by no means invariably living under the protection of a male household head.

Indeed, a significant feature of our findings is the high percentage of households that were headed by women. As Table 11 shows, 23 per cent of households in 1851 were headed by a woman, and by 1891 this had risen to no less than 40 per cent of all households. In some parts of the area, the proportion was even higher, with a marked difference according to socio-economic status. In Stanley and Carnarvon Streets, which housed the families of the lower middle class, 29.2 per cent of households were headed by a woman in 1851, compared with the overall figure of 23 per cent. By 1891 the percentage was nearly 50 compared with 40 per cent overall. Furthermore, in Stanley Street by 1891 there were more female- than male-headed households. Clearly, the new housing in Stanley and Carnarvon Streets, which was smaller and often in the form of tenement flats, attracted lone women with or without families. Significantly, in the larger terraced houses of the substantial bourgeoisie there also was an increasing proportion of households headed by women, rising from just over 20 per cent in 1851 to over 30 per cent by 1891.

In the early part of the period, the majority of female household heads, 77 per cent, were widows. However, the corresponding figure for 1891 was just under 60 per cent. The increase in female heads in the more affluent streets, where industrial magnates, merchants and professionals lived, was largely made up of unmarried women, while the number of widows remained more or less constant. By 1891 widows only just outnumbered spinsters in the more substantial properties. In Carnarvon and Stanley Streets, however, widowed and single women increased in very similar proportions, although widows consistently outnumbered spinsters by two to one as household heads. Thus, although widows made up an increasing proportion of household heads in the lower middle-class area, female-headed households were by no means confined to the less well-off streets and smaller houses. In 1891 the mean house size across the area was 8.3 rooms: for female-headed houses the figure was not much less at 7.1.

Far from being socially and economically dependent on a man, many of these women apparently had dependants of their own. Just over half of single women over thirty (51.4 per cent) lived with a female head in 1851, and this figure rose steadily until 1891, when two-thirds (66.7 per cent) of such women lived in a female-headed household. Of widowed women, only a minority lived in a male-headed household: never more than a quarter of all widows, the proportion fell as low as 6.4 per cent in 1881. Therefore of all lone women over thirty, whether widowed or unmarried, the proportion living in a household headed by a man fell from a third at the start of the period to a quarter by the end, a social reality which belied the cultural convention of female dependence.

Furthermore, there were numerous men living in households headed by women. Table 12 shows their relationships to the head of household: there were wider kin − brothers, brothers-in-law, uncles and nephews of the head − as well as adult sons. In addition, the number of men living as boarders in female-headed households peaked in 1881, with an even greater number of lodgers recorded for 1871. In fact, the percentage of all single *men* over thirty living in a female-headed household was between 30 and 38 per cent across the period. This raises the question of the social reality lying behind the formal categorisation of the census. To what extent were these men really seen as 'subordinate' or 'dependent' members of these female-headed households? It seems to us that the 'head of household' designation did have real empirical force: most male kin,

Table 12 Males in female-headed households, 1851–1891

	1851	1861	1871	1881	1891
Brother	–	1	6	7	5
Brother-in-law	1	–	1	1	1
Father	–	–	–	–	1
Grandson	2	–	4	4	8
Great-nephew	–	1	–	–	–
Nephew	2	5	4	8	5
Son-in-law	1	–	–	1	–
Son (adult)	24	29	39	50	51
Stepson	–	1	–	–	–
Uncle	–	–	–	–	2
Visitor	4	2	3	7	6
Boarder	1	12	12	20	15
Lodger	4	7	37	30	28
Total	39	58	106	128	122

for instance, were at least one generation younger than the female household head. Boarders and lodgers, although part of an economic relationship, were in no sense involved in running the household. Furthermore, if the same designation is to be taken as meaningful when the household head is a man, it seems perverse to deny it significance when applied to a woman. The fact that between a third and a half of all households in the area were, at various periods, headed by women *must* have impacted upon notions of female dependence. Contemporaries could see that widows and spinsters did not invariably live under the aegis of male social and economic protection: indeed they often offered such protection to others. At times, parts of this middle-class area must have resembled the village of Mrs Gaskell's *Cranford*, where 'all the holders of houses above a certain rent are women'.[7]

The widespread view of spinsters as constituting a 'social problem' was fuelled both by demographic realities and by a popular perception which exaggerated these realities. W. R. Greg complained of the 'enormous and increasing number of single women in the nation [. . .] which, positively and relatively, is indicative of an unwholesome social state, and is both productive and prognostic of much wretchedness and wrong'.[8] The existence of an increasing number of women who were 'compelled to live an independent and incomplete existence of their own' was viewed as symptomatic of a greater social malaise.[9]

Never-married women did indeed considerably outnumber never-married men in the second half of the nineteenth century. There were just over a million unmarried women aged twenty-five and over in Britain in 1851: it has been reckoned that this amounted to over 400,000 'surplus' women.[10] In Scotland, ratios of never-married in 1861 were 135 per 1,000 and 201 per 1,000 for males and females respectively: in 1891 the figures were 134 per 1,000 for men and 187 per 1,000 for women.[11] In England, the trend was for more rather than fewer unmarried women as the century progressed.[12] In particular, however, it was the middle-class spinster who was the focus of social commentary, and who has attracted most attention from historians. As discussed in chapter 2, it has even been argued that among the upper middle class only a minority of women ever married.[13] Vicinus, however, argues that their numbers were actually not large, and the attention given to them was disproportionate: they were a highly visible group.[14] Their numbers, too, were perhaps increasing more rapidly than among the working class. It is indeed the case that, in our middle-class area, numbers of spinsters rose across the period, in contrast to the figures for Scotland as a whole.

When did an unmarried woman become an old maid? Mean age at first marriage for women in Victorian Scotland was consistently just over twenty-five years.[15] In this study of Glasgow, the percentage of all women of twenty-six and over who were never married rose steadily from just over a third (35.3%) in 1851 to half in 1891 (50.9%). Given the relatively late age at first marriage, it is probably more meaningful to take thirty as the cut-off point beyond which single women were definitely 'on the shelf' in popular perception, even if some (like Charlotte Brontë, spokeswoman for the Victorian spinster) did marry after that age. Table 13 shows never-married women over thirty as a proportion of all women over that age: it also reiterates the proportion who lived in female-headed households.

These are very revealing figures. Spinsterhood was common, and increasingly so through the later part of the century. By 1891 44 per cent of all women over thirty had never married. The increasing incidence of celibacy is shown also in a detailed analysis of the 1891 census returns (see Table 14): to some extent the falling proportion of never-married women by decadal cohort may be an indication that some women did indeed marry in their thirties and forties; but it also suggests that celibacy had been less common in women born in the first three decades of the century. Victorian commentators were right: there *were* large numbers of

Table 13   **Never-married women over 30 years old, 1851–1891**

	Number of women	% of cohort	% in female-headed households
1851	71	31.7	50.7
1861	95	31.7	52.6
1871	139	41.0	60.9
1881	145	40.5	59.3
1891	187	44.1	65.2

Table 14   **Never-married women by age cohort, 1891**

Age	31–40	41–50	51–60	61–70	71+
Number	83	44	38	9	13
% of all	60.1	46.8	40.4	17.7	35.1

single women in the middle class; and these numbers *were* increasing as the century progressed. Contemporaries, however, were too prone to seeing these 'redundant' or 'surplus' women as single simply because they could not get a husband. But women did not outnumber men in anything like these proportions. In fact, in our study area in 1891, there were eighty-nine never-married men over the age of thirty and twenty-six widowers – altogether comprising 43.6 per cent of all men over thirty. There were thus not enough men to go round, to be sure: but there were marriageable men as well as marriageable women who remained unwed. The 'problem' of surplus women, while resting on a numerical reality, was socially constructed in that it derived from perceptions of spinsters as economically dependent. The eighty-nine ageing bachelors of the Claremont estate were not seen as constituting an economic problem.

By way of explanation for the prevalence of spinsters, demographers have pointed to the disparity in mortality rates between the sexes, especially among infants. In addition, rates of emigration were higher for males than for females.[16] Stephen Ruggles has argued that the 'problem' was particularly great among the middle class: 'Bourgeois men delayed marriage: many bourgeois women did not marry at all.'[17] Because the possibility of upward social mobility via marriage was greater for women, and because these men often chose brides younger than themselves, he maintains that the pool of women competing for husbands was greater than the demand.

While there is no doubt that demographic and social factors played a part in accounting for 'surplus' women in Victorian middle-class society, such explanations rest on an assumption that all women would have chosen to marry if only they could have succeeded in snaring the glittering prize of a husband. That is certainly the view underlying many contemporary attitudes towards spinsters, those who had failed to 'compete' successfully. Not even a more positive view of spinsterhood makes it sound attractive: virtues of denial, selflessness and sublimation may have served to improve its image without necessarily providing powerful motives for remaining single. As shown in chapter 3, however, there is evidence that women were aware of the loss of independence, the removal from the parental home and the sheer uncertainty that for them accompanied marriage. Some women *chose* not to marry.

Missing out on motherhood, especially when that role had been elevated to mythic status in Victorian domestic ideology, was generally agreed to be the hardest part of the spinster's lot. Motherhood, rather than sex, was the urge that spinsters were primarily supposed to be sublimating. However, in an era before widespread contraception, the two were virtually inseparable, and there was a subtext which tacitly acknowledged the dangers of suppressed sexuality.[18] Nevertheless, motherhood was the largest missing piece in the 'incomplete life'. It was Ruskin's depriving his wife Effie of children, rather than sexual gratification, by refusing to consummate the marriage that was presented as grounds for its annulment.[19] In fact, the almost inevitable arrival of children shortly after marriage may have acted as a deterrent for some women. Frances Murray, visiting a friend in the London suburbs, wrote disparagingly of the 'conventional dullness' of her hostess's domestic life, which she described as 'the apotheosis of babydom'.[20] Even Queen Victoria regarded pregnancy and childbirth as unfortunate concomitants of wedded bliss.

Marriage was recognised as being something of a lottery, and women were conscious of the legal, social and financial restrictions that followed from it. Ruth Freeman and Patricia Klaus have pointed to the influence of the suffrage movement and the proto-feminist movement accompanying it, and Cecile Dauphin to the advent of the 'New Woman', as signs of a growing readiness among middle-class women to forgo marriage.[21] They and Vicinus evidence the rise of female communities for 'independent women' in both Britain and America in the later part of the century.[22] For the increasing band of women who wished to pursue higher education, an independent career or the social and sexual companionship of other women, marriage was at best a hindrance and at worst an impossibility.

Women who chose not to marry constituted an even more challenging problem than those who simply could not. Even before the advent of the 'New Woman', there were those who elected to remain single.[23] Perhaps as a consequence of increased expectations of the marital state, married women themselves were increasingly expressing dissatisfaction with it.[24] By the end of the century, gender relations and gender identities were, it is argued, in a state of flux. Female scepticism about marriage and women's growing sense of independence supposedly led to a 'crisis in masculinity', and to the social construction of homosexualities.[25]

Choosing not to marry was easier for the well-to-do. Jane Austen (who herself turned down at least one offer of marriage) gave Emma an ironic but telling riposte to Harriet's exclamation of dread: 'Never mind, Harriet, I shall not be a poor old maid, and it is poverty only which makes celibacy contemptible to a generous public! [. . .] a single woman of good fortune is always respectable, and may be as sensible and pleasant as anybody else.'[26] Two generations later, although concern centred on the social as well as financial plight of spinsters, some truth remained in Emma's assessment. For the better off, spinsterhood could bestow a degree of autonomy that marriage never could. The unmarried woman who headed a household had real social independence. By 1891 there were forty of these women in our area – more than one in eight of all household heads. Miss Mary Perry, who features in the story of Madeleine Smith, had inherited the family home in West Renfrew Street (half a mile east of our area) – or at least a liferent in it, for she had married siblings living elsewhere. In the mid-1850s she developed a friendship with Madeleine's lover Emile L'Angelier, who often visited her in her home, sometimes staying for dinner. When he lay dying, it was Miss Perry who was summoned and who kissed and wept over his body. It was also Miss Perry who then went to Blythswood Square and demanded an interview with Madeleine's mother. Clearly this was a woman who enjoyed the freedom to form her own friendships, carry on an independent social life, and take decisive action when she felt it necessary. Nigel Morland acknowledged this in his book *That Nice Miss Smith* in noting that she had 'an adequate allowance and complete freedom'.[27] Various writers on the Madeleine Smith case have therefore seen Miss Perry as a sentimental old lady with a maternal interest in L'Angelier and his love affairs.

Douglas MacGowan describes her as 'matronly' and Henry Blyth states that she had always seen L'Angelier as a son.[28] In fact, Mary Perry, born in Glasgow in 1817, was thirty-nine at the time of L'Angelier's death: he was five years younger. Women in their late thirties seldom look maternally on men some five years younger than themselves (unless, of course, they are married to them). Whatever Miss Perry's feelings, she was free to pursue this relationship – whatever its nature – with a man widely considered to be disreputable, without apparent loss of that respectability which contemporaries saw as her defining characteristic.

Another spinster involved in a murder case headed a household in our study area. Marion Gilchrist was the victim in what became known as the Oscar Slater case. She lived at 15 Queen's Terrace, and in 1891 was fifty-eight years old and of 'independent means'. She also lived alone, except for one servant. One evening in December 1908 Miss Gilchrist, now seventy-six, sent the servant out for a newspaper. In the brief time she was away, someone entered the flat and bludgeoned her to death with a chair leg. The case became a *cause célèbre* when, after Slater's conviction, Sir Arthur Conan Doyle and others campaigned for his release on the reasonable grounds that there was nothing whatsoever to connect him with the murder. Slater was eventually freed in 1927.

Like Mary Perry, Marion Gilchrist had sole occupation of what had been the parental home: in 1881 she had been at the same address, the daughter of an absent parent or parents. She was in financially comfortable circumstances. Robbery was agreed to have been the motive for murder: some jewellery was missing, and at least one writer on the case speaks darkly of a missing will and the possible involvement of a young male relative.[29] According to another source, her collection of jewellery was worth £3,000 at the time of her death.[30] Miss Gilchrist also owned property on what became the site of Glasgow's Barras market.[31] The catalogue of her possessions, which were sold by auction in 1909, reinforces the impression of material wealth. The jewellery collection ran to sixty-four lots, and included such items as a 'superb diamond necklace, with large centre stone, in all 45 stones, with gold mounts'. In all, her estate was valued at £15,578.[32] Unfortunately, little is known of her personality or daily life, beyond her disastrous interest in the evening news.

Spinsters who lived in households headed by others may have enjoyed less autonomy than did Miss Perry and Miss Gilchrist. Table 15 shows the household situation of all unmarried women over thirty. The two most frequent categories, apart from household head itself, were clearly those of daughter and sister. (The table also shows these as a percentage of all

Table 15 Relationship of never-married women over 30 to head of household, 1851–1891

	1851	1861	1871	1881	1891
Aunt	1	2	3	1	4
Boarder	–	2	1	3	4
Cousin	–	–	2	2	–
Daughter	21	21	39	37	59
Governess	1	1	1	–	1
Great-aunt	1	–	–	–	–
Housekeeper	1	–	–	–	–
Head	10	16	31	31	40
Lodger	–	2	2	–	5
Niece	3	2	6	4	6
Nurse	–	1	–	–	6
Sister-in-law	5	3	6	5	6
Sister	22	30	37	50	43
Visitor	6	13	10	11	13
Percentage					
Daughter	29.6	22.6	25.3	25.5	31.5
Sister	31.0	32.3	27.3	34.5	23.0

never-married women.) This fits with the conventional picture of spinsters as usually living at home with parents or siblings, of acting 'primarily as surrogate mother and housewife'.[33] In particular, unmarried sisters are seen as frequently acting as 'wives' to their brothers.[34] As Table 13 makes clear, however, closer examination of the domestic situation of spinsters does not square with this view. As pointed out in chapter 2, this was not a common scenario. A majority of daughters and sisters lived in *female*-headed households, and were not the social dependants of men.

The stereotypical sister housekeeping for her brother was more likely to be living (and sometimes working) with one or more sisters, thus putting the relationship on a more equal footing than the conventional view of the stereotype would imply. The daughter who remained in the family home was likely, in the demographic way of things, to spend longer living with Mother than with Father. Margaret White of Woodside Terrace lived with her widowed mother in 1861, 1871 and 1881. At some point before 1891 Mrs White must have died, for at that date Margaret lived alone – except for the housemaid, tablemaid and cook.

The cyclical nature of family formation and the ways in which the form of the family and the status of individuals within it changed over time (see chapter 2) applies equally to the situation of single women. The daughter who stayed in the family home in due course became the head of household. In 1851 Agnes Arnot lived with her parents and worked as a teacher of languages: in 1861, now forty, she lived with her widowed mother of seventy-four and was an annuitant. She left the area (or married) presumably after the death of her mother. Sisters Elizabeth and Dorothea Auchterlonie did stay on together. In 1861, aged thirty and twenty-four, they lived with both parents and their younger brother. By 1871 Elizabeth, as the elder daughter, had become head of household, and Dorothea lived with her. Thus two 'daughters' became one 'head' and one 'sister'.

As Table 15 shows, not all unmarried women lived as daughters or sisters of the household head. In 1861 Janet Pattison, aged forty and single, lived with her unmarried aunt in Woodlands Terrace. Margaret Smith lived in the household headed by her bachelor uncle Thomas McClymont. Census returns from 1861 to 1881 show that her two nephews also lived with them throughout their childhood, and it looks very much as if Margaret had been largely responsible for their upbringing. There are at least two analogous instances of this. The prevailing levels of mortality and concomitant reliance on kin (described in chapter 2) meant that some unmarried women were very closely involved with children and could become surrogate mothers, especially to nephews and nieces. Janet Gallacher, who was single and forty-one in 1881, lived with her widowed brother-in-law and his seven children, whose ages ranged from twenty-four down to eight. However, this was not as common as literary and anecdotal evidence might suggest: there was only one other example in the whole of the 1881 census sample.

The census also provides evidence that, especially in the later decades of the century, there were employment opportunities for single middle-class women. The range of acceptable employment for women, especially of the lower middle class, cited as crucial in permitting women to delay or reject marriage, was widening.[35] For some women employment was a necessity rather than a vocation, something to be done before or, at worst, instead of marriage. For others, however, it was the preferred option. In 1892, having worked in the East End of London, Frances Murray's youngest sister Evelyn went to China to work in the China Inland

Mission.[36] Single women by this time were beginning to express a desire for the independence that employment brought. Frances Murray herself wrote to her father as early as 1867, urging him to 'remember that if your daughter is not earning a fortune, the desire is strong enough in her to do so. I would like [. . .] to take up something that will earn me a living, if it be nothing more than sewing machine work for a shop!'[37] Kate Maitland, having fulfilled familial obligations as 'orphan-cousin' by keeping house for Joseph Coats until his marriage, used her freedom not to marry but to train as a nurse.[38]

As Ellen Jordan argues, middle-class women – individually and, especially, collectively – were active agents in claiming a place in the labour market, rather than merely being the beneficiaries of the changing requirements of capital.[39] Their desire for employment was rooted in existing middle-class values, not running counter to them. Notions of independence, self-reliance and industriousness were integral to those values. One way in which they could be given expression, still within the ideology of separate spheres, was by a devotion to philanthropy.

For others, who sought alternative routes to independence and self-fulfillment, religious and political ideology could conjoin with middle-class values to provide powerful alternatives to that of domesticity. Nineteenth-century Christianity's exaltation of women as the moral and spiritual superiors of men could be appropriated and reconceived to give women licence to enter the public sphere and to create a public identity which could encompass productive work. Similarly, the language of radical liberalism, with its stress on liberty, independence and free will, could be mobilised to sanction involvement in paid employment. Certainly for the women of the Murray family, the right to employment flowed naturally from the family's long-held religious and radical liberal principles.

Whether out of necessity or vocation, many single women in the Claremont estate did have paid work. Census returns show that of the 233 unmarried women between the ages of twenty-five and sixty in 1891, thirty-one were employees, thirty-four were self-employed, and fifteen employed others – in all some 34 per cent of the total. The limitations of census returns as a complete guide to women's involvement with the labour market were pointed out in relation to married women in the previous chapter. The record of single women's employment, summarised in Table 16, should therefore also be treated as representing a minimum figure for women who earned money: such occasional paid work as giving lessons or sewing, for instance, would not have been recorded. The table further illustrates the inadequacies of the census when the numbers

Table 16 **Employment of never-married women aged over 16, 1851–1891***

Occupation	1851	1861	1871	1881	1891
Governess	11	13	12	12	8
Teacher	14	14	20	23	23
Dressmaker etc.	3	10	19	13	55
Landlady	–	1	2	7	2
Companion	–	–	3	1	–
Retail trade	1	2	1	1	1
Shop assistant	–	3	–	5	20
Clerical	–	–	–	5	20
Nurse	–	–	–	2	7
Artist	–	1	–	–	3
Student	–	–	–	–	4
Other	–	–	2	–	3
Total	29	44	59	69	146
% of all never-married women	14.1	16.7	19.0	24.0	37.8

*Excluding domestic servants

of single women recorded as landladies are taken into account. While the maximum is reflected as only seven in 1881, the same censuses show many cases where no formal occupation is listed but women were clearly acting in that capacity. The unmarried Buchanan sisters in 1881, for example, had two boarders; and in 1891 there were thirty-eight lodgers and eighteen boarders living in female-headed households.

Table 16 bears out the view that towards the end of the century there was an opening-up of opportunities in education and employment for middle-class women. Certainly more single women over sixteen had a formal occupation: over a third of all women in this category worked even according to the rigorous criteria of the census. There are also signs of the formalising and professionalising of female occupations. By 1891 there were 'certificated' teachers and 'infants' teachers as well as those giving private lessons or working in small private schools. In 1891, too, the first instance of female 'students' is recorded. And nursing was becoming professionalised: nurses all described themselves as 'trained' or 'certificated'. Even dressmaking offered training and qualifications of a sort, at such institutions as the Anglo-Parisian School of Dresscutting,

Dressmaking and Millinery (Proprietrix Madam Grohe) at Charing Cross Mansions, adjoining the study area, or at the Rodmure School of Dress, which was advertised as 'the Principal School in Britain', with Madame Levine as manageress.[40]

Throughout the period, education and dressmaking were the staple occupations for single middle-class women. They were often cited as providing little more than poverty wages.[41] However, both occupations provided employment at several levels. In education, this varied from live-in governesses to those women running boarding schools who were effectively businesswomen. There were several of the latter in our area at different periods, many more in Glasgow as a whole. One random edition of the local newspaper in 1871 carried advertisements for twelve 'schools for young ladies' in the city, nearly all run by women.[42] Running a boarding school required not only capital outlay and premises, but some measure of business acumen. In 1851 four sisters – Jane, Agnes, Margaret and Elizabeth Miller – kept a school at 8 Woodside Crescent, a large house in one of the most prestigious terraces in the area. They, like other school heads, employed men: they advertised that when the school reopened on 2 August 1853 it would 'have the attendance of the same eminent masters'.[43] Schools were often run by unmarried sisters, for whom it was important to establish their respectability and middle-class credentials:

> The Misses Reid (daughters of the late Hugh Reid Esq, Town Clerk, Ayr) beg leave to intimate to the Ladies of Sandyford and the vicinity, that they intend opening an Establishment for the Board and Education of Young Ladies, at No 3 Corunna St, St Vincent Crescent, on Tuesday the 10th May, when they hope, by strict attention to the mental and moral culture of the Young Ladies placed under their charge, to merit a share of public patronage.[44]

At the other end of the scale, the Victorian governess has been portrayed as occupying a lonely and insecure position somewhere between servant and social equal.[45] 'Going as a governess' has been seen as a desperate last resort for the genteel spinster reduced by the death or bankruptcy of parents to making her own financial way in the world. Countless novels, with *Jane Eyre* and *Agnes Grey* as the best-known examples, have made the governess a still-familiar figure, whether awaiting tribulations or rewards. In fact, as table 6 shows, there were never large numbers of governesses in our middle-class area; and several of those women who were recorded as such in fact lived and worked in schools as teachers rather than in the classic situation with a family. Others were daughters of the household, who must have been either working elsewhere on a daily basis, or at home briefly from a residential post.

The socially anomalous position of governesses is reflected in the way they are recorded in census returns – some as 'servant', some as 'visitor' and some simply as 'governess' or 'domestic governess', the latter nicely echoing 'domestic servant'. There are also some indications that it was desirable to have a non-Scots governess: of the eleven governesses in 1851, four were born in England and two in the West Indies, a proportion similarly reflected in subsequent censuses. The distance between 'down-trodden' governess and independent keeper-of-school was not great and could often be bridged. Charlotte Brontë herself turned down the chance of co-ownership of the school in Roe Head at which she had taught.[46] In our area, Euphemia Turnbull was in 1851 a twenty-year-old 'governess' in the Misses Millers' school at Woodside Crescent; two years later, when the elder Miss Miller gave notification of her retirement, the 'interest of her business' was to pass to Miss Turnbull.[47] By the later decades of the century governesses might be well-educated professionals and be expected to teach considerabably more than basic genteel accomplishments.[48] In 1880 'ladies requiring governesses holding University certificates' were invited to apply to Miss Galloway, Secretary of the Glasgow branch of the Association for the Higher Education of Women.[49]

The other 'staple' occupation for single middle-class women was dress-making and millinery: by 1891 it made up by far the largest group of working single women. Like education, the occupation could encompass a range of situations, from successful businesswoman to sweated worker.[50] Given the nature of the study area, one would expect to find more of the former than the latter. Indeed, in 1891 twelve of the fifty-five unmarried women dressmakers were employers of others, and a further nineteen were self-employed. Because it could be done from home, dressmaking could be combined with other money-making activities, especially taking lodgers. Sisters Magdaline and Elizabeth Swinton were both self-employed dressmakers, but they also had one boarder and two lodgers in their Stanley Street home. Also in Stanley Street, Mary McCulloch and her two sisters were all dressmakers: Mary, the household head, was an employer; her two sisters were self-employed and were doing well enough to keep a resident domestic servant. Dressmaking, like the keeping of a school, was something that sisters living together often undertook. It cannot have been terribly lucrative – all unmarried dress-makers in 1891 lived in Claremont, Carnarvon or Stanley Streets – but the fact that they lived in this area at all, alongside professional and clerical men, illustrates that dressmaking and millinery could provide an adequate income for single women. This seems to represent a change from the situation in mid-century, when there were only three unmarried dressmakers in the area, one visitor and two sisters, the latter living with their widowed mother.

The chief differences across the period lie in the increased numbers of women who were employed, and in the range of jobs at which they worked. In 1851 almost the only work available to single women was as a teacher or dressmaker. This range expanded in the last quarter of the century, with jobs as shop assistants and in clerical work featuring prominently after 1871. To some extent this is a result of the expansion of the lower middle-class part of the study area: women of the upper bourgeoisie generally did not take jobs as shop assistants. But it is also indicative of a growing range of opportunities for women in non-manual occupations. This reflects a national trend: as Freeman and Klaus argue, middle-class spinsters were 'no longer restricted to needlework or governessing'.[51] Jobs like telegraphist and typist appear by 1891. Establishments like that of the 'Misses Bertram' offered classes in typewriting and shorthand.[52] Single women worked as assistants in shops selling fruit, stationery, ironmongery and, above all, clothes, hats and shoes. As explained below, this is indicative of the range of retail businesses actually run by women.

To some extent, male attitudes towards women's employment and independence were also changing in the light of this increased involvement in the labour market. Sir William MacEwen, addressing nurses in 1891, voiced the opinion that 'Every girl, whatever her station in life may be, ought to be trained not only to be a useful member of society, but to be self-supporting. She ought to be taught a profession, an occupation or a trade whereby she could earn her own livelihood.'[53] No doubt tailoring his speech to his audience, Sir William evidently wanted to endorse the idea of careers for single women: 'The unmarried woman who quietly and perseveringly makes her own way through life, unsupported by others [. . .] is worthy of the highest respect. [. . .] There are numerous channels into which a woman's energy may be tuned and many which have not yet been tapped.' However, his relatively enlightened view is still informed by notions of biological determinism. The single woman must 'retain her womanly characteristics'. Some occupations 'may afford but a barren field for her womanly nature'. Nursing, of course, is an occupation for which women are uniquely suited: it is 'a sphere for women's work'. Indeed 'a woman is a born nurse'.

Thus for MacEwen 'separate spheres' could accommodate changes in women's employment: women working outside the home could be reconciled with existing ideologies about gender roles, provided that they were working in occupations which mirrored their domestic responsibilities (caring for the sick, teaching children and so on) and did not run counter to received notions of their 'natural' role. Just as women could use current ideologies to justify being 'self-supporting', so too could men come to terms with a new role for women if that was forged within existing ideological parameters.

It was in particular the financial plight of middle-class spinsters that exercised social commentators in the second half of the nineteenth century.[54] Working-class single women could find employment, at least while they were relatively young.[55] For the middle class there were during much of the period few culturally acceptable routes to employment, and it is here that the 'redundant woman' was thought to create a particular problem. Even after the turn of the century, Ada Moore found it necessary to write her plea on behalf of 'decayed gentlewomen'.[56] She argued for better education and training for women, and better female wages. Clara Collet similarly drew attention to the poor pay of graduate women teachers, at around £120 a year.[57] Moore referred to 'a large army of unmarried gentlewomen who are practically destitute'.[58] Vicinus, while taking care not to exaggerate their plight and acknowledging some increased opportunities in education and employment towards the end of the century, also argues that middle-class spinsters often lived in genteel poverty, which as they aged became desperate.[59] Others echo this view of the 'desperation' of the ageing spinster.[60]

There is, however, no compelling evidence from the census returns for our study area that these concerns reflected reality. It may be the case that the truly impoverished moved out into solidly working-class districts, despite the existence of modest tenement flats in the area. Spinster-headed households were distributed fairly evenly across the area: in 1891 they comprised 15.2 per cent of households in Carnarvon and Stanley Streets, and 13.9 per cent over the whole area. It is difficult to test the assertion, made by Vicinus and others, that single women, especially from the lower end of the middle-class spectrum, lapsed into desperate poverty as they aged. In 1881, for example, there were twenty-seven unmarried women aged sixty and over in the study area. Twenty-one lived in households headed by women – either as heads themselves or as sisters of heads. Their households had a mean of 1.4 resident servants and 8.2 rooms. The fact that so many spinsters were able to remain in an area which, although

Table 17 Retail businesses in Sauchiehall and Buchanan Streets, 1851–1891

	1851	1861	1871	1881	1891
Total Buchanan St	124	138	135	90	63
Female retailers	10	5	10	2	2
Percentage	8.1	3.6	7.4	2.2	3.2
Total Sauchiehall St	92	155	202	133	86
Female retailers	21	34	47	12	14
Percentage	22.8	22.0	23.3	9.0	16.3
Percentage female overall	14.4	13.3	16.9	6.3	10.7

varied in its socio-economic composition, was solidly middle class, suggests that many unmarried women were able to maintain a reasonable standard of living.

While census returns for our study area mention only a handful of women engaged in retail trade, other sources provide a more complete picture.[61] Post Office Directories and Valuation Rolls of Glasgow from the 1860s to the 1880s show that there was a range of female-run businesses, especially in Sauchiehall Street, one of the main and most prosperous shopping thoroughfares. A good number dealt with clothing – dressmakers, milliners, staymakers, clothiers, hosiers, furriers, sellers of baby-linen. The domestic interior, too, was a principal focus of female businesses: there were furnishers, upholsterers, china shops, a lace warehouse and a specialist in Berlin wool. Women were also fruiterers, greengrocers, poulterers. And the Dining Rooms of Mrs McIntosh, recorded in 1872, were a forerunner of the teashop movement, that, by the early years of the twentieth century, had become 'so prominent a feature of Glasgow life' that the 'business career' of Miss Cranston made her one of only five women in a contemporary list of the 500 prominent citizens of Glasgow.[62] In short, the evidence from these and other directories suggests that much of the retail commerce of the city was based on the public servicing of the domestic world, and involved women selling to women.[63]

Table 17 sets out the results of an analysis of retail businesses in Sauchiehall and Buchanan Streets, the city's main shopping area, from directories across the census period. Unfortunately, by the last quarter of the century many businesses are listed only by company names, and neither the nature of the business nor the sex of the owner is recorded. This may help to account for the drop in the percentage of female shop-keepers, which on Sauchiehall Street had earlier been consistent at 22–23 per cent. The directories do indicate that women's involvement in retail did not decline before 1871, and in terms of absolute numbers, their involvement increased until 1871.

The Valuation Rolls provide a fuller picture than the Post Office Directories of the extent of female involvement in retail, being a record of the value of all property in the city with the occupational details of the tenants. For example the directories of 1861 and 1881 contain twenty-three and seven women respectively who owned coffee houses, eating houses or restaurants, whereas the Valuation Rolls for the same years have respective figures of thirty-six and forty-five. Not only does this indicate that the directories underestimate the number of women in the restaurant and coffee-shop trades, but that they erroneously indicate a trend of decline after 1871. Indeed, an analysis of the Valuation Rolls for the years 1861 and 1881 reveals that between those years the numbers of women in business in Glasgow trebled from 600 to just over 1,500.[64] Most of these businesses were in retail and were concentrated in the area of food, drink and clothing. Nonetheless, Valuation Rolls also show that some women worked outside these traditional areas as plumbers, dentists, drug-gists, coal dealers, accountants, photographers and designers. The vast majority of these businesses would have been small-scale and would have been run by women from the lower middle class or even working class. However, owners of retail businesses in the more prosperous areas would have had substantial concerns and of course there were the exceptions such as Miss Cranston who were at the helm of large and prosperous businesses.

The persistence of small businesses and family-owned businesses in the British economy has been well established.[65] The rise of the department store and large retail outlets towards the end of the century did not signal the demise of small-scale concerns and the 'corner shop'. Women may have played a marginal role in business because of their preponderance in petty retail, although, as Charles Wilson has argued, developments in retailing and consumer industries have had a much more significant role in economic growth and development than had previously been acknowledged.[66] What is clear is that there is no evidence of any with-drawal of women from the retail business in Victorian Glasgow. Women continued to occupy a significant role in the city's retail industry, even if concentrated in petty retail with a sprinkling in other areas. However, women's occupations had always clustered in these areas, as Peter Earle's research on late seventeenth- and early eighteenth-century London has shown.[67]

Both contemporaries and modern historians have given less attention to the Victorian widow than to the spinster, perhaps because widows were not seen as exuding the aura of social, moral and psychological dubiety that clung to unmarried women. There was also, of course, the iconic figure of the Widow Queen who, having provided an example of the ideal wife and mother, was between her husband's death in 1861 and her own in 1901 the epitome of widowhood. They were, nevertheless, women who were not living in that desired state of dependence and servitude portrayed by William Greg and others as women's natural and essential role, and in that sense constituted another 'problem'.

In fact, the Victorian widow, although enjoying the same property rights as men, has generally been viewed as economically vulnerable and lacking the legal rights enjoyed by her seventeenth-century counterpart.[68] Ada Moore, writing in 1904, argued that the plight of 'poverty stricken' widows, unlike that of elderly spinsters, was well known and had properly attracted sympathy.[69] Cynthia Curran paints a very bleak picture of the middle-class widow, left almost penniless, unable to work, and forced onto the grudging hospitality of relatives.[70] She argues that it was difficult for widows to remain in the family home after the death of their husband, and that in a period with no state pensions and little use of insurance, they were unlikely to be left with enough money to live on.[71] Olwen Hufton found a similar reliance on charity among middle-class widows of the eighteenth century.[72] Davidoff and Hall refer to widows being forced to move in with a male relative after the death of their husbands in order to seek social and economic support.[73]

However, it is worth reiterating that, among our sample, it was relatively rare for widows to do so: only sixteen of the ninety-five widows in 1891 lived in a male-headed household, while seventy-four headed their own household. This had been the case throughout the census period, for in 1851 only ten of the forty-nine widows were recorded in male-headed households, and of those three were only visiting. A mere three widows lived as 'mother' or 'mother-in-law' with their offspring. Indeed, widows could offer support as well as seek it: when William MacEwen's mother died in 1863, he and his father went to live with an elderly widowed aunt.[74] This all suggests that middle-class widows of the second half of the nineteenth century were in a position to retain more

Table 18   Widows, 1851–1891

	1851	1861	1871	1881	1891
Widows	49	63	85	78	95
Married women	148	169	150	162	162
Widows as % of all ever-married	24.9	27.2	36.2	32.5	37.0
Mean age of widows	56.8	57.6	59.2	60.4	61.9

financial and social independence than a conventional picture would allow.

There was no shortage of widows. Women outlived men in Victorian Britain.[75] Furthermore, husbands tended to be older than wives: as mentioned above, in our sample, married men were an average of seven years older than married women. Table 18 shows that the absolute number of widows was rising: more tellingly, they made up an increasing proportion of all ever-married women (excluding servants). As the age-profile of the population as a whole was getting older, one would expect more widows. This is supported by the mean age of widows, which increased steadily across the period. The additions to the housing stock in the area were mostly for the less wealthy, which may have led to a differential take-up by lone women. Nevertheless, it is instructive to note that widows comprised a quarter of all ever-married women in mid-century, and well over a third by its closing decade.

Widowhood naturally became a more likely prospect with age. By 1891 there were ninety-eight women over the age of sixty (there were only sixty-four men); fifty-five of them were widows, twenty-two were spinsters and only twenty-one were married. The employment of servants meant that even in old age, many of these women continued to live independently, in the sense that they headed their own households. The oldest head of household in 1891 was Janet Fullarton, a ninety-nine-year-old widow, who lived alone except for a cook and a housemaid.

The family situation of widows was far less varied than that of spinsters. Contrary to the view that widows had to seek a home with relatives, in our sample they were overwhelmingly heads of household. As discussed in chapter 2, widowed mothers generally did not move in with their offspring. From 1851 to 1881 the percentage of widows living as mother or mother-in-law was always a mere 6 or 7 per cent. In 1891 this jumped to nearly 15 per cent. It is hard to see any particular reason for this change, though it may be related to the increasing age of widows: resident mothers and mothers–in–law were older on average than widows in general (ten years older in 1891 and fourteen years older in 1881); this suggests that mothers tended to move in with offspring – if at all – only in extreme old age. By 1891 there were more very elderly widows in the area.

It is difficult to test this suggestion by tracing resident mothers through successive censuses to see if they did indeed spend some time living independently before moving in with offspring. Of the fourteen mothers and mothers–in–law of 1891, only one can be found in the area ten years earlier, which may lend some support to the thesis. Those widows who eventually moved in with adult children seem to have done so literally as a last resort.

Not all widows were particularly elderly, and some headed households with dependent children. Ten of the forty-nine widows in 1851 were under fifty years old. The youngest was Eliza Hamilton, aged only twenty-two and with two infant daughters; they were living with her in-laws. The remaining 'young widows' all headed their own households, and seven had dependent children. In fact, in 1851, forty-three children under the age of sixteen lived in a female-headed household. By 1891 this had risen to sixty-one children. The widowed Elizabeth Bannerman lived with as many as nine children in Stanley Street. Others were in a better financial position: Frances Orr had five children at home in Woodside Crescent (three of them under sixteen), but also had seven servants to help care for them.

Rates of remarriage for our sample cannot be computed. In England, they seem to have been lower in the nineteenth century than they had been in the early modern period, although Barbara Todd finds a decrease in remarrying from the seventeenth century.[76] For the earlier period, this has been attributed as much to women's lesser need to remarry as to any inability to do so. For the nineteenth century, however, there has been a tendency to explain the phenomenon in terms of widows' lack of appeal to men who were increasingly looking to young brides (if indeed they were not eschewing marriage altogether), and to their financially poor position.[77] Certainly, like spinsters, widows faced a shortage of eligible men, which worsened as they aged.

As for length of widowhood, Jane Bannerman of Woodside Place was widowed by the time of the 1851 census, when she was thirty-eight, and appears on each successive census up to 1881. Throughout this time, she

Table 19 Widows' sources of income, 1851–1891*

	1851	1861	1871	1881	1891
Blank	11	33	38	42	15
Annuitant	24	16	23	19	12
Companion	–	–	1	–	2
Dividends	–	–	8	6	–
Dressmaker	–	1	3	1	2
Landlady	1	2	3	2	2
Military pension	–	–	1	–	2
Nurse	–	2	1	2	–
Private means	4	–	2	1	48
Proprietrix	6	7	3	4	9
Retail trade	2	–	–	–	2
Retired	–	2	–	–	–
Teacher	1	–	2	1	1
Total widows	49	63	85	78	95
% with formal occupation	8.2	7.9	8.5	7.7	9.5

* excludes domestic servants

headed the household, and always had three servants. Evidently childless, at the time of the 1851 and 1861 censuses, she had a female visitor staying with her, and in 1871, two nieces were apparently living with her. She presumably died some time between 1881 and 1891, and never remarried.

Among the reasons for widows choosing not to remarry were possible financial penalties (Peter Fisher in 1877 left his wife a life interest in his estate, but if she remarried 'it shall cease as if she were naturally dead'[78]) and certainly a loss of financial independence. The chief difficulty facing the less well-provided-for middle-class widow was her inability to obtain employment outside the home. Curran points to the (very real) obstacles in her way, and traces them to the operation of the separate spheres ideology – although it is an exaggeration to say that the widow 'was required to remain hidden from public view'.[79] It is certainly the case that widows in our sample were less likely than spinsters to have a formal occupation. Table 19 shows the sources of income of widows as recorded in the census.

The caveats about the inadequacies of the census apply as much to the employment of widows as to that of spinsters. The two or three widows in each census who were officially 'landladies', for example, were only a fraction of those with boarders or lodgers in their household. Ann McAndrew, a widow of forty-eight, had three lodgers in 1881, but nothing recorded as an occupation. Widows, even more likely than spinsters to head their own household, were in a good position to take in boarders or lodgers if it were necessary to supplement their income. They could also work. Margaret Robertson, a widow of Stanley Street, was a dressmaker in 1871 and headed a household of nine, including four children at school and one working as a clerk, a boarder who was a dressmaker and probably an employee, and two servants. Catherine Sutherland, another widowed dressmaker, employed nine women in 1881. Both women seem to have been doing considerably more than scratching a living. A few widows also worked in education. In 1851 Jane Graham, a fifty-year-old widow, shared with her unmarried sister the keeping of a school at 6 Claremont Terrace. On census night there were three other resident 'governess/teachers', ten boarding pupils, and seven domestic servants. Above all, Table 19 shows that widows commonly lived on annuities, investments or pensions – as carefully drawn-up marriage contracts intended that they should. Thus their lack of formal employment might indicate less that they were shackled by a restrictive ideology which denied them access to the labour market, but more that they were well provided for and simply free from the need to try to obtain employment.

Whether they had an occupation or not, spinsters and widows have often been portrayed as financially vulnerable and economically powerless. Even lone women who were professionally and financially successful were viewed through this dominant cultural representation. The Midlothian-born novelist Margaret Oliphant was widowed in 1859 aged thirty-one, but through her copious writings was able to support her children, educate them at Eton and Oxford, and provide financially for a small army of extended relatives, including her widowed brother and his four children, as well as adopting the children of a close friend who had died. Janet Story, a friend of the novelist, documented her largesse, caustically noting of Mrs Oliphant's decision to educate her boys at Eton that she 'was prepared for any sacrifice on her part for what she fondly imagined the good of her boys'. Janet Story commented of Mrs Oliphant's decision to adopt her friend's children that, 'she was not a rich woman, and she had children of her own.' Mrs Oliphant patently was a fairly rich woman, but it was more in keeping with the stereotype of the widow with dependants to represent her as beleaguered and financially embattled.[80] Of course not all lone women were as successful as Mrs Oliphant, but were concerns about the vulnerability of lone women well-founded, or were they influenced by conceptions of women as the dependants of men and unable to survive financially unless provided for by a male sponsor?

Some of the lone women in our area who worked for a living would also have had access to unearned income. The area encompassed wide variations in wealth, although it was solidly middle class, and this is reflected in the estates which women left behind when they died. A non-systematic sample of 452 records of Confirmations in the Glasgow Commissary Court, covering the years 1876–88, 1900 and 1914, was extracted, nearly all relating to testators resident in the west of Glasgow and a majority from our census area. Of these 452 cases (just over half of them of women), fifty-five individuals left estates valued at more than £20,000 – the very rich – a quarter of them women. In the group of estates valued between £5,000 and £20,000, women actually outnumber men by thirty-nine to thirty-four. Most of these women were widows. Some, the widows of the city's business elite, were probably the wealthiest women in Glasgow during the last quarter of the nineteenth century. They could be very wealthy indeed. Eliza Smith, a widow of Woodside Terrace, left £372,000 in 1883 – one of the largest estates in the census area, if not the whole of the city.[81] In 1914, when Janet MacLellan of Claremont Gardens left £62,305, her sole executrix was her unmarried daughter Eleonora.[82]

Thirty of these confirmations register the estates of women with a formal occupation. Although marital status is not always absolutely clear, it seems that twenty of the women were widows and ten single. Their estates were valued at between £37 (an upholsterer) and £12,982 (a hotel keeper). The mean value was £1,110 – or £700 if the unusually wealthy hotel keeper is excluded. These represent middle-class finances comparable with those of male testators employed as Army captain, auctioneer, insurance broker, commission merchant, writer, physician, warehouseman, ironmerchant, ship broker and so on. Clearly, these women had achieved a comfortable standard of living and often left thriving businesses behind them.

Some occupations feature prominently. Nine of the thirty women were wine and/or spirit merchants; five were or had been teachers; and four kept hotels. Most of the others seem to have kept shops of some sort – two fishmongers, a butcher, bootmaker, confectioner, tobacconist, draper, butter seller and dairy keeper.[83] Perhaps surprisingly, in view of the occupations recorded in censuses and directories, only one was a dressmaker, and one a nurse.

The estates of spinsters reveal the same pattern of variation in wealth among women in the area. Margaret Pinkerton, who died in 1882, left movable estate worth £43,760: she was obviously a very wealthy woman.[84] There is no record of the estate of Elizabeth Buchanan, but it is known that she lived with her sister Rebecca Fyfe, who left £21,732 in 1885.[85] Anna Playfair, who died in 1894, had inherited over £10,000 from her father Patrick, which together with stock held in her own name, meant a total personal estate of £12,237.[86] Single women could be in possession of considerable wealth in their own right, even when their parents were still alive. When Isabella Paterson of Claremont Gardens died intestate in 1878, her father, a manufacturing chemist, was granted administration of her estate of £15,343.[87] These women lived in the more prosperous streets of the area. At the other end of the middle-class spectrum, in Carnarvon Street, Isabella Stewart died in 1881 leaving £838 in various bank accounts.[88] It is difficult to estimate her annual income, but we can attempt to do this for Miss Agnes Buchanan, who died in 1876 leaving a similar estate of £882. She had shares in railways, paying a dividend. In addition, she was receiving a liferent from the estates of both her late parents, and a share of rents from property. It looks as if she was getting £206 per annum in liferents, as well as the share dividends – perhaps some £5 per week in total.[89] Many working-class women were obliged to maintain a family on 'round about a pound a week' at this date and later. Even ageing, unmarried, lower-middle class women in our study area were very much better off than that.

The wills of widows and spinsters offer further details about their wealth, the source of it, and the influence it allowed them to exercise.[90] They reveal that many of these women, including those of relatively modest means, invested in stocks, shares and property. Margaret Tannahill, a widow who died in 1878, had investments in three railway companies and a waterworks, as well as income from property in Glasgow and two annuities. This corroborates the evidence of a number of historians who have argued that women have played a prominent role in investment markets and as property owners since at least the seventeenth century and suggests that this role did not diminish in the course of the nineteenth century.[91] Property was a favoured choice of investment and wealthy women played a significant role in Glasgow's property market in the nineteenth century. Women of no stated occupation as a percentage of property owners in the city increased from 18.5 in 1861 to 24.9 in 1911.[92] Not all of these female property owners would have lived in Glasgow, but there were also Glasgow women who owned property outside the city. Robert Brown, a Paisley businessman, in common with his Glasgow counterparts, usually rented a holiday house on the Firth of Clyde for the summer months, and on at least two of these occasions that property was rented directly from a woman.[93] Many of these women were single or widowed. Some would have inherited the property from husbands or fathers, and others would have exercised the choice to invest and become rentiers. The Glasgow Register of Sasines, which recorded all land transfers in the city, indicates that a significant proportion of those involved in land transfers were women. The type of transfer varied, with some women receiving property through bequest and others selling off land to construction firms.[94]

Women also comprised a significant number of investors in stocks and shares. Of the 1,358 investors in the City of Glasgow Bank in 1878, just over 25 per cent were women. There is no clear record of the marital status of these women. Of those who were married, some invested jointly with their husbands, while others were investors in their own right. Most female investors however, are likely to have been single or widowed.[95] The amounts invested ranged widely from sums as small as £10 to fairly sizeable investments of over £1,000; in 1851 Mrs Jane Grieve, marital status uncertain, invested £2,400. Investments in property and shares were as popular as those in annuities. The records of the Glasgow Water Commission in 1856 reveal that women were an important source of capital for municipal utilities. Overall women represented almost 30 per cent of annuitants and provided almost 14 per cent of the funds. As with the City of Glasgow Bank, the majority of women (two-thirds) provided loans of below £500 and only about 10 per cent provided loans of over £1,000. This pattern is the reverse of men's, where almost 80 per cent provided large sums of over £1,000.[96]

Testaments also reveal something of the extent to which women were free to dispose of wealth as they wished and a little about how they used that freedom. Making one's will while still relatively young could leave scope for several changes of heart. By the time she died in 1901, Euphemia Bulley or Guthrie had added five codicils in the previous twenty-three years.[97] The ability to make such changes must have given well-to-do widows considerable authority, within the family and elsewhere. Davidoff and Hall have argued that the terms and conditions of men's wills severely curtailed widows' ability to dispose of property freely.[98] Some husbands left everything to their wives for the duration of their life, and then to their children. David Cargill in 1904 left his wife £10,000 and an annuity of £2,500 per annum if she did not remarry, £1,250 per annum if she did.[99] As mentioned above, Peter Fisher in 1877 left his wife a life interest in his estate, which ceased completely if she remarried.[100]

However, marriage settlements, as discussed in chapter 5, often provided wives with independent wealth and sometimes made detailed provision for the event of widowhood, stipulating the amount of their annuity (though sometimes more was given). Money which a woman had brought to a marriage could be seen as exclusively hers and reserved to her, like the widow of Alexander Anderson, who 'also had an income from the estate of the late Misses Jane and Lilias Campbell, her aunts'.[101] Catherine Miller or Ure, when she died in 1880, still had untouched the £1,000 conferred on her by the Deed of Settlement of her late father. Indeed a noticeable feature of wills is the frequency with which bequests are left to women exclusive of the *jus mariti* whereby the property and wealth of the woman was passed to the husband on marriage. The way in which Eliza Service Smith chose to dispense her extensive wealth is an illuminating example of priorities: she left her married daughter the entire contents of her house, but no money; £25,000 was to be divided among her widowed sister-in-law and her three children; each of her nieces and nephews was left £2,500; and the remainder of her estate was divided among her grandchildren; for female relatives, the legacy was exclusive of the *jus mariti*. Note the focus on providing for lone women.

Among other examples showing how concerned testators were to provide adequately for unmarried female relatives is that of Mrs Helen Gibb, who died in 1878. She left virtually everything ('all my lands, goods etc') to her two single daughters, and made them sole executors.[102] Her two sons and two married daughters received £10 each from an insurance policy – presumably having had their shares earlier. Dr James Adams, who died in 1901, was explicit about favouring his unmarried daughter, Barbara 'residing with me', over his other children: 'It is my duty, I consider, to make special provision for my daughter Barbara, and [. . .] it is my hope that what I have done in her favour will be considered fair and reasonable.'[103] In fact the whole of his estate went in liferent to Barbara for as long as she remained unmarried.

Although the interests of male relatives were not neglected, the expectation that they would earn their living affected the timing of gifts, with male relatives more likely to receive *inter vivos* gifts than legacies. Sometimes this was to provide funds for setting up in business or, on occasion, to assist a business to expand or to bail it out of trouble. Many businesses benefited from an injection of cash from a female relative. Adam Heugh & Co., for example, borrowed £600 in 1897 from Adam Heugh's two daughters.[104] Elizabeth MacLellan of Royal Crescent, when her son George suffered loss in his investments in a steamship company, offered

Table 20   Executors, 1876–1914

Executors	Female estates	Male estates	Total
Male only	146	80	226
Female only	74	65	139
Both male and female	25	33	58
Total	**245**	**178**	

to pay off the share which would have fallen to her other son had the partnership between the two brothers not been dissolved some four years earlier: 'After giving the matter due consideration I have resolved to share with you all the loss in the above which would have fallen to my son James i.e. all that sum of money as at the respective dates on which they were paid and I shall feel obliged if you will debit my account in your books accordingly.'[105] One of Eliza Service Smith's codicils was to increase to £2,000 her bequest to John Service (relationship not specified) of Smith Sons & Laughland, warehousemen.[106]

Women, whatever their marital status, were frequently named as execu-tors in testaments, or appointed executors as next of kin. This was the case right across the spectrum of middle-class wealth. It was equally common, at all economic levels, for women to come forward to register the estate of a relative who died intestate. The executors were not, of course, sole legatees, but they held considerable responsibility and indeed power, especially if the estate was large. This obviously involved consid-erable liaison with legal and other professional men. Meinhard Robinow, a merchant of Park Circus, left £85,000 in 1886 to be solely administered by his wife Therese.[107] Stuart Foulis of Park Circus in 1914 left £50,000 to be administered by his unmarried sister Eliza.[108] In this respect, at least, there is little difference discernible between the practice of upper and lower middle classes. As Table 20 shows, men do outnumber women as executors overall, but not by a very large margin. Men as well as women seemed happy to appoint women as their executors, a position of trust and responsibility which presumably required the appointee having some knowledge of the financial affairs of the testator.

Concentration on the plight of married women disadvantaged by the law and on the genteel poverty of spinsters has tended to present a one-sided view of Victorian middle-class lone women's economic role.

Generally they are seen as having little or no economic role to play, and little or no financial independence. Those who have acknowledged that women made an economic contribution have claimed that it was 'shadowy' and largely hidden. We have demonstrated that in Glasgow there were considerable numbers of widowed and single women with occupations, running businesses and engaging directly in the market. Women's money supported family firms; women were major investors in enterprises like the railways. Some women ran successful small (or occasionally large) businesses. Women owned property; they employed lawyers and accountants; they administered large estates. There were, of course, social constraints upon the economic freedom of women. But it was possible – indeed common – to work within these constraints to achieve real economic autonomy and influence. The middle-class women of Victorian Glasgow were by no means without money, control of money, or the power that goes with it.

So to what extent were often-expressed concerns about the financial insecurity of lone women in general well founded? It must be re-emphasised that our study area was a middle-class one, even if that did encompass great variation in wealth. Yet where are the legions of desperate widows forced to move in with unwilling relatives? If they became too poor to remain in this area as household heads, this is precisely the kind of area where the sheltering relatives would have lived. Where are the ageing spinsters living in genteel starvation? Relatively, some spinsters may have been less well off than if they had married; some widows may have been in more straitened circumstances than when their husbands were alive. Some may even have been forced to leave the area to live more cheaply elsewhere. But those who remained in our area were not living in absolute poverty. In addition, they had a financial independence that was not guaranteed to be available to the married woman.

Similarly, lone middle-class women had considerable social independence. Widows who lived in the home of offspring, or even more rarely of a more distant relative, were a small minority. Most headed their own households, kept servants, and came and went as they pleased. Even spinsters were likely to head households or live as 'joint' heads with siblings. Lone women were free to choose their own friends, pursue their own interests and take up causes of their own choosing. A conventional view of these women sees them as essentially passive, not as agents of their own destiny. It is too simplistic to portray the spinster as embittered, the widow as helpless, and both as dependent on (male) relatives for financial support and social protection. Indeed, whether by eschewing marriage in the first place, or by declining to live with married offspring, many women consciously rejected such social protection.

It is vital to recognise the diversity that middle-class women in the nineteenth century experienced. It varied according to their position on the socio-economic scale, their stage of life, their marital status and the familial and cultural worlds they inhabited. All of these could change during any individual's life. The daughter long resident in the family home, the sister who was housekeeper to her brother, and the wife who set up a new home could all expect independence at some stage. This was likely to be earlier for the daughter than the wife; and of course not all wives outlived their husbands. But however much the status of wife was lauded, to whatever extent the 'little woman', the 'angel in the home' was held up as an example, she was always in a minority. All women knew legions of lone women: all women could reasonably expect to *be* lone women at some stage. Such women could enjoy considerable social independence without sacrificing respectability, and be at least as active as married women in the wide range of social, cultural and philanthropic activities in which middle-class women participated.

7

Downtown

THE MIXTURE OF 'PUBLIC' AND 'PRIVATE' social events undertaken by most middle-class Victorian women during the space of a single day, and sometimes well into the night, must have required considerable stamina. Janet Story, for example, looking back on her youth in the 1850s, recalled

> remaining at a ball till the morning was so far advanced, that the various workmen and labourers were all setting out on their different avocations, and I felt so ashamed of myself sitting in full view, decked in all my ball frippery, that I slipped to the floor of the cab, and tried to hide myself as well as I could from what I felt must be the disapproving eyes of those honest sons and daughters of toil.[1]

She had literally danced the night away. The 'sons and daughters of toil' might have been similarly disapproving of a fairly typical 'working' day as she described it in her diary for 13 March 1856: 'We had a luncheon party today [. . .]. Dined at Dr Simpson's. A good deal of music. We then went to a dance at Red Bob's. [. . .] I danced loads and enjoyed it very much. Pretty good day's work.'[2] A fortnight later, after a wedding, 'We had a very merry breakfast [. . .] broke up about four. In the evening we returned to a very large party [. . .]. Then we went to the assembly. It was most delicious. I danced the whole night, and with all my favourite partners, and enjoyed myself thoroughly though tolerably fatigued by the end of the proceedings.'[3] One can well imagine that she was. 'After this', she wrote, 'came the usual winter of unlimited gaiety; dinners, lunches, evening parties, balls, the same thing over and over again till even my own constitution showed signs of exhaustion [. . .] my father as a rule contenting himself with dinner parties and an occasional evening affair, while I did everything.'[4]

Janet was twenty-seven and single at this time of 'unlimited gaiety', and living in Edinburgh. A similarly hectic social whirl was available to the Glasgow middle class. In the same month, March 1856, Madeleine Smith wrote: 'I have been so engaged, never in bed a night before 2 or 3 o'clock and all day long going about. We were at the Exhibition every afternoon.'[5] Elizabeth Thomson described her life as a young woman in Glasgow at the beginning of Victoria's reign as 'a constant round of pleasure'.[6] Such activities were not confined to young, single women, nor to the early years of the period. Having been laid up after an accident in 1909, the sixty-six-year-old Frances Murray recounted what she had been forced to miss in a presumably typical week.

Monday – King's Theatre (opera)
Tuesday – Seeing grandchild in a play. Evening orchestral concert.
Wednesday – a.m. – discussion at the Christian Union on the Insurance Bill. Evening – party in Dumbarton
Thursday – Nothing special
Friday – Musical practice in Cardross. Evening – an entertainment at Provand's Lordship, a Glasgow club of which I am a member.
Saturday – a lecture on Egyptology given by Miss Buchanan [a friend]. Followed by going to Edinburgh to spend Sunday with friends.[7]

Other things, presumably, might have cropped up during the week – this is just what Frances had already in her diary. She had always revelled in a busy social round. Visiting an old friend in Streatham in 1870, she wrote to her father: 'The change from London life to this suburban quiet is very great; I do not like it.' Yet on the same day she wrote to David Murray that on Friday she had 'received three invitations to dinner parties and a box at the Prince of Wales'.[8] All things are relative.

This busyness and sociability is at odds with a conventional picture of Victorian middle-class women languishing at home, enfeebled by lack of activity and enervated by boredom. Such a view, informed by notions of withdrawal from the world, is difficult to reconcile with the young Janet Story 'doing everything' to the point of exhaustion.

Numerous historians have noted that the ideology of domesticity did not involve a conception of separate spheres which hinged on a simple spatial contrast between a domestic and non-domestic setting with women immured in the confines of the home. Moreover, Victorian middle-class ideology *required* a public role for women. In order to acquire the goods and attributes essential to her domestic role, the middle-class woman *had* to enter the public realm of shops, churches, concert halls and so on. Furthermore, these realms were seen as benefiting from her presence. Just as middle-class identity was partly forged around a sense of difference from and obligation towards the 'uncivilised' at home and abroad, so middle-class women, as the gentler and more spiritual sex, had a mission to 'civilise' the public spaces and public intercourse of the Victorian city.[9]

However, it is vital to consider what the term 'public' meant to contemporaries, for whom it had several different connotations. It is therefore more profitable to speak of 'public realms' and by the same token of 'public spheres': the cultural, political, social and philanthropic spheres as well as that of economic life. Female involvement in some of these realms was an integral part of 'middle classness'. Simon Gunn argues that the middle class used culture both to differentiate itself from the working class and to forge a common identity in a group otherwise riven by economic, political and religious differences.[10] Shared taste and cultural interests were essential factors in this process, as was the ritualised and formal display of them. However, historians who have focused on the centrality of culture, particularly civic and public culture, in constituting middle-class identity, have rarely discussed women's role in this process. Yet a public role for women was a key feature in the *creation* of the middle class. Thus the cultural imperative precluded adherence to an ideology of domesticity which demanded that women remain incarcerated in the home. We have already emphasised the contradictions within the ideology of domesticity, the existence of which does not preclude the coexistence of other ideologies. Middle-class values of industry and 'usefulness' and to a religious ethos which lauded female moral virtues could be a powerful tools for the woman negotiating entry into the labour market. Similarly, women's involvement in public spheres was mediated through class ideologies which both justified and demanded her participation. Thus scholars must remain alert not only to the existence of a multiplicity of public spheres, but also to the possibility of interaction and conflict between them.[11]

Some public roles for women were considered more acceptable than others. Chosen activities would, of course, vary according to personal ambition and personality, and to position within the socio-economic spectrum of the middle class. What is perhaps surprising to modern readers, particularly if they have taken on board an unproblematic view of the public/private dichotomy, is the extent of what *was* acceptable, and the multiplicity of what Mary Ryan calls 'points of access' to public realms that women negotiated.[12] This chapter aims to investigate those 'points of access'; the ways in which middle-class women engaged with the world outside the home, and how these changed over the period.

For Mrs Story in the 1850s, 'doing everything' meant going to parties, balls, weddings and dinners, often in the homes of friends and acquaintances. There was, as described in chapter 4, a flourishing social life centred on people's homes, where entertaining was often large-scale and lavish. Young women regularly went out to dinner with acquaintances of the family, not necessarily with a male escort. Such social events fall into a category somewhere between 'public' and 'private': they were domestic in setting, and one attended only by invitation – there was no public scrutiny, and so one might think of them as being essentially 'private'. Yet there was an element of public display about them, and women performed a public function by attending. Dinners and parties could be used to cement business ties – the Smith sisters went to dine with the Houldsworths who were business contacts of their father. Unmarried women in particular were expected to display their charm. On Boxing Day 1865 John Stephen attended a private dinner where he 'had Miss E. Wilson as a partner at table and I succeeded in one of the great events of my life'.[13] They were married the following March.

Women also engaged in the practice of 'calling' on each other, although there is little evidence of the rituals that are supposed to have accompanied this practice – the leaving of cards, being 'at home' and so on. Perhaps there was some social obligation to receive callers. Lilias Scotland of Partick in Glasgow wrote to her mother: 'I had Miss Smart and her friend Mrs Fisher out calling last Friday. They want a house in Partick. I hope they don't get one.'[14]

Even the social life that centred on home and family was clearly not devoid of contact with a wider social world. But not only did the world – in the shape of dinner guests and visiting family and friends – come to women: they themselves went out into a world whose horizons, while ultimately bounded, were far wider than those suggested by the discourse of separate spheres. Dancing was a favoured pastime: Madeleine Smith's correspondence is full of references to attending balls, both in Glasgow and in Edinburgh. These were often attended or hosted by military men. In a letter to Emile L'Angelier she wrote about a ball on 11 March 1856: 'I danced a good deal. There is no use going to a Ball if you don't dance. It was with the officers we danced.'[15] A couple of weeks later, on 30 March: 'There were few at the Ball, we had only two gentlemen to attend us (one of the 72nd and the other of the 93rd), a great many of the militia were there, we left at half past 2.'[16] People were happy to travel considerable distances to attend balls. The Smith family provided accommodation in Glasgow for friends en route to a ball in Stirling. When the Smith parents attended this ball without their daughters, Madeleine wrote: 'I think it is very foolish of M and P going about to Balls.' At the other end of the age scale, there seems to have been little need for formal 'coming-out' in late teens, for her sister Janet, then aged fourteen, was to dance 'at D'Albert's Ball' in Glasgow.[17] James Smith occasionally acted as a much-needed chaperone to his daughters. But chaperonage seems to have been only irregularly observed. Madeleine and Bessie Smith went 'without a matron' to 'a luncheon party' with the garrison at Edinburgh Castle. Madeleine knew that L'Angelier would not approve of them 'going to the Castle today by ourselves among so many gents'. When he unexpectedly caught her out in doing so, she apologised: 'I acted wrong in going to the Castle without a Matron.'[18] Neither their hosts, nor the girls' parents, seem to have objected, and the sisters had happily gone off to lunch with the officers unchaperoned. Madeleine expressed regret and a sense of wrongdoing only when reproached by her sanctimonious (and jealous) lover. Madeleine's letters suggest that parents allowed considerable latitude to daughters unless they had particular reason – as they did in Madeleine's case – to be suspicious of her. After all, Madeleine had met L'Angelier when out and about unchaperoned in the city.

Other references to chaperones occur, particularly in the earlier years of the period. In 1837, when Elizabeth and Anna Thomson were 'overwhelmed with invitations' and 'led very gay lives', one evening they 'went to a dinner party with our father, thence to a private dance for two hours, after which we went to Mrs James Graham's in the middle of the night to dress for our first subscription ball to which her daughter, Mrs Bartholomew, chaperoned us.'[19] Mrs Story, however, does not specify any chaperone accompanying her to parties and balls in the Edinburgh of the 1850s, after her father had to some extent withdrawn from the full social round.

Frances Murray's sister, at school in Edinburgh, wrote to Frances in 1861: 'On Saturday I went to the Bensons and enjoyed it *excessively*. I met a good many nice fellows, who when I meet I always bow to, to the great annoyance of the Misses G. especially as they prohibit bowing to gentlemen.'[20] It sounds as if the Misses G., if present as chaperones, were powerless to control the behaviour of their young charges. We have already noted Madeleine Smith's flirting, and her virtuous pride in having abstained from it for a fortnight. In fact young women seem to have enjoyed considerable latitude in their deportment in public. They appear to have been able to choose dancing partners freely, for instance. Chaperones, where they existed, seem not to have objected when one partner was shown particular favour. Madeleine mentioned that her sister Bessie 'danced with Pagan all night at the last Ball'.[21] Mrs Story even had 'favourite partners'. It appears to have been quite acceptable for unaccompanied women to attend concerts, and some certainly seem to have felt at home: J. J. Bell recalled an orchestral concert at St Andrew's Hall in the 1870s when 'two very musical-looking ladies' in front of him, while waiting for the concert to begin, 'produced little parcels and whiled away the time by eating oatcakes and kippers – and running down Wagner.'[22] It looks as if chaperonage was something of an empty gesture, used largely for form's sake at formal public events.

Balls and assemblies were a feature of the winter, when the middle class were mostly in town. The *Glasgow Herald* carried notices throughout the season, which seems to have begun immediately after Christmas. 'Glasgow Assemblies: The first Assembly of the Season will be held in the Merchants Hall on Thursday evening January 5 [1854].'[23] Five 'lady patronesses' were named, and tickets cost 5s for ladies and 7s 6d for gentlemen.

At the beginning of January 1859, a new venue for balls and other social activities was opened at the end of Woodside Place. The Queens Rooms was an imposing building with several halls for concerts and lectures, and had a ballroom with a fine sprung floor. At the first ball held there, revellers became alarmed, as the dancing got more frantic, at the way the floor appeared to 'give' beneath their pounding feet. Given their proximity, the Queens Rooms must have been frequented by at least the upper middle class from our sample population.

Balls were expensive to attend: 'Glasgow Celtic Society – Second Annual Ball and Assembly at City Galleries of Art, 206 Sauchiehall St, on Friday 24th Feb. Tickets admitting one gentleman and two ladies – 1 guinea.'[24] Similarly, the dress codes for social events of the Glasgow season were designed to confine such entertainments to the well-to-do. The newspaper notice for a pre-Christmas concert in 1863 made this clear. 'Operatic recital in Queens Rooms – Full dress only permitted.'[25] (In other words, no riff raff.) Opera seems also to have been popular among the middle class, as is implied in an advertisement which appeared on Boxing Day 1853: 'Italian Opera: Applications for private boxes for the season (12 nights) ought to be made immediately to prevent disappointment.'[26] Madeleine Smith clearly did not enjoy it. As she wrote in 1856:

'Jack [her brother] took me to the Opera this evening. When he came home for dinner he told me that he had 2 seats in the Boxes. But I did not like it at all.'[27]

The theatre, however, was more likely to be open to the full spectrum of the middle class as represented in our study area. According to Bell's memoirs, there were five theatres in Glasgow in the 1870s.[28] By March 1900 seven theatres were advertised in a single issue of the *Glasgow Herald*.

There were also, of course, entertainments open to all except the poorest. Not all on offer in the city was 'highbrow': particularly over holiday seasons, there were pantomimes, circuses and ice-shows. Middle-class women did attend these more popular entertainments, and did not need a male companion, especially if they were mothers with children. In the summer of 1873, Archibald Allan's mother took his younger siblings to see the visiting Wombwell's Menagerie.[29] Other circus companies visited too: Henglers Grand Cirque offered a 'Carnival on the Ice' plus various 'scenes in the circle by Henglers Equestrian Company'.[30] The 'Last night of the Engagement at the Equestrian Company, Theatre Royal' was for the 'Benefit of M. Pablo Fanque', whose name might have been forgotten without its later association with The Beatles' *Sergeant Pepper's Lonely Hearts Club Band*.[31] Among local entertainers were James Jee, his Italian-born wife and their four children (the youngest aged seven), all 'equestrians' living in Bath Street in the city centre in spring 1881. Other 'artistes', of both sexes, were in lodgings all over the city centre. There was clearly a lively popular entertainment scene where classes could mingle. Of course, some venues were off-limits to middle-class women: indeed, as Bell remembered from his youth, middle-class *men* felt adventurous in visiting certain music halls.[32]

By the later years of the period, the cinema had arrived. In 1912 the Cinema House, Renfield Street (showing *Vengeance of the Mafia*), was described as 'the Finest Picture House in Glasgow'.[33] Nevertheless, it would be some time before its advent took its toll on other forms of entertainment: the *Glasgow Herald* of 19 January 1914 advertised ten theatres, a circus and a 'winter carnival' as well as four cinemas. The latter did not attract an entirely working-class audience: 'Stalls 6d, back seats 9d, balcony 1s, private box seats 1/6d.' Despite some democratisation of leisure, the middle class could still pay to preserve class distinctions.

As well as professional performances, middle-class women could attend and even take part in amateur concerts and theatricals, usually put on for the benefit of a local charity. The following is a typical notice from the local press, in this case from as early as 1860:

> The MacDonald Fund – an amateur dramatic performance by Gentlemen connected with the Glasgow Press and other friends of the late Hugh MacDonald. At the Princes Theatre, Sat May 12th. The following ladies, who have kindly volunteered their services, will appear –
> Miss Aitken, Miss Cleaver, Miss Josephs, Miss Hodson, and Mrs Ashley. The second act of Guy Mannering, 'All that Glitters is not Gold' and 'Diamond Cut Diamond'.[34]

It is slightly surprising that the women were listed in the press. Presumably the charitable nature of the venture was sufficient guarantee of its respectability; but amateur dramatics had moved on considerably from the furore over the purely domestic performance of *Lovers' Vows* in *Mansfield Park* (1814)!

As described in earlier chapters, women were also involved in rather more serious and 'improving' activities. The *Waverley Journal* regularly praises and recommends to its (female) readers the Glasgow Royal Polytechnic Institute, which held public lectures and exhibitions. Here too, women speakers were widely advertised. Miss Lydia Becker gave the Glasgow Athenaeum Lecture on women in Walter Scott, as announced in the *Glasgow Herald* in 1871. Some societies actively encouraged women lecturers and participants. Ella Burton wrote to her father John in 1877:

> The Philosophical Society in Aberdeen have asked me to read a paper to them next Tuesday evening on some literary or antiquarian subject so I have chosen the Bayeux Tapestry. The Society are anxious that ladies should attend their meetings so they think if a lady read a paper it would be a good beginning to 'encourager les autres' to listen or speak. I would be very grateful if you can suggest any book I could consult on the Tapestry subject.[35]

Similarly, the Edinburgh Philosophical Institution in 1851 advertised ('to the ladies') that its directors encouraged ladies' membership at 10s 6d per annum, to include attendance at lectures and use of the library.

Nenadic argues that middle-class women in Glasgow resented the access that men enjoyed to male-only social worlds, and sought to enter these worlds themselves.[36] She cites examples where women's participation in similar activities remained only partial well after mid-century. The implication is that men resisted this female incursion. However, the chief agents of change in these examples seem to have been the male societies themselves, whose committees expressed the desire for more female participation. Such societies were, of course, only one aspect of male social worlds. Nevertheless, it seems that in some areas at least, women were encouraged to take their place alongside men. Gentlemen's clubs and the like remained as male-only preserves: but in other cultural settings the 'civilising influence' of women could be evinced to justify and even encourage their presence.

As far as administrative tasks were concerned, the example of Frances Murray has already been mentioned: she not only gave lectures, but made all the arrangements. She complained in 1878 that 'I have been busy with concerts and lectures. Every detail has to be attended to. The seating of the hall, the sale of tickets, a hundred and one things on my shoulders.'[37] Yet there is little sign of an exclusively female associational life of an anonymous, non-subscriptional nature, and little advertising of women-only public events of this kind, until near the end of our period. An unusual lecture advertised in 1914 sounds as if it might be a coded reference to contraception:

> Of interest to women – Arrangements have been made for Mrs K. E. Whyte (London) to give one illustrated lecture especially for and of particular interest to women, in the Charing Cross Halls. Subject 'Some Causes and the Main Cause of Illhealth in Women'.
>
> Mrs Whyte has had a wide experience in the lecture field. These lectures are entertaining and instructive. All women interested in advancement and success in life are cordially invited to attend. Admission free. Action will resolve the doubt that theory cannot solve.[38]

This is a striking example of how women could use a public setting for the dissemination of 'private' information. What might have once been whispered mother-to-daughter is now the subject of an advertised lecture, from which men are tacitly but clearly excluded.

The only other area where women-only public lectures and meetings were frequent was, of course, the suffragist movement. Increasing agitation for female suffrage has been cited as important both in practical and social terms for women: it brought women together in a public campaign, and provided both an outlet for their energies and a climate in which women could more easily justify a single life.[39] The Glasgow Branch of the National Society for Women's Suffrage was formed in 1870. As early as February 1871 Robert Brown of nearby Paisley 'went and heard Miss Taylor, from the south of Scotland, deliver a lecture in favour of women's rights, and particularly that those who had to pay taxes should

have a vote.'[40] He found it 'a clever and eloquent address'. By the beginning of the twentieth century there were also the Women's Freedom
League and the Women's Social and Political Union, both of which had
headquarters in Sauchiehall Street. All of these organisations advertised
their public meetings. On 3 February 1909 the *Glasgow Herald* announced:

> Votes for Women
> Public meeting in Hillhead Burgh Hall on Feb 10th.
> Challenge: – The Hillhead Branch W.F.L. is prepared to arrange a public
> debate with an anti-Suffragist – no sex disability shown – on the
> Question of Women's Suffrage. Expenses and hospitality given. Reply
> Branch Secretary, offices, 30 Gordon St.[41]

And on 21 January 1914:

> Glasgow Society for Women's Suffrage, National Union of Women's
> Suffrage Societies – non-party, law abiding. Public meeting in St
> Andrews Halls, Thurs 5th Feb.
> Chair Mrs Henry Fawcett LL.D., President, NUWSS
> Speakers Miss Maude Royden, Rt Hon W. H. Dickenson Esq. Tickets
> from Suffrage Office, 202 Hope St.[42]

The Conservative and Unionist Women's Franchise Association was also
active from 1909, when at their first meeting 'there was a numerous attendance of ladies'.[43] The rhetoric at this meeting was careful to stress that
women need not neglect their 'proper' role: however, to be completely
'bound up in their own small life' was 'feckless'. 'The woman whom they
all admired, while she looked well after the ways of her household, had
broadened her outlook and was the better and not the worse of taking
an interest in matters dealing with the lives of the whole community.'
The meeting joined Lady Frances Balfour in abhorring 'the class of
women who could not look beyond the top of their bonnet'. So engagement with the public world was no longer merely a privilege: it had
become a requirement for the middle-class woman. The pejorative terms
were reserved for the woman who did *not* look beyond her bonnet. Yet
even in a radical cause, women sought to accommodate existing ideologies about their 'proper role' and extend them to justify involvement in
a wider sphere.

Women were well aware, however, that this process involved a struggle.
Frances Murray backed her daughter's activity in the suffragist cause –
she headed a procession in Edinburgh in 1910 at a demonstration where
Eunice was a speaker. She felt herself 'unable to enthuse for causes' but

encouraged her daughter, to whom she felt she had passed on 'the love of a fight and the ability to work for abstract justice' from her own father. 'Go ahead my daughter', she wrote. 'You possess on both sides fighting blood.' That these were 'masculine' characteristics inherited from male forebears did not make them any less desirable attributes in her daughter. As long before as 1877, around the time of Eunice's birth, Frances had written to her own parents: 'David and I wonder what your lecturer said upon the political situation of ladies in England? What advance have we made except that women are on the School Board? Yet better days are surely ahead: before I die I look forward to the fulfilment of sex equality.' Indeed, despite professing to have 'lapsed into indifference' to the suffragist cause, Frances did live to vote in the 1918 election.[44]

Another struggle was that for access to higher education. In the early part of the period, participation in the more serious public social events, lectures and such like, could shade into semi-formal higher education. As early as the 1830s, Lord Kelvin's father James Thomson – a mathematician at Glasgow University – taught an afternoon course for ladies, on geography and astronomy, given twice a week in his classroom: 'All the belles of Glasgow were among the students.'[45] This makes it sound as if attending lectures had more to do with fashion and the appeal of the widowed Thomson than it did with a thirst for learning. Yet the middle-class women of Glasgow clearly cared about education. Queen's College was established in 1842 and was the first institution in Britain to attempt to provide a comprehensive higher education for women. Although there were classses for pupils aged twelve to fifteen, there were also classes 'for ladies over 18 years', taught by staff drawn from such establishments as the Andersonian Institute and its medical school, Glasgow High School and the Western Academy.[46] Classes taught included religion, classical language and literature, natural philosophy, chemistry, physiology, botany, natural history, logic and rhetoric.[47] That the venture proved short-lived was less to do with the lack of a market and much to do with the refusal of the Andersonian Institute's managers to permit their staff to teach in a second educational establishment.[48]

Women in Glasgow continued to be enthusiastic about education and to have an appetite for fairly meaty stuff. In 1868 a series of 'lectures for ladies' was instituted, given by professors of Glasgow University.[49] This led to the formation in 1877 of the Glasgow Association for the Higher Education of Women. Lectures were open only to women: they could attend on a one-off basis or as part of a course. In 1877–8, a total of 318 attended lectures, 'counting only once those who attended more than one class'.[50]

Such subjects as the psychology of the nervous system and the senses, philosophy and logic were particularly popular. In 1879–80 there were as many as forty-three lectures on physiology, attended by fifty-four 'ladies'. The topics do not sound geared towards dilettantes: in the early 1880s chemistry, logic, moral philosophy and Latin literature were included, as were music, fine art and literature. One feels that considerable intellectual as well as physical stamina was required to lead a 'life of leisure' in Victorian Glasgow.

In 1883, through the Association for the Higher Education of Women, Queen Margaret College (for women) was established in premises donated by Isabella Elder and with her financial backing.[51] This formalised higher education for women, and led eventually to the award of degrees. Initially only arts subjects were taught, but science subjects were added in 1888 and medicine in 1890. The College merged with Glasgow University in 1892, and the first female graduate, Marion Gilchrist, graduated in medicine in 1894. It was a long but continuous road from the belles of the 1830s, and led to that increasing professionalisation of women's employment in teaching and medicine noted above. Higher education qualifications were the entrée to several fields of endeavour. The rather formidable-sounding Miss Margaret Kerr introduced herself to a Royal Commission in 1909:

> I hold the Girton Certificate (Math. Tripos 1881). I was engaged in school teaching in England and Canada 1880–99. Settled in Glasgow 1900. Collected Savings Bank deposits in Anderston in connection with Queen Margaret College Settlement Association 1901–04. Elected member of Glasgow Parish Council for Blythswood and Broomielaw Dec 1904, since when I have been engaged in Poor Law administration.[52]

Even when qualified and working in a profession, some women pursued further education. Miss Agnes Brown, a schoolteacher, witness in the case of Miss Gilchrist's murder, was on her way to an evening class at 7.10 p.m. on 21 December 1908.[53] Attending college, and even gaining a degree, was the apogee of educational attainment, of course, and only achieved by a few. However, it seems to be the tip of an iceberg of academic *interest* indicated by women's involvement in lectures, exhibitions and societies which had a long history in the city. Engagement with the world of 'culture' was a requirement for the middle-class woman. Her home and her conversation had to demonstrate membership of a shared community of cultural consumption.[54] Because 'middle-classness' resided in such attributes, attendance at concerts and exhibitions became more than a pleasure: it was her work, and she took it seriously.

Reference libraries, museums and galleries catered for and helped to establish shared cultural tastes, and also gave women the opportunity not just to visit but to linger in a public setting. In the early years of the period, the range of such settings was relatively narrow, but always encompassed art exhibitions. In 1853, for example, the *Glasgow Herald* announced: 'The Exhibition of Works of Modern Artists is now Open, at St Enoch's Hall, 11 Dixon St.'[55] The McLellan Galleries opened in 1856, providing both shops and exhibition space in the heart of Sauchiehall Street; Madeleine Smith's father was the architect of the building. The Hunterian Museum was removed to the west end of the city with the rest of Glasgow University in 1870, and the enormous Mitchell Library was founded in 1874. The great exhibitions of 1881, 1901 and 1911 were held in West End (later Kelvingrove) Park at the foot of the Claremont estate, where the Kelvingrove Museum and Art Gallery opened in 1901. This burgeoning of public bourgeois culture from the 1870s is also noted in English industrial cities. However, insufficient attention is paid there to the participation of women and their role in establishing this public culture.[56] Even though the way in which these spaces was experienced was gendered, access to them was not; the presence of middle-class women was instrumental in shaping these public institutions.[57]

It is perhaps the extent, rather than the nature, of activities outside the home that is at odds with the picture of the house-bound middle-class woman. There is nothing surprising, perhaps, in even the most domesticated of angels occasionally leaving her hearth for a visit to the theatre. But, as diaries and correspondence indicate, many women were out at some function (maybe more than one) almost every night of the week, often in the afternoon too, going from dinner party to ball until even the most robust flagged under the regime of constant activity and late nights.

If women were to some extent 'displayed' in a domestic setting when visiting or being visited, this was amplified when they engaged in truly 'public' social life. The box at the theatre or the opera is a prime example of this, being as much about being seen as about seeing. Maureen Montgomery draws attention to the way in which New York elite women of the late nineteenth century were on display at such venues.[58] Similarly, the middle-class women in our study *had* to be seen in public, in the appropriate settings and appropriately attired.

A key element of this public visibility was simply walking in the town, in suburban parks or city streets. We have mentioned Kelvingrove Park, opened in 1852 on the doorstep of the Claremont estate, and deliberately created to add to its amenities and attract the middle classes to the area. There was in fact some unrest at the time that so much public money was being spent on such an exclusively middle-class amenity.[59] Public parks attracted the bourgeoisie with 'promenade concerts', such as the 'Grand Promenade with the 8th Light Infantry Band' advertised for September 1871 in the Royal Botanic Gardens, a little further west than Kelvingrove.[60] Strolling in the park was essentially a bourgeois pastime, where status and family could legitimately be displayed, and women were 'on show'.

Emile L'Angelier was well aware of this aspect of 'walking in town' when he urged Madeleine Smith not to do it: he did not want her to be 'on display' to others. She replied on 21 February 1856: 'I did promise not to go on S, R and B Sts but it was necessity that took me there on Saturday. I went to town at 12 o'clock to make some purchases. I do promise I shall not walk for pleasure. I told Mama and B this day I did not intend to walk S[auchiehall] Road. B. said she would go herself.'[61] It seems that Madeleine and her sister were in the habit of walking on Sauchiehall Street most afternoons 'for pleasure', although she professes not to like 'household shopping' – presumably ordering food – or 'making markets' as she called it.

Erika Diane Rappaport makes the point (with regard to London's West End) that during the second half of the nineteenth century, the city came to be seen as a site of pleasure which created a public form of bourgeois femininity.[62] Women were 'natural' shoppers and so for them pleasure 'naturally' resided in the experience of city shopping. This experience encompassed far more than the actual purchase of goods: space and time were consumed as well as objects. By the 1850s Madeleine Smith was clearly alive to this, distinguishing between going 'out of necessity' to do 'household shopping' and 'walking' in the city for the enjoyment of being out and about, seeing and being seen. While owners of large stores at the turn of the century would argue that *they* had been responsible for the fusion of necessity and pleasure that their stores represented, shopping-as-entertainment had become part of some families' leisure regime shortly after mid-century.

Furthermore, as Lore Anne Loeb argues, shopping – acquiring the goods for that display of consumption which typified the Victorian middle class – was primarily seen as a female task. For her it formed an intersection between the public and the private not least because consumption (and advertising) both creates and draws upon a 'community of consumers'.[63] The 'right' goods had to be bought and the 'right' appearance achieved. It was imperative to know what that was, so knowledge as well as tangible goods had to be acquired by the woman of 'taste' and 'fashion', as Frances Murray acknowledged: 'I have been altering my bonnet and now feel more in the height of fashion.'[64] Middle-class women, in particular, were beginning to go out to acquire the latest fashionable look, with more goods being available ready-made to be purchased over the counter. There was even the beginning of a service industry: one could visit the hairdresser's and enjoy 'A New Sensation! Rotary Hair Brushing, by Camp's Patent Machinery. Now in operation at Sturrock and Sons.'[65] Even in the early years of the period, a plethora of shops catered exclusively or particularly to women. The Glasgow Post Office Directory of 1857 listed the following retail businesses dealing mainly with female fashion.

artificial flower/feather makers – 7	boot and shoemakers – about 300
button factors – 2	dressmakers – about 145
embroiderers/pattern makers – 5	furriers – 11
hairdressers – 65	hosiers and glovers – 82
jewellers – 83	milliners – about 250
muslin embroiderers – 3	perfumers – 24
shawl warehouses – 30	silkmercers – 6
stay and corset makers – 40	straw hat makers – 54
umbrella and parasol – 21	woollen & linen drapers – 125

Yet the baldness of the directory entries does not convey the glamour suggested by the same firms' advertising. H. Salomon & Co. appear in the 1857 directory as a 'boot warehouse'. Yet on Boxing Day 1853 the *Glasgow Herald* carried a notice that the company had 'much pleasure in announcing the arrival on Thursday last from Paris of a new supply of the most Chaste and Elegant Coiffures in Wreaths, Plumes, Peignes, Epingles, etc. Also the celebrated "Corset Imperial" so much recommended by the Faculty. Maison de Paris, 267 Sauchiehall St.'[66] The lure of the Maison de Paris was infinitely greater than the boot warehouse, and many other delights may lurk behind the prosaic descriptions provided by the Post Office Directories.

In order to entice female customers, the magic of French fashion was in fact often invoked. New styles had come 'from Paris', and female costumiers styled themselves as 'Madame' or adopted pseudo-French names, for example: 'Madame Veitch, Sauchiehall St, model gowns, boleros, blouses and mantles.'[67] And:

Mademoiselle E. Agier (From Paris) late W. D. Kemp and Son, now 1 University Avenue, Byars Rd. Invites the Ladies of Glasgow to visit the beautiful selection, in the new premises, of all the latest novelties in Day and Evening Gowns, Mantles, Millinery, Furs and Lingerie. All cutting and fitting done under Personal Supervision.[68]

Interestingly, the process was two-way: Margaret Allan on her Paris trip of 1891 wrote of 'notices in the most fashionable shops saying "London Fashions" or "As worn by the Queen of England"'.[69] In both cities, retailers were keen to attract women by reference to the exotic and stylishly foreign. The consumption and display of 'fashion' in personal appearance is of course recognised as a key feature of modernity.[70] However, long before the arrival of department stores and galleries there was a multitude of individual shops and 'bazaars' catering to the female shopper.

Glasgow had long had shopping arcades and large 'warehouses', the precursors of department stores. Argyle Arcade, linking Argyle and Buchanan Streets, was built in 1827, while retail warehouses were popular from the 1840s and 1850s. Wylie and Lochhead, which opened on Buchanan Street in 1855, had an interior arcade surrounded by three levels of open galleries – and an elevator.[71] Certainly the warehouses sound architecturally very like department stores, even if their stock, ambience and target market were different. In 1857 the Wylie and Lochhead warehouse sold furniture, wallpaper, carpets, floor-cloths, bed and table linen, wax- and hair-cloth, and down and feathers.[72] As the 'tasteful' furnishing of the home was regarded as a largely female obligation, it seems likely that women visited such establishments.

So from the very beginning of our period, Glasgow's middle-class women could and did go shopping in person, not just for household necessities but also for pleasure. Except with hindsight, no one seems to have found it odd that the twenty-one-year-old single Madeleine Smith went more than once to chemists' shops to buy arsenic for killing rats. The inventory taken after the death in 1883 of Andrew Chrystal, wine merchant, and presented by his wife Jean, details household bills still to be paid: four dressmakers and two milliners were owed a total of £36 12s 6d.[73] Mrs Chrystal may also have been responsible for purchases from the lithographer, painter, cabinet maker, silversmith, warehousemen, butcher, newsagent and druggist. Similarly, Anna Playfair died in 1894 still owing money to Kemp & Sons, silk mercers (the shop which had by 1899 given way to Mlle Agier from Paris) and J. Stewart & Co., Ladies' Tailors – as well as to her dentist.[74] Thus middle-class women clearly engaged with the world of retail commerce on different levels and in different ways.

The development of department stores built upon and extended the concept of shopping as entertainment. Fraser's on Buchanan Street in Glasgow was established in 1849, originally as a draper's. Others followed, such as Copland & Lye's Caledonian House and the pseudo-French Tréron & Cie., both on Sauchiehall Street. Their rise is acknowledged to be a consequence not only of middle-class women's greater spending power but also of their increased leisure time. Such stores allowed women to shop unaccompanied, to socialise with other women, to take a leisurely tour and look at goods, not necessarily to purchase them. The stores appealed to woman's 'aesthetic eye', and allowed her to be a spectator as well as a consumer.

Rappaport stresses the department store as a place of entertainment for women; like the city itself, a site of pleasure – and importantly a site of legitimate, *respectable* pleasure.[75] Shopping came to be seen as a cultural pursuit rather than simply an economic one. Selfridges opened in London in 1909, and particularly stressed this transformation from chore to pleasure – but it was the expression of a rationale which had underlain the whole department store movement for the previous decades. Since at least the 1880s, stores had promoted self-selection and self-service.[76] Here women were taking the initiative: they were buying rather than being sold to.

While the middle-class women of Glasgow had shopped unaccompanied or with female friends, taking pleasure in strolling, looking and choosing since at least mid-century, the introduction of department stores greatly facilitated these activities. They responded to, rather than created, women as shoppers. They were doubtless more attractive than the warehouses that preceded them, and they did increase women's opportunities to turn shopping into a social event: but this was a continuation and development of a trend, not a radical innovation.

There were some new features. Department stores were open longer hours: in 1886 in London they were generally open from 8.15 a.m. to 7.30 p.m.[77] It was thus possible to travel from considerable distances to spend a day shopping; and important that the stores also offered restaurants and cloakrooms, especially in view of the paucity of public lavatories for women. The first 'public conveniences' in Glasgow were installed in 1850, but it was not until 1877 that any were provided for women, and they remained few in number.[78]

Department stores thus came to portray themselves as places of rest, refreshment and sociability for women – a sort of 'gentlewoman's club'.[79] In doing so, they set out to blur the distinction between public and private, advertising themselves as providing an arena where women could feel 'at home', despite the fact that women had evidently long been comfortable in this public arena.

Teashops, too, were locating themselves somewhere between public and private. Cynthia A. Brandimarte stresses the way in which tearooms (particularly in North America) 'looked like home and felt like home'.[80] She argues that, with their 'homely' atmosphere and approximation to home cooking and entertaining, they 'mediated between dining in private and dining in public' and as a consequence were suitable not only for women to visit but also to run. Brandimarte cites Kate Cranston and her Glasgow tearoom empire as the originator of this movement in the 1880s. However, Miss Cranston was by no means the only proprietor of tearooms in the city, although she was extraordinarily successful and has remained well known for her patronage of Glasgow School designers. Furthermore, the point about Kate Cranston is that she was *not* an enthusiastic amateur who believed that because she could run a home she could run a teashop: she was first and foremost a shrewd businesswoman whose expertise was drawn from a family background in catering and the tea trade. It took business acumen and artistic foresight to create the artifice of 'homeliness'. Certainly the tearoom very quickly became established in Glasgow: in 1889 it was 'among the newer features of Glasgow life'; by 1901 Glasgow was 'a very Tokyo for tea-rooms'.[81] A feature of tearooms was that, even when they did not cater exclusively to women, they provided 'ladies' rooms' which were for single-sex use. This fact was advertised, for example: 'Central Dining and Tea Rooms, 51 Buchanan St. Ladies Room – no gratuities – no delay';[82] and 'Grosvenor Restaurant and Tea Rooms – opposite Central Station/Breakfasts, Luncheons, Dinners, Teas, Ladies Rooms, Smoking Room, Billiard Room.'[83]

A logical extension of the 'ladies' rooms' in teashops (where Miss Cranston provided a telephone and writing desk) was the ladies' club. If gentlemen's clubs remained as a male bastion, why should women not enjoy the same amenities and comradeship in their own clubs? The Kelvin Club was founded in 1897, and initially rented premises in Buchanan Street, in the heart of the city centre.[84] Its members hailed from all over the west of Scotland and even from the corners of the Empire, although of course Glasgow and its environs predominated.[85] Several of the original committee lived in the Claremont/Woodside area. Members used the club premises to lunch when in town, to change before going out in the evening, and to conduct business such as interviewing domestic servants. There were also bedrooms for those who needed to stay overnight in the city.

A similar club was run by the Glasgow Lady Artists' Society. This began in 1882 as a group of ex-students of Glasgow School of Art who met to encourage each others' artistic efforts and shortly afterwards was renting premises in which to hold its own exhibition.[86] In 1893 the society was sufficiently flourishing to open its own premises in Blythswood Square. It became a social as well as an artistic club, and offered meals to members in addition to hosting exhibitions and concerts. The committee and all the club office holders were women. In 1908 they had a contretemps with the celebrated architect Charles Rennie Macintosh, whom they had invited to submit designs for redecoration. Macintosh's proposal was thought to be too expensive and rather too avant-garde. However, after some hard bargaining, his designs were implemented – at a reduced cost.[87]

There are two ways of looking at such institutions as ladies' clubs: on the one hand, they can be seen as closing down public space by herding women into enclaves within it; on the other, as opening up the public sphere to women, and allowing women to enter the masculine world of the city.[88] It is important to remember, however, that women had been a presence in the city long before the setting-up of women-only places of entertainment and sociability. What was new, perhaps, was that they could enable women to look out, to become 'spectators of the city'. Like department stores, they allowed women to take on something of the role of the *flâneur/se*, the urban stroller and observer.[89] Thus women developed a female gaze, rather than simply being the passive object of a male gaze.

'Seeing everything' was to become as important and desirable as 'doing everything' – certainly when travelling. But even at home, women engaged with the bustle of the city: Glasgow was a great city, larger not only than any other in Scotland, but also with a bigger population than nearly every English city. It was smoky, noisy, smelly – yet vibrant and frantic with activity in which middle-class women took part.

Outside the city, country walking was a favoured pastime in which Victorian women proved to be more hardy and energetic than is generally acknowledged. They covered considerable distances, often over rough terrain. In May 1866 Frances Murray went with her brother on a tour of the Highlands: she climbed Cruachan, apparently alone, while her brother fished, and on another day walked 13 miles to Oban; in the 1870s she and her husband David loved to 'tramp the moors'.[90] Madeleine Smith also referred to an 8-mile walk with her brother 'without fatigue'.[91]

Women expected to be out and about, and needed to dress accordingly. Alison Aldburgham makes the point that by the 1850s 'women were beginning to feel the *need* for more practical clothes'.[92] She cites the fashion for the 'Balmoral' or 'Alpine' walking boot, and quotes 'The Habits of Good Society: A Handbook of Etiquette for Ladies and Gentlemen' of about 1860: 'It was formerly thought ungenteel to wear anything but thin morocco shoes.' The author adds that with the addition of a warm cloak and a looped dress 'the high-born lady may [. . .] take a good walk with pleasure and safety.'[93] It was a Glasgow firm, Charles Mackintosh & Co., that patented waterproofing in the 1820s. These developments in fashion were well before the 'Rational Dress' movement of the 1880s, and more widely adopted.

Glasgow retailers were happy to offer women outfits tailored to as many activities as possible. David Kemp & Sons of Buchanan Street advertised in 1886: 'Young Ladies Walking Dresses, Yachting, Tennis, Garden Party and Summer Dinner dresses, in great variety.'[94] Even though women's dress remained in many ways wildly impractical – and its restrictive nature is often cited as evidence of the limitations on its wearers – it is instructive to remember these innovations in outdoor clothing and what they say about the increasingly active (and public) nature of women's lives.

David Kemp knew his market: his prospective customers were indeed taking part in various sports. Twenty years before his 'yachting dresses' were advertised, the diary of John Stephen for July 1866 records that Maggie Stephen went on a three-day yachting trip with Mr and Mrs Cowan.[95] In October 1862 Frances Murray went to 'a croquet party'.[96] Mrs Story mentioned that: 'Colonel Goodham of Fairlie [. . .] originated a club of archery of ladies and gentleman residing in the neighbourhood [. . .] called the Zingari Club.'[97] Her daughters played golf in the early nineties,[98] and Mina Brown of Paisley enjoyed trout fishing with her father in the early 1870s.[99] Women also enjoyed riding. Although this was less of a new departure than tennis, archery or croquet, it remained popular as much for the freedom it gave as for the physical activity. When living in Edinburgh before her marriage, Mrs Story recorded on 12 May 1857: 'Rode today with Major Harman of the 34th, all through Princes Street down to Portobello, where we rode on the sands, returning along the coast.'[100] There seems to have been no chaperone. Frances Murray was 'fond of horses and had a thorough knowledge of them. It was she, and not her husband, who superintended the stables.'[101] Madeleine Smith in April 1856 announced her intention to take up the activity: 'I think I shall ride this summer.'[102]

The range of women's sports expanded later in the century, and physical exercise, at least for girls, came to be seen as so beneficial as to be included in the school curriculum. The Brown sisters enthusiastically took up tennis in 1881 and 'took an active part in the playing'.[103] Bell's memoirs state that in the early 1880s 'young ladies' holidaying on the Clyde coast hired boats and 'rowed athletically and seriously'.[104] By this date, he explains, swimming (or at least submersion) in the sea was an established part of the holiday. Much earlier, in November 1864, Walter Crum wrote to his daughter: 'I am glad you are taking advantage of the sea bathing.'[105] She seems not to have been abroad at the time, so was presumably bathing somewhere near her Cheshire home, which would seem to require exceptional hardiness.

Women's energy was similarly displayed in their readiness to undertake foreign travel. Whether accompanied by relatives or alone, whether touring Europe, journeying to America or simply visiting other parts of Britain, the middle-class women of Glasgow were great travellers. This seems to have become more acceptable and more frequently undertaken as the century progressed. In 1839 Lord Kelvin's father took all his children to Paris, but only the girls went on with him to Switzerland 'because he thought the girls would have less chance than boys of travelling in later life'.[106] On their return the sisters were 'very gay, being invited to many dinners [. . .] balls and evening parties', where they were 'not a little lionised for a time as great travellers'.[107] His daughter Elizabeth records that in 1835 she met a Miss Gibson, then aged fifty, who had 'made the Grand Tour of Europe', noting that 'it was a rare distinction in those days to have seen so much of the world'.[108] So perhaps from the perspective of 1839 their father was right: but within a couple of decades middle-class women, whether married or single, were travelling widely and often. Walter Crum wrote to his daughter Jessie in 1864: 'You have been in towns I never saw.'[109] The advent of organised tourism may have helped: when Robert Brown went on a 'Cook's continental tour' in 1866, 'a number of females' was among the party of forty.[110]

Young, single women could and did travel together unescorted. Georgiana Coats accompanied her younger sister Victoria on travels designed to improve the latter's health; they visited Trinidad, Italy and Malta, where Victoria sadly died. In 1867 Frances Murray (then aged twenty-four) and her sister went to America for eighteen months; they presumably visited their American relatives, though their parents did not accompany them. Twenty years later Frances wrote home: 'Here in Cannes there is scarce a specimen of the genus Englishman, but on the contrary

Englishwomen swarm so as to blot out the natives.'[111] Frances herself was travelling without her husband. Similarly, Isabella Elder in her widow-hood travelled the continent with only a female companion.

Women could travel alone to further their education. As mentioned in the previous chapter, Lord Kelvin's Aunt Agnes went to Brussels to improve her French (shades of *Villette*). By the turn of the century, this could be more official education. Dorothy Murray and her friend Chrystal MacMillan went to Berlin to attend lectures at the university in 1901. The same Chrystal accompanied Frances Murray on a tour of Greece five years later: Frances was married and middle-aged; but there was no male escort.

Women were becoming active observers, emphasising seeing rather than being seen. Margaret Allan and her daughter wrote home from Paris: 'Be assured we are missing nothing that has been in our power to see, and we intend to see all we have not seen.'[112] As indefatigable tourists, women often went to the great cultural centres of Europe, following the path of the Grand Tour undertaken by their male counterparts in the eighteenth century. But they also ventured further afield. Maria Ewing, widow of Alexander, died in 1878 in Wadi Halfa, Sudan. Georgiana Coats and her husband visited Australia, New Zealand, America, Norway and Algeria. Shortly after being widowed in 1899, she took her daughters abroad 'for a year or two'.[113]

Women did, of course, often travel with a male companion, usually father, husband or brother. The 'holiday on the Continent' outlined in John Stephen's diaries from 28 September 1865 seems to have been with his sister Janet. They went to Rotterdam, Cologne, Bonn, Frankfurt, Heidelberg and then on to tour Switzerland, arriving back in Glasgow on 18 October. They visited museums, cathedrals, castles, zoological gardens, the opera, and travelled by carriage, rail and steamer. Six months later Stephen married Eliza Wilson; they spent their long honeymoon — thirty-six days — travelling across France and Switzerland, and through Italy as far as Rome.

Fathers often accompanied their children, especially, it seems, their daughters. In 1864 Walter Crum and his daughter Elizabeth were in Paris together. Robert Brown and his daughter Isabella toured southern and midland England in 1869, and in 1876, joined by another daughter, they travelled in France, Italy, Switzerland and Germany for nearly two months. The following year the trio spent nearly three months touring the USA and Canada together.[114] So although married couples often travelled extensively together, for wives this was likely to be a continuation of a practice begun long before marriage.

In fact many middle-class women's first experience of travel had been in their teens, going away to boarding school; whether in England or more distant parts of Scotland, several of the women in this study kept in touch with old schoolfriends. In 1870 Frances Murray, then twenty-seven, went to London to visit family friends, saw her sister then at school, then stopped off in Cheshire with her 'old school friend Emily Higs, now married and become Mrs Bellhouse'. She was away over a month at least.

Nineteenth-century travel was of course made much easier by developments in transport, especially the railway. It was this that made the frequent trips to London, Manchester and so on possible, and greatly facilitated the continental tours. Similarly transatlantic travel was becoming safer and swifter. In Glasgow it became easier for women to move around the city, often unescorted, when private companies started running omnibuses from mid-century.[115] According to Alison Aldburgham, 'By 1850, it was quite respectable for a lady to go in an omnibus.'[116] There were hackney carriage stands in Claremont, Woodlands and Woodside Terraces, from which fares to central Glasgow were 1s 6d in 1857.[117] Later in the century, other forms of transport were introduced – trams from 1872 and the Glasgow underground in 1896.[118]

So if women needed to use public transport, there was plenty available and no apparent barriers to them taking it. Many middle-class families, however, were 'carriage folk', and had their own private transport. The inventory of James Watson of Woodside Terrace in 1869 included an 'old carriage', and Mrs Margaret Mackenzie had a brougham and carriage at her 'other' house at Ayr in 1902. The 'lanes' at the back of the houses in the more prosperous Claremont/Woodside streets were in fact mews – there were six or seven coachmen and their families in Woodside Terrace Lane alone in 1881. Women also seem to have enjoyed freedom of access to this transport. Madeleine Smith had the use of some sort of family carriage: 'On Thursday I intend to drive down to Partick and make B. walk home so as she may be tired and go to bed at 10 o'clock.'[119] Walter Crum wrote: 'Your Mother and Agnes are just off to Dalry to meet the brougham for Largs.'[120]

The view of Victorian middle-class women as debilitated and virtually housebound managed to accommodate knowledge of the exceptional 'lady explorers' who set off with their stout shoes and parasols for distant countries simply by seeing them *as* exceptional. Insofar as they travelled, often alone, to remote and relatively unexplored destinations, they were certainly out of the ordinary. Yet their exploits were not far removed from those of the women swarming to the continent and hiking through demanding terrain in their own country. For many middle-class women, making lengthy visits abroad shaded into actually living there. Wives accompanied husbands to the corners of the Empire and across Glasgow's extensive trading routes. Jessie Gow or Elsden, wife of Thomas Elsden, a ship's captain, died at sea in 1873.[121] John Stephen's sister Mina married on 31 October 1866, and five days later the couple left for South Africa.[122] Despite their unsatisfactory marriage, Lord Kelvin's Aunt Agnes lived with her husband in Brazil and Portugal in the early years of the period.[123] In the early twentieth century Frances Murray's daughter Dorothy lived with her husband in India.[124]

Frances Murray's three daughters provide good examples of the variety of discourse which could sanction a public role for women. Dorothy supported her husband in the service of Empire, while Sylvia eschewed marriage and travelled to China as part of the China Inland Mission. This society actively recruited single women missionaries, claiming that in some circumstances they could be more effective than men.[125] Imperialism and Evangelicism were key influences not only on those women who travelled to distant lands, but also on those who read about their experiences and who used the language and concepts of both to sanction an active female role at home as well as abroad.[126] What Jane Haggis calls the 'meshed discourses' of religion and Empire together permitted an extension of the female sphere far beyond the confines of the home.[127] Not only were women thus given licence to exert influence over their own lives, but over those of (especially) women in other countries.

Religious discourses could also underwrite women's claims to have a political role. Sylvia and Eunice Murray were ardent feminists whose family tradition of radical liberalism and committed Christianity has already been emphasised. As Laura Nym Mayhall put it, their philanthropic and suffrage beliefs were 'underwritten by a sense of moral urgency and religious calling'.[128] The importance of religion in the lives of the Victorian middle class should not be underestimated. Principally through moral precepts, church-goers felt united as a community. Religious and philanthropic imperatives conjoined to allow – indeed to demand – a public role for women. Just as they had to engage with the public world to acquire the 'tasteful' furnishings that defined the home, so they had to engage with a different public realm in order to acquire and to demonstrate their spirituality. Aesthetic, religious and moral sensibility needed to be on the one hand nurtured and on the other hand displayed. Church attendance is merely the most obvious manifestation of this. Virtually all the families in this study are recorded as regular churchgoers. Clearly, genuine piety motivated much church-going. However, the form was also important – the rituals of dressing-up and processing to church, which Bell describes as a fixed and key feature of the family week.[129] Like the theatre and the promenade, church provided the opportunity both to see and be seen, and to make a statement about the secular as well as the spiritual well-being of the family.

Weekly attendance at church was only one part of the communal religious life. Philanthropy was not entirely organised through churches, but religious organisations were a principal outlet for philanthropic activities for much of the period. Although women's involvement in philanthropy had long been accepted, Davidoff and Hall find that in England in the first half of the nineteenth century 'the male and female philanthropic worlds remained substantively different'.[130] They argue that female philanthropy was carried out within parameters set by men: 'the more prestigious, public and formal associations were started and run by men [. . .]. when women moved in it was usually because men were moving out.'[131] Thus although women were 'testing the boundaries of female social action', they were not engineering social change.

The philanthropic activities of Glasgow's middle-class women in the second half of the century only partly support such a view. There was indeed a clear gendering within this sphere, with women's associations taking up such causes as the plight of women and children. The charitable associations attached to the Claremont United Presbyterian Church illustrate this very clearly. The Dorcas Society, founded in 1839, aimed to relieve poverty and distress among, especially, women and children who were members of the congregation by providing coal, cloth and some foodstuffs. In 1862 'Ladies connected with the congregation' set up a Female Industrial School. 'Mothers' Meetings' are recorded around this time too. A 'Bible Woman' was appointed in 1861 to carry out home visits in a poor 'mission district' of the city. Later a committee was formed to distribute religious tracts, and a Young Women's Guild was set up in 1894.[132]

In the last two decades of the century, the focus of Claremont Church's activities widened somewhat. A Temperance Society was founded in 1882 as an offshoot of the Mothers' Meeting. Around the same date, a Zenana Mission was formed and 'an efficient staff of eleven collectors' was gathered. Among the mission's aims was to 'increase and deepen the interest of the women of our church in their sisters abroad'.[133] Africa next received attention, with the establishing of a Ladies Kaffrarian Society to promote the education of females in that vast continent.[134] Antoinette Burton has shown how imperial ideals encouraged the involvement of British women in the lives of, in particular, women in India and Africa.[135] The Claremont ladies were no exception.

Other, city-wide charitable associations included the Glasgow Female Anti-Slavery Association and the Ladies Auxiliary to the Glasgow City Mission.[136] Their activities were also differentiated along gender lines. Women, it was argued, could visit working-class homes when men were out at work, and provide counselling on matters that were 'of too intimate a character to be tolerant of print'.[137] The (male) minister of the Claremont United Presbyterian Church described how the 'Bible Woman' was able to offer 'her womanly sympathies to the mother' in homes where she 'has been made a confidant, where I could never have hoped to gain a hearing'.[138]

Women could move more easily than men between the public and private worlds, and their association with the home made home visiting seem 'natural'. In a similar spirit, women would visit hospitals, care homes and orphanages. The Claremont ladies also did much collecting of subscriptions by calling on other middle-class families, an extension of the ritual of 'calling' in which they were already engaged. In other words, the gendering of philanthropy did not necessarily imply female inferiority and subordination. Women could appropriate existing ideologies of 'naturally' female virtues to establish areas of activity where they were seen as superior to men. Evangelical ideology stressed women's purity and spirituality, and made the care of others their 'proper sphere'. Thus notions of female moral superiority and of 'woman's mission' led to the idea of a 'distinct ministry' for women – different from and parallel to that of men. While this did not challenge notions of separate spheres for men and women, it did allow the development of women's engagement with public life.[139] Single-sex charitable societies allowed 'women's authority and autonomy to develop as alternatives to the model of male domestic patriarchy'.[140] The gendered nature of much of this philanthropic activity has furthermore tended to obscure its extent and scope. In terms of hours, this could amount to almost full-time employment. Between April and December 1861, for example, Miss Dougall of the Claremont Missionary Association 'paid nearly 3,000 visits [. . .] being occupied several hours a day'.[141] In its early years, the Claremont Female Industrial School met for two hours on Monday and Friday evenings, had 200 scholars on the roll and an average attendance of 125 with eighteen teachers.[142]

Another fund-raising speciality was the charity bazaar. Organisers and sponsors were listed in the local newspapers as part of the advertising of these events, which sometimes supported individual churches but were also in aid of other more secular endeavours like the Temperance League, where women played a prominent part.[143] Male attitudes towards these bazaars could be patronising, for example Bell's fond indulgence of his 'maiden aunt' doing crewel-work, fretwork, macrame, oil painting and decoupage for charity sale.[144] However, some women were 'promoters' of large bazaars held in Glasgow's City Halls, as Miss Beatrice Clugston was for that in 1871.[145] With the use of city-wide publicity, involvement with a bazaar was also a very public activity.

Individual women often undertook more than one philanthropic venture. In 1909 the charitable efforts of Lady Chisholm (daughter of a teacher, she married Sir Samuel Chisholm as her second husband) were listed in *Who's Who in Glasgow*: she was president or board member of new fewer than thirteen organisations. As outlined in chapter 1, Isabella Elder was not only instrumental in financing Queen Margaret College, but created Elder Park in Govan; in this venture she directed operations, took crucial decisions and gave a speech at the park's opening before a vast crowd. A statue commemorating her contributions to public life was erected in Govan in 1906, apparently the first in the city to a woman other than Queen Victoria.

It is noticeable that increasing formality and 'professionalism' is also associated with charity towards the end of the century, while before that women would make spontaneous gestures of generosity, acting on their own initiative. When Mrs Story moved to the Ayrshire countryside in the 1860s, for example, she had visions of 'endeavouring as far as lay in my power to brighten the lives of our humbler neighbours, and act in some measure as a modified Lady Bountiful.' She 'made friendly invasions on some of the cottages [. . .] who took my advances in good part and were generally quite well pleased to see me.'[146] In 1864 Walter Crum similarly described his wife's activities: '4 pm. I have dined since I came home without being able to startle your mother in her missionary labours. William told me she had gone out at 11.30 with some parcels of tea, and I now learn that she is in the village.'[147]

The Claremont Dorcas Society in the 1850s met only between October or November and April, as, presumably, members were away during the summer. In 1857, 'as there was little to be done' in January, they stopped meeting until late October.[148] However, later in the century their activities became more formalised. By the late 1880s, although home visiting continued, some applicants also attended the society's meetings to receive aid. A system of 'cards' for those applying for aid was introduced, and in 1894 rules were drawn up to regulate admission to benefits. By this date, too, the society had links with other agencies to whom they referred cases: by the early years of the twentieth century this included 'the Corporation', as private philanthropy gave way to State involvement.

Other organisations too increased in both scale and formality. The YWCA (President Mrs Mirrlees, Vice-President Mrs Gumprecht in 1900) had refreshment and reading rooms open daily, held educational and religious meetings, ran a large boarding house for 'young women engaged in business', and a registry for female servants. This was clearly a 'professional' operation. Female societies adopted the language of the boardroom, appointing presidents, secretaries and treasurers. The philanthropic roles of these women became increasingly public, with names and addresses of office holders, subscribers and supporters published in Post Office Directories and newspapers as well as in the records of the societies themselves. The immense amount of charitable effort undertaken by middle-class women throughout the period is testament to their energy and their success in creating a public philanthropic sphere for themselves.

The gendering of much philanthropic work should not blind one to the role of women as active in shaping middle-class ideology and to the impact of their cultural prescriptions on working-class women. In their choice of recipients and in the conditions they imposed on their benevolence, middle-class women were in a position to prescribe a particular morality upon those in need of their aid. In this respect, they were far from passive. In 1900 the Glasgow Home for Deserted Mothers pointed out: 'only those who, for the first time, have been led astray are admitted, and it is no part of the home to make matters light and easy for the girls and therefore probably encourage sin.'[149]

This sense of agency can be found throughout the minutes of the Claremont Dorcas Society. Aid could be withdrawn for whatever the committee decided was 'misconduct'. In 1869 the society withdrew support from the church's 'missionary district' in a poorer area because 'so bad a use was made' of the assistance that they decided to confine help to their own congregation.[150] It was the ladies' practice to visit and report on all cases so that only those they described as 'the deserving poor' received aid. The recipients knew how to respond: their 'heartfelt gratitude' was often recorded.

Virtues of self-help and frugality were encouraged. The Claremont Dorcas Society routinely gave *half* the cost of clothing, leaving beneficiaries to find the other half, which they might pay in small sums in advance. The Industrial School taught some basic literacy, but concentrated on sewing, so that girls could make their own clothing and produce articles for sale. They were also taught to cook 'plain substantial dishes suitable for use in the households to which they belong'. It was, of course, the Claremont ladies who decided what dishes were suitable for humble homes. They also noted with approval how the 'neatness and thrift' instilled into the girls remained with them into their 'after life'.[151]

Philanthropy, therefore, was an excellent vehicle for imposing middle-class values on the working class. Although the Claremont church philanthropists spoke occasionally of those they helped as 'sisters' in a spirit of Christian equality, they also brought to bear their own ideas both of how the recipients of charity should behave and of what they should receive. Tea was distributed because it was 'the cup that cheers but not inebriates'. Throughout the summer of 1896 they provided flowers to be given to the old and sick in poor districts – no doubt welcome, but perhaps less so than some other form of aid to those struggling to feed and clothe themselves. The Glasgow Female Society in 1857 afforded 'relief to aged and destitute women, who are visited monthly at their dwellings by a committee of ladies, and to whom pecuniary aid is afforded [. . .] with which is combined reading of the Scriptures and prayer.'[152]

The role of these women as *active* in shaping middle-class ideology and the impact of their cultural prescriptions on working-class women undermines the assumption of female passivity inherent in many conceptions of 'separate spheres'. It has been suggested that philanthropy was also crucial in allowing women to 'see' as well as be seen: that in entering working-class homes and scrutinising working-class lives women were enabled to develop a gaze and to become spectators of the (different) urban scene, just like the male *flâneur*.[153] Yet this view too denies women's agency: the *flâneur* is a detached observer of the social scene, not an active participant in its creation. The Claremont Dorcases were both establishing and enforcing middle-class values: in this context, class dichotomies and allegiances cut across those of gender.

In many ways, the social life of the Glasgow middle class conformed to the pattern of change over the second half of the century noted for English industrial cities. It is generally argued that this period saw a shift from small-scale social life, based on the home or on clubs and societies, to an expanded and more anonymous one, based on cash payment and

with more emphasis on formality and display.[154] Elements of this pattern
in the experience of middle-class women in Glasgow can certainly be
identified. The increasing professionalism in female employment is para-
llelled by greater formality and seriousness in women's social activities.
They became more involved in political activity, especially the suffrage
movement, and increasingly engaged in higher education. They undertook even more philanthropic activities, and tended to do so in a less
frivolous or dilettante spirit. The daughters of the sociable and active Mrs
Story led 'public' lives that were very different from their mother's: Elma
served on a multitude of church committees, was President of the Lady
Artists' Society, and was involved in social work and the Girls' Guildry
among many other areas of public service; Helen was instrumental in the
setting up of social services and the training of social workers in Glasgow
and was awarded an Honorary LLD from Glasgow University in recognition of her services. The sisters recognised that philanthropy had moved
on since their mother's day, and become formalised and professionalised.
Helen wrote: 'We must not dream of playing the Lady Bountiful now-
a-days.'[155]

While the middle class increasingly took part in a more inclusive, more
anonymous social life, this was in addition to – not instead of – the old
'subscription' sociability. In some respects – notably the mixture of
domestic entertaining (dinners, musical evenings, dancing) and public
assemblies – little seems to have changed between the social world
of Jane Austen and the end of the nineteenth century. At the beginning
of our period, social life revolved around membership of a select group.
The same people attended balls, took part in amateur dramatics,
visited each others' houses and undertook charitable ventures together.
They continued to do so. The chief difference was that a whole range of
other activities became open to middle-class women as the century
progressed.

The other realms where women were increasingly taking a place – the
department stores, libraries, teashops, lecture halls – were less dependent
on membership of an exclusive group than were the public activities of
mid-century. New forms of public transport made it less essential to have
one's own carriage. New activities which became popular towards the
end of the century and beyond, like the cinema, bicycling, hiking and so
on, were well within the financial compass of lower middle-class women,
especially those who were now earning their own salaries. Crucially, lower
middle-class women – those from Carnarvon and Stanley Streets, for
instance – by the end of the century had access to higher education, and

were able to enjoy the greater autonomy and participation in public life that it brought.

This democratrisation of leisure (for men as well as for women) is an important trend. It is a key part of the shift from interiority to anonymity in middle-class social life.[156] Cash, rather than cachet, now gained admittance to theatres, cinemas, restaurants and the like. Indeed, in some cases even the working classes might attend the same venue, and so it was important to preserve a tiered pricing structure in entertainment, transport and so on. How the middle class behaved – and perhaps especially how middle-class women behaved – in public was an important means of preserving class differentiation.

It has been argued that, paradoxically, as upper- and middle-class women became more visible and more socially active, so their behaviour became more policed. If 'respectable' women could be out and about in the city, as 'disreputable' women were, then the former would need to take care to preserve the distinction.[157] Thus, Maureen Montgomery argues, New York society adopted European ideas of chaperonage only in the 1880s. Yet, as discussed above, chaperonage – while occasionally observed – seems never to have been particularly restrictive on Glasgow middle-class women, and was breaking down in Britain at much the same period that it was being adopted in America.[158] Similarly, Judith R. Walkowitz argues that women's freedom in the city was constrained by the ever-present danger of being mistaken for a prostitute.[159] It is true that many of the social activities in which Glasgow women participated required them to be accompanied by men: but it is also true that they could and did venture into the city alone or with a female companion. In any case, one wonders how likely it was that women from the Claremont estate, with their carriages, silks and furs, would be mistaken for streetwalkers. As Simon Gunn points out: 'codes of dress and conduct [. . .] were clearly crucial in maintaining class and status distinctions in the highly visible world of the city.'[160] These codes could be read, one assumes, with sufficient ease by all classes. Nevertheless, middle-class women campaigned to make the city safe for 'respectable' women: moral purification of the city was a means as well as an end of women's involvement in its social life.[161] The indications are that Glasgow middle-class women became *less* rather than more policed as the century progressed, certainly in the sense that they were more likely to be out and about in the city unescorted.

The increase in range and frequency of the activities described above in the last decades of the century does not appear to support the view that domestic ideology fostered a sisterhood among women, who gathered together in their homes because they were denied much chance to socialise outside them. Women still met each other in a domestic setting, but they were also more likely to be socialising in tearooms, clubs and department stores, enjoying public places in exclusively female company. Rappaport nevertheless argues that middle-class respectability continued to depend on the idea that women 'remain apart from the market, politics and public space' and that therefore the female urban stroller and shopper was particularly subversive.[162] Yet middle-class women throughout the second half of the century had certainly not remained apart from urban public space. Not only as shoppers, but as consumers of a wide range of entertainments and participators in a host of activities, they had an active and established place in public life. Indeed in many aspects they were not subverting or challenging ideologies of public and private: their role arose *from* such ideologies. What middle-class women did – their moral mission, their civilising of social life, their culture – helped define the middle class. Competing discourses derived from religion, feminism, liberal politics, individualism all cut across tidy delineations of women's 'proper role' and any simplistic interpretation of public and private activity.

Ultimately, as already noted, much depends on how one defines 'public'. Women had a multiplicity of points of entry to the world outside the home. If women were excluded from a 'public realm', then that realm must be seen as chiefly constituting areas of the labour market, parliamentary politics, and some masculine clubs and societies. This would be subscribing to a narrow and male-defined view of the public. By the turn of the century, middle-class women had created their own 'public worlds', an act that is easily overlooked. Women were active agents in shaping not only metaphorical 'social circles' in the public sphere: they also played their part in the construction of the physical space of the city.

While women's participation in public spheres clearly changed over the course of the century, it is perhaps unhelpful to frame the issue in terms of the extent of their involvement. It is perhaps equally unhelpful to argue whether women in the second half of the century were in revolt against narrowing opportunities for participation in public life in the early years of the nineteenth century.[163] Discourses of domesticity and separate spheres were certainly influential in shaping women's identities and experience, although they were located within an array of discursive practices. However, it is by no means clear that notions of 'private' woman and 'public' man were as pivotal to the organisation of gender differences as has been assumed. More importantly, definitions of 'private' and 'public' were not eternal but mutable and shifting, as well as gendered. Women in public did not see themselves as breaking the rules, but regarded themselves as having a legitimate place there, and it is their interpretations and understanding of the concepts of public and private which are most telling.

Epilogue

As THE STEREOTYPES OF THE Victorian family and Victorian gender relations – the angel in the home, the ivy and the tower – have proved unreliable in relation to the experience of middle-class women, it is worth recapitulating our view of that experience.

First, it is remarkable for its diversity. Experience varied according to socio-economic standing, and the middle class encompassed a wide range. Life for the women of Claremont Terrace was in some ways quite different from life for women in Carnarvon Street. Nevertheless, other factors cut across this stratification, notably marital status. Conventional views have concentrated on the Victorian wife: it is salutary to remember that wives comprised a minority of adult women, and that single women and widows merit equal consideration. In some respects life for the spinsters of Carnarvon Street *and* Claremont Terrace differed from that of the wives of the same streets. Wealth and social status were not the only sources of diversity, or of identity. There were in fact multiple, competing identities, derived also from familial and cultural worlds, religious affiliation and so on. Furthermore, individuals experienced change within their lives: families moved up and even down the socio-economic hierarchy; spinsters became wives and often ultimately widows. So it is hard to say that *this* is what middle-class women's lives were like, or *this* is how middle-class families lived. Our study does not claim to contribute to studies of the formation of the middle class and its definition: the diversity of political, cultural and economic life across the spectrum of the streets investigated here is so great that it is difficult to subsume it into a neat category of 'middle class' or indeed 'middle classes'.

This is not to say that there were no factors in common, of course. Neither should our challenging of the extent of the purchase of ideologies of domesticity be taken to argue that there was no 'cult of the home', no equating of women with the private domestic sphere. But the home was a permeable realm, penetrated by social and professional association.

The family does not seem to have 'turned in on itself' and become intensely privatised and nuclear in focus. Contact with wider kin was considerable; the home was the locus of a host of social activities; and professional and business life was intertwined with home life for many families. There were many household forms, and most people experienced living in several, both nuclear and extended, at different times of their lives. At any point only a minority of households were two-parent nuclear families headed by the paterfamilias. Virtually all contained members who were not related to the family at all; the great majority had resident domestic servants; many had boarders, visitors, governesses. Many households were headed by women – and all women must have been aware that they might themselves be household heads at some stage. It has been assumed that marriage and motherhood formed the height of ambition for women: but, powerful as images of motherhood were, not all women saw these roles as their destiny. They had recourse to alternative discourses to legitimate other roles; and material circumstances meant that they were enabled to undertake them.

Domestic ideology, then, did not have the effect of isolating nuclear families in 'fortress' homes, nor of stripping them of close association with the extended family. Neither did it inevitably elevate the status of the 'man of the house' to that of demi-god. Gender relations were indeed played out within a context of male dominance, both legal and cultural: for all the diversity of their experience, women shared the same disadvantaged situation vis-à-vis men. But, while the legal and institutional framework of marriage was patriarchal, married couples could mediate and modify the 'rules'. Women, whether married or single, whether inside or outside the home, were active – both in the sense of energetic and in the sense of 'not passive'. They were actively involved in child-care, in running the household, in economic matters and in a range of public spheres. Middle-class women were in some respects better placed to counter male dominance than were women of the working class, and more able to negotiate a satisfying role for themselves within marriage or during widowhood. Similarly, the exaltation of motherhood could be empowering for women, but the meaning of motherhood varied not only across the hierarchy of the middle classes, but according to family culture, social ambition, religiosity, individual predilections and so on.

The danger of over-reliance on prescriptive literature to understand social relations in any era, and the inevitability of a gap between precept and practice, have been rehearsed many times.[1] People can pay lip-service to a set of ideals while behaving quite differently in their own lives. They might have *said* that the family was 'entire unto itself' but they did not *behave* as if it was, just as they may have used the rhetoric of male supremacy while consciously or unconsciously belying it in their every-day life.[2]

So how useful is the 'separate spheres' paradigm as a way of under-standing the organising principles of Victorian gender relations? Just as with the ideology of domesticity, we do not wish to argue that it has no relevance or usefulness in examining the nineteenth-century middle class. No one would seriously argue that. But it was not the only ideology in town. Certainly women's identities were negotiated around the meanings embedded in dominant discourses, but it must be re-emphasised that those discourses were multiple and diverse. Self-help, citizenship, indus-triousness, public service, religious leadership (to cite a few) sometimes reinforced but often competed with the paradigm. Furthermore, there is danger in conflating 'separate spheres' with an ideology of domesticity. The gendering of 'proper' spheres of activity for men and women is not *necessarily* the same as equating the female with the domestic.

Those who have challenged the extent and impact of separate spheres ideology have focused on its supposed adoption in the late eighteenth and early nineteenth centuries. Vickery is critical of the outlook in which separate spheres are seen as putting 'the middle in the middle class'– as being crucial to the formation of a middle-class identity – and questions the extent to which there was an increased restriction on women, or indeed the creation of a middle class, in the early nineteenth century.[3] Neither a separate spheres ideology nor the formation of a specifically middle-class identity can, she argues, be seen as products expressly of the early nineteenth century.

Similarly, Linda Colley and Amanda Foreman both argue that women (albeit often of the aristocracy rather than the middle class) were more active in political and social life in the late eighteenth and early nine-teenth centuries than contemporary literature would suggest.[4] Foreman argues that public and private in this period were in practice blurred – a view which is gaining currency at least for the early nineteenth century, where a body of work now questions the impermeability of separate spheres.

There has been greater acceptance of the view that the separate spheres paradigm is a key concept in understanding social life in the period from the start of Victoria's reign, particularly the notion that these spheres equated to public man and private woman. However, the gendering of identities and activities did not preclude diverse public roles for women. Women were equated with the domestic in a particularly subtle way; they were not necessarily kept immured within their homes. Even the most vocal proponents of separate spheres could argue that 'home' was not a concrete place: it was located wherever the woman was. 'Wherever a true wife comes, home is always round her [. . .] home is yet wherever she is.'[5] Not only did this view not automatically confine women to domestic space, it could also justify a public role for them. The ideology of domesticity had as much salience for men as for women, and it did not proscribe a public role for women.

Women acknowledged distinct spheres of influence and activity within 'the public' and indeed used this to claim a role based in some areas on an assertion of female superiority. They were comfortable in spheres that were at once female and public. Similarly, men's domestic role was greater, and more important to their construction of self, than in archetypal depictions of Victorian manhood. Thus the equation of public/private with male/female is not helpful in understanding women's *or* men's lives. The ideology of separate spheres, supposedly integral to an understanding of Victorian middle-class society, is in fact of limited usefulness if it is used as a universal paradigm, a sort of 'one size fits all' guide to gender roles.

It is important to avoid a simplistic interpretation of public and private. Categories were not static: they were malleable and amenable to variation. As Lawrence Klein has argued, contemporaries had multiple meanings for the terms 'public' and 'private'.[6] It is not helpful to impose dualisms on the past: there is more fluidity, and more room for overlapping meanings, than oppositional dichotomies permit. Discourses are *not* all-powerful, even though they are important, both because they can be resisted, and because the material context means that some things are not shaped by discourse alone. The women in this study played many public roles for which they found legitimation in a range of ideologies, discourses and practices. There is no sign that they regarded themselves as aberrant or transgressive. Furthermore, discourses and practices changed over time, for example the way in which opportunities of 'suitable' employment for women widened considerably across the period.

Nevertheless, change came at different times for different women. While there certainly was, as many have noted, a widening sphere in education and employment towards the end of the nineteenth century, this was almost entirely for single women. The view of spinsters bursting their bonds in the 1880s carries two problems. First, it tends to imply that before that time they had led unduly confined lives, which was not

necessarily the case. Second, it also supposes that married women continued to have restricted lives – ignoring the way that before and after
this watershed, married women carved out an influential role in the formation and perpetuation of family culture and identity, in philanthropy
and other public spheres. Trawling the slums, travelling the Empire, they
wielded influence abroad as well as at home.

The view of the Victorians as strait-laced, conventional and repressed
did not gain widespread currency until the twentieth century. Retro-
spection about the Victorian period began almost before it was over. The
largely disparaging tone of these observations prevailed for decades and
arguably they still colour some views today. Michael Mason argues that
anti-Victorianism was entrenched before the First World War, particularly
among intellectuals.[7] But the people who lived through these years had
different perceptions: 'I have been reading a clever article laughing at the
Victorian Age', Frances Murray wrote to her daughter in 1917. She then
set out a lengthy and spirited defence of the Victorian era – an 'age of
great progress', a 'live and throbbing age', listing its major social, political
and cultural achievements.[8] Born in 1843, Frances had, after all, lived
through nearly all of Victoria's reign.

J. J. Bell, looking back from the 1930s on his youth in the 1870s and
1880s, similarly defended the good sense, prudence and selflessness of
Victorian Glaswegians against what he claimed were often pitiless criticisms of the 'sins and weaknesses' of that period.[9] Nevertheless, it became
fashionable to denigrate the era, and 'Victorian' became generally synonymous with hypocrisy, sentimentality, prudery and self-satisfaction.

It has become difficult to uncouple 'Victorian' from pejorative associations and from the ready stereotypes that flow from them. Certainly the
Victorians have suffered at the hands of naïve interpretations of the
emblematic categories of their period – public, private, domestic and so
on. These have also been seen as the *only* defining features of the era, so
that the complexity of Victorian social life has been obscured. More
detailed work is emerging, and we hope that this study contributes to
the further opening-up of categories and undermining of stereotypes. By
demonstrating the richness of lived experience, we have aimed to illustrate and to do justice to the diversity and contradictions of Victorian
middle-class life.

Appendix I

Biographical Notes

Note on names: In Scotland it was the custom for married women to retain their family name and to use it alongside their husband's name, particularly in official correspondence. For example the testament of Mrs Eliza Smith refers to her as Eliza Service or Smith.

Allan, Hugh Builder and brickmaker of Crosshill. He married Margaret Binnie in 1845. Their children included Archibald, James, Peter and Maryanne (b. 1853), later the wife of **William McEwen**.

Blackie, Robert (1820–96) Publisher. Resident in Lynedoch Street in 1861. His daughter Constance married **Hugh Ewing** in 1888.

Brown, Robert (1810–95) Brickmaker, builder and stockbroker of Paisley. Active in local politics and civic affairs, he was also a keen antiquary. He was a friend and business associate of **James Watson**.

Cameron, Hector (1843–1928) Surgeon, Professor at Glasgow University. Having lived on the fringes of the Claremont estate (with the **Macfarlane** family as neighbours), he moved to Woodside Crescent. Friend and relative by marriage of the **Murray** family, he also knew **Joseph Coats**. He was knighted in 1900.

Coats, Joseph (1846–1899) Professor of Pathology, Glasgow University. He married Georgiana Taylor (1852–1927). Before moving to live at the university, they lived at 31 Lynedoch Street. She had been born and brought up in Royal Crescent, adjacent to the Claremont estate, where she went to church. Their daughters Olive Mary and Victoria compiled *A Book of Remembrance* (Jackson, Wylie & Co., 1929), using the family correspondence. The first twenty-five pages are extracts from a notebook compiled by Joseph Coats over two and a half years, not intended for publication. The remainder consists, *inter alia*, of letters to each other, their children and some later letters of Mrs Coats.

Crum, Walter (1796–1867) Cotton spinner, owner of the Thornliebank works and house at Rouken Glen. His nephew Alexander and several other branches of the Crum Ewing clan lived in Claremont Terrace and Woodside Crescent. One of Walter's daughters married into the **Houldsworth** family and another married **William Thomson (Lord Kelvin)**. See figs 2 and 3.

Elder, Isabella [née Ure] (1828–1905) Philanthropist. She moved to 6 Claremont Terrace after the death of her husband John, shipbuilder and marine engineer, in 1869. She was also prominent in civic and educational activities.

Ewing family Descended from Walter Ewing (see fig. 3), the family were West Indies merchants. They intermarried with the **Crum** dynasty.

Gilchrist, Marion (1832–1908) Resident at 15 Queen's Terrace. Victim in the Oscar Slater murder case, she was a well-to-do spinster who lived alone except for a servant.

Houldsworth Family of cotton spinners and iron masters.

Houldsworth, William (1798–1853) and his wife Mary [née Trueman] (d. 1879) were resident at 9 Claremont Terrace. The architect James Smith (**Madeleine Smith's** father) and William Minnoch (her fiancé) were business partners of William's brother John. Their nephew married Elizabeth, daughter of **Walter Crum**. See fig. 2.

Kelvin, Lord See **William Thomson**

L'Angelier, Emile See **Madeleine Smith**.

Lister, Joseph, Lord (1827–1912). He and his wife Agnes [née Syme] were resident at 17 Woodside Place.

McCallum [née Macewan], **Margaret** Resident in St Vincent Crescent, Glasgow. She married John McCallum in 1862. Their children attended school in the Claremont estate.

Macewan, Mollie Resident in Alabama, USA. Through her marriage to Henry Macewan, she became the sister-in-law of **Margaret McCallum**, with whom she enjoyed an extensive correspondence.

McEwen, William (1848–1924) Regius Professor of Surgery, Glasgow University. He grew up at 3 Stanley Street and later lived with his wife Maryanne [née Allan] and family at 3 Woodside Crescent. He was knighted in 1902.

Macfarlane, George Commission agent. He and his wife Mary Ann were members of the Free Church and active in temperance and philanthropy. They lived in Renfrew street as neighbours of **Sir Hector Cameron**. Their daughter Catherine Carswell (1879–1946) was a journalist and novelist, author of *Lying Awake*.

MacFie, Helen [née Wahab] (1844–96) She married John W. MacFie, Greenock sugar broker, in 1867. Their daughter Janet was born in 1869.

Minnoch, William See **Madeleine Smith**.

Mirrlees Buchanan, James (1822–1903) He was a partner in a firm of mechanical engineers, Mirrlees, Watson & Co. Ltd. His first wife died in 1853, and in 1859 he married Helen Gumprecht, daughter of Julius and Dorothea of Lynedoch Crescent.

Murray [née Stoddard], **Frances** (b. 1843) Born in the USA, she moved to Scotland with her parents in her early childhood. In 1872 she married David Murray, a lawyer. They lived in Fitzroy Place, less than 100 yards from the area of this study, and later in Cardross. Her girlhood friend Frances Macdonald married **Sir Hector Cameron**, whose daughter Hester became the wife of Murray's son Anthony; that couple lived in Woodside Crescent. This book draws strongly on the memoir to Frances Murray, compiled by her daughter Eunice.

Napier, Edith (b. 1849) Daughter of Robert, engineer and shipbuilder, and his wife Emma.

Perry, Mary (b. 1817) Resident in West Renfrew Street, friend of Emile L'Angelier, victim in the **Madeleine Smith** murder case.

Smith, Madeleine (b. 1835) Daughter of the architect James Smith. She was tried for the murder of her lover, Emile L'Angelier, in 1857. Her fiancé William Minnoch had planned for them to live in the Claremont estate. Instead it was he and his wife Mary who settled there at 6 Woodside Crescent. Minnoch also worked for the **Houldsworth** family, with whom the Smiths had business and social connections.

Smith, Robert (1801–73) Shipowner, co-founder of the City Line. He married **Eliza Service** (d. 1883) and lived at 15 Woodside Terrace. Their daughter Jane married Alexander Allan, shipowner, grandson of the founder of the Allan Line. The family were committed to evangelical causes and the temperance mission. See fig. 1.

Stephen Family of shipbuilders. Messrs Alexander Stephen & Sons, mostly resident in Park Terrace, adjoining the Claremont streets. John Stephen (b. 1835) was at one time a lodger at 7 Woodside Crescent.

Story [née Maughan], **Janet** (b. 1828) This book draws extensively on her two volumes of reminiscences. Born in Bombay, she spent her youth in Edinburgh. In 1863 she married Robert Story, Minister of Roseneath, who was appointed to the Chair of Church History in 1886 and later became Principal of Glasgow University. Their daughters Elma and Helen compiled a *Memoir of Robert Herbert Story*.

Templeton, John (1832–1918) Carpet manufacturer. Resident at 7 Woodside Crescent, he was related by marriage to the **Stephen** family. The carpet factory subsequently merged with that set up by **Frances Murray's** father to become Stoddard Templeton.

Thomson, William (Lord Kelvin) (1824–1907) Physicist, Professor at Glasgow University. His sister Elizabeth Thomson King compiled a volume of memoirs, *Lord Kelvin's Early Home Life.* He married Margaret, daughter of **Walter Crum**, in 1852.

Watson, James (1801–89) Lord Provost of Glasgow. Resident at 9 Woodside Terrace and acquainted with the Revered Robert and **Janet Story**. He was knighted in 1874.

Appendix 2

Residents of the Claremont/ Woodside Estate

The following is a selective list of residents in the Claremont/Woodside estate. It is intended to illustrate the many geographical and social links between the families discussed in this book.

7 Claremont Terrace 1861, 1871 Alexander Ewing

6 Claremont Terrace 1861 Elizabeth Ewing

8 Woodside Crescent 1861 Alexander Ewing

26 Woodside Place 1871 Jessie Crum Ewing

20 Woodside Terrace 1851 Humphrey Ewing Crum

9 Claremont Terrace William and Mary Houldsworth

6 Claremont Terrace Isabella Elder

16 Claremont Terrace James Templeton

5 Lynedoch Crescent Julius and Dorothea Gumprecht

9 Lynedoch Crescent Peter Clouston, Lord Provost of Glasgow, 1860–63

34 Lynedoch Street Robert Blackie

31 Lynedoch Street Joseph and Georgiana Coats

3 Stanley Street Childhood home of Sir William MacEwen

Woodside Crescent Sir Hector Cameron

Woodside Crescent Anthony and Hester [née Cameron] Murray

3 Woodside Crescent Sir William and Maryanne [née Allan] MacEwen

6 Woodside Crescent William and Mary Minnoch

7 Woodside Crescent John Templeton; John Stephen

17 Woodside Place Joseph [Lord] Lister and Agnes Lister [née Syme]

9 Woodside Terrace Sir James Watson

15 Woodside Terrace Robert and Eliza [née Service] Smith

15 Queen's Terrace Marion Gilchrist

Notes

INTRODUCTION

1   For a critical discussion of the utility of the concept, see A. J. Vickery, 'From Golden Age to Separate Spheres: A Review of the Categories and Chronology of English Women's History', *Historical Journal*, 36, 2 (1993), pp. 383–414; for a discussion of the confining and constraining effects of the ideology of separate spheres, see Susan Moller Okin, 'Women and the Making of the Sentimental Family', *Philosophy and Public Affairs*, 11, 1 (1982), pp. 65–88, and, for a more positive appraisal, Sylvana Tomaselli, 'The Enlightenment Debate on Women', *History Workshop Journal*, 20 (1985), pp. 101–24.

2   John Ruskin, one of the Victorian ideologues of 'separate spheres', advocated a definition of the ideology of domesticity which transcended physical space and place and argued essentially that home was where woman was. Quoted in Thad Logan, *The Victorian Parlour* (Cambridge University Press, 2001), p. 25.

3   Leonore Davidoff and Catherine Hall, *Family Fortunes: Men and Women of the English Middle Class, 1780–1850* (Routledge, 1987), p. 403.

4   Judith Butler, *Gender Trouble: Feminism and the Subversion of Identity* (Routledge, 1993); Terry Lovell, 'Thinking Feminism with and against Bourdieu', in Bridget Fowler (ed.), *Reading Bourdieu on Society and Culture* (Blackwell, 2000), pp. 27–48.

5   Lawrence E. Klein, 'Gender and the Public/Private Distinction in the Eighteenth Century: Some Questions about the Evidence and Analytic Procedure', *Eighteenth Century Studies*, 29, 1 (1995), pp. 97–109.

6   Ibid., p. 99.

7   Doreen Massey, 'Masculinity, Dualisms and High Technology', in Nancy Duncan (ed.), *Body Space: Destabilising Geographies of Gender and Sexuality* (Routledge, 1996), p. 113.

8   Sue Morgan, 'Faith, Sex and Purity: The Religio-Feminist Theory of Ellice Hopkins', *Women's History Review*, 9, 1 (2000), pp. 13–34; essays by Eileen Janes Yeo, Alison Twells and Helen Rogers in Eileen Janes Yeo (ed.), *Radical Femininity: Women's Self-Representation in the Public Sphere* (Manchester University Press, 1998).

9   Ibid. See the articles in Sandra Stanley Holton, Alison Mackinnon and Margaret Allan (eds), 'Between Rationality and Revelation: Women, Faith and Public Roles in the Nineteenth Centuries', special issue of *Women's History Review*, 7, 2 (1998).

10   Quoted in Phillip Mallet, 'Women and Marriage in Victorian Society', in Elizabeth Craik (ed.), *Marriage and Property* (Aberdeen University Press, 1984), p. 166.

11   Holton *et al.* (eds), 'Between Rationality and Revelation'; Megan Smitley, 'Women's Mission: The Temperance and Women's Suffrage Movements in Scotland, c. 1870–1914', unpublished PhD thesis, University of Glasgow, 2002.

12 Kathryn Gleadle, *The Early Feminists: Radical Unitarians and the Emergence of the Women's Rights Movement, 1831–51* (Macmillan, 1995); Clare Midgley, *Women against Slavery: The British Campaigns, 1780–1870* (Routledge, 1992).

13 See the various articles in Clare Midgley (ed.), *Gender and Imperialism* (Manchester University Press, 1998); Antoinette Burton, *Burdens of History: British Feminists, Indian Women and Imperial Culture, 1865–1915* (University of Carolina Press, 1994).

14 Jane Haggis, '"A heart that has felt the love of God and longs for others to know it": Conventions of Gender, Tensions of Self and Constructions of Difference in Offering to be a Lady Missionary', *Women's History Review*, 7, 2 (1998), pp. 171–92.

15 John Tosh, *A Man's Place: Masculinity and the Middle-Class Home in Victorian England* (Yale University Press, 1999), pp. 141–2.

16 See the essays in Joseph H. Carens (ed.), *Democracy and Possessive Individualism: The Intellectual Legacy of C. G. Macpherson* (State University of New York Press, 1993).

17 John Seed, 'Unitarianism, Political Economy and the Antimonies of Liberal Culture in Manchester, 1830–50', *Social History*, 7, 1 (1982), pp. 1–25.

18 John Stuart Mill, as quoted in Phillip Mallet, 'Women and Marriage in Victorian Society', p. 164.

19 Simon Gunn, 'The Public Sphere, Modernity and Consumption: New Perspectives on the History of the English Middle Class', in Alan Kidd and David Nicholls (ed.), *Gender, Civic Culture and Consumerism: Middle-Class Identity in Britain 1800–1940* (Manchester University Press, 1999), pp. 12–29.

20 Much may hinge on the definition of 'public sphere'. Even in its classic Habermassian formulation, however, women could be said to have a presence. See Lawrence Klein, 'Gender, Conversation and the Public Sphere in Early 18th century England', in Judith Still and Michael Worton (ed.), *Textuality and Sexuality*

(Manchester University Press, 1993); for a discussion of 'the feminine public sphere' and the role of middle-class women in temperance, suffrage and philanthropy in Scotland, see Megan Smitley, 'Woman's Mission'.

21 The essays in Kidd and Nicholls (ed.), *Gender, Civic Culture and Consumerism* exemplify the approach which focuses on culture and identity as the key categories of analysis in studies of the middle classes.

22 George Eliot, *Middlemarch* [1871–2], ed. B. G. Hornsback (W. W. Norton & Co., 2000), p. 515.

1 LIFE IN THE CITY

1 N. F. R. Crafts, *British Economic Growth during the Industrial Revolution* (Oxford, 1985). For the counter-argument, see Pat Hudson, 'Rehabilitating the Industrial Revolution', *Economic History Review*, 45, 1 (1992), pp. 24–50.

2 W. H. Fraser and Irene Maver (ed.), *Glasgow*, vol. II: *1830–1912* (Manchester University Press, 1996), chapters 2 and 3.

3 Ibid., chapter 4, p. 141.

4 M. A. Simpson, 'The West End of Glasgow 1830–1914', in M. A. Simpson and T. H. Lloyd (ed.), *Middle-Class Housing in Britain* (David and Charles, 1977), p. 44.

5 Nicholas Morgan and Richard Trainor, 'The Dominant Classes', in W. Hamish Fraser and R. J. Morris (ed.), *People and Society in Scotland*, vol. II: *1830–1914* (John Donald, 1990), pp. 103–37.

6 J. Forbes Munro, 'Scottish Overseas Enterprise and the Lure of London: The Mackinnon Shipping Group, 1847–1893', *Scottish Economic and Social History Journal*, 8 (1988), pp. 73–87.

7 Perilla Kinchin and Juliet Kinchin, *Glasgow's Great Exhibitions 1888, 1901, 1911, 1938, 1988* (White Cockade 1988), p. 34.

8 Ibid., p. 34.

9 Ibid., p. 35.

10 Stana Nenadic, 'The Small Family Firm in Victorian Britain', *Business History*, 35, 4 (1993), pp. 86–114.

11 Irene Sweeney, 'The Municipal Administration of Glasgow 1833–1912: Public Service and the Scottish Civic Identity', unpublished PhD thesis, University of Strathclyde, 1990, biographical appendix; the Madeleine Smith case is discussed in chapter 3.

12 Peter L. Payne, *The Early Scottish Limited Companies 1856–1895* (Scottish Academic Press, 1980).

13 Richard Saville, *The History of the Bank of Scotland* (Edinburgh University Press, 1996), pp. 422–4.

14 Guy McCrone, *Wax Fruit* [1947] (Black & White Publishing, 1993), pp. 190–92.

15 Quoted in Kinchin and Kinchin, *Glasgow's Great Exhibitions*, p. 56.

16 James Schmiechen, 'Glasgow of the Imagination: Architecture, Townscape and Society', in Fraser and Maver (ed.), *Glasgow*, p. 500.

17 Introduction to Fraser and Maver (ed.), *Glasgow*, p. 5.

18 Ibid., p. 4.

19 Irene Maver, 'Glasgow Town Council in the Nineteenth Century', in T. M. Devine, *Scottish Elites* (John Donald, 1994), p. 122.

20 Ibid., p. 122.

21 W. W. Knox, *The Industrial Nation* (Edinburgh University Press, 1998), chapter 18; Eleanor Gordon, *Women and the Labour Movement in Scotland 1850–1914* (Oxford University Press, 1991), chapter 7.

22 Callum G. Brown, *Religion and Society in Scotland since 1707* (Edinburgh University Press, 1997), chapter 5.

23 Peter Hillis, 'Presbyterianism and Social Class in Mid-Nineteenth Century Glasgow: A Study of Nine Churches', *Journal of Ecclesiastical History*, 32 (1981), pp. 42–64.

24 Brown, *Religion and Society*, p. 120.

25 Some historians have argued that religious differences within the working class in Glasgow were not particularly divisive before the war: J. J. Smyth, *Labour in Glasgow, 1896–1936: Socialism, Suffrage,* *Sectarianism* (Tuckwell Press, 2000) and Joan Smith, 'Labour Traditions in Glasgow and Liverpool', *History Workshop*, 17 (1984), pp. 32–56.

26 Brown, *Religion and Society*, chapter 5.

27 R. Q. Gray, *The Labour Aristocracy in Victorian Edinburgh* (Oxford University Press, 1976).

28 W. W. Knox, 'The Political and Workplace Culture of the Working Class, 1832–1914', in W. Hamish Fraser and R. J. Morris (ed.), *People and Society in Scotland*, vol. 11: *1830–1914* (John Donald, 1990), pp. 138–66.

29 Geoffrey Ingham, *Capitalism Divided?* (Macmillan, 1984); David Rubinstein, 'Wealth, Elites and the Class Structure of Modern Britain', *Past and Present*, 76 (1977), pp. 99–126; R. J. Morris, *Class, Sect and Party: The Making of the British Middle Class, Leeds, 1820–50* (Manchester University Press, 1990); Leonore Davidoff and Catherine Hall, *Family Fortunes: Men and Women of the English Middle Class, 1780–1850* (Routledge, 1987).

30 See the essays in Alan Kidd and David Nicholls (ed.), *Gender, Civic Culture and Consumerism: Middle-Class Identity in Britain 1800–1940* (Manchester University Press, 1999); Simon Gunn, *The Public Culture of the Victorian Middle Class* (Manchester University Press, 2000).

31 Davidoff and Hall, *Family Fortunes*.

32 Gareth Stedman Jones, *Languages of Class: Studies in English Working Class History, 1832–1983* (Cambridge University Press, 1983); Patrick Joyce, *Visions of the People: Industrial England and the Question of Class, 1840–1914* (Cambridge University Press, 1994); Dror Wahrmann, 'National Society, Communal Culture: An Argument about the Recent Historiography of Eighteenth-Century Britain', *Social History*, 17, 1 (1992), pp. 43–72.

33 Ibid., p. 47.

34 Gunn, *Public Culture*, p. 16.

35 R. H. Trainor, 'The Elite', in Fraser and Maver (ed.), *Glasgow*, pp. 227–64.

36 Stana Nenadic, 'The Victorian Middle Classes', in ibid, pp. 265–99.

37 Ibid., p. 272.

38 *Scotsman*, 18 August 1849.

39 R. H. Trainor, 'The Elite', in Fraser and Maver (ed.), *Glasgow*, p. 233.

40 Simpson, 'West End of Glasgow', pp. 44–85.

41 M. A. Simpson, 'Urban Transport and the Development of Glasgow's West End, 1830–1914', *Journal of Transport History*, n.s. I (1971–2), pp. 146–60.

42 Simpson, 'West End of Glasgow', p. 52; Catherine Carswell, *Lying Awake* (Canongate, 1997).

43 Davidoff and Hall, *Family Fortunes*; Simpson, 'The West End of Glasgow'.

44 Davidoff and Hall, *Family Fortunes*, *passim*; despite their emphasis on the separation of work and home, Davidoff and Hall found that the majority of the middle classes lived at or adjacent to their place of work in 1851. See Tosh, *A Man's Place*, p. 17, n. 17.

45 Peter Reed, 'The Victorian Suburb', in Reed (ed.), *Glasgow: The Forming of a City* (Edinburgh University Press, 1992), pp. 62–83.

46 Ibid., p. 68.

47 David Ward, 'Environs and Neighbours in the "Two Nations": Residential Differentiation in Mid-Nineteenth Century Leeds', *Journal of Historical Geography*, 6 (1980), pp. 133–62; J. G. Robb, 'Suburb and Slums in Gorbals', in George Gordon and Brian Dicks (ed.), *Scottish Urban History* (Aberdeen University Press, 1983), pp. 133–62.

48 GCA T/MR/197, Trust book of Alexander Johnston; *Glasgow and West of Scotland Property Index*, 1892.

49 *Glasgow and West of Scotland Property Index*, 1897.

50 Simpson, 'West End of Glasgow', p. 83.

51 NAS SC 36/48/104, Inventory of Andrew Chrystal, 1883, pp. 253–7.

52 GCA T-HH 24/6, Inventory of James Thomson, March 1905.

53 GCA TD 862/70, Inventory of William Houldsworth, Jan 1854.

54 GCA T-HB/121, Inventory of Miss Isabella Campbell, May 1890.

55 GCA T-HB/655, Inventory of Mrs Margaret Wilson, Oct 1889.

56 GCA T-BK-8, Sederunt book of Alexander Anderson.

57 GCA TD 976/98/1, Inventory of Andrew Jack, Dec 1885.

58 *Calendar of Confirmations and Inventories 1876–1936*.

59 *Memoirs and Portraits of One Hundred Glasgow Men* (1886), p. 165.

60 Ibid., p. 282.

61 Anthony Slaven, 'The Origins of Scottish Business Leaders 1860–1960', in T. M. Devine (ed.), *Scottish Elites* (John Donald, 1994), p. 293.

62 John L. Carvel, *Stephen of Linthouse* (Alexander Stephen & Sons Ltd, 1950), p. 90.

63 Ibid., p. 89.

64 Slaven, 'The Origins', p. 168.

65 GCA PA/190, 'Crum's Land: A History of Thornliebank', p. 7.

66 R. D. Anderson, *Education and Opportunity in Victorian Scotland: Schools and Universities* (Oxford University Press, 1983).

67 *Memoirs and Portraits*, pp. 165–6; GCA TD 1073/4, Crum family correspondence; Anthony Slaven and Sidney Checkland (ed.) *Dictionary of Scottish Business Biography* (Aberdeen University Press, 1986–90), vol. 2, p. 263.

68 Obituary, *British Medical Journal*, 29 March 1924.

69 Slaven, 'The Origins', pp. 152–69; Introduction to Fraser and Maver (ed.), *Glasgow*, p. 6.

70 Quoted in Arthur Herman, *The Scottish Enlightenment: The Scots' Invention of the World* (Fourth Estate, 2001), p. 293.

71 School certificate from 1909. We are grateful to Valerie McClure for bringing this to our attention.

72 See Megan Smitley, '"Women's Mission": The Temperance and Women's Suffrage Movements in Scotland, c. 1870–1914', unpublished PhD thesis, University of Glasgow, 2002.

73 Fred H. Young, *A Century of Carpet Making 1839–1939* (James Templeton, 1944).

74 Evidence to Royal Commission on Poor Laws and Relief of Distress, 1909.

75 NAS SC 36/51/70, Testament of Susannah C. Allan, 1876, pp. 27–35.

76 Joan McAlpine, *The Lady of Claremont House* (Argyll Publishing, 1997), p. 69.

77 Ibid., p. 84.

78 Ibid., pp. 199–200.

79 Davidoff and Hall, *Family Fortunes*, chapter 2; Simon Gunn, 'The Ministry, the Middle Class and the "Civilising Mission" in Manchester, 1850–80', *Social History*, 21, 1 (1996), pp. 22–36; Sue Morgan, 'Faith, Sex and Purity: The Religio-Feminist Theory of Ellice Hopkins', *Women's History Review*, 9, 1 (2000), pp. 13–34; Callum G. Brown, *The Death of Christian Britain* (Routledge, 2001).

80 D. W. Bebbington, *The Baptists in Scotland* (Baptist Union of Scotland, 1988), p. 4.

81 Brown, *Death of Christian Britain*, p. 105.

82 Brown, *Religion and Society*.

83 Peter Hillis, 'Presbyterianism and Social Class in Mid-Nineteenth Century Glasgow: A Study of Nine Churches', unpublished PhD thesis, University of Glasgow, 1978.

84 A number of historians have argued for the centrality of religious belief and culture to nineteenth-century society and the need to accord it centre stage in discussions of how individuals constructed their identities. Morgan, 'Faith, Sex and Purity'; Gunn, 'The Ministry, the Middle Class and the "Civilising Mission"'; Lesley A. Orr MacDonald, *A Unique and Glorious Mission: Women and Presbyterianism in Scotland 1830–1930* (John Donald, 2000); Eileen Janes Yeo (ed.), *Radical Femininity: Women's Self-Representation in the Public Sphere* (Manchester University Press, 1998), chapters 1, 2, 4; and Jane Haggis, '"A heart that has felt the love of God and longs for others to know it": Conventions of Gender, Tensions of Self and Constructions of Difference in Offering to be a Lady

Missionary', *Women's History Review*, 7, 2 (1998), pp. 171–92. For a persuasive argument against the late nineteenth-century secularisation thesis, see for example, Brown, *Death of Christian Britain*.

85 Brown, *Death of Christian Britain*, chapter 4.

86 Carswell, *Lying Awake*, editor's introduction.

87 Ibid., chapter 2.

88 Ibid., p. 26.

89 Ibid., p. 19.

90 Slaven and Checkland (ed.), *Dictionary of Scottish Business Biography*, vol. 2, pp. 262–4; Smitley, 'Women's Mission'.

91 *Dr and Mrs Coats: A Book of Remembrance* (Jackson, Wylie & Co., 1929), p. 237.

92 Ibid., p. 20.

2 It's a Family Affair

1 Peter Laslett, *The World We Have Lost* (Methuen, 1973); Alan Macfarlane, *The Origins of English Individualism* (Blackwell, 1978); Peter Laslett and Richard Wall (ed.), *Household and Family in Past Time* (Cambridge University Press, 1972).

2 Michael Anderson, *Approaches to the History of the Western Family 1500–1914* (Cambridge University Press, 1995), p. 11.

3 Barry Reay, 'Kinship and the Neighbourhood in Nineteenth-Century Rural England: The Myth of the Autonomous Nuclear Family', *Journal of Family History*, 21 (1996), pp. 87–104; Zvi Razi, 'The Myth of the Immutable English Family', *Past and Present*, 140 (1993), pp. 3–44.

4 Gwyneth Nair, *Highley: The Development of a Community 1550–1880* (Blackwell, 1988); Keith Wrightson and David Levine, *Poverty and Piety in an English Village: Terling 1525–1700* (Oxford University Press, 1995).

5 Michael Anderson, *Family Structure in Nineteenth Century Lancashire* (Cambridge University Press, 1971).

6 Richard Sennett, *Families against the City: Middle Class Homes of Industrial Chicago, 1872–90* (Harvard University Press, 1970).

7 Richard Sennett, *The Face of Public Man* (Faber, 1993), quoted in Simon Gunn, *The Public Culture of the Victorian Middle Class* (Manchester University Press, 2000).

8 Stephen Ruggles, *Prolonged Connections: The Rise of the Extended Family in Nineteenth Century England and America* (University of Wisconsin Press, 1987).

9 Anderson, *Family Structure*; John Foster, *Class Struggle and the Industrial Revolution: Early Industrial Capitalism in Three English Towns* (Methuen, 1974).

10 Anthony Howe, *The Cotton Masters, 1830–1860* (Clarendon Press, 1984).

11 Ruggles, *Prolonged Connections*.

12 Laslett and Wall, *Household and Family*, pp. 29–31.

13 Marguerite Dupree, *Family Structure in The Staffordshire Potteries, 1840–1880* (Clarendon Press, 1995). Anderson, *Family Structure*; Foster, *Class Struggle*.

14 Ruggles, *Prolonged Connections*.

15 Michael Mason, *The Making of Victorian Sexuality* (Oxford University Press, 1995); John Gillis, Louise Tilly and David Levine, *The European Experience of Declining Fertility 1850–1970* (Blackwell, 1992).

16 Leonore Davidoff, Megan Doolittle, Janet Fink and Katherine Holden, *The Family Story: Blood, Contract and Intimacy, 1830–1960* (Longman, 1999).

17 Stana Nenadic, 'The Victorian Middle-Classes', in W. H. Fraser and Irene Maver, (ed.), *Glasgow* vol. II: *1830–1912* (Manchester University Press, 1996), pp. 227–64.

18 Ruggles, *Prolonged Connections*.

19 Leonore Davidoff and Catherine Hall, *Family Fortunes: Men and Women of the English Middle Class, 1780–1850* (Routledge, 1987).

20 Howe, *Cotton Masters*.

21 Dorothy Crozier, 'Kinship and Occupational Succession', *Sociological Review*, 13 (1965), pp. 15–43.

22 NAS SC 36/51/81, Testament of George Thomson, 1881, pp. 661–4.

23 Eunice G. Murray, *Frances Murray: A Memoir* (Maclehose, 1920), *passim*.

24 John Gillis, *A World of their own Making* (Oxford University Press, 1997).

25 Catherine Carswell, *Lying Awake* (Canongate, 1997), pp. 26–7.

26 In Scotland women were referred to legally by their own name as well as their married name. Thus Gow would have been Jane's maiden name and Smith her married one.

27 NAS SC 36/51/83, Testament of James Fraser, 1882, pp. 995–1003.

28 Di Cooper and Moira Donald, 'Households and "Hidden" Kin in Early Nineteenth Century England: Four Case Studies in Suburban Exeter, 1821–1861', *Continuity and Change*, 10, 2 (1995), pp. 257–78.

29 GUAS UGD 4/7/1, Diary of John Stephen.

30 Davidoff *et al.*, *Family Story*, p. 32.

31 NAS SC 36/61/85, Testament of Margaret Pinkerton, 1882, pp. 54–62.

32 Crozier, 'Kinship and Occupational Succession'.

33 *Memoirs and Portraits of One Hundred Glasgow Men* (John Tweed, 1886), vol. 1, pp. 5–8.

34 NAS SC 36/51/86, Testament and confirmation of Eliza Service or Smith, pp. 825–36.

35 GCA TD 62/2, Marriage contract of Robert Smith Allan and Lizzie Kincaid Greenhorn.

36 Razi, 'The Myth of the Immutable English Family', pp. 3–44; Reay, 'Kinship and the Neighbourhood in Nineteenth-Century Rural England', pp. 87–104.

37 GCA TD 1073/3/15, Letter from Walter Crum, 4 Sept 1864.

38 GCA TD 1073/4/1, Letter from Walter Crum, 21 May 1862.

39 GCA TD 1073/3/15, Letter from Walter Crum, 7 Sept 1864.

40 GUAS DC 79/70, Letter from Hugh Allan to his son, 23 July 1874.

41 *Dr and Mrs Coats: A Book of Remembrance* (Jackson, Wylie & Co.), p. 247.

42 GUAS UGD 4/7/1, Diary of John Stephen, 1864.

43 John Gillis, *A World of Their Own Making: A History of Myth and Ritual in Family Life* (Oxford University Press, 1997); Nenadic, 'The Victorian Middle Classes'.

44 GUAS UGD 4/7/1, Diary of John Stephen, 1864.

45 Letter from Anderson McCallum to John McCallum, 24 Dec 1862 (kind permission of Allan Campbell-Smith).

46 GUAS DC 79/71, Letter from Archibald Allan to James Allan, 27 June 1874.

47 GUAS DC 79/71, Letter from Archibald Allan to James Allan, 20 June 1873.

48 J. L. Story, *Early Reminiscences* (Maclehose, 1911), pp. 17–18.

49 NAS CS 247/5453, Aliment case between Andrew Stephen and his father Alexander Stephen, 1862.

50 GUAS DC 79/71, Letter from Hugh Allan to James Allan, 16 Aug 1880.

51 GCA TD 1063/3/15, Letter from Walter Crum to Jessie Crum, 2 Sept 1864.

52 NAS AD 14/57/255/1, Letters of Madeleine Smith to Emile L'Angelier.

53 Letters from Mollie de Winter Macewan to Margaret McCallum, 1869–73. We have been able to consult the Macewan correspondence by kind permission of Alan Campbell-Smith.

54 Letter from John Macewan to Margaret Macewan, 19 June 1855.

55 GCA TD 1073/4/4, Correspondence from William Graham Crum.

56 GCA TD 1073/4/1, TD 1073/4/10, Crum family correspondence.

57 GCA TD 1073/3/14, Crum family correspondence.

58 GCA TD 1073/8, Letter from William G. Crum to Agnes Crum, 29 April 1859.

59 GCA TD 1073/3/15, Letter from Walter Crum to Jessie Crum, 4 Sept 1864.

60 GUAS DC 79/70, Letters from Hugh Allan to James Allan, Oct 1869, and M. D. Allan to James Allan, 31 Oct 1874.

61 GUAS DC 79/131, Letter from James Allan to Peter Allan, Oct 1869.

62 Davidoff and Hall, *Family Fortunes*, pp. 348–53.

63 GCA TD 1073/4/4, Letter from William Crum to Margaret Crum Thomson, 16 Oct 1862.

64 GCA TD 1073/4/4, Letter from William Crum to Margaret Crum Thomson, 28 June 1864.

65 Ibid.

66 John Tosh, *A Man's Place: Masculinity and the Middle-Class Home in Victorian England* (Yale University Press, 1999).

67 A. J. Hammerton, *Cruelty and Companionship: Conflict in Nineteenth-Century Married Life* (Routledge, 1995), p. 79.

68 GUAS DC 79/33, Biographical note by W. MacDonald.

69 GUAS UGD 61/9/36, Blackie & Son Ltd, Letters from Robert Blackie to John Blackie.

70 GUAS UGD 4/7/1–6, Diaries of John Stephen.

71 Ibid.

72 GUAS DC 79/26, Letter from James Allan, 27 July 1874.

73 GUAS DC 79/26, Letter from James Allan, July 1907.

74 GUAS DC 79/131, Letter from James Allan, 1 Aug 1870.

75 Elizabeth Thomson King (ed.), *Lord Kelvin's Early Home Life* (Macmillan, 1909), p. 87.

76 GUAS DC 79/26, Letter from James Allan to Maryanne MacEwen, 27 July 1874.

77 GUAS DC 79/33, Biographical note by W. MacDonald.

78 Gillis, *A World of Their Own Making*, p. 190.

79 Thomson King, *Lord Kelvin's Early Life*, pp. 87 and 89.

80 GUAS DC 79/70, Letter from Hugh Allan to James Allan, 24 Sept 1869. Emphasis in original.

81 *Dr and Mrs Coats*, p. 135.

82 Ibid., p. 134.

83 Ibid., p. 262.

84 Ibid., p. 135.

85 Ibid., p. 269.

86 Ibid., p. 262.

87 GCA TD 1073/3/15, Letter from Walter Crum to Mary Crum, 31 Aug 1864.

88 GCA TD 1073/3/15, Letter from Walter Crum to Mary Crum, 18 Nov 1864.

89 GCA T-HB 352, Sederunt book of Mrs Janet Mathieson or Broom.

90 NAS SC 36/51/76, Testament of Anna Loudoun, pp. 812–20.

91 GCA T-BK-8, Sederunt book of Alexander Anderson.

92 NAS SC 36/51/126, Testament of Mrs Euphemia Halliburton Bulley or Guthrie, 1901, pp. 707-9.

93 NAS SC 36/51/85, Testament of Euphemia Gunn or Johnstone, 1883, p. 971.

94 NAS SC 51/84, Testament of Janet Mitchell, 1881, pp. 95–101.

95 NAS SC 36/51/83, Testament of James Fraser, 1881, pp. 995–1003.

96 NAS SC 36/48/90, Testament and inventory of Mrs Anne Abernethie Pirie or Munro, 1880, pp. 700–703.

97 NAS SC 36/48/147, Inventory of Miss Anna Mary Playfair, 1894, pp. 107–10.

98 GCA TD 1073/3/15, Letter from Walter Crum, 6 Nov 1864.

99 GCA TD 1073/3/15, Letter from Walter Crum, 17 May 1864.

100 GCA TD 1073/3/3, Letter from David Wilkie, 8 May 1871.

101 GCA TD 1073/10, Letter from Walter Crum junr, 1872; GCA TD 1073/3/3, Letter from Charles Mathieson, 17 June 1857.

102 Gillis, *A World of Their Own Making*, p. 70.

103 P. L. Payne, 'Family Business in Britain: An Historical and Analytical Survey', in M. B. Rose (ed.), *Family Business* (Edward Elgar, 1995), pp. 69–104.

104 Ibid.

105 GCA T/MR/197, Letter from Walter Paterson to the trustees of the estate of Alexander Johnston, Nov 1851.

106 Stana Nenadic, 'The Small Family Firm in Victorian Britain', *Business History*, 35, 4 (1993), p. 93.

107 Payne, 'Family Business in Britain', p. 173.

108 John L. Carvel, *Stephen of Linthouse* (Alexander Stephen & Sons Ltd, 1950), p. 85.

109 Ibid.; Anthony Slaven and S. G. Checkland (ed.), *Dictionary of Scottish Business Biography* (Aberdeen University Press, 1986–90), vol. 1, pp. 105–7.

110 Foreword to Carvel, *Stephen of Linthouse*.

111 Fred H. Young, *A Century of Carpet Making 1839–1939* (James Templeton, 1944).

112 Ibid., p. 61.

113 Carswell, *Lying Awake*, p. 39.

114 Nenadic, 'The Small Family Firm', p. 101.

115 Alfred D. Chandler, *Scale and Scope: The Dynamics of Industrial Capitalism* (Belknap Press, 1990); William Lazonick, *Business Organisation and the Myth of the Market Economy* (Cambridge University Press, 1991).

116 Nenadic, 'The Small Family Firm', p. 86.

117 Yoran Ben-Porath, 'The F-Connection: Families, Friends and Firms and the Organisation of Exchange', *Population and Development Review*, 6 (1980), p. 12.

118 Peter L. Payne, *The Early Scottish Limited Companies 1856–1895* (Scottish Academic Press, 1980).

119 Gillis, *A World of Their Own Making*, p. 70.

120 Amanda Vickery, 'From Golden Age to Separate Spheres: A Review of the Categories and Chronology of English Women's History', *Historical Journal*, 36, 2 (1993), pp. 383–414.

121 Rosemary O'Day, *The Family and Family Relationships, 1500–1900* (Macmillan, 1994), p. 300.

3 What's Love Got to Do with it?

1 For this view of the development of marital relations, see Lawrence Stone, *Family, Sex and Marriage in England 1500–1800* (Weidenfeld & Nicolson, 1977).

2 See, *inter alia*, Keith Wrightson, *English Society, 1580–1680* (Unwin Hyman, 1982); Ralph A. Houlbrooke, *The English Family, 1450–1700* (Longman, 1984); Alan Macfarlane, *Marriage and Love in England, 1300–1840* (Harlow, 1984), whose common critical thread is the importance of love as the foundation of marriage in earlier centuries.

3 Quoted in Sylvana Tomaselli, 'The Enlightenment Debate on Women', *History Workshop Journal*, 20 (1985), p. 120.

4 Lord Kames, *Loose Hints upon Education chiefly concerning the Culture of the Heart* (Edinburgh, 1781), pp. 228 and 246.

5 Susan Moller Okin, 'Women and the Making of the Sentimental Family', *Philosophy and Public Affairs*, 11, 1 (1982), pp. 65–88.

6 A. J. Hammerton, *Cruelty and Companionship: Conflict in Nineteenth-Century Married Life* (Routledge, 1995), chapter 3.

7 David Baird Smith, 'The Reformers and Divorce', *Scottish Historical Review*, 9 (1912), pp. 10–36.

8 Leah Leneman, 'Disregarding the Matrimonial Vows', *Journal of Social History*, 30, 2 (1996), pp. 465–82.

9 Eric M. Clive, *The Law of Husband and Wife in Scotland* (W. Green, 1982), p. 12.

10 Baron David Hume, *Lectures on the Law of Scotland, 1786–1822*, quoted in ibid., p. 12.

11 Clive, *The Law of Husband and Wife*, p. 285.

12 Quoted in ibid., p. 178.

13 Quoted in Lesley A. Orr Macdonald, *A Unique and Glorious Mission: Women and Presbyterianism in Scotland 1830–1930* (John Donald, 2000), p. 25.

14 Lord Kames, *Loose Hints upon Education*, p. 228.

15 Lecture delivered by the Reverend F. West in Liverpool, 'Woman: Her Position, Power and Privileges', reprinted in the *Waverley Journal*, 15 Nov 1856.

16 Hammerton, *Cruelty and Companionship*, p. 72.

17 Ibid., *passim*.

18 Carol Dyhouse, *Feminism and the Family in England 1880–1939* (Blackwell, 1989); Hammerton, *Cruelty and Companionship*; Judith Walkowitz, *City of Dreadful Delight* (Virago, 1992).

19 Clive, *The Law of Husband and Wife*, p. 288.

20 Quoted in ibid., p. 178.

21 Michael Mason, *The Making of Victorian Sexuality* (Oxford University Press, 1995), p. 50; N. L. Tranter, *Population and Society 1750–1940: Contrasts in Population Growth* (Longman, 1985), p. 51.

22 Fiona Dobbie, 'Divorce in Scotland 1830–1890', undergraduate dissertation, Department of Economic and Social History, University of Glasgow, 1998, p. 19.

23 Leah Leneman, *Alienated Affections* (Edinburgh University Press, 1998).

24 Dobbie, 'Divorce in Scotland 1830–1890'.

25 John Gillis, *A World of Their Own Making: A History of Myth and Ritual in Family Life* (Oxford University Press, 1997), p. 135; Macfarlane, *Marriage and Love*.

26 Amanda Vickery, *The Gentleman's Daughter: Women's Lives in Georgian England* (Yale University Press, 1998), p. 44.

27 Pat Jalland, *Women, Marriage and Politics 1860–1914* (Oxford University Press, 1988).

28 Richard Fisher, *Joseph Lister 1827–1912* (MacDonald & Jane's, 1977), p. 79.

29 Nancy Fix, 'Cousin Marriage in Victorian England', *Journal of Family History*, 11–12 (1986–7), pp. 285–301.

30 Elizabeth Thomson King (ed.), *Lord Kelvin's Early Home Life* (Macmillan, 1909), *passim*.

31 Eunice Murray, *Frances Murray: A Memoir* (Maclehose, 1920), p. 225.

32 GCA TD 1073, Crum family papers; GUA DC 79, MacEwen family papers; GUAS UGD 4, Alexander Stephen & Co.

33 The literature on the 'rational recreation' movement of the early and mid-Victorian period discusses the problems of social segregation and social distance

between classes. See Peter Bailey, *Popular Culture and Performance in the Victorian City* (Cambridge University Press, 1998); Hugh Cunningham, *Leisure in the Industrial Revolution* (Croom Helm, 1980).

34 Douglas MacGowan, Prelude to *Murder in Victorian Scotland: The Trial of Madeleine Smith* (Praeger, 1999).

35 Ibid., p. 14.

36 NAS AD 14/57/255/1, Letters of Madeleine Smith to Emile L'Angelier, 4 March 1856.

37 MacGowan, *Murder in Victorian Scotland*, p. 21.

38 Ibid., p. 14.

39 Ibid., p. 59.

40 Quoted in ibid., p. 38.

41 Ibid., p. 8.

42 Ibid., pp. 75–6.

43 For a discussion of the response of the press to Madeleine Smith, see Mary S. Hartman, 'Murder for Respectability: The Case of Madeleine Smith', *Victorian Studies*, 16 (1972–3), pp. 381–400.

44 Peter Borscheid, 'Romantic Love and Material Interest: Choosing Partners in Nineteenth-Century Germany, *Journal of Family History*, 11–12 (1986–7), pp. 157–68.

45 NAS AD 14/57/255/1, 15 June 1855.

46 Ibid., 14 Jan 1856.

47 Ibid., 14 Feb 1856, 18 June 1855, 8 Aug 1855.

48 Ibid., 30 Dec 1855.

49 Karen Lystra, *Searching the Heart: Women, Men and Romantic Love in Nineteeth Century America* (New York, 1989); Nicole Eustace, '"The Cornerstone of a Copious Work": Love and Power in Eighteenth-Century Courtship', *Journal of Social History*, 34, 3 (2001), p. 527.

50 MacGowan, *Murder in Victorian Scotland*, p. 22.

51 Quoted in MacGowan, *Murder in Victorian Scotland*, p. 45.

52 NAS AD 4/57/255/3, Precognitions against Madeleine Smith, evidence of Christina Haggart.

53 Ibid., Letter from Madeleine Smith to L'Angelier, 18 June 1855.

54 Murray, *Memoir*, p. 89.

55 Mason, *The Making of Victorian Sexuality*; Jalland, *Women, Marriage and Politics*; M. Jeanne Peterson, *Family, Love, and Work in the Lives of Victorian Gentlewomen* (Indiana University Press, 1989); Peter Gay, *The Bourgeois Experience: Victoria to Freud*, vol. 1: *Education of the Senses* (Cambridge University Press, 1984).

56 NAS AD 4/57/255/3, 5 Dec 1855.

57 MacGowan, *Murder in Victorian Scotland*, p. 33.

58 Quoted in ibid., p. 41.

59 GUAS DC 79/26, Letter to Mary MacEwen from her brother, 27 Nov 1873.

60 *Dr and Mrs Coats: A Book of Remembrance* (Jackson, Wylie & Co., 1929), p. 227.

61 Murray, *Memoir, passim.*

62 J. L. Story, *Later Reminiscences* (Maclehose, 1913), p. 4.

63 Thomson King, *Lord Kelvin's Early Home Life*, p. 213.

64 Ibid.

65 Ibid., p. 224.

66 Murray, *Memoir*, p. 88.

67 Ibid., p. 78.

68 Letter of March 1872, quoted in ibid., p. 141.

69 Ibid., p. 98.

70 Ibid., p. 119.

71 *Dr and Mrs Coats*, pp. 32–3.

72 NAS AD 14/57/255/1, 30 Jan 1855.

73 Ibid., 30 Dec 1855.

74 MacGowan, *Murder in Victorian Scotland*, p. 43.

75 Ibid., p. 42.

76 Ibid., p. 46.

77 Ibid., p. 46.

78 Ibid., pp. 35–6.

79 NAS AD 14/57/255/1, Sept 1855.

80 *Dr and Mrs Coats*, p. 130.

81 ibid., p. 134.

82 Ibid., p. 227.

83 Ibid., p. 140.

84 Ibid., p. 216.

85 Ibid., p. 248.

86 Ibid., p. 238.

87 Letter of 3 Feb 1896, quoted in ibid., p. 251.

88 *Dr and Mrs Coats*, p. 251.

89 D. W. Bebbington, Introduction to *The Baptists in Scotland: A History* (Baptist Union of Scotland, 1988).

90 *Dr and Mrs Coats*, p. 24.

91 Ibid., p. 136.

92 Ibid., p. 130.

93 Ibid., p. 22.

94 *Waverley Journal*, 6 Sept 1856.

95 Ibid., 1 Nov 1856.

96 Ibid., 9 Aug 1856.

97 Ibid., 20 Sept 1856.

98 Ibid., 6 Sept 1856.

99 Murray, *Memoir*, p. 75.

100 Ibid., p. 153.

101 Ibid., p. 245.

102 Ibid., p. 147.

103 Ibid., p. 143.

104 Ibid., p. 89.

105 Ibid., p. 194.

106 Ibid., p. 264.

107 Story, *Later Reminiscences*, p. 5.

108 Ibid., p. 9.

109 Thomson King, *Lord Kelvin's Early Home Life*, p. 73.

110 Story, *Early Reminiscences*, p. 40.

111 Elaine Showalter, *Sexual Anarchy: Gender and Culture at the Fin de Siecle* (Bloomsbury, 1991); Hammerton, *Cruelty and Companionship*; Harry Brod (ed.), *The Making of Masculinities: The New Men's Studies* (Allen & Unwin, 1987); John Tosh, *A Man's Place: Masculinity and the Middle-Class Home in Victorian England* (Yale University Press, 1999).

112 Mason, *The Making of Victorian Sexuality*, pp. 48–52.

113 Tosh, *A Man's Place*, chapter 8.

114 *Glasgow Herald*, 11 May 1906.

115 GUAS DC 79, William MacEwen Collection; *Dr and Mrs Coats*, pp. 229–32.

116 W. D. Brooker (ed.), *A Century of Scottish Mountaineering: An Anthology from the Scottish Mountaineering Club Journal* (Scottish Mountaineering Trust, 1988).

4 LET ME ENTERTAIN YOU

1 Elizabeth Thomson King (ed.), *Lord Kelvin's Early Home Life* (Macmillan, 1909), p. 50.

2 John Gillis, *A World of Their Own Making: A History of Myth and Ritual in Family Life* (Oxford University Press, 1997), chapter 6; Mary Ryan, *Cradle of the Middle Class: The Family in Oneida County, New York, 1790–1865* (Cambridge University Press, 1981), chapter 4.

3 Jane Rendall, *The Origins of Modern Feminism* (Lyceum Books, 1985), chapter 3.

4 Leonore Davidoff and Catherine Hall, *Family Fortunes: Men and Women of the English Middle Class, 1780–1850* (Routledge, 1987), p. 180.

5 Ibid.; Gillis, *A World of Their Own Making*, p. 113.

6 *Waverley Journal*, 6 Sept 1856, p. 40.

7 Davidoff and Hall, *Family Fortunes*, prologue; John Tosh, *A Man's Place: Masculinity and the Middle-Class Home in Victorian England* (Yale University Press, 1999), p. 47.

8 Simon Gunn, *The Public Culture of the Victorian Middle Class* (Manchester University Press, 2000), p. 26.

9 Davidoff and Hall, *Family Fortunes*, passim; Gillis, *A World of Their Own Making*, p. 69; Bonnie Smith, *Ladies of the Leisure Class: The Bourgeoisie of Northern France in the Nineteenth century* (Princeton University Press, 1981), chapter 4; Tosh, *A Man's Place*, part 2.

10 Gillis, *A World of Their Own Making*, p. 71.

11 Davidoff and Hall, *Family Fortunes*, p. 181.

12 NAS AD 14/57/255/1, Letters of Madeleine Smith to Emile L'Angelier.

13 Catherine Carswell, *Lying Awake* (Canongate, 1997), p. 36.

14 Ibid., p. 35.

15 Ibid., p. 35.

16 Ibid., p. 36.

17 NAS AD 14/57/255/1, Letters of Madeleine Smith.

18 GUAS DC 79/33, Sir William MacEwen Collection, 'Early Life and Marriage' (written by his grandson W. M. R. MacDonald).

19 Ibid.

20 Thomson King (ed.), *Lord Kelvin's Early Home Life*, p. 107.

21 M. A. Crowther and Marguerite Dupree, *Lister's Men* (forthcoming).

22 Ibid.

23 GCA T-HB/655, Inventory of George Wilson, 1889.

24 GCA T-BK-8, Inventory of Alexander Anderson, 1870.

25 Sir Robert Bryce Walker, 'Servus Servorum Populi', p. 14. We are grateful to Joyce Walker for giving us access to this unpublished manuscript.

26 GCA T-HH24/6, Inventory of James Thomson, 1905.

27 J. L. Story, *Early Reminiscences* (James Maclehose, 1911).

28 His daughters compiled a *Memoir of Robert Herbert Story* (Maclehose, 1909); diary entry, p. 88.

29 G. E. R. Young, *Elma and Helen Story: A Recollection* (Blackie & Son, 1948).

30 GCA PA5/190, Crum's Land: A History of Thornliebank.

31 'Brief Notes of the Autobiography of Robert Brown Underwood Park Paisley'. We are grateful to Mr Fred Hay of the Department of Economics, University of Glasgow, for allowing us access to this manuscript.

32 Joan McAlpine, *The Lady of Claremont House* (Argyll, 1997), p. 25.

33 Ibid., p. 45.

34 *Glasgow Post Office Directory*, 1879–80.

35 *Holmwood House* (The National Trust for Scotland, 1998).

36 James Carroll, Nicholas Morgan and Michael Moss, 'Building by Numbers: The Lifecycle of Scottish Building Firms, 1793–1913', in Phillippe Jobert and Michael Moss (ed.), *The Birth and Death of Companies* (Parthenon Publishing, 1990), p. 201.

37 GCA TD 976/98/1, Sederunt book of Andrew Jack.

38 GUAS UGD 4/7/1, Diaries of John Stephen.

39 Ian Gow, 'The Dining Room', in Annette Carruthers (ed.), *The Scottish Home*

(National Museums of Scotland, 1996), pp. 125–54.

40 Quoted in Richard Fisher, *Joseph Lister 1827–1912* (MacDonald & Jane's, 1977), p. 163.

41 Joan B. Landes, 'The Public and the Private Sphere: A Feminist Reconsideration', in Joan B. Landes (ed.), *Feminism: The Public and the Private* (Oxford University Press, 1998), pp. 135–163.

42 Carswell, *Lying Awake*, pp. 26–7.

43 For a discussion of the practice of 'drawing room' meetings held by the women of the Scottish Christian Union and the Scottish Federation of Women's Suffrage Societies, see Megan Smitley, ' "Women's Mission": The Temperance and Women's Suffrage Movements in Scotland c. 1870–1914', unpublished PhD thesis, University of Glasgow, 2002, pp. 85–7.

44 GUAS DC 90/3/8/9, Napier family papers.

45 GUAS DC 120/1/10, MacFie family papers.

46 Story, *Early Reminiscences*, p. 20.

47 Ibid., pp. 145–6.

48 J. L. Story, *Later Reminiscences* (Maclehose, 1913), p. 29.

49 NAS AD 14/57/255/3, Precognition against Madeleine Smith, evidence of Isabella Thomson.

50 NAS AD 14/57/253, Criminal precognitions against Madeleine Smith.

51 Eunice Murray, *Frances Murray: A Memoir* (Maclehose, 1920), pp. 112–13.

52 Murray, *Memoir*, pp. 112–13.

53 Leonore Davidoff, *The Best Circles: Society, Etiquette and the Season* (Cresset Library, 1986).

54 Davidoff and Hall, *Family Fortunes*, p. 437.

55 Ibid., p. 23.

56 Ibid., pp. 25–7.

57 Story, *Later Reminiscences*, p. 226.

58 For a discussion of this trend, see Michael Mason, *The Making of Victorian Sexuality* (Oxford University Press, 1995), chapter 1.

59 NAS AD 14/57/253, Precognitions

against Madeleine Smith, evidence of Mr Middleton.

60 NAS AD 14/57/255/1, Letters of Madeleine Smith to Emile L'Angelier.

61 Ibid., Jan 1856.

62 Story, *Later Reminiscences*, p. 228.

63 Brown, 'Brief Notes', p. 98.

64 Ibid., p. 19.

65 Story, *Later Reminiscences*, pp. 231–2.

66 Ibid., p. 226.

67 Story, *Early Reminiscences*, p. 248.

68 J. J. Bell, *I Remember* (Porpoise Press, 1932), p. 100.

69 Ibid., p. 111.

70 Felicity Heal, *Hospitality in Early Modern England* (Oxford University Press, 1990), p. 350.

71 Story, *Later Reminiscences*, p. 105.

72 Stana Nenadic, 'Middle Rank Consumers and Domestic Culture in Edinburgh and Glasgow 1720–1840', *Past and Present*, 145 (1994), pp. 122–56.

73 Karen Halttunen, 'From Parlor to Living Room: Domestic Space, Interior Decoration, and the Culture of Personality', in Simon Bronner (ed.), *Consuming Visions* (W. W. Norton, 1989), pp. 157–89.

74 Amanda Vickery, 'Women and the World of Goods: A Lancashire Consumer and Her Possessions, 1751–81', in John Brewer and Roy Porter (ed.), *Consumption and the World of Goods* (Routledge, 1993), pp. 274–303.

75 Juliet Kinchin, 'Interiors: Nineteenth Century Essays on the "Masculine" and the "Feminine" Room', in Pat Kirkham (ed.), *The Gendered Object* (Manchester University Press, 1996), pp. 12–29; Juliet Kinchin, 'The Drawing Room', in Carruthers (ed.), *Scottish Home*, pp. 155–80; Joanna Banham, Sally MacDonald and Julia Porter MacDonald, *Victorian Interior Design* (Crescent Books, 1991).

76 Kinchin, 'Interiors', p. 18.

77 Kinchin, 'The Drawing Room', p. 161.

78 Jean-Christophe Agnew, 'A House of Fiction: Domestic Interiors and the Commodity Aesthetic', in Bronner (ed.), *Consuming Visions*, pp. 157–89.

79 NAS AD 14/57/255/1, Letter from Madeleine Smith to Emile L'Angelier, 7 March 1856.

80 Bell, *I Remember*, pp. 84–5.

81 Carswell, *Lying Awake*, p. 27.

82 *Glasgow Herald*, 2 May 1860.

83 Bell, *I Remember*, pp. 62–3.

84 Carswell, *Lying Awake*, p. 58.

85 *Glasgow Herald*, 2 May 1860.

86 Carswell, *Lying Awake*, p. 51.

87 Bell, *I Remember*, p. 65.

88 Alastair J. Durie, 'The Development of the Scottish Coastal Resorts in the Central Lowlands, c1770–1880: From Gulf Stream to Golf Stream', *Local Historian*, 24, 4 (1994), pp. 206–16.

89 Brown, 'Brief Notes'.

90 *Glasgow Herald*, 9 Sept 1871.

91 GUAS UG 4/7/1, Diaries of John Stephen.

92 GUAS DC 79/26, MacEwen family papers.

93 Carswell, *Lying Awake*, p. 46.

94 Story, *Later Reminiscences*, p. 15.

95 Brown, 'Brief Notes'.

96 For an exposition of this view, see Thad Logan, *The Victorian Parlour* (Cambridge University Press, 2001).

5 A Woman's Touch

1 *Waverley Journal*, Sept 1856.

2 Callum G. Brown, *The Death of Christian Britain* (Routledge, 2001), especially chapter 4; R. H. Bloch, 'Ideals in Transition: The Rise of Moral Motherhood, 1785–1815', *Feminist Studies*, 4 (1978), pp. 101–27.

3 Philippe Aries, *Centuries of Childhood* (Penguin, 1982); Edward Shorter, *The Making of the Modern Family* (Basic Books, 1975); L. A. Pollock, *Forgotten Children: Parent Child Relations from 1500–1900* (Cambridge University Press, 1983); L. A. Pollock, *A Lasting Relationship: Parents and Children over Three Centuries* (University Press of New England, 1987); Ralph Houlbrooke, *The English Family 1450–1700* (Longman, 1984); Elisabeth Badinter, *The*

Myth of Motherhood: An Historical View of the Maternal Instinct (Souvenir Press, 1981); Bloch, 'Ideals in Transition', pp. 101–27; Hugh Cunningham, *Children and Childhood in Western Society since 1500* (Longman, 1995); Anthony J. Fletcher, *Gender, Sex and Subordination in England, 1500–1800* (Yale University Press, 1995).

4 Cunningham, *Children and Childhood*; Patricia Crawford, 'The Construction and Experience of Maternity in Seventeenth Century England', in Valerie Fildes (ed.), *Women as Mothers in Pre-Industrial England: Essays in Memory of Dorothy McLaren* (Routledge, 1990), pp. 3–38; Stephen Wilson, 'The Myth of Motherhood: The Historical View of European Child-Rearing', *Social History*, 9, 2 (1984), pp. 181–98.

5 Wilson, 'The Myth of Motherhood'.

6 Cunningham, *Children and Childhood*.

7 Lord Kames, *Loose Hints upon Education chiefly concerning the Culture of the Heart* (Edinburgh, 1781), p. 8.

8 Ibid., p. 228.

9 Quoted in ibid., p. 66.

10 Cunningham, *Children and Childhood*, p. 17.

11 Eunice Murray, *Frances Murray: A Memoir* (Maclehose, 1920), p. 14.

12 J. L. Story, *Later Reminiscences* (Maclehose, 1913), p. 21.

13 N. L. Tranter, *Population and Society, 1750–1940* (Longman, 1985), p. 47.

14 Story, *Early Reminiscences*, p. 24.

15 Murray, *Memoir*, pp. 27–8.

16 Cunningham, *Children and Childhood*, p. 77.

17 Pat Jalland, *Women, Marriage and Politics* (Oxford University Press, 1988), p. 10.

18 Jane McDermid, 'Women and Education', in June Purvis (ed.), *Women's History: Britain 1850–1945* (University College London Press, 1995), pp. 107–30.

19 *Glasgow Herald*, 15 April 1853.

20 Lindy Moore, 'Researching the Education of Middle-Class Girls: With Particular Reference to Private Schools', *Scottish Archives*, 3 (1977), pp. 77–86.

21 Lindy Moore, 'Young Ladies' Institutions: The Development of Secondary Schools for Girls in Scotland, 1833–c 1870'. We are grateful to Lindy Moore for allowing us access to this unpublished work.

22 Ibid., p. 15.

23 Ibid., p. 3.

24 Ibid., p. 3.

25 Ibid., p. 3.

26 Ibid., p. 4.

27 *Glasgow Post Office Directory*, 1857.

28 Lindy Moore, 'Young Ladies' Institutions', p. 9.

29 Ibid., p. 4.

30 GUAS DC 79/33, Sir William MacEwen collection.

31 We are grateful to Joseph Melling for providing us with this information.

32 Elizabeth Thomson King (ed.), *Lord Kelvin's Early Home Life* (Macmillan, 1909), p. 43.

33 Murray, *Memoir*, p. 25.

34 Ibid.

35 Ibid., p. 196.

36 GUAS DC 120/1/15, Diaries of Helen MacFie.

37 Catherine Carswell, *Lying Awake* (Canongate, 1997), p. 47; Letter from Mollie Macewan to Margaret McCallum, 6 Feb 1872. Access to the correspondence of the Macewan/McCallum family was kindly provided by Allan Campbell-Smith, who provided the genealogical notes.

38 GUAS DC 120/1/15, Diaries of Helen MacFie.

39 Letter to the *Scotsman*, 18 Aug 1849, which gave a breakdown of expenses for a typical middle-class household.

40 Letter from Mollie Macewan to Margaret McCallum, 7 June 1873.

41 Ibid., 13 Jan 1869.

42 Ibid., 6 Feb 1872.

43 Ibid., 18 Feb 1873.

44 Ibid., 7 June 1873.

45 Carswell, *Lying Awake*, p. 66, recounts how her parents differed from their peers in allowing her and her siblings to play freely in the nearby streets.

46 *Dr and Mrs Joseph Coats: A Book of Remembrance* (Jackson, Wylie & Co., 1929), p. 225.

47 Amanda Vickery, *The Gentleman's Daughter: Women's Lives in Georgian England* (Yale University Press, 1998), p. 110.

48 Ibid., p. 236.

49 Carswell, *Lying Awake*, p. 15.

50 Murray, *Memoir*, p. 173.

51 GUAS DC 79/26, Letter to Maryanne MacEwen.

52 Murray, *Memoir*, p. 27.

53 Letter from John Mcewan to Margaret Mcewan, 19 June 1855.

54 GUAS DC 79/128, Letters from Mrs Margaret Allan to her children.

55 NAS AD 14/57/255, Letters of Madeleine Smith to Emile L'Angelier.

56 GUAS DC 120, MacFie family papers, preamble to catalogue in GUAS.

57 Patricia Branca, 'Image and Reality: The Myth of the Idle Victorian Woman', in Mary S. Hartman and Lois Banner (ed.), *Clio's Consciousness Raised: New Perspectives on the History of Women* (Harper & Row, 1974), pp. 179–910.

58 Pamela Horn, *Rise and Fall of the Victorian Servant* (Alan Sutton, 1990).

59 Elizabeth Roberts, *Women's Work 1840–1940* (Cambridge University Press, 1995).

60 *Glasgow Post Office Directory*, 1857.

61 *Glasgow Herald*, 31 March 1900.

62 Shirley Nicholson, *A Victorian Household* (Alan Sutton Publishing, 1994), pp. 65–8.

63 Carswell, *Lying Awake*, p. 47.

64 Horn, *Victorian Servant*, pp. 130–35.

65 *Dr and Mrs Coats*, p. 245. Elsewhere in the memoir, the plumber's name is spelt 'Leach'.

66 Carswell, *Lying Awake*, p. 46.

67 *Dr and Mrs Coats*, p. 234.

68 Bonnie Smith, *Ladies of the Leisure Class: The Bourgeoises of Northern France in the Nineteenth Century* (Princeton University Press, 1981), pp. 42–5.

69 Carswell, *Lying Awake*, pp. 39–40.

70 Rachel Bowlby, *Carried Away: The Invention of Modern Shopping* (Faber, 2000); Erika Diane Rappaport, *Shopping for Pleasure: Women and the Making of London's West End* (Princeton University Press, 2000); Geoffrey Crossick and Serge Toumain (ed.), *Cathedrals of Consumption: The European Department Store* (Ashgate, 1999).

71 *Dr and Mrs Coats*, pp. 253–4.

72 Ibid., p. 247.

73 Rappaport, *Shopping for Pleasure*.

74 GUAS DC 79/33, MacEwen papers, 'Early Life and Marriage', written by his grandson W. M. R. MacDonald.

75 *Waverley Journal*, 20 Sept 1856.

76 J. L. Story, *Early Reminiscences* (Maclehose, 1911), p. 42.

77 Elizabeth Thomson King (ed.), *Lord Kelvin's Early Home Life* (Maclehose, 1909), p. 116.

78 *Dr and Mrs Coats*, pp. 233–4.

79 *Bridge of Allan Reporter*, Jan 1896. We are grateful to Alistair Durie for this reference.

80 Letter from Mollie Macewan to Maggie McCallum, 18 Feb 1873.

81 Glasgow Valuation Rolls, 1881.

82 For discussions of the social construction of the census, see Edward Higgs, *A Clearer Sense of the Census: Victorian Censuses and Historical Research* (HMSO, 1996), and Eleanor Gordon, *Women and the Labour Movement in Scotland 1850–1914* (Oxford University Press, 1991), pp. 16–21.

83 Gordon, ibid.

84 Lindy Moore, 'Young Ladies' Institutions', Appendix.

85 Story, *Early Reminiscences*, p. 339.

86 M. Jeanne Peterson, *Family, Love, and Work in the Lives of Victorian Gentlewomen* (Indiana University Press, 1989), chapter 6.

87 NLS ACC 10495, Geddes papers, 25 Oct 1897.

88 Peterson, *Family, Love, and Work*, p. 176.

89 GUAS DC21, Robert Herbert Story Collection.

90 Richard Fisher, *Joseph Lister 1827–1912* (MacDonald & Jane's, 1977).

91 Sir Rickman Godlee, *Lord Lister* (Macmillan, 1917), p. 73.

92 Fisher, *Joseph Lister*, p. 78.

93 NAS SC 36/48/104, Inventory of Andrew Chrystal, 1883, pp. 253–7.

94 Joan McAlpine, *The Lady of Claremont House* (Argyll, 1997), p. 15.

95 Pamela Robertson, 'Catherine Cranston', *Journal of the Decorative Arts Society*, 10 (1980).

96 Sir Robert Bryce Walker, 'Servus Servorum Populi', p. 14.

97 Mary Ryan, *Cradle of the Middle Class: The Family in Oneida County, New York, 1790–1865* (Cambridge University Press, 1981), p. 201.

98 Peterson, *Family, Love, and Work*, p. 166.

99 For the persistence of a sexual division of labour through centuries, but also the importance of women's economic role, see the essays in Pamela Sharpe (ed.), *Women's Work: The English Experience 1650–1914* (Arnold, 1995).

100 Eric M. Clive, *The Law of Husband and Wife in Scotland* (W. Green, 1982), pp. 285–7.

101 The following discussion draws heavily on Clive and Wilson, ibid., chapter 10.

102 Susan Staves, *Married Women's Separate Property in England 1660–1833* (Harvard University Press, 1990). Maxine Berg, however, has questioned this position and argues that, contrary to the formal legal position, women did own and control property in the early nineteenth century; see her 'Women's Property and the Industrial Revolution', *Journal of Interdisciplinary History*, 24, 2 (1993), pp. 233–50.

103 David Murray, *The Law Relating to the Property of Married Persons, with an Appendix of Statutes and Notes* (Maclehose, 1891), p. 53.

104 Clive, *The Law of Husband and Wife*, p. 345.

105 Story, *Early Reminiscences*, pp. 8–9.

106 Hansard, 1880/3/252, p. 1548, quoted in Craig Young, 'Middle-class "Culture", Law and Gender Identity:

Married Women's Property Legislation in Scotland, c1850–1920', in Alan Kidd and David Nicholls (ed.), *Gender, Civic Culture and Consumerism: Middle-Class Identity in Britain 1800–1940* (Manchester University Press, 1999), pp. 133–45.

107 Amy Erickson, 'Common Law versus Common Practice: The Use of Marriage Settlements in Early Modern England', *Economic History Review*, 43 (1990), pp. 21–39.

108 GCA T-MR/362, Marriage contract between Robert Orr Sawyer and Jessie Patrick White, sederunt book, 1862–1903; GCA TD 162/33, Marriage contract trust between Humphrey Ewing Crum Ewing and Janet Creelman Robson.

109 GCA TD 862/71, Marriage contract between William Henry Houldsworth and Elizabeth Graham Crum, sederunt book, 1862–1925.

110 Leonore Davidoff and Catherine Hall, *Family Fortunes: Men and Women of the English Middle Class* (Routledge, 1987), p. 209.

111 GCA TD 862/71, Marriage contract between William Henry Houldsworth and Elizabeth Graham Crum.

112 GCA TD 1189/9, Marriage contract between Hugh McMaster Ewing and Constance Robertson Blackie, sederunt book, 1888–1921.

6 I Will Survive

1 Jane Austen, *Emma* [1816], ed. James Kinsley (Oxford University Press, 1995), p. 77.

2 Christine Adams, 'A Choice not to Wed? Unmarried Women in Eighteenth-Century France', *Journal of Social History*, 29 (1995–6), p. 884.

3 Cecile Dauphin, 'Single Women', in Geneviève Fraisse and Michelle Perrot (ed.), *A History of Women in the West* (Harvard University Press, 1993), pp. 427–42.

4 Virginia Lee, *Liberty, a Better Husband* (Yale University Press, 1984).

5 Martha Vicinus, *Independent Women: Work and Community for Single Women 1850–1920* (Virago, 1985), p. 5.

6 William Greg, *Literary and Social Judgements* (Trubner, 1868), quoted in Michael Anderson, 'The Social Position of Spinsters in Mid-Victorian Britain', *Journal of Family History*, 9 (1984), pp. 377–93. Italics in original.

7 Elizabeth Gaskell, *Cranford* [1851–3] (Wordsworth Editions, 1993), p. 15.

8 Greg, *Literary and Social Judgements*.

9 Ibid.

10 Anderson, 'Social Position of Spinsters'; Pauline Simonsen, 'Elizabeth Barrett Browning's Redundant Women', *Victorian Poetry*, 35, 4 (1997), pp. 509–32.

11 N. L. Tranter, *Population and Society 1750–1940: Contrasts in Population Growth* (Longman, 1985), pp. 53–4.

12 Anderson, 'Social Position of Spinsters'.

13 Dorothy Crozier, 'Kinship and Occupational Succession', *Sociological Review*, 13 (1965), pp. 15–43.

14 Vicinus, *Independent Women*.

15 M. W. Flinn (ed.), *Scottish Population History* (Cambridge, 1977).

16 Patricia Jalland, 'Victorian Spinsters: Dutiful Daughters, Desperate Rebels and the Transition to the New Women', in Patricia Crawford (ed.), *Exploring Women's Past* (Allen & Unwin, 1983), pp. 129–70.

17 Stephen Ruggles, *Prolonged Connections: The Rise of the Extended Family in Nineteenth Century England and America* (University of Winsconsin Press, 1987), p. 214.

18 Leonore Davidoff and Catherine Hall, *Family Fortunes: Men and Women of the English Middle Class, 1780–1850* (Routledge, 1987), p. 114.

19 Jennifer M. Lloyd, 'Conflicting Expectations in Nineteenth-Century British Matrimony: The Failed Companionate Marriage of Effie Gray and John Ruskin', *Journal of Women's History*, 11, 2 (1999), pp. 86–109.

20 Eunice Murray, *Frances Murray: A Memoir* (Maclehose, 1920), p. 113.

21 Ruth Freeman and Patricia Klaus, 'Blessed or Not? The New Spinster in England and the United States in the Nineteenth and Early Twentieth Centuries', *Journal of Family History*, 9 (1984), pp. 331–44; Dauphin, 'Single Women', pp. 427–42.

22 Dauphin, ibid.; Freeman and Klaus, 'Blessed or Not?'; Vicinus, *Independent Women*.

23 Sheila Jeffries, *The Spinster and her Enemies: Feminism and Sexuality 1880–1930* (Pandora, 1985).

24 A. J. Hammerton, *Cruelty and Companionship: Conflict in Nineteenth-Century Married Life* (Routledge, 1995).

25 Elaine Showalter, *Sexual Anarchy: Gender and Culture at the Fin de Siecle* (Bloomsbury, 1991).

26 Austen, *Emma*, p. 77.

27 Nigel Morland, *That Nice Miss Smith* (Souvenir Press, 1957), p. 31.

28 Douglas MacGowan, *Murder in Victorian Scotland: The Trial of Madeleine Smith* (Praeger, 1999), p. 9; Henry Blyth, *Madeleine Smith: A Famous Victorian Murder Trial* (Duckworth, 1977), p. 116.

29 Filson Young, 'Oscar Slater', in Harry Hodge and James Hodge (ed.) *Famous Trials* (Penguin, 1984).

30 Http://www.crimefiction.com/slater.html.

31 Jack McLean, 'The Barrowers', *Sunday Herald*, 1 April 2001.

32 Richard Whittington-Egan, *The Oscar Slater Murder Story* (Neil Wilson Publishing, 2001).

33 Lee, *Liberty*, p. 26.

34 Adams, 'A Choice not to Wed?'; Davidoff and Hall, *Family Fortunes*.

35 Lee, *Liberty*.

36 Murray, *Memoir*, p. 202.

37 Ibid., p. 86.

38 *Dr and Mrs Joseph Coats: A Book of Remembrance* (Jackson, Wylie & Co., 1929), p. 33.

39 Ellen Jordan, *The Women's Movement and Women's Employment in Nineteenth Century Britain* (Routledge, 1999).

40 *Glasgow Herald*, 31 March 1900.

41 Ada Moore, 'The Decayed Gentlewoman: An Appeal to England's Chivalry', *Westminster Review* (London, 1904).

42 *Glasgow Herald*, 11 Sept 1871.

43 *Glasgow Herald*, 15 April 1853.

44 *Glasgow Herald*, 2 May 1853.

45 Kathryn Hughes, *The Victorian Governess* (Hambledon, 1993).

46 Lyndall Gordon, *Charlotte Brontë: A Passionate Life* (Vintage, 1995).

47 *Glasgow Herald*, 15 April 1853.

48 Hughes, *Victorian Governess*.

49 *Glasgow Evening Times*, 4 Oct 1880.

50 Sally Alexander, *Women's Work in Nineteenth Century London* (Journeyman Press, 1983).

51 Freeman and Klaus, 'Blessed or Not?', pp. 394–414.

52 *Glasgow Herald*, 29 March 1900.

53 GUAS DC 79/33, William MacEwen collection, biographical note by his grandson W. M. R. MacDonald.

54 Clara Collet, 'The Social Status of Women Occupiers', *Journal of the Royal Statistical Society*, 71, Part 3 (1908), pp. 513–15; Greg, *Literary and Social Judgements*; Moore, 'Decayed Gentlewoman'.

55 Anderson, 'Social Position of Spinsters'.

56 Moore, 'Decayed Gentlewoman'.

57 Collet, 'The Social Status of Women Occupiers', p. 514.

58 Moore, 'Decayed Gentlewoman'.

59 Vicinus, *Independent Women*.

60 Freeman and Klaus, 'Blessed or Not?', p. 407.

61 Alice Clark, *Working Life of Women in the Seventeenth Century* (Routledge, 1982); Alexander, *Women's Work*.

62 *Who's Who in Glasgow 1901* (Glasgow, 1901).

63 Stana Nenadic, 'The Victorian Middle-Classes', in W. H. Fraser and Irene Maver (ed.), *Glasgow*, vol. 2: 1830–1912 (Manchester University Press, 1996), pp. 227–64.

64 Glasgow Valuation Rolls, GCA D-CAI, 1861 and 1881.

65 P. L. Payne, 'Family Business in Britain: An Historical and Analytical Survey', in M. B. Rose (ed.), *Family Business* (Edward Elgar, 1995), pp. 69–104.

66 Charles Wilson, 'Economy and Society in Late Victorian Britain', *Economic History Review*, 18 (1965), pp. 183–98.

67 Peter Earle, 'The Female Labour Market in the Later Seventeenth and Early Eighteenth Centuries', *Economic History Review*, 42 (1989), pp. 328–53.

68 Davidoff and Hall, *Family Fortunes*, p. 276.

69 Moore, 'Decayed Gentlewoman'.

70 Cynthia Curran, 'Private Women, Public Needs: Middle-Class Widows in Victorian England', *Albion*, 25, 2 (1993), pp. 217–36.

71 Ibid.

72 Olwen Hufton, 'Women without Men: Widows and Spinsters in Britain and France in the Eighteenth Century', *Journal of Family History*, 9 (1984), pp. 355–75.

73 Davidoff and Hall, *Family Fortunes*, p. 285.

74 GUAS DC 79/33, William MacEwen collection, biographical note by W. M. R. MacDonald.

75 Rosalind Mitchison, *British Population Change since 1860* (Macmillan, 1977).

76 E. A. Wrigley and R. S. Schofield, *The Population History of England 1541–1871* (Cambridge, 1981), p. 258; Curran, 'Private Women'; Barbara Todd, 'The Remarrying Widow: A Stereotype Reconsidered', in Mary Prior (ed.), *Women in English Society 1500–1800* (Methuen and Co., 1985), pp. 54–92.

77 Curran, 'Private Women', n. 33.

78 NAS SC 36/51/73, Testament of Peter Fisher, Oct 1877, pp. 826–8.

79 Curran, 'Private Women', p. 228.

80 J. L. Story, *Later Reminiscences* (Maclehose, 1913), p. 49.

81 Glasgow Confirmations, 1883.

82 Ibid., 1914.

83 Of these nine examples, six were widows, two spinsters, and one whose status is not clear.

84 *Calendar of Confirmations and Inventories*, 1882.

85 Ibid., 1885.

86 NAS SC 36/48/147, Testament of Anna Playfair, pp. 107–10.

87 Annual Register of Confirmations, 1878.

88 NAS SC 36/48/98, Inventory of Isabella Stewart, pp. 4–7.

89 NAS SC 36/48/81, Inventory of Agnes Buchanan, pp. 286–8.

90 Full transcripts were made of sixty-four testaments and inventories, virtually all relating to individuals who lived within the census area, thirty-six of whom were women.

91 Peter Earle, *The Making of the English Middle Class: Business, Society and Family Life in London, 1660–1730* (Methuen, 1989), pp. 171–4; Maxine Berg, 'Women's Property and the Industrial Revolution', *Journal of Interdisciplinary History*, 24, 2 (1993), pp. 233–50; C. W. Chalklin, *The Provincial Towns of Georgian England: A Study of the Building Process 1740–1820* (Edward Arnold, 1974), p. 9; Davidoff and Hall, *Family Fortunes*, p. 211.

92 Nicholas Morgan, 'Property Ownership in Victorian and Edwardian Glasgow', ESRC End of Award Report D00232126, quoted in Callum Brown, 'Residential Differentiation in Nineteenth Century Glasgow', End of Award Report R000232733, pp. 20–21.

93 Robert Brown, 'Brief Notes' (see chapter 4, n. 31 above).

94 GCA B10/4/331–341, Burgh Register of Sasines (new series).

95 GUL Sp Coll MU2-d.13, City of Glasgow Bank, list of shareholders.

96 We are grateful to Steven Salzman of John Jay College of Criminal Justice for allowing us access to this information, drawn from his forthcoming thesis.

97 NAS SC 36/51/126, Testament of Mrs Euphemia Halliburton Bulley or Guthrie, pp. 707–9.

98 Davidoff and Hall, *Family Fortunes*, pp. 211–12.

99 NAS SC 36/48/190, Testament of David Cargill, pp. 826–8.

100 NAS SC 36/51/73, Testament of Peter Fisher, Oct 1877, p. 28.

101 GCA T-BK-8, Sederunt book of Alexander Anderson.

102 NAS SC 36/51/74, Testament of Mrs Helen Wright Hutcheson or Gibb, Feb 1878, pp. 465–8.

103 NAS SC 36/51/123, Testament of James Adams M.D., Feb 1900, pp. 838–41.

104 NAS SC 36/48/169, Inventory of Jessie Bald Heugh and Jane McDonald Heugh, pp. 769–71.

105 GCA TD 512, George MacLellan papers.

106 NAS SC 36/51/86, Testament of Eliza Service Smith, pp. 825–36.

107 Annual Register of Confirmations, 1886.

108 Ibid., 1914.

7 DOWNTOWN

1 J. L. Story, *Early Reminiscences* (Maclehose, 1911), p. 247.

2 Ibid., p. 250.

3 Ibid., p. 252.

4 Ibid., p. 265.

5 NAS AD 14/57/255/1, Letters of Madeleine Smith to Emile L'Angelier.

6 Elizabeth Thomson King (ed.), *Lord Kelvin's Early Home Life* (Macmillan, 1909), p. 139.

7 Eunice Murray, *Frances Murray: A Memoir* (Maclehose, 1920), p. 237.

8 Ibid., p. 113.

9 Alan Kidd and David Nicholls (ed.), *Gender, Civic Culture and Consumerism: Middle-class Identity in Britain 1800–1940* (Manchester University Press, 1999).

10 Simon Gunn, *The Public Culture of the Victorian Middle Class* (Manchester University Press, 2000).

11 Jane Rendall, 'Women and the Public Sphere', *Gender and History*, 11, 3 (1999), pp. 475–88.

12 Mary Ryan, 'Gender and Public Access: Women's Politics in Nineteenth-Century America', in Craig Calhoun (ed.), *Habermas and the Public Sphere* (MIT Press, 1992), p. 264.

13 GUA UGD 4/7/1–6, Diaries of John Stephen.

14 GCA GD 1/626/30, Letters from Lilias Scotland, 1848–52.

15 NAS AD 14/57/255/1, Letters of Madeleine Smith.

16 Ibid.

17 Ibid.

18 Ibid.

19 Thomson King (ed.), *Lord Kelvin's Early Home Life*, p. 139.

20 Murray, *Memoir*, p. 43.

21 NAS AD 14/57/255/1, Letter from Madeleine Smith to L'Angelier, 8 April 1856.

22 J. J. Bell, *I Remember* (Porpoise Press, 1932), p. 141.

23 *Glasgow Herald*, 26 Dec 1853.

24 *Glasgow Herald*, 23 Feb 1860.

25 *Glasgow Herald*, 19 Dec 1863.

26 *Glasgow Herald*, 26 Dec 1853.

27 NAS AD 14/57/255/1, Letters of Madeleine Smith.

28 Bell, *I Remember*, p. 122.

29 GUA DC 79/71, Letter from Archibald Allan, 19 July 1873.

30 *Evening Times*, 1 Jan 1880.

31 *Glasgow Herald*, 26 Dec 1853.

32 Bell, *I Remember*, p. 131.

33 *Glasgow Herald*, 15 April 1912.

34 *Glasgow Herald*, 5 May 1860.

35 NLS MS 9413, Letter to John Burton from his daughter Ella, 14 Feb 1877.

36 Stana Nenadic, 'The Victorian Middle-Classes', in W. Hamish Fraser and Irene Maver (ed.), *Glasgow*, vol. 2: *1830 to 1912* (Manchester University Press, 1996), pp. 227–64.

37 Murray, *Memoir*, p. 167.

38 *Glasgow Herald*, 9 Feb 1914.

39 Virginia Lee, *Liberty, a Better Husband* (Yale University Press, 1984).

40 Robert Brown, 'Brief Notes' (see chapter 4, n. 31 above).

41 *Glasgow Herald*, 3 Feb 1909.

42 *Glasgow Herald*, 21 Jan 1914.

43 *Glasgow Herald*, 1 Feb 1909.

44 Murray, *Memoir*, pp. 164, 98.

45 Thomson King (ed.), *Lord Kelvin's Early Home Life*, p. 99.

46 Lindy Moore, 'Young Ladies' Institutions: The Development of Secondary Schools for Girls in Scotland, 1833–c 1870' (see chapter 5, n. 21 above).

47 Ibid., p. 12.

48 Ibid.

49 Michael Moss, Moira Rankin and Lesley Richmond, *Who, Where and When: The History and Constitution of the University of Glasgow* (University of Glasgow, 2001).

50 GUA DC 233/1/2/5, Annual report, 1877–8.

51 Moss, Rankin and Richmond, *Who, Where and When*.

52 Evidence to Royal Commission on Poor Laws and Relief of Distress, 1909.

53 Richard Whittington-Egan, *The Oscar Slater Murder Story* (Neil Wilson Publishing, 2001), p. 228.

54 Lore Anne Loeb, *Consuming Angels: Advertising and Victorian Women* (Oxford University Press, 1994).

55 *Glasgow Herald*, 26 Dec 1853.

56 Gunn, *Public Culture*.

57 Abigail van Slyck, 'The Lady and the Library Loafer: Gender and Public Space in Victorian America', *Winterthur Portfolio: A Journal of American Material Culture*, 31, 4 (1996), pp. 221–42.

58 Maureen Montgomery, *Displaying Women: Spectacles of Leisure in Edith Wharton's New York* (Routledge, 1998).

59 'Noremac' (ed.), *The Public Parks of Glasgow* (James Cameron Ltd, 1908).

60 *Glasgow Herald*, 13 Sept 1871.

61 NAS AD 14/57/255/1, Letters of Madeleine Smith.

62 Erika Diane Rappaport, *Shopping for Pleasure: Women in the Making of London's West End* (Princeton University Press, 2000), p. 5.

63 Loeb, *Consuming Angels*, p. 141.

64 Murray, *Memoir*, p. 44.

65 *Glasgow Herald*, 7 Dec 1863.

66 *Glasgow Herald*, 26 Dec 1853.

67 *Glasgow Herald*, 31 March 1900.

68 *Glasgow Herald*, 27 Dec 1899.

69 GCA DC 79/128, Letter from Margaret Allan, 1891.

70 David Frisby and Mike Featherstone (ed.), *Simmel on Culture: Selected Writings* (Sage, 1997); Elizabeth Wilson, *Adorned in Dreams: Fashion and Modernity* (Virago, 1985).

71 James Schmiechen, 'Glasgow of the Imagination: Architecture, Townscape and Society', in Fraser and Maver (ed.), *Glasgow*, pp. 486–518.

72 *Glasgow Post Office Directory*, 1857.

73 NAS SC 36/48/104, Inventory of Andrew Chrystal, 1883, pp. 253–7.

74 NAS SC 36/48/147, Testament of Anna Playfair, 1894, pp. 107–10.

75 Erika Rappaport, '"A New Era of Shopping": The Promotion of Women's Pleasure in London's West End, 1909–1914', in Leo Charney and Vanessa Schwartz, *Cinema and the Invention of Modern Life* (University of California Press, 1999), pp. 130–55.

76 Loeb, *Consuming Angels*.

77 Alison Aldburgham, *Shops and Shopping 1800–1914* (George Allen & Unwin, 1989).

78 Peter Kearney, *The Glasgow Cludgie: A History of Glasgow's Public Conveniences* (People's Publications, 1985).

79 Rappaport, 'A New Era of Shopping'.

80 Cynthia A. Brandimarte, 'To Make the World Homelike: Gender, Space and America's Tearoom Movement', *Winterthur Portfolio: A Journal of American Material Culture*, 30, 1 (1995), pp. 1–19.

81 Pamela Robertson, 'Catherine Cranston', *Journal of the Decorative Arts Society*, 10 (1986).

82 *Evening Times*, 1 Jan 1880.

83 *Glasgow Herald*, 29 Dec 1899.

84 Moira R. Smith, *Kelvin Club Western Club* (Dunkeld Cathedral Press, 1997).

85 Ibid., p. 8.

86 DeCourcy Lewthwaite Dewar, *History of the Glasgow Society of Lady Artists' Club* (Glasgow University Press, 1950).

87 Ibid., p. 23.

88 Carolyn Brucken, 'In the Public Eye: Women and the American Luxury Hotel', *Winterthur Portfolio: A Journal of American Material Culture*, 31, 4 (1996), pp. 203–220.

89 Rappaport, *Shopping for Pleasure*.

90 Murray, *Memoir*, p. 126.

91 Douglas MacGowan, *Murder in Victorian Scotland: The Trial of Madeleine Smith* (Praeger, 1999), p. 54.

92 Aldburgham, *Shops and Shopping*, p. 79.

93 Ibid., p. 80.

94 *Glasgow Herald*, 10 May 1886.

95 GUA UGD 4/7/1, Diaries of John Stephen.

96 Murray, *Memoir*, p. 56.

97 Story, *Early Reminiscences*, p. 289.

98 G. E. R. Young, *Elma and Helen Story: A Recollection* (Blackie, 1948).

99 Brown, 'Brief Notes'.

100 Story, *Early Reminiscences*, p. 274.

101 Murray, *Memoir*, p. 154.

102 NAS AD 14/57/255/1, Letters Madeleine Smith.

103 Brown, 'Brief Notes'.

104 Bell, *I Remember*, p. 59.

105 GCA TD 1063/3/5, Letter from Walter Crum.

106 Thomson King (ed.), *Lord Kelvin's Early Home Life*, p. 154.

107 Ibid., p. 161.

108 Ibid., p. 122.

109 GCA TD 1073/3/15, Letter from Walter Crum to Jessie Crum, 4 Sept 1864.

110 Brown, 'Brief Notes'.

111 Murray, *Memoir*, p. 194.

112 GCA DC 79/128, Letter from Margaret Allan, 1891.

113 *Dr and Mrs Joseph Coats: A Book of Remembrance* (Jackson, Wylie & Co., 1929), p. 171.

114 Brown, 'Brief Notes'.

115 Irene Maver, *Glasgow* (Edinburgh University Press, 2000).

116 Aldburgham, *Shops and Shopping*, p. 79.

117 *Post Office Directory of Glasgow*, 1857.

118 Fraser and Maver (ed.), *Glasgow*.

119 NAS AD 14/57/255/1, Letter from Madeleine Smith to L'Angelier, 21 Feb 1856.

120 GCA TD 1073/3/15, Letter from Walter Crum, 21 Sept 1864.

121 *Calendar of Confirmations and Inventories*, 1878.

122 GUAS UGD 4/7/1–6, Diaries of John Stephen.

123 Thomson King (ed.), *Lord Kelvin's Early Home Life*.

124 Murray, *Memoir*, p. 237.

125 Delia Davin, 'British Women Missionaries in Nineteenth-Century China', *Women's History Review*, 1, 2 (1992), pp. 257–71.

126 Antoinette Burton, 'Women and "Domestic" Imperial Culture: The Case of Victorian Britain', in Marilyn Boxer and Jean Quataert (ed.), *Connecting Spheres: European Women in a Globalizing World, 1500 to the Present* (Oxford University Press, 2000), pp. 174–84.

127 Jane Haggis, '"A heart that has felt the love of God and longs for others to know it": Conventions of Gender, Tensions of Self and Constructions of Difference in Offering to be a Lady Missionary', *Women's History Review*, 7, 2 (1998), pp. 171–92.

128 Laura Nym Mayhall, 'The Making of a Suffragette: The Uses of Reading and the Legacy of Radicalism, 1890–1918', in Fred Leventhal and George Behlmer (ed.), *Singular Continuities: Tradition, Nostalgia and Society in Modern Britain* (Stanford University Press, 2001).

129 Bell, *I Remember*, p. 42.

130 Leonore Davidoff and Catherine Hall, *Family Fortunes: Men and Women of the English Middle Class, 1780–1850* (Routledge, 1987), p. 434.

131 Ibid.

132 GCA CH3/480/49/1, Report of societies connected with Claremont Church, 1888, p. 17.

133 Ibid., p. 13.

134 Ibid., 1889, p. 25.

135 Burton, 'Women and "Domestic" Imperial Culture'.

136 Both listed in the *Glasgow Post Office Directory*, 1857.

137 GCA CH3/480/53/2, 1902, p. 47.

138 Ibid., p. 13.

139 Megan Smitley, '"Woman's Mission": The Temperance and Women's Suffrage Movements in Scotland, c. 1870–1914', unpublished PhD thesis, University of Glasgow, 2002.

140 Jenny Daggers, 'The Victorian Female Civilising Mission and Women's Aspiration towards Priesthood in the Church of England', *Women's History Review*, 10, 4 (2001), p. 657.

141 GCA CH3/480/53/2, 1861, p. 10.

142 GCA CH3/480/49/1, 1868, p. 16.

143 Maver, *Glasgow*, p. 164.

144 Bell, *I Remember*, pp. 211–18.

145 *Glasgow Herald*, 12 Sept 1871.

146 Story, *Early Reminiscences*, p. 284.

147 GCA TD 1073/3/15, Letter from Walter Crum to Mary Crum, 21 Aug 1864.

148 GCA CH3/480/45, Claremont Dorcas Society minute book.

149 *Glasgow Post Office Directory*, 1900.

150 GCA CH3/480/45, Claremont Dorcas Society minute book.

151 GCA CH3/480/49/1, 1896, p. 46.

152 *Glasgow Post Office Directory*, 1857.

153 Mica Nava, 'Modernity's Disavowal: Women, the City and the Department Store', in Mica Nava and Alan O'Shea (ed.), *Modern Times: Reflections on a Century of English Modernity* (Routledge, 1996), pp. 38–76.

154 Gunn, *Public Culture*.

155 Young, *Elma and Helen Story*, p. 16.

156 Gunn, *Public Culture*.

157 Montgomery, *Displaying Women*.

158 Erika Rappaport, 'Travelling in the Lady Guides' London: Consumption, Modernity and the Fin-de-Siècle Metropolis', in Martin Daunton and Bernhard Dieger (ed.), *Meanings of Modernity* (Berg, 2001), pp. 25–43.

159 Judith R. Walkowitz, 'Going Public: Shopping, Street Harrassment and Street Walking in Late Victorian London', *Representations*, 62 (1998), pp. 1–30.

160 Simon Gunn, 'The Public Sphere, Modernity and Consumption', in Kidd and Nicholls, *Gender, Civic Culture and Consumerism*, pp. 12–19.

161 Lucy Bland, '"Purifying" the Public World: Feminist Vigilantes in Late Victorian England', *Women's History Review*, 1, 3 (1992), pp. 397–412.

162   Rappaport, *Shopping for Pleasure*, p. 6.

163   Davidoff and Hall, *Family Fortunes*, p. 453, see the middle of the century as a 'world more rigidly divided into separate spheres for men and women' and the women of the generation born in the 1820s and 1830s as reacting against these restrictions, whereas Amanda Vickery disputes this and points to an increasing public role for women in the late eighteenth and early nineteenth centuries. Amanda Vickery, 'Golden Age to Separate Spheres?', in Pamela Sharpe (ed.), *Women's Work: The English Experience 1650–1914* (Arnold, 1998), p. 297.

EPILOGUE

1   John Tosh, *A Man's Place: Masculinity and the Middle-Class Home in Victorian England* (Yale University Press, 1999); Lawrence E. Klein, 'Gender and the Public/ Private Distinction in the Eighteenth Century: Some Questions about Evidence and Analytic Procedure', *Eighteenth Century Studies*, 29, 1 (1995), pp. 97–109.

2   Or, as cited in Leonore Davidoff and Catherine Hall, *Family Fortunes: Men and Women of the English Middle Class, 1780–1850* (Routledge, 1987), pp. 321–56, that it was 'a little world'.

3   Amanda Vickery, 'Golden Age to Separate Spheres?', in Pamela Sharpe (ed.), *Women's Work: The English Experience 1650–1914* (Arnold, 1998), p. 297.

4   Linda Colley, *Britons: Forging the Nation, 1707–1837* (Yale University Press, 1992); Amanda Foreman, *Georgiana, Duchess of Devonshire* (HarperCollins, 1999), p. 403.

5   John Ruskin, quoted in Thad Logan, *The Victorian Parlour* (Cambridge University Press, 2001), p. 25.

6   Klein, 'Gender and the Public/ Private Distinction'.

7   Michael Mason, *The Making of Victorian Sexuality* (Oxford University Press, 1995).

8   Eunice Murray, *Frances Murray: A Memoir* (Maclehose, 1920), pp. 264–5.

9   J. J. Bell, *I Remember* (Porpoise Press, 1932), p. 71.

Bibliography

PRIMARY SOURCES

Glasgow City Archive (GCA)
T-HB/121, Inventory of valuation of Miss Isabella Campbell
T-HH 24/6, Inventory of valuation of James Thomson
T-HB/646, Inventory of valuation of J. G. Watson
TD 862/70, Inventory of valuation of William Houldsworth
T-MS/172, Inventory of valuation of Margaret Law or Mackenzie
T-MR/325, Sederunt book of Walter Paterson
T/MR/197, Sederunt book of Alexander Johnston
T/MR/331, Sederunt book of James Pinkerton senior
T-HB/655, Sederunt book of Mrs Margaret Gibbs or Wilson
TD 976/98/1, Sederunt book of Andrew Jack
T-HB 352, Sederunt book of Mrs Janet Mathieson or Broom
T-BK-8, Sederunt book of Alexander Anderson
TD 974/81, Sederunt book of David Grieg
T-MR/362, Marriage contract, Robert Orr Sawyer and Jessie Patrick White
TD1189/9, Marriage contract, Hugh McMaster Ewing and Constance
  Robertson Blackie
TD162/33, Marriage contract trust, Humphrey Ewing Crum Ewing and Janet
  Creelman Robson
TD862/71, Marriage contract, William Henry Houldsworth and Elizabeth
  Graham Crum
TD 62/2, Marriage contract, Robert Smith Allan and Lizzie Kincaid Greenhorn
TD 974/3, Marriage contract, William Aikman and Jessie Robertson Blackie
TD 1073, Crum Collection
CH3/480, Reports of societies connected with Claremont United Presbyterian
  Church
CH3/1267, Reports of societies connected with Downhill United Presbyterian
  Church
CH3/1238, Reports of societies connected with Wellington Free Church

B 10/4/331–41, The Burgh Register of Sasines (new series)
D-CA1, Glasgow Valuation Rolls, 1861 and 1881

Glasgow University Archive Services (GUAS)
UGD61, Blackie & Sons Ltd
UGD3, William Denny & Brothers
UGD 131, Ellerman Lines
DC 66, Glasgow Archaeological Society
DC 227, Glasgow Athenaeum and Royal Scottish Academy of Music and Drama
DC 79, Sir William MacEwen Collection
DC 120, MacFie family papers
DC 90, Napier family collection
DC233, Queen Margaret College Collection
DC 118, Royal Philosophical Society
DC 21, Robert Herbert Story Collection
UGD4, Alexander Stephen & Sons Ltd
UGD265, Templeton & Co. Ltd

Glasgow University Library Special Collections (GUL Sp Coll)
Bh 12, *The Bailie*, 1878–1900
Mu22-C.20, Catalogue of Auction of Goods of Marion Gilchrist (Morrison, Dick & McCulloch, Auctioneers)
MU2-d.13, City of Glasgow Bank, list of shareholders
MU1-g.40, J. S. Jeans: *Western Worthies: A Gallery of Biographical and Critical Sketches of West of Scotland Celebrities* (1872)
MU 46-f.22, Lord Kames, *Loose Hints upon Education chiefly concerning the Culture of the Heart* (Edinburgh, 1781)
MU8-g.11, Thomson King, Elizabeth, *Lord Kelvin's Early Home Life: Being the Recollections of his Sister, the late Mrs. Elizabeth King / together with some family letters and a supplementary chapter by the editor, Elizabeth Thomson King* (Macmillan, 1909)
MU24-b6.77, Murray, Eunice G., *Frances Murray: A Memoir* (Maclehose, 1920), printed for private circulation.
BG 50-a.2, *The Waverley Journal*, 1856

Mitchell Library
Glasgow Amateur, Public Amusements Record and General Miscellany, 1856
Glasgow Census Enumerators' Returns, 1851, 1861, 1871, 1881, 1891
Hay, M. H., *Glasgow Theatre and Music Halls: A Guide* (Mitchell Library Glasgow, n.d.)
Ladies Own Journal and Miscellany 1851–72
United Presbyterian Magazine, 1864–5

National Archive of Scotland (NAS)
AD 14/57/255/1-5, Precognition of Madeleine Smith
AD 2/28, High Court Indictment of Madeleine Smith
JC 26/1031/1, Justiciary Court process, letters of Madeleine Smith to Emile L'Angelier
SC 36, Testaments and inventories
CS 247/5453, Aliment Case, Andrew Stephen Alexander Stephen, 1862

National Library of Scotland (NLS)
ACC 10495, Geddes Papers
MS 9413 (ii), 9414 (i–iii), 9416 (iii), Hill Burton Papers

Private Collections
Macewan family correspondence
Sir Robert Bryce Walker, 'Servus Servorum Populi'. Unpublished typescript
'Brief Notes of the Autobiography of Robert Brown of Underwood of Park Paisley'. Unpublished typescript

Contemporary Published Sources
Biographical Sketches of the Honourable of the Lord Provosts of Glasgow (John Tweed, 1883)
Bridge of Allan Reporter (January 1896)
British Medical Journal (March 1924)
Calendar of Confirmations of Estates, 1878–88, 1900, 1914
Collet, Clara, 'The Social Status of Women Occupiers', *Journal of the Royal Statistical Society*, 71, 3 (1908), pp. 513–15
Edinburgh Medical Journal, 5 (1899), 8 (1912)
Glasgow Evening Times, 1877–80
Glasgow Herald, 1853–1914
Glasgow Medical Journal, 51 (1899), 101 (1924)
Glasgow Post Office Directory, 1801, 1841, 1851, 1861, 1871, 1881, 1891, 1901, 1911
Glasgow and West of Scotland Property Index, 1892
Greg, William, *Literary and Social Judgements* (Trubner, 1868)
Memoirs and Portraits of One Hundred Glasgow Men (John Tweed, 1886)
Moore, Ada, 'The Decayed Gentlewoman: An Appeal to England's Chivalry', *Westminster Review* (1904)
Murray, David, *The Law Relating to the Property of Married Persons, with an Appendix of Statutes and Notes* (Maclehose, 1891)
'Noremac' (ed.), *The Public Parks of Glasgow* (James Cameron Ltd, 1908)
The Royal Commission on the State of Schools in Scotland 1865–67: Report on Glasgow Education 1867 [3845–II], xxv. 345
Smith, David Baird, 'The Reformers and Divorce', *Scottish Historical Review*, 9 (1912), pp. 10–36

Story, J. L., *Early Reminiscences* (Maclehose, 1911)

Story, J. L., *Later Reminiscences* (Maclehose, 1913)

Who's Who in Glasgow in 1909 (Gowan & Gray, 1909)

Walton, Frederick P., *A Handbook of Husband and Wife according to the Law of Scotland* (William Green & Son, 1893)

BOOKS

Aldburgham, Alison, *Shops and Shopping 1800–1914* (Allen & Unwin, 1989)

Alexander, Sally, *Women's Work in Nineteenth Century London* (Journeyman Press, 1983)

Anderson, Michael, *Family Structure in Nineteenth Century Lancashire* (Cambridge University Press, 1971)

Anderson, Michael, *Approaches to the History of the Western Family 1500–1914* (Cambridge University Press, 1995)

Anderson, R. D., *Education and Opportunity in Victorian Scotland: Schools and Universities* (Oxford University Press, 1983)

Ariès, Phillipe, *Centuries of Childhood* (Penguin, 1982)

Aspinwall, Bernard, *Portable Utopia: Glasgow and the United States 1820–1920* (Aberdeen University Press, 1984)

Auerbach, Nina, *Private Theatricals: The Lives of the Victorians* (Harvard University Press, 1990)

Badinter, Elizabeth, *The Myth of Motherhood: An Historical View of the Maternal Instinct* (Souvenir Press, 1981)

Bailey, Peter, *Popular Culture and Performance in the Victorian City* (Cambridge University Press, 1998)

Banham, Joanna, Sally MacDonald and Julia Porter, *Victorian Interior Design* (Crescent Books, 1991)

Basch, Françoise, *Relative Creature: Victorian Women in Society and the Novel 1833–67* (Allen Lane, 1974)

Bebbington, David, (ed.), *The Baptists in Scotland: A History* (Baptist Union of Scotland, 1988)

Bebbington, David, *Evangelicalism in Modern Britain: A History from the 1730s to the 1980s* (Allen & Unwin, 1989)

Bebbington, David, and G. A. Rawlyk, *Evangelicalism: Comparative Studies of Popular Protestantism in North America, the British Isles and beyond 1700–1990* (Oxford University Press, 1994)

Bell, J. J., *I Remember* (Porpoise Press, 1932)

Benson, John, *The Rise of the Consumer Society in Britain, 1880–1980* (Longman, 1994)

Blackie, Agnes A. C., *Blackie & Son 1809–1959: A Short History of the Firm* (Blackie, 1959)

Bladgett, Harriet, *Centuries of Formal Days: English Women's Private Diaries* (Rutgers University Press, 1988)

Blyth, Henry, *Madeleine Smith: A Famous Victorian Murder Trial* (Duckworth, 1977)

Bowlby, Rachel, *Carried Away: The Invention of Modern Shopping* (Faber, 2000)

Boxer, Marilyn, and Jean H. Quataert (ed.), *Connecting Spheres: European Women in a Globalizing World, 1500 to the Present* (Oxford University Press, 2000, 2nd edn)

Boyd, Kenneth, *Scottish Church Attitudes to Sex, Marriage and the Family 1850–1914* (John Donald, 1980)

Branca, Patricia, *Silent Sisterhood: Middle Class Women in the Victorian Home* (Croom Helm, 1975)

Breward, Christopher, *The Hidden Consumer: Masculinities, Fashion and City Life 1860–1914* (Manchester University Press, 1999)

Brod, Harry (ed.), *The Making of Masculinities: The New Men's Studies* (Allen & Unwin, 1987)

Brooker, W. D. (ed.), *A Century of the Scottish Mountaineering Club: An Anthology from the Scottish Mountaineering Club Journal* (Scottish Mountaineering Trust, 1988)

Brown, Callum G., *Religion and Society in Scotland since 1707* (Edinburgh University Press, 1997)

Brown, Callum G., *The Death of Christian Britain* (Routledge, 2001)

Burton, Antoinette, *Burdens of History: British Feminists, Indian Women and Imperial Culture, 1865–1915* (University of Carolina Press, 1994)

Butler, Judith, *Gender Trouble: Feminism and the Subversion of Identity* (Routledge, 1993)

Butler, Marilyn, *Jane Austen and the War of Ideas* (Clarendon Press, 1975)

Calder, Jenni, *The Victorian Home* (Batsford, 1977)

Carens, Joseph H. (ed.), *Democracy and Possessive Individualism: The Intellectual Legacy of C. B. Macpherson* (State University of New York Press, 1993)

Carswell, Catherine, *Lying Awake* (Canongate, 1997)

Carvel, John L., *Stephen of Linthouse* (Alexander Stephen & Sons, 1950)

Chalklin, C. W., *The Provincial Towns of Georgian England: A Study of the Building Process 1740–1820* (Edward Arnold, 1974)

Chandler, Alfred D., *Scale and Scope: The Dynamics of Industrial Capitalism* (Belknap Press, 1990)

Clark, Alice, *Working Life of Women in the Seventeenth Century* (Routledge, 1982)

Clive, Eric M., *The Law of Husband and Wife in Scotland* (W. Green, 1982)

Coats, Olive Mary, and Victoria Taylor Coats, *Dr and Mrs Joseph Coats: A Book of Remembrance/Compiled by their Daughters* (Jackson, Wylie & Co., 1929)

Colley, Linda, *Britons: Forging the Nation, 1707–1837* (Yale University Press, 1992)

Corbett, Mary Jean, *Representing Femininity: Middle-Class Subjectivity in Victorian and Edwardian Women's Autobiography* (Oxford University Press, 1992)

Crafts, N. F. R., *British Economic Growth during the Industrial Revolution* (Oxford University Press, 1985)

Craik, Elizabeth (ed.), *Marriage and Property: Women and Marital Customs in History* (Aberdeen University Press, 1984)

Crossick, Geoffrey, and Serge Jaumain (ed.), *Cathedrals of Consumption: The European Department Store, 1850–1939* (Ashgate, 1999)

Cunningham, Hugh, *Leisure in the Industrial Revolution* (Croom Helm, 1980)

Cunningham, Hugh, *Children and Childhood in Western Society since 1500* (Longman, 1995)

Davidoff, Leonore, *The Best Circles: Society, Etiquette and the Season* (Cresset Library, 1986)

Davidoff, Leonore, Megan Doolittle, Janet Fink and Katherine Holden, *The Family Story: Blood, Contract and Intimacy, 1830–1960* (Longman, 1999)

Davidoff, Leonore, and Catherine Hall, *Family Fortunes: Men and Women of the English Middle Class, 1780–1850* (Routledge, 1987)

Dewar, De Courcy Lewthwaite (ed.), *The History of the Glasgow Society of Lady Artists' Club* (Maclehose, 1950)

Dunbar, Janet, *The Early Victorian Woman: Some Aspects of Her Life 1837–57* (Harrap, 1953)

Dupree, Marguerite, *Family Structure in the Staffordshire Potteries, 1840–1880* (Clarendon Press, 1995)

Dyhouse, Carol, *Feminism and the Family in England 1880–1939* (Oxford University Press, 1989)

Dyhouse, Carol, *Girls Growing up in Late Victorian and Edwardian England* (Routledge & Kegan Paul, 1981)

Earle, Peter, *The Making of the English Middle Class: Business, Society and Family Life in London, 1660–1730* (Methuen, 1989)

Fisher, Richard B., *Joseph Lister, 1827–1912* (Macdonald & Jane's, 1977)

Flatcher, Anthony J., *Gender, Sex and Subordination in England, 1500–1800* (Yale University Press, 1995)

Flinn, M. W., *Scottish Population History from the Seventeenth Century to the 1930s* (Cambridge University Press, 1977)

Foreman, Amanda, *Georgiana, Duchess of Devonshire* (Harper Collins, 1999)

Foster, John, *Class Struggle and the Industrial Revolution: Early Industrial Capitalism in Three English Towns* (Methuen, 1974)

Foy, Jessica H., and Thomas J. Schlereth (ed.), *American Home Life 1880–1930: A Social History of Spaces and Services* (University of Tennessee Press, 1992)

Fraser, Derek (ed.), *A History of Modern Leeds* (Manchester University Press, 1980)

Fraser, W. Hamish, and Irene Maver (ed.), *Glasgow*, vol. II: *1830–1912* (Manchester University Press, 1996)

Frisby, David, and Mike Featherstone (ed.), *Simmel on Culture: Selected Writings* (Sage, 1997)

Frost, Ginger, *Promises Broken: Courtship, Class, and Gender in Victorian England* (University Press of Virginia, 1995)

Gay, Peter, *The Bourgeois Experience: Victoria to Freud*, vol. I: *Education of the Senses* (Cambridge University Press, 1984)

Gay, Peter, *The Bourgeois Experience: Victoria to Freud*, vol. II: *The Tender Passion* (Oxford University Press, 1984–6)

Gillis, John, *A World of Their Own Making: A History of Myth and Ritual in Family Life* (Oxford University Press, 1997)

Gillis, John, Louise Tilly and David Levine, *The European Experience of Declining Fertility 1850–1970* (Blackwell, 1992)

Gleadle, Kathryn, *The Early Feminists: Radical Unitarians and the Emergence of the Women's Rights Movement, 1831–51* (Macmillan, 1995)

Godlee, Sir Rickman, *Lord Lister* (Macmillan, 1917)

Gordon, Eleanor, *Women and the Labour Movement in Scotland 1850–1914* (Oxford University Press, 1991)

Gordon, Eleanor, and Esther Breitenbach (ed.), *The World is Ill Divided: Women's Work in Scotland in the Nineteenth and Early Twentieth Centuries* (Edinburgh University Press, 1990)

Gordon, Lyndall, *Charlotte Brontë: A Passionate Life* (Vintage, 1995)

Gray, Marion, W., *Productive Men, Reproductive Women: The Agrarian Household and the Emergence of Separate Spheres in the German Enlightenment* (Berghahn Books, 2000)

Gray, R. Q. *The Labour Aristocracy in Victorian Edinburgh* (Oxford University Press, 1976)

Greig, Geordie, *Louis and the Prince* (Hodder & Stoughton, 1999)

Gunn, Simon, *The Public Culture of the Victorian Middle Class* (Manchester University Press, 2000)

Hall, Catherine, Keith McClelland and Jane Rendall, *Defining the Victorian Nation: Class, Race, Gender and the British Reform Act of 1867* (Cambridge University Press, 2000)

Hall, Lesley A., *Sex, Gender and Social Change in Britain since 1880* (Macmillan, 2000)

Halttunen, Karen, *Confidence Men and Painted Women: A Study of Middle Class Culture in America 1830–1870* (Yale University Press, 1982)

Hammerton, A. J., *Emigrant Gentlewomen: Genteel Poverty and Female Emigration 1830–1914* (Croom Helm, 1979)

Hammerton, A. J., *Cruelty and Companionship: Conflict in Nineteenth Century Married Life* (Routledge, 1995)

Harrison, Carol E., *The Bourgeois Citizen in Nineteenth Century France: Gender, Sociability and the Use of Emulation* (Oxford University Press, 1999)

Heal, Felicity, *Hospitality in Early Modern England* (Oxford University Press, 1990)

Helland, J., *The Studios of Frances and Margaret McDonald* (Manchester University Press, 1996)

Helland, J., *Professional Woman Painters in Nineteenth-Century Scotland* (Ashgate, 2000)

Hendrickson, Robert, *The Grand Emporiums: The Illustrated History of American Great Department Stores* (Stein & Day, 1979)

Higgs, Edward, *A Clearer Sense of the Census: Victorian Censuses and Historical Research* (HMSO, 1996)

Hill, Bridget, *Servants: English Domestics in the Eighteenth Century* (Oxford University Press, 1996)

Hodge, Harry, and James Hodge (ed.), *Famous Trials* (Penguin, 1984)

Holcombe, Lee, *Victorian Ladies at Work: Middle-Class Working Women in England and Wales 1850–1914* (David & Charles, 1973)

Holmwood House (The National Trust for Scotland, 1998)

Holton, Sandra Stanley, Alison Mackinnon and Margaret Allan (ed.), *Between Rationality and Revelation: Women, Faith and Public Role in the Nineteenth Century*, Special issue of *Women's History Review*, 7, 2 (1998)

Horn, Pamela, *Ladies of the Manor: Wives and Daughters in Country-House Society 1830–1918* (Sutton Publishing, 1977)

Horn, Pamela, *Rise and Fall of the Victorian Servant* (Alan Sutton, 1990)

Houlbrooke, Ralph A., *The English Family 1450–1700* (Longman, 1984)

Howe, Anthony, *The Cotton Masters, 1830–1860* (Clarendon Press, 1984)

Hughes, Kathryn, *The Victorian Governess* (Hambledon, 1993)

Ingham, Geoffrey, *Capitalism Divided?* (Macmillan, 1984)

Jalland, Pat, *Women, Marriage and Politics 1860–1914* (Oxford University Press, 1988)

Jeffries, Sheila, *The Spinster and Her Enemies: Feminism and Sexuality 1880–1930* (Pandora, 1985)

Jeremy, David, *Religion, Business and Wealth in Modern Britain* (Routledge, 1998)

Jones, Gareth Stedman, *Languages of Class: Studies in English Working-Class History, 1832–1983* (Cambridge University Press, 1983)

Jordan, Ellen, *The Women's Movement and Women's Employment in Nineteenth-Century Britain* (Routledge, 1999)

Joyce, Patrick, *Visions of the People: Industrial England and the Question of Class, 1840–1914* (Cambridge University Press, 1994)

Kaplan, Anne E., *Motherhood and Representation: The Mother in Popular Culture and Melodrama* (Routledge, 1992)

Kearney, Peter, *The Glasgow Cludgie: A History of Glasgow's Public Conveniences* (People's Publications, 1985)

Kidd, Alan, and David Nicholls (ed.), *Gender, Civic Culture, and Consumerism: Middle Class Identity in Britain, 1800–1940* (Manchester University Press, 1999)

Kidd, Alan J., and K. W. Roberts (ed.), *City, Class and Culture: Studies of Social Policy and Cultural Production in Victorian Manchester* (Manchester University Press, 1985)

Kinchin, Pirella, *Tea and Taste: The Glasgow Tea Rooms 1875–1975* (White Cockade, 1991)

Kinchin, Pirella, and Juliet Kinchin, *Glasgow's Great Exhibitions 1888, 1901, 1911, 1938, 1988* (White Cockade, 1988)

Kirkham, Pat, (ed.), *The Gendered Object* (St Martin's Press, 1996)

Knox, W. W., *The Industrial Nation: Work, Culture and Society in Scotland, 1800–Present* (Edinburgh University Press, 1999)

La Bossa, Ralph, *The Modernization of Fatherhood: A Social and Political History* (University of Chicago Press, 1991)

Lancaster, William, *The Department Store: A Social History* (Leicester University Press, 1995)

Landes, Joan, *Women and the Public Sphere in the Age of the French Revolution* (Cornell University Press, 1988)

Langland, Elizabeth, *Nobody's Angels: Middle Class Woman and Domestic Ideology in Victorian Culture* (Cornell University Press, 1995)

Laslett, Peter, *The World We Have Lost* (Methuen, 1973)

Laslett, Peter, and Richard Wall (ed.), *Household and Family in Past Time* (Cambridge University Press, 1972)

Lazonick, William, *Business Organisation and the Myth of the Market Economy* (Cambridge University Press, 1991)

Lee, Virginia, *Liberty, a Better Husband* (Yale University Press, 1984)

Leneman, Leah, *Alienated Affections* (Edinburgh University Press, 1998)

Lochhead, Marion, *The Scottish Household in the Eighteenth Century* (Moray Press, 1948)

Lochhead, Marion, *The Victorian Household* (J. Murray, 1964)

Loeb, Lore Anne, *Consuming Angels: Advertising and Victorian Women* (Oxford University Press, 1994)

Logan, Thad, *The Victorian Parlour* (Cambridge University Press, 2001)

Lovell, Terry, *Consuming Fiction* (Verso, 1987)

Lystra, Karen, *Searching the Heart: Women, Men and Romantic Love in Nineteeth Century America* (New York, 1989)

Macdonald, Lesley A. Orr, *A Unique and Glorious Mission* (John Donald, 2000)

MacElroy, David, *Scotland's Age of Improvement: A Survey of Eighteenth Century Literary Clubs and Societies* (Washington, DC, 1969)

Macfarlane, Alan, *The Origins of English Individualism* (Blackwell, 1978)

Macfarlane, Alan, *Marriage and Love in England, 1300–1840* (Harlow, 1984)

Macfarlane, Alan, *The Culture of Capitalism* (Blackwell, 1987)

MacGowan, Douglas, *Murder in Victorian Scotland: The Trial of Madeleine Smith* (Praeger, 1999)

MacLeod, Dianne, *Art and the Victorian Middle Class* (Cambridge University Press, 1996)

Mananzan, Sr Mary J., (ed.), *Woman and Religion: A Collection of Essays, Personal Histories, and Contextualised Liturgies* (Manila, Institute of Woman's Studies, St Scholastica's College, 1988)

Marsden, Gordon, *Victorian Values: Personalities and Perspectives in Nineteenth Century Society* (Longman, 1990)

Mason, Michael, *The Making of Victorian Sexuality* (Oxford University Press, 1984)

Massey, Doreen B., *Space, Place and Gender* (Polity, 1994)

Matus, Jill L., *Unstable Bodies: Victorian Representation of Sexuality and Maternity* (Manchester University Press, 1995)

McAlpine, Joan, *The Lady of Claremont House* (Argyll Publishing, 1997)

Melville, J. D., *The Use and Organisation of Domestic Space in Late Seventeenth Century London* (University of Cambridge Press, 1999)

Midgley, Clare, *Women against Slavery: The British Campaigns, 1780–1870* (Routledge, 1992)

Midgley, Clare (ed.), *Gender and Imperialism* (Manchester University Press, 1998)

Mintz, Steven, *A Prison of Expectations: The Family in Victorian Culture* (New York University Press, 1983)

Mitchell, J. C., *Regality Club* (Maclehose, 1899)

Mitchison, Rosalind, *British Population Change since 1860* (Macmillan, 1977)

Mitterauer, Michael, and Reinhard Sieder, *The European Family* (Blackwell, 1989)

Montgomery, Maureen, *Displaying Women: Spectacles of Leisure in Edith Wharton's New York* (Routledge, 1998)

Morland, Nigel, *That Nice Miss Smith* (Souvenir Press, 1957)

Morris, R. J., *Class, Sect and Party: The Making of the British Middle Class, Leeds, 1820–50* (Manchester University Press, 1990)

Morton, Graham, *Unionist-Nationalism: Governing Urban Scotland 1830–1860* (Tuckwell, 1999)

Moss, Michael, Moira Rankin and Lesley Richmond, *Who, Where and When: The History and Constitution of the University of Glasgow* (University of Glasgow, 2001)

Nair, Gwyneth, *Highley: The Development of a Community 1550–1880* (Blackwell, 1988)

Nead, Lynda, *Myths of Sexuality: Representations of Women in Victorian Britain* (Blackwell, 1988)

Nead, Lynda, *Victorian Babylon: People, Streets and Images in Nineteenth Century London* (Yale University Press, 2000)

Newton, Stella M., *Health, Art and Reason* (London, 1974)

Nicholson, Shirley, *A Victorian Household* (Alan Sutton Publishing, 1994)

O'Day, Rosemary, *The Family and Family Relationships, 1500–1900* (Macmillan, 1994)

Outhwaite, William, *Habermas: A Critical Introduction* (Polity, 1991)

Pacione, Michael, *Glasgow: The Socio-Spatial Development of the City* (John Wiley & Sons, 1995)

Pateman, Carole, *The Disorder of Women; Democracy, Feminism and Political Theory* (Polity, 1989)

Payne, Peter, *The Early Scottish Limited Companies* (Scottish Academic Press, 1980)

Perkin, Joan, *Women and Marriage in Nineteenth-Century England* (Routledge, 1989)

Peterson, M. Jeanne, *Family, Love and Work in the Lives of Victorian Gentlewomen* (Indiana University Press, 1989)

Phillips, Patricia, *The Scientific Lady: A Social History of Women's Scientific Interests 1520–1918* (Weidenfeld & Nicolson, 1990)

Pointon, Marcia, *Strategies for Showing: Women, Possession and Representation in English Visual Culture 1650–1800* (Oxford University Press, 1997)

Pollock, Linda A., *Forgotten Children: Parent Child Relations from 1500–1900* (Cambridge University Press, 1983)

Pollock, Linda A., *A Lasting Relationship: Parents and Children over Three Centuries* (University Press of New England, 1987)

Purvis, June (ed.), *Women's History: Britain, 1850–1945* (University College London Press, 1995)

Rappaport, Erika, *Shopping for Pleasure: Women and the Making of London's West End* (Princeton University Press, 2000)

Reader, W. J., *The Weir Group: A Centenary History* (Weidenfeld & Nicolson, 1971)

Reed, Peter (ed.), *Glasgow: The Forming of a City* (Edinburgh University Press, 1992)

Rendall, Jane, *The Origins of Modern Feminism* (Lyceum Books, 1985)

Richards, Thomas, *The Commodity Culture of Victorian England: Advertising as Spectacle 1851–1914* (Stamford University Press, 1990)

Roberts, Elizabeth, *Women's Work 1840–1940* (Cambridge University Press, 1995)

Robertson, Edna, *Glasgow's Doctor: James Burns Russell, 1837–1904* (Tuckwell, 1998)

Robinson, Michael G., *Acting Women: The Performing Self in the Late Nineteenth Century* (Loughborough University Press, 1991)

Robson, John M., *Marriage or Celibacy* (University of Toronto Press, 1995)

Rothman, Ellen, *Hands and Hearts: A History of Courtship in America* (Basic Books, 1984)

Rubik, Margarete, *The Novels of Mrs Oliphant: A Subversive View of Traditional Themes* (Peter Lang, 1994)

Rubinstein, David, *Victorian Homes* (David & Charles, 1974)

Ruggles, Stephen, *Prolonged Connections: The Rise of the Extended Family in Nineteenth Century England and America* (University of Wisconsin Press, 1987)

Ryan, Mary, *Cradle of the Middle Class: The Family in Oneida County New York 1790–1865* (Cambridge University Press, 1981)

Sanders, Valerie, *The Private Lives of Victorian Women: Autobiography in Nineteenth-Century England* (Harvester Wheatsheaf, 1989)

Sanderson, Elizabeth C., *Women and Work in Eighteenth-Century Edinburgh* (Macmillan, 1996)

Saville, Richard, *Bank of Scotland: A History, 1695–1995* (Edinburgh University Press, 1996)

Sennett, Richard, *Families against the City: Middle Class Homes of Industrial Chicago, 1872–90* (Harvard University Press, 1970)

Sharein, Harold I., *Lord Kelvin: The Dynamic Victorian* (Pennsylvannia State University Press, 1979)

Sharpe, Pamela (ed.), *Women's Work: The English Experience 1650–1914* (Arnold, 1995)

Shevelow, K. *The Construction of Femininity in the Early Periodical* (London, 1989)

Shires, Linda (ed.), *Rewriting the Victorians: History, Theory and the Politics of Gender* (Routledge, 1992)

Shorter, Edward, *The Making of the Modern Family* (Fontana Books, 1977)

Showalter, Elaine, *Sexual Anarchy: Gender and Culture at the Fin de Siècle* (Bloomsbury, 1991)

Sklar, Kathryn K., *Catherine Beecher: A Study in American Domesticity* (Yale University Press, 1973)

Slaven, Anthony, and Sidney Checkland (ed.), *Dictionary of Scottish Business Biography*, 2 vols (Aberdeen University Press, 1986–90)

Smith, Bonnie, *Ladies of the Leisure Class: The Bourgeoisie of Northern France in the Nineteenth Century* (Princeton University Press, 1981)

Smith, Bonnie, *Changing Lives* (D. C. Heath & Co., 1989)

Smith, Crosbie W., *Energy and Empire: A Biographical Study of Lord Kelvin* (Cambridge University Press, 1989)

Smith, Moira R., *Kelvin Club Western Club* (Dunkeld Cathedral Press, 1997)

Smyth, J. J., *Labour in Glasgow, 1896–1936: Socialism, Suffrage, Sectarianism* (Tuckwell Press, 2000)

Spain, Daphne, *Gendered Spaces* (University of North Caroline Press, 1992)

Staves, Susan, *Married Women's Separate Property in England 1660–1833* (Harvard University Press, 1990)

Stephen, Frank, *Life with Father: Parenthood and Masculinity in the Nineteenth-Century American North* (Johns Hopkins University Press, 1998)

Still, Judith, and Michael Worton (ed.), *Textuality and Sexuality* (Manchester University Press, 1993)

Stone, Lawrence, *Family, Sex and Marriage in England 1500–1800* (Weidenfeld and Nicolson, 1977)

Sweet, Matthew, *Inventing the Victorians* (Faber, 2001)

Szreter, Simon, *Fertility, Class and Gender in Britain, 1860–1940* (Cambridge University Press, 1996)

Tanner, Tony, *Adultery and the Novel: Contract and Transgression* (Johns Hopkins University Press, 1979)

Thompson, F. M. L., *Gentrification and the Enterprise Culture* (Oxford, 2001)

Thornton, Margaret, *Public and Private: Feminist Legal Debates* (Oxford University Press, 1995)

Tosh, John, *A Man's Place: Masculinity and the Middle Class Home in Victorian England* (Yale University Press, 1999)

Toughill, Thomas, *Oscar Slater: The Mystery Solved* (Canongate, 1993)

Tranter, N. L., *Population and Society 1750–1940: Contrasts in Population Growth* (Longman, 1985)

Vicinus, Martha (ed.), *Suffer and Be Still: Women in the Victorian Age* (Methuen & Co., 1980)

Vicinus, Martha, *Independent Women: Work and Community for Single Women 1850–1920* (Virago, 1985)

Vickery, Amanda, *The Gentleman's Daughter: Women's Lives in Georgian England* (Yale University Press, 1998)

Wahrman, Dror, *Imagining the Middle Class: The Political Representation of Class in Britain (1780–1840)* (Cambridge University Press, 1995)

Walkowitz, Judith, *City of Dreadful Delight* (Virago, 1992)

Walton, Frederick P., *A Handbook of Husband and Wife According to the Law of Scotland* (William Green & Son, 1893)

Weatherill, Lorna, *Consumer Behaviour and Material Culture 1660–1760* (Routledge, 1997)

White, Gavin, *The Scottish Episcopal Church: A New History* (Edinburgh General Synod of the Scottish Episcopal Church, 1998)

Whittington-Egan, Richard, *The Oscar Slater Murder Story* (Neil Wilson Publishing, 2001)

Williams, Rosalind H., *Dream Worlds: Mass Consumption in Late Nineteenth Century France* (University of California Press, 1982)

Wilson, Elizabeth, *Adorned in Dreams: Fashion and Modernity* (Virago, 1985)

Wilson, Elizabeth, *The Sphinx in the City* (Virago, 1991)

Wrightson, Keith, *English Society, 1580–1680* (Unwin Hyman, 1982)

Wrightson, Keith, and David Levine, *Poverty and Piety in an English Village: Terling 1525–1700* (Oxford University Press, 1995)

Wrigley, E. A., and R. S. Schofield, *Population History of England 1541–1871* (Cambridge University Press, 1981)

Yeo, Eileen Janes, *Contest for Social Science in Britain: Relation and Representation of Gender and Class in the Nineteenth and Twentieth Centuries* (Rivers Oram Press, 1996)

Yeo, Eileen Janes (ed.), *Radical Femininity: Women's Self-Representation in the Public Sphere* (Manchester University Press, 1998)

Young, Fred H. Y., *A Century of Carpet Making 1839–1939* (James Templeton & Co., 1944)

Young, G. E. R., *Elma and Helen Story: A Recollection* (Blackie & Son, 1948)

ARTICLES AND ESSAYS

Adams, Christine, 'A Choice not to Wed? Unmarried Women in Eighteenth-Century France', *Journal of Social History*, 29 (1995–6), pp. 883–94

Agnew, Jean-Christophe, 'A House of Fiction: Domestic Interiors and the Commodity Aesthetic', in Simon Bronner (ed.), *Consuming Visions* (W. W. Norton & Co., 1989), pp. 157–89

Anderson, Michael, 'The Social Position of Spinsters in Mid-Victorian Britain', *Journal of Family History*, 9 (1984), pp. 377–93

Ben-Porath, Yoran, 'The F-Connection: Families, Friends and Firms and the Organisation of Exchange', *Population and Development Review*, 6 (1980), pp. 1–30

Berg, Maxine, 'Women's Property and the Industrial Revolution', *Journal of Interdisciplinary History*, 24 (1993), pp. 233–50

Bland, Lucy, ' "Purifying" the Public World: Feminist Vigilantes in Late Victorian England', *Women's History Review*, 1, 3 (1992), pp. 397–412

Bloch, R. H., 'Ideals in Transition: The Rise of Moral Motherhood, 1785–1815', *Feminist Studies*, 4 (1978), pp. 101–27

Borscheid, Peter, 'Romantic Love and Material Interest: Choosing Partners in Nineteenth-Century Germany', *Journal of Family History*, 11–12 (1986–7), pp. 157–68

Branca, Patricia, 'Images and Reality: The Myths of the Idle Victorian Woman', in Mary S. Hartman and Lois Banner (ed.), *Clio's Consciousness Raised* (Harper & Row, 1974), pp. 179–91

Brandimarte, Cynthia A., 'To Make the World Homelike: Gender, Space and America's Tearoom Movement', *Winterthur Portfolio: A Journal of American Material Culture*, 30, 1 (1995), pp. 1–19

Brucken, Carolyn, 'In the Public Eye: Women and the American Luxury Hotel', *Winterthur Portfolio*, 31, 4 (1996), pp. 203–220

Burton, Antoinette, 'Women and "Domestic" Imperial Culture: The Case of Victorian Britain', in Marilyn Boxer and Jean Quataert (ed.), *Connecting Spheres: European Women in a Globalizing World, 1500 to the Present* (Oxford University Press, 2000), pp. 174–84

Carroll, James, Nicholas Morgan and Michael Moss, 'Building by Numbers: The Lifecycle of Scottish Building Firms, 1793–1913', in Phillippe Jobert and Michael Moss (ed.), *The Birth and Death of Companies* (Parthenon Publishing, 1990)

Checkland, S. G., 'The British Industrial City as History: The Glasgow Case', *Urban Studies*, 1 (1964), pp. 34–54

Cooper, Di, and Moira Donald, 'Households and "Hidden" Kin in Early Nineteenth-Century England: Four Case Studies in Suburban Exeter, 1821–1861', *Continuity and Change*, 10, 2 (1995), pp. 257–78

Crawford, Patricia, 'The Construction and Experience of Maternity in Seventeenth Century England', in Valerie Fildes (ed.), *Women as Mothers in Pre-Industrial England: Essays in Memory of Dorothy McLaren* (Routledge, 1990), pp. 3–38

Crozier, Dorothy, 'Kinship and Occupational Succession', *Sociological Review*, 13 (1965), pp. 5–43

Curran, Cynthia, 'Private Women, Public Needs: Middle-Class Widows in Victorian England', *Albion*, 25, 2 (1993), pp. 217–36

Daggers, Jenny, 'The Victorian Female Civilising Mission and Women's Aspiration towards Priesthood in the Church of England', *Women's History Review*, 10, 4 (2001), pp. 651–70

Dauphin, Cecile, 'Single Women', in Geneviève Fraisse and Michelle Perrot (ed.), *A History of Women in the West* (Harvard University Press, 1993), pp. 427–42

Davin, Delia, 'British Women Missionaries in Nineteenth-Century China', *Women's History Review*, 1, 2 (1992), pp. 257–71

Durie, Alastair J., 'The Development of the Scottish Coastal Resorts in the Central Lowlands, *c*1770–1880: From Gulf Stream to Golf Stream', in *Local Historian*, 24, 4 (1994), pp. 206–16

Earle, Peter, 'The Female Labour Market in the Later Seventeenth and Early Eighteenth Centuries', *Economic History Review*, 42 (1989), pp. 328–53

Erickson, Amy, 'Common Law versus Common Practice: The Use of Marriage Settlements in Early Modern England', *Economic History Review*, 43 (1990), pp. 21–39

Eustace, Nicole, '"The Cornerstone of a Copious Work": Love and Power in Eighteenth-Century Courtship', *Journal of Social History*, 34, 3 (2001), pp. 517–46

Fix, Nancy, 'Cousin Marriage in Victorian England', *Journal of Family History*, 11–12 (1986–7), pp. 285–301

Freeman, Ruth, and Patricia Klaus, 'Blessed or Not? The New Spinster in England and the USA in the Late Nineteenth and Early Twentieth Centuries', *Journal of Family History*, 9 (1984), pp. 331–44

Garrard, John, 'Urban Elites 1850–1914: The Rise and Decline of a New Squirearchy?', *Albion*, 27 (1995), pp. 583–621

Gordon, Eleanor, and Gwyneth Nair, 'The Myth of the Victorian Patriarchal Family', History of the Family, 7 (2002), pp. 125–38

Gordon, Eleanor, and Gwyneth Nair, 'The Economic Role of Middle-Class Women in Victorian Glasgow', Women's History Review, 9, 4 (2000), pp. 791–813

Gow, Ian, 'The Dining Room', in A. Carruthers (ed.), *The Scottish Home* (National Museums of Scotland, 1996), pp. 125–54

Gunn, Simon, 'The Ministry, the Middle Class and the "Civilising Mission" in Manchester, 1850–80', *Social History*, 21, 1 (1996), pp. 22–36

Gunn, Simon, 'The Public Sphere, Modernity and Consumption: New Perspectives on the History of the English Middle Class', in Alan Kidd and David Nicholls (ed.), *Gender, Civic Culture and Consumerism: Middle-Class Identity in Britain 1800–1940* (Manchester University Press, 1999), pp. 12–29

Haggis, Jane, '"A heart that has felt the love of God and longs for others to know it": Conventions of Gender, Tensions of Self and Constructions of Difference in Offering to be a Lady Missionary', *Women's History Review*, 7, 2 (1998), pp. 171–92

Halttunen, Karen, 'From Parlor to Living Room: Domestic Space, Interior Decoration and the Culture of Personality', in Simon Bronner (ed.), *Consuming Visions* (W. W. Norton, 1989) pp. 157–89

Hammerton, A. J., 'The English Weakness? Gender, Satire and "Moral Manliness" in the Lower Middle-Class, 1870–1920', in Alan Kidd and David Nicholls (ed.), *Gender, Civic Culture and Consumerism: Middle-Class Identity in Britain 1800–1940* (Manchester University Press, 1999), pp. 164–82

Hartman, Mary S., 'Murder for Respectability: The Case of Madeline Smith', *Victorian Studies*, 16 (1972–3), pp. 381–400

Hillis, Peter, 'Presbyterianism and Social Class in Mid-Nineteenth Century Glasgow: A Study of Nine Churches', *Journal of Ecclesiastical History*, 32 (1981), pp. 47–64

Hudson, Pat, 'Rehabilitating the Industrial Revolution', *Economic History Review*, 45, 1 (1992), pp. 24–50

Hufton, Olwen, 'Women without Men: Widows and Spinsters in Britain and France in the Eighteenth Century', *Journal of Family History*, 9 (1984), pp. 355–75

Jalland, Patricia, 'Victorian Spinsters: Dutiful Daughters, Desperate Rebels and the Transition to the New Women,' in Patricia Crawford (ed.), *Exploring Women's Past* (Allen & Unwin, 1983), pp. 129–70

Kinchin, Juliet, 'Interiors: Nineteenth Century Essays on the "Masculine" and the "Feminine" Room', in Pat Kirkham (ed.), *The Gender of Object* (Manchester University Press, 1996), pp. 12–29

Kinchin, Juliet, 'The Drawing Room', in A. Carruthers (ed.) *The Scottish Home* (National Museums of Scotland, 1996), pp. 155–80

Klein, Lawrence, 'Gender, Conversation and the Public Sphere in Early Eighteenth-Century England', in Judith Still and Michael Worton (ed.), *Textuality and Sexuality: Reading Theories and Practices* (Manchester University Press, 1993), pp. 100–15

Klein, Lawrence, 'Gender and the Public/Private Distinction in the Eighteenth Century: Some Questions about the Evidence and Analytic Procedure', *Eighteenth Century Studies*, 29, 1 (1995), pp. 97–109

Knox, William, 'The Political and Workplace Culture of the Working Class, 1832–1914', in W. Hamish Fraser and R. J. Morris (ed.), *People and Society in Scotland*, vol. 2: *1830–1914* (John Donald, 1990), pp. 138–66

Landes, Joan B., 'The Public and the Private Sphere: A Feminist Reconsideration', in Joan B. Landes (ed.), *Feminism: The Public and the Private* (Oxford University Press, 1998), pp. 135–63

Leach, William, 'Transformations in a Culture of Consumption: Women and Department Stores 1890–1925', *Journal of American History*, 7 (1984), pp. 319–42

Leneman, Leah, 'Disregarding the Matrimonial Vows', *Journal of Social History*, 30, 2 (1996), pp. 465–82

Lloyd, Jennifer M., 'Conflicting Expectations in Nineteenth-Century British

Matrimony: The Failed Companionate Marriage of Effie Gray and John Ruskin', *Journal of Women's History*, 11, 2 (1999), pp. 86–109

Lohan, Maria, 'Come Back Public/Private: (Almost) All is Forgiven: Using Feminist Methodologies in Researching Information Communication Technologies', *Women's Studies International Forum*, 23, 1 (2000), pp. 107–17

Lovell, Terry, 'Thinking Feminism with and against Bourdieu', in Bridget Fowler (ed.), *Reading Bourdieu on Society and Culture* (Blackwell, 2000), pp. 27–48

Lummis, Trevor, 'The Historical Dimension of Fatherhood: A Case Study 1892–1914', in Lorna McKee and Margaret O'Brien (ed.), *The Father Figure* (Tavistock, 1982), pp. 43–56

Mallett, Phillip, 'Women and Marriage in Victorian Society', in Elizabeth Craik (ed.), *Marriage and Property* (Aberdeen University Press, 1984), pp. 159–89

Massey, Doreen, 'Masculinity, Dualisms and High Technology', in Nancy Duncan (ed.), *Body Space: Destabilising Geographies of Gender and Sexuality* (Routledge, 1996), pp. 109–26

Maver, Irene, 'Glasgow Town Council in the Nineteenth Century', in T. M. Devine (ed.), *Scottish Elites* (John Donald, 1994), pp. 98–130

Maver, Irene, 'Glasgow's Parks and the Community 1850–1914: A Case Study', *Urban History*, 25, 3 (1998), pp. 323–47

Mayhall, Laura Nym, 'The Making of a Suffragette: The Uses of Reading and the Legacy of Radicalism, 1890–1918', in George Behlmer and Fred Leventhal (ed.), *Singular Continuities: Tradition, Nostalgia and Society in Modern Britain* (Stanford University Press, 2000)

McBride, Teresa, ' "As the Twig is Bent": The Victorian Nanny', in Anthony S. Wohl (ed.), *The Victorian Family: Structure and Stresses* (St Martin's Press, 1978)

McCrum, Ann, 'Inheritance and the Family: The Scottish Urban Experience in the 1820s', in Jan Stobart and Alastair Owen (ed.), *Urban Fortunes: Property and Inheritance in the Town, 1700–1900* (Ashgate, 2000), pp. 149–71

McDermid, Jane, 'Women and Education', in June Purvis (ed.), *Women's History: Britain 1850–1945* (University College London Press, 1995), pp. 107–30

Moore, Lindy, 'Researching the Education of Middle-Class Girls: With Particular Reference to Private Schools', *Scottish Archives*, 3 (1977), pp. 77–86

Morgan, Nicholas, and Richard Trainor, 'The Dominant Classes', in W. Hamish Fraser and R. J. Morris (ed.), *People and Society in Scotland*, vol. 2: *1830–1914* (John Donald, 1990), pp. 103–37

Morgan, Sue, 'Faith, Sex and Purity: The Religio-Feminist Theory of Ellice Hopkins', *Women's History Review*, 9, 1 (2000), pp. 13–34

Morris, R. J., 'The Middle Class and the Property Cycle during the Industrial Revolution', in T. C. Smout (ed.), *The Search for Wealth and Stability* (Macmillan, 1979), pp. 91–113

Munro, J. Forbes, 'Scottish Overseas Enterprise and the Lure of London: The Mackinnon Shipping Group, 1847–1893', *Scottish Economic and Social History Journal*, 8 (1988), pp. 73–87

Nava, Mica, 'Modernity's Disavowal: Women, the City and the Department Store', in M. Nava and A. O'Shea (ed.), *Modern Times: Reflections on a Century of English Modernity* (Routledge, 1996), pp. 38–76

Nenadic, Stana, 'The Small Family Firm in Victorian Britain', *Business History*, 35, 4 (1993), pp. 86–114

Nenadic, Stana, 'Middle Rank Consumers and Domestic Culture in Edinburgh and Glasgow 1720–1840', *Past and Present*, 145 (1994), pp. 122–56

Nenadic, Stana, 'The Victorian Middle Classes', in W. Hamish Fraser and Irene Maver (ed.), *Glasgow*, vol. 2: *1830 to 1912* (Manchester University Press, 1996), pp. 265–99

Okin, Susan Moller, 'Women and the Making of the Sentimental Family', *Philosophy and Public Affairs*, 11, 1 (1982), pp. 65–88

Okin, Susan Moller, 'Gender, the Public and the Private', in D. Held (ed.), *Political Theory Today* (Stanford University Press, 1991), pp. 67–90

Owens, Alastair, 'Property, Gender and the Life Course: Inheritance and Family Welfare Provision in Early Nineteenth-Century England', *Social History*, 26, 3 (2001), pp. 299–317

Palazzi, Maura, 'Female Solitude and Patrilineage: Unmarried Women and Widows during the Eighteenth and Nineteenth Centuries', *Journal of Family History*, 15, 4 (1990), pp. 443–59

Payne, Peter, 'Family Business in Britain: An Historical and Analytical Survey', in M. B. Rose (ed.), *Family Business* (Edward Elgar, 1995), pp. 69–104

Rappaport, Erika, '"A New Era of Shopping": The Promotion of Women's Pleasure in London's West End, 1909–1914', in Leo Charney and Vanessa Schwartz (ed.), *Cinema and the Invention of Modern Life* (University of California Press, 1999), 130–55

Rappaport, Erika, 'Travelling in the Lady Guides' London: Consumption, Modernity and the Fin-de-Siècle Metropolis', in Martin Daunton and Bernhard Dieger (ed.), *Meanings of Modernity* (Berg, 2001), pp. 25–43

Razi, Zvi, 'The Myth of the Immutable English Family', *Past and Present*, 140 (1993), pp. 3–44

Reay, Barry, 'Kinship and the Neighbourhood in Nineteenth-Century Rural England: The Myth of the Autonomous Nuclear Family', *Journal of Family History*, 21 (1996), pp. 87–104

Reed, Peter, 'The Victorian Suburb', in Reed (ed.), *Glasgow: The Forming of a City* (Edinburgh University Press, 1992), pp. 62–83

Rendall, Jane, 'Nineteenth Century Feminism and the Separation of Spheres: Reflections on the Public/Private Dichotomy', in Tayo Andreasen et al. (ed.), *Moving On: New Perspectives on the Women's Movements* (Aarhus University Press, 1991), pp. 17–37

Rendall, Jane, 'Citizenship Culture and Civilisation: The Language of British Suffragists 1866–74', in Melanie Nolan and Caroline Daly (ed.), *Suffrage and Beyond: International Feminist Perspectives* (New York University Press, 1994), pp. 127–50

Rendall, Jane, 'Women and the Public Sphere', *Gender and History*, 11, 3 (1999), pp. 475–88

Robb, J. G., 'Suburb and Slums in Gorbals', in George Gordon and Brian Dicks (ed.), *Scottish Urban History* (Aberdeen University Press, 1983), pp. 130–67

Roberts, David, 'The Paterfamilias of the Victorian Governing Classes', in A. S. Wohl (ed.), *The Victorian Family: Structure and Stresses* (St Martin's Press, 1978), pp. 59–81

Robertson, Pamela, 'Catherine Cranston', *Journal of the Decorative Arts Society*, 10 (1980)

Rose, Michael E., 'Culture, Philanthropy and the Manchester Middle Classes', in Alan J. Kidd and K. W. Roberts (ed.), *City, Class and Culture: Studies of Social Policy and Cultural Production in Victorian Manchester* (Manchester University Press, 1985)

Rubinstein, David, 'Cycling in the 1890s', *Victorian Studies*, 21 (1977), pp. 47–71

Rubinstein, W. D., 'Wealth, Elites and the Class Structure of Modern Britain', *Past and Present*, 76 (1977), pp. 99–126

Ryan, Mary, 'Gender and Public Access: Women's Politics in Nineteenth-Century America', in Craig Calhoun (ed.), *Habermas and the Public Sphere* (MIT Press, 1992), pp. 259–88

Schmiechen, James, 'Glasgow of the Imagination: Architecture, Townscape and Society', in W. Hamish Fraser and Irene Maver (ed.), *Glasgow*, vol. 2: *1830–1912* (Manchester University Press, 1996), pp. 486–518

Seed, John, 'Unitarianism, Political Economy and the Antimonies of Liberal Culture in Manchester, 1830–50', *Social History*, 7, 1 (1982), pp. 1–25

Sharpe, Pamela, 'Dealing with Love: The Ambiguous Independence of the Single Woman in Early Modern England', *Gender and History*, 11, 2 (1999), pp. 209–32

Simonsen, Pauline, 'Elizabeth Barrett Browning's Redundant Women', *Victorian Poetry*, 35, 4 (1997), pp. 509–32

Simpson, M., 'Urban Transport and the Development of Glasgow's West End, 1830–1914', *Journal of Transport History*, 1 (1971–2), pp. 146–60

Simpson, M. A., 'The West End of Glasgow 1830–1914', in M. A. Simpson and T. H. Lloyd (ed.), *Middle-Class Housing in Britain* (David & Charles, 1977), pp. 44–85

Slaven, Anthony, 'The Origins of Scottish Business Leaders 1860–1960', in T. M. Devine (ed.), *Scottish Elites* (John Donald, 1994), pp. 152–69

Slyck, Abigail van, 'The Lady and the Library Lodger: Gender and Public Space in Victorian America', *Winterthur Portfolio: A Journal of American Material Culture*, 31, 4 (1996), pp. 221–42

Smith, Joan, 'Labour Traditions in Glasgow and Liverpool', *History Workshop*, 17 (1984), pp. 32–56

Smith-Rosenberg, Carroll, 'The Female World of Love and Ritual,' *Signs*, 1 (1975), pp. 1–29

Smith-Rosenberg, Carroll, 'Disorderly Conduct: Visions of Gender in Victorian America', Book Review of Gerda Lerner's *Single Woman in Nineteenth-Century*

Society: Pioneers or Deviants, *Reviews in American History*, 15, 1 (1987), pp. 94–100

Tadmor, Naomi, ' "Family" and "Friends" in *Pamela*', *Social History*, 14 (1989), pp. 289–306

Thane, Pat, and Jane Mackay, 'The Englishwoman', in Robert Colls and Philip Dodd (ed.), *Englishness, Politics and Culture 1880–1920* (Croom Helm, 1986), pp. 191–229

Todd, Barbara, 'The Remarrying Widow: A Stereotype Reconsidered', in Mary Prior (ed.), *Women in English Society 1500–1800* (Methuen and Co., 1985), pp. 54–92

Tomaselli, Silvana, 'The Enlightenment Debate on Women', *History Workshop*, 20 (1985), pp. 101–24

Tosh, John, 'Domesticity and Masculinity in the Victorian Middle Class', in Michael Roper and John Tosh (ed.), *Manful Assertions: Masculinities in Britain since 1800* (Routledge, 1991), pp. 44–73

Tosh, John, 'Authority and Nurture in Middle Class Fatherhood: The Case of Early and Mid-Victorian England', *Gender and History*, 8, 1 (1996), pp. 48–64

Vickery, Amanda, 'Golden Age to Separate Spheres? A Review of the Categories and Chronology of English Women's History', in Pamela Sharpe (ed.), *Women's Work: The English Experience 1650–1940* (Arnold, 1988), pp. 294–331

Vickery, Amanda, 'Golden Age to Separate Spheres? A Review of the Categories and Chronology of English Women's History', *Historical Journal*, 36, 2 (1993), pp. 383–414

Vickery, Amanda, 'Women and the World of Goods: A Lancashire Consumer and Her Possessions 1751–91', in John Brewer and Roy Porter (ed.), *Consumption and the World of Goods in the Seventeenth and Eighteenth Centuries* (Routledge, 1993), pp. 274–303

Wahrman, Dror, 'National Society, Communal Culture: An Argument about the Recent Historiography of Eighteenth-Century Britain', *Social History*, 17, 1 (1992), pp. 43–72

Walkowitz, Judith R., 'Going Public: Shopping, Street Harassment and Street Walking in Late Victorian London', *Representations*, 62 (1998), pp. 1–30

Ward, David, 'Environs and Neighbours in the "Two Nations": Residential Differentiation in Mid-Nineteenth Century Leeds', *Journal of Historical Geography*, 6 (1980), pp. 133–62

Wilson, Charles, 'Economy and Society in Late Victorian Britain', *Economic History Review*, 18 (1965), pp. 183–98

Wilson, Stephen, 'The Myth of Motherhood: The Historical View of European Child-Rearing', *Social History*, 9, 2 (1984), pp. 181–98

Yeatman, Anna, 'Gender and the Differentiation of Social Life into Public and Private Realms', *Social Analysis Journal of Culture and Social Practice*, 15 (1984), pp. 32–50

Yeo, Eileen Janes, 'The Creation of "Motherhood" and Women's Responses in Britain and France, 1750–1914', *Women's History Review*, 8, 2 (1999), pp. 201–18

Young, Craig, 'Middle-Class "Culture", Law and Gender Identity: Married Women's Property Legislation in Scotland, c.1850–1920', in Alan Kidd and David Nicholls (ed.), *Gender, Civic Culture and Consumerism: Middle Class Identity in Britain 1800–1940* (Manchester University Press, 1999), pp. 133–45

Young, Filson, 'Oscar Slater', in Harry Hodge and James Hodge (ed.), *Famous Trials* (Penguin, 1984)

UNPUBLISHED THESES, DISSERTATIONS AND PAPERS

Brown, Callum G., 'Residential Differentiation in Nineteenth Century Glasgow' (ESRC Award Report, R000 232733, 1993)

Dobbie, Fiona, 'Divorce in Scotland 1830–1890' (Undergraduate dissertation, Department of Economic and Social History, University of Glasgow, 1998)

Hillis, Peter, 'Presbyterianism and Social Class in Mid-Nineteenth Century Glasgow: A Study of Nine Churches' (Unpublished PhD thesis, University of Glasgow, 1978)

Moore, Lindy, 'Young Ladies' Institutions: The Development of Secondary Schools for Girls in Scotland, 1833–c1870' (Unpublished paper)

Pattison, D. A., 'Tourism in the Firth of Clyde' (Unpublished thesis, University of Glasgow, 1967)

Ross, Fiona, 'Representations of Middle Class Single Women in the Novel from the Mid-Nineteenth Century to the Early Twentieth' (Unpublished PhD thesis, University of Glasgow, 1996)

Smith, Sarah J., '"Weary of the Petticoat": Women in Higher Education in Glasgow c1796–1845' (Unpublished BA Honours dissertation, University of Strathclyde, 1997)

Smitley, Megan, '"Women's Mission": The Temperance and Women's Suffrage Movements in Scotland, c1870–1914' (Unpublished PhD thesis, University of Glasgow, 2002)

Sweeney, Irene, 'The Municipal Administration of Glasgow 1833–1912: Public Service and the Scottish Civic Identity' (Unpublished PhD thesis, University of Strathclyde, 1990)

Illustration Acknowledgements

1   Map. *Glasgow Post Office Directory*, 1883.

2   Woodside Terrace, 1852. Photograph courtesy of the Mitchell Library, Glasgow.

3   The hall of Marion Gilchrist's home in Queen's Terrace, 1907. Photograph courtesy of the Signet Library, Edinburgh.

4   Great Western Road, *c*.1905. Photograph courtesy of Glasgow Conservation Trust West.

5   Wellington Church, 1905. Photograph courtesy of Glasgow Conservation Trust West.

6   Glasgow International Exhibition, 1901. Photograph courtesy of Special Collections, Glasgow University Library.

7   The Coats family, 1856. Photograph by kind permission of the family.

8   Family group on holiday, *c*.1880s, GUAS DC 116/1/114. Photograph courtesy of Glasgow University Archive Services.

9   The Napier family, *c*.1880s. Photograph courtesy of Glasgow University Archive Services.

10 The wedding of Rosa Mirrlees, 1901, GGHBA HB 10/5/1. Photograph courtesy of Greater Glasgow Health Board Archive.

11 Joseph and Georgiana Coats, 1879. Photograph by kind permission of the family.

12 David Murray, *The Bailie*, 1893. Photograph courtesy of Glasgow University Special Collections.

13 William MacEwen, *The Bailie*, 1888. Photograph courtesy of Glasgow University Special Collections.

14 Janet Story's table setting, 1847, GUAS DC 21. Photograph courtesy of Glasgow University Archive Services.

15 The dining room of the Mirrlees home, *c*.1890, GGHBA HB 10/5/1. Photograph courtesy of Greater Glasgow Health Board Archive.

16 The dining room of Marion Gilchrist's flat in Queen's Terrace, 1907. Photograph courtesy of the Signet Library, Edinburgh.

17 The interior of the Edgar family home, 1895. Photograph courtesy of Calum Crawford.

18 'Our Coastal Residences', *The Bailie*, 1890. Photograph courtesy of Glasgow University Special Collections.

19 Helen MacFie and her daughter Janet, 1870, GUAS DC 120/4. Photograph courtesy of Glasgow University Archive Services.

20 Maryanne MacEwen and her children, *c.*1890, GUAS DC 79/175. Photograph courtesy of Glasgow University Archive Services.

21 Professor William Thomson (Lord Kelvin) and his second wife, Frances Blundy, *c.*1890. GUAS PH 7002. Photograph courtesy of Glasgow University Archive Services.

22 The Taylor family, *c.*1870. Photograph by kind permission of the family.

23 Isabella Elder, 1894. Photograph courtesy of Glasgow University Archive Services.

24 Miss Cranston's tearoom, *The Bailie*, 1885. Photograph courtesy of Glasgow University Special Collections.

25 Dr Joseph Coats, 1897. Photograph by kind permission of the family.

26 'Royal Clyde Yacht Club Ball', *The Bailie*, 1891. Photograph courtesy of Glasgow University Special Collections.

27 Various bill posters for Glasgow theatres. Photographs courtesy of Glasgow University Special Collections.

28 'Cooper, Hunter and Rodger', Ladies shopping, *The Bailie*, 1896. Photograph courtesy of Glasgow University Special Collections.

29 'Bazaar, Kelvinside United Presbyterian Church', *The Bailie*, 1895. Photograph courtesy of Glasgow University Special Collections.

30 Napier family cycling, *c.*1900, GUAS, DC 90/4/2/9. Photograph courtesy of Glasgow University Archive Services.

31 Two women in a rowing boat, *c.*1900, GUAS DC 116/1/209. Photograph courtesy of Glasgow University Archive Services.

Index

290

Index